New Perspectives on

X M L

Introductory

New Perspectives on

X M L

Introductory

PATRICK CAREY
Carey Associates, Inc.

THOMSON
COURSE TECHNOLOGY

Australia • Canada • Mexico • Singapore • Spain • United Kingdom • United States • Japan

THOMSON

COURSE TECHNOLOGY

New Perspectives on XML-Introductory

is published by Course Technology.

Managing Editor:
Rachel Crapser

Senior Editor:
Donna Gridley

Senior Product Manager:
Kathy Finnegan

Product Manager:
Karen Stevens

Technology Product Manager:
Amanda Shelton

Associate Product Manager:
Brianna Germain

Editorial Assistant
Emilie Perreault

Marketing Manager:
Rachel Valente

Developmental Editor:
Paul Griffin

Production Editor:
Catherine G. DiMassa

Composition:
GEX Publishing Services

Text Designer:
Meral Dabcovich

Cover Designer:
Efrat Reis

Preface

Course Technology is the world leader in information technology education. The New Perspectives Series is an integral part of Course Technology's success. Visit our Web site to see a whole new perspective on teaching and learning solutions.

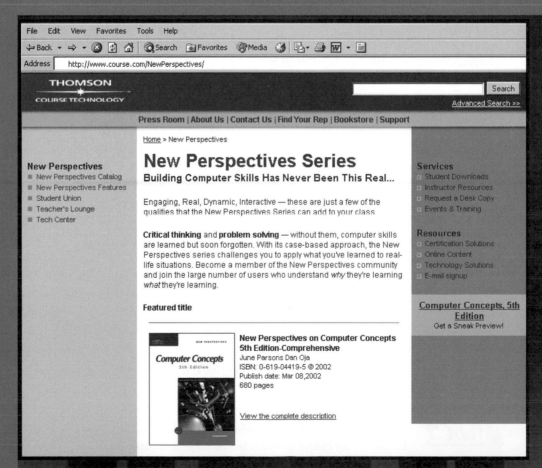

New Perspectives—Building Computer Skills Has Never Been This Real

Why New Perspectives will work for you.

Critical thinking and **problem solving**—without them, computer skills are learned but soon forgotten. With its **case-based** approach, the New Perspectives Series challenges students to apply what they've learned to real-life situations. Become a member of the New Perspectives community and watch your students not only **master** computer skills, but also **retain** and carry this **knowledge** into the world.

New Perspectives catalog
Our online catalog is never out of date! Go to the Catalog link on our Web site to check out our available titles, request a desk copy, download a book preview, or locate online files.

Complete system of offerings
Whether you're looking for a Brief book, an Advanced book, or something in between, we've got you covered. Go to the Catalog link on our Web site to find the level of coverage that's right for you.

Instructor materials
We have all the tools you need—data files, solution files, figure files, a sample syllabus, and ExamView, our powerful testing software package.

How well do your students know Microsoft Office?
Experience the power, ease, and flexibility of SAM XP and TOM. These innovative software tools provide the first truly integrated technology-based training and assessment solution for your applications course. Click the Tech Center link to learn more.

Get certified
If you want to get certified, we have the titles for you. Find out more by clicking the Teacher's Lounge link.

Interested in online learning?
Enhance your course with rich online content for use through MyCourse 2.0, WebCT, and Blackboard. Go to the Teacher's Lounge to find the platform that's right for you.

Your link to the future is at
www.course.com/NewPerspectives

What you need to know about this book.

- Students will appreciate the real-world scenarios that provide the context of the case problems in each tutorial.

- Students will gain confidence as they learn how to bind XML fields with specific elements in an HTML document, and to populate tables with the content of XML documents.

- ExamView testing software gives you the option of generating a printed test, LAN-based test, or test over the Internet.

- This book provides extensive coverage of DTDs, namespaces, schemas, CSS, and XSLT.

- Students learn how to validate a single document, combined from the contents of several XML files. XML documents are validated using the validation commands in XML Spy.

- Student Online Companion takes students to the Web for additional work.

- Includes a 120-day evaluation copy of XML Spy 4.3 — a leading XML editor.

CASE	TROUBLE?	SESSION 1.1	QUICK CHECK	RW
Tutorial Case Each tutorial begins with a problem presented in a case that is meaningful to students. The case sets the scene to help students understand what they will do in the tutorial.	**TROUBLE? Paragraphs** These paragraphs anticipate the mistakes or problems that students may have and help them continue with the tutorial.	**Sessions** Each tutorial is divided into sessions designed to be completed in about 45 minutes each. Students should take as much time as they need and take a break between sessions.	**Quick Check Questions** Each session concludes with conceptual Quick Check questions that test students' understanding of what they learned in the session.	**Reference Windows** Reference Windows are succinct summaries of the most important tasks covered in a tutorial. They preview actions students will perform in the steps to follow.

BRIEF CONTENTS

TABLE OF CONTENTS

Tutorial 3   XML 3.01

Creating a Valid XML Document

Working with a Document Type Definition

Tutorial 4   XML 4.01

Working with Namespaces and Schemas

Creating a Patient Report Document

XML

Tutorial 5   XML 5.03

Working with Cascading Style Sheets
Formatting Your XML Documents with CSS

Tutorial 6   XML 6.01

Working with XSLT
Transforming an XML Document

Acknowledgments

This book would not have been started without the support and enthusiasm of Greg Donald, who initially proposed the project. Special thanks to Developmental Editor, Paul Griffin, who improved the book with his editorial skill and insight, and Technology Product Manager, Amanda Shelton, who kept the project on track and was indispensable with her suggestions and assistance. Other people at Course Technology who deserve credit are Rachel Crapser, Managing Editor; Donna Gridley, Senior Editor; Kathy Finnegan, Senior Product Manager; Brianna Germain, Associate Product Manager; Catherine DiMassa, Production Editor; John Bosco, Quality Assurance Project Leader; and John Freitas, Jeff Schwartz, and Matt DeGraff, Quality Assurance Testers.

Feedback is an important part of writing any book, and thanks go to the following reviewers for their ideas and comments: Risa Blair of Champlain College, Eric Johnston, Candace Garrod of Red Rocks Community College, Craig Shaw of Central Community College–Hastings, WJ Patterson of Sullivan University, and John Whitney of Fox Valley Technical College. Special thanks to reviewer Robert Cormia of Foothill College, who was instrumental with advice on the schema and namespace material.

Finally, I want to thank my wife Joan for her encouragement and love, and my six children: John Paul, Thomas, Peter, Michael, Stephen, and Catherine, to whom this book is dedicated.

New Perspectives on

XML

Read This Before You Begin

To the Student

Data Disks

To complete the Level I tutorials, Review Assignments, and Case Problems, you need two Data Disks. Your instructor will either provide you with these Data Disks or ask you to make your own.

If you are making your own Data Disks, you will need **two** blank, formatted high-density disks. You will need to copy a set of files and/or folders from a file server, standalone computer, or the Web onto your disks. Your instructor will tell you which computer, drive letter, and folders contain the files you need. You could also download the files by going to www.course.com and following the instructions on the screen.

The information below shows you the Data Disks you need so that you will have enough disk space to complete all the tutorials, Review Assignments, and Case Problems:

Data Disk 1

Write this on the disk label:
Data Disk 1: XML Tutorials 1 and 2

Data Disk 2

Write this on the disk label:
Data Disk 2: XML Tutorials 3 and 4

When you begin each tutorial, Review Assignment, or Case Problem, be sure you are using the correct Data Disk. Refer

to the "File Finder" chart at the back of this text for more detailed information on which files are used in which tutorials. See the inside front cover of this book for more information on Data Disk files, or ask your instructor or technical support person for assistance.

Using Your Own Computer

If you are going to work through this book using your own computer, you need:

■ **Computer System** A text editor and a Web browser (preferably Netscape Navigator or Internet Explorer, versions 4.0 or higher) must be installed on your computer. If you are using a non-standard browser, it must support frames and HTML 4.0 or higher.

■ **Data Disks** You will not be able to complete the tutorials or exercises in this book using your own computer until you have your Data Disks.

Visit Our World Wide Web Site

Additional materials designed especially for you are available on the World Wide Web.
Go to www.course.com/NewPerspectives.

To the Instructor

The Data Disk Files are available on the Instructor's Resource Kit for this title. Follow the instructions in the Help file on the CD-ROM to install the programs to your network or standalone computer. For information on creating Data Disks, see the "To the Student" section above.

You are granted a license to copy the Data Files to any computer or computer network used by students who have purchased this book.

OBJECTIVES

In this tutorial you will:

- Learn about the history of XML

- Compare the features of XML and HTML

- Learn how XML documents are structured

- Create your own XML elements and attributes

- Link an XML document to a cascading style sheet

- Display an XML document in a Web browser

CREATING AN XML DOCUMENT

Developing an XML Document for the Jazz Warehouse

CASE

The Jazz Warehouse

The Jazz Warehouse is a store located in Kansas City specializing in jazz recordings and collectibles. The store is famous for locating hard-to-find records as well as current releases. The store has also had recent success in offering items on the World Wide Web.

Richard Brooks manages the Jazz Warehouse's Web site. When the site was first created, it was developed using standard HTML code. Since then, Richard has heard of several Web sites that are changing from HTML documents to XML documents that incorporate style sheets. Richard has learned that XML has some advantages over HTML in presenting structured content. XML is more flexible, allowing authors to create their own document tags specifically tailored to their needs. XML also supports tools that ensure any data entered into an XML document follows well-defined rules for both structure and content. This feature will make it easier for Richard to create documents that accurately reflect the Jazz Warehouse's inventory.

Richard believes that the company will eventually move from HTML to a combination of XML and style sheets, so he wants to start investigating how to display the company's recording inventory using an XML document. He has asked for your help in creating a small demonstration document for this purpose.

SESSION 1.1

In this session, you'll study the history and theory of XML as well as compare the features of XML and HTML. You'll also learn how XML documents are created and review some of the XML editors available to you. Finally, you'll learn about well-formed and valid XML documents and how XML ensures the integrity and consistency of your data.

Introducing XML

You and Richard meet to discuss how XML can help him in developing content for the Jazz Warehouse's Web site. First, Richard wants to know what XML is and how it can help his business.

XML stands for **Extensible Markup Language**. A **markup language** is a computer language that specifies the structure and content of a document by breaking the document down into a series of **elements**, where each element represents a different part of the document. The term **extensible** means that the language can be used to create a wide variety of document types by using elements tailored to each document. The following XML history lesson may help you better understand the XML of today.

A Short History of XML

XML has its roots in the Standard Generalized Markup Language (SGML). Introduced in the 1980s, SGML was used to create the general structure of markup languages. SGML can be thought of as the parent or umbrella technology for both XML and HTML (see Figure 1-1).

Figure 1-1	THE ROOTS OF XML AND HTML

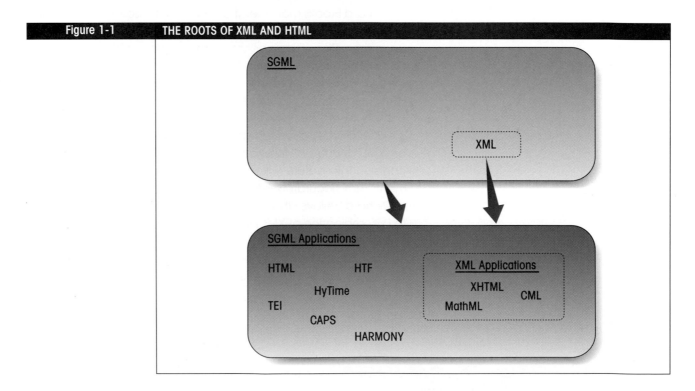

SGML is device independent and system independent, which means that it can be used with almost any type of document stored in almost any format. SGML has been the chosen vehicle for creating documents in businesses and government organizations of all sizes. For example, think of the daunting task of documenting all of the parts used in creating the space shuttle while at the same time creating a structure that shuttle engineers can use to quickly retrieve and edit that information. SGML provides tools to manage documentation projects of this magnitude.

But, there is a price to pay for this type of complex system; thus, SGML is limited to those organizations that can afford the cost and overhead of maintaining complex SGML environments. SGML is often most useful in creating applications, based on the SGML architecture, that apply to specific types of documents. The most famous of these applications is Hypertext Markup Language, or HTML, the language of the World Wide Web.

The success of the World Wide Web is due in no small part to HTML. HTML allows Web authors to easily create documents that can be displayed across different operating systems. Creating Web sites with HTML is a straight-forward process that does not require a programming background. This ease of use has made HTML popular with many different types of users. Millions of Web sites, including the Jazz Warehouse Web site, were created with HTML, and there is every indication that HTML will continue to be an important language of the Web for a long time to come.

The Limits of HTML

Despite its popularity, HTML is not without limitations and flaws, which continue to frustrate Web developers. The major problem is that people are interested in Web pages not only for their appearance but also for their content, and HTML was not designed with data content in mind. For example, if Richard wants to display information on music sold by the Jazz Warehouse, he might use the following HTML code in his Web page:

```
<H2>Kind of Blue</H2>
<H3>Miles Davis</H3>
<OL>Tracks
      <LI>So What (9:22)</LI>
      <LI>Freddie Freeloader (9:46)</LI>
      <LI>Blue in Green (5:37)</LI>
      <LI>All Blues (11:33)</LI>
      <LI>Flamenco Sketches (9:26)</LI>
</OL>
```

The HTML tags <H2>, <H3>, <OL>, and <LI> merely format the information, they do not describe it. After all, those same tags could be used in a grocery Web page:

```
<H2>HiValue Foods</H2>
<H3>Fresh Produce</H3>
<OL>Products
      <LI>Apples ($1.99/bag)</LI>
      <LI>Grapes ($1.49/bag)</LI>
      <LI>Onions ($1.99/bag)</LI>
      <LI>Red Leaf Lettuce ($0.50/bunch)</LI>
      <LI>Mushrooms ($0.79/carton)</LI>
</OL>
```

As long as your only concern is formatting, it makes no difference whether your page is about music or mushrooms. But, what if Richard wants to develop a Web application that can easily access the company's inventory of a particular recording artist? Without being able to determine whether an HTML tag refers to a CD title, music track, price, or artist, it may be difficult to locate the information. In response to this limitation, developers have added features to HTML, such as the CLASS attribute, which allow Web authors to attach descriptive information to each tag. Web authors can also make use of the <META> tag to record information about a document's contents. These additional HTML features are helpful, but they don't entirely solve the problem of effectively describing and cataloging data in an HTML document.

A second problem of HTML is that it is not extensible and, therefore, can't be modified to meet specific needs. As a result of the demands of the market and competition, the various Web browsers have developed their own unique flavors of HTML. Netscape Communicator saw a need for frames, so it introduced a version of HTML that included the <FRAMESET> and <FRAME> tags, both of which were not part of standard HTML. Internet Explorer saw a need for internal frames and introduced the <IFRAME> tag, and that innovation also represented a departure from standard HTML.

The result was a confusing mix of competing HTML standards, one for each browser and, indeed, each browser version. The innovations offered by Netscape, Internet Explorer, and others certainly increased the scope and power of HTML but did so at the expense of clarity. Web authors could not easily create Web sites without taking into account the cross-browser compatibility of the code in the Web pages.

Finally, HTML can be inconsistently applied. Some browsers require all tag attributes to be enclosed within quotes; some don't. Some browsers require all paragraphs to include an ending </P> tag; others do not. The lack of standards can make it easier to write HTML code, but it also means that code read by one browser may be rejected by another.

Partly because of the reasons outlined above, the Web was in need of a language that could more effectively handle data content, be easily customized by developers, and hold developers accountable to well-defined standards. In response to these needs, XML was created.

Exploring the Concepts Behind XML

Like HTML, XML was developed by the **W3C** (**World Wide Web Consortium**), an organization created in 1994 to develop common protocols and standards for sharing information on the World Wide Web. You can learn more about the W3C and view specifications for XML, HTML, and other languages at *http://www.w3.org*.

XML Design Goals

The W3C established ten primary design goals for XML:

1. XML must be easily usable over the Internet.

   XML was developed with the Web in mind and supports major Web protocols such as HTTP and MIME.

2. XML must support a wide variety of applications.

   Although XML was developed for the Web, it can also be used for other applications such as databases, financial transactions, and voice mail.

3. XML must be compatible with SGML.

   Because XML is a subset of SGML, many of the software tools developed for SGML can be adapted for XML.

4. It must be easy to write programs that process XML documents.

   One of HTML's greatest strengths is its simplicity. XML has tried to emulate this by making it easy for even nonprogrammers to write XML code.

5. The number of optional features in XML must be kept to the absolute minimum, ideally zero.

   SGML supports a wide range of optional features, which means that SGML software can be large and cumbersome. XML removed this aspect of SGML, which makes it a more suitable Web-development tool.

6. XML documents should be clear and easily understood by nonprogrammers.

   Like HTML, XML documents are text files. The contents of an XML document follow a logical, tree-like structure. As you'll see later, XML authors can specify element names whose meanings are intuitively clear to anyone reading the XML code.

7. The XML design should be prepared quickly.

   XML was only going to be a viable alternative to HTML if the Web community adopted it as a standard. For that to happen, W3C had to quickly settle on a design for XML before other competing standards emerged.

8. The design of XML must be exact and concise.

   XML can be easily processed by computer programs, which makes it easy for programmers to develop applications.

9. XML documents must be easy to create.

   For XML to be practical, XML documents must be as easy to create as HTML documents.

10. Terseness in XML markup is of minimal importance.

    Because of the speed in which information can be exchanged over the Internet, keeping document size small is not as important as keeping the document code understandable and easy to use.

Although XML is sometimes referred to as a markup language, it is actually more of a meta-markup language because it is a markup language that is used to create other markup languages. Unlike HTML, which is an SGML application, XML should be considered a subset of SGML—without SGML's complexity and overhead.

Comparing XML and HTML

As you can see, XML and HTML share many of the same design goals. So, how does XML differ from HTML? HTML is a language used for data presentation and formatting, whereas XML's emphasis is on data content only. Figure 1-2 shows how the same data content from the Jazz Warehouse can be encoded in both HTML and XML. The HTML code tells us that the first line should be displayed using an H2 heading, followed by an H3 heading. The document concludes with an ordered list of text.

Figure 1-2	SAMPLE HTML AND XML CODE
HTML CODE	**XML CODE**

```
<H2>Kind of Blue</H2>
<H3>Miles Davis</H3>
<OL>Tracks
  <LI>So What (9:22)</LI>
  <LI>Freddie Freeloader (9:46)</LI>
  <LI>Blue in Green (5:37)</LI>
  <LI>All Blues (11:33)</LI>
  <LI>Flamenco Sketches (9:26)</LI>
</OL>
```

```
<CDTITLE>Kind of Blue</CDTITLE>
<ARTIST>Miles Davis</ARTIST>
<CONTENTS>
  <TRACK>So What (9:22)</TRACK>
  <TRACK>Freddie Freeloader (9:46)</TRACK>
  <TRACK>Blue in Green (5:37)</TRACK>
  <TRACK>All Blues (11:33) </TRACK>
  <TRACK>Flamenco Sketches (9:26) </TRACK>
</CONTENTS>
```

HTML code describes the format of the data, but not the data content	XML code describes the data content, but not the data format

The same data encoded with XML tells us about the type of information in the document. Without knowing anything about the document, you can quickly see that this contains data on a music CD named *Kind of Blue* by the artist Miles Davis and that the CD has five tracks, starting with "So What" and concluding with "Flamenco Sketches." The document doesn't tell you anything about how this information should be rendered on a page, or even with what media the data is to be presented.

The <CDTITLE>, <ARTIST>, <CONTENTS>, and <TRACK> tags in this example do not come from any particular XML specification, rather they are custom tags that Richard could create specifically for one of his documents. Richard could create additional tags describing the selling price of the CD, the CD label, and the date the CD was recorded. Because an XML document doesn't indicate how data is to be formatted or displayed, it must be linked to a style sheet containing formatting instructions for each element.

One final point of comparison between HTML and XML: a document created with HTML has no mechanism for monitoring the document's content. If Richard neglects to include the name of the artist in an HTML document about the company's music CDs, no one will be the wiser. However, with XML one can force a document to follow a defined structure. This is done by attaching either a **document type definition (DTD)** or a **schema** to the XML document containing the data. Both DTDs and schema define rules for how data in the document should be structured. For example, Richard can create a DTD or schema to require his documents to list the title, the artist, a list of tracks, and the price of each CD. DTDs and schemas are not required, but they can be helpful to ensure that your XML documents follow a uniform structure. You'll learn how to create and apply DTDs and schemas in upcoming tutorials.

Creating an XML Document

Like HTML, XML documents are text files. Therefore, an XML author needs no more than a simple text editor, like Notepad, Emacs, or vi, to get started. There are more sophisticated XML editors available that may make it easier to design your document, but they are not required. Figure 1-3 lists some of the XML editors and the associated URL that are available to you today. The XML Spy application is included with this book, and you'll have a chance to work with XML Spy later on.

Figure 1-3	XML EDITORS	
XML EDITOR	**URL**	**TYPE**
Amaya	http://www.w3.org/Amaya/	Windows, UNIX
BBEdit	http://www.bbedit.com/	Macintosh
EditML Pro	http://www.editml.com/	Windows
Emilé	http://www.in-progress.com/emile/	Macintosh
Merlot	http://www.merlotxml.org/	Java
Visual XML	http://www.pierlou.com/visxml/index.html	Java
XML Pro	http://www.vervet.com/xmlpro.html	Windows
XML Spy	http://www.xmlspy.com/	Windows
XMLwriter	http://www.xmlwriter.net/	Windows

XML Parsers

After the XML document is created, it needs to be evaluated by an application known as an **XML processor** or **XML parser**. Part of the function of the parser is to interpret the document's code and verify that it satisfies all of the XML specifications for document structure and syntax. XML parsers are strict. If one tag is omitted or a character is lowercase when it should be uppercase, the parser will report an error and reject the document. This may seem excessive, but that rigidity was built into XML to correct the flaw in HTML that gave Web browsers too much discretion interpreting HTML code. The end result is that XML code accepted by the parser is sure to work the same everywhere.

Microsoft developed an XML parser called **MSXML** for its Internet Explorer browser. MSXML was introduced as an add-on for Internet Explorer version 4.0 and then was built directly into the Web browser for Internet Explorer versions 5.0 and above. The current release of MSXML is MSXML 4.0. Netscape also introduced its own XML parser, called **Mozilla**, which is available starting with version 6.0 of the browser. In addition, any of the editors listed in Figure 1-3 can process and interpret XML code.

Well-Formed and Valid XML Documents

XML documents fall into one of two categories: well-formed documents or valid documents. A **well-formed document** contains no syntax errors and satisfies the specifications for XML code as laid out by the W3C. A **valid document** is a well-formed document that also satisfies the rules laid out in the DTD or schema attached to the document. An XML parser that can verify whether an XML document is valid is called a **validating parser**. If the parser can only check for well-formedness, it is referred to as a **nonvalidating parser**. Netscape's parser is a nonvalidating parser, whereas Internet Explorer checks for both well-formedness and validity in some cases.

Richard is only concerned with creating well-formed documents for his project at the Jazz Warehouse. You'll learn how to create valid documents in upcoming tutorials.

Once the XML document is parsed, it can be displayed to the user. Figure 1-4 outlines the complete process from document creation to final presentation.

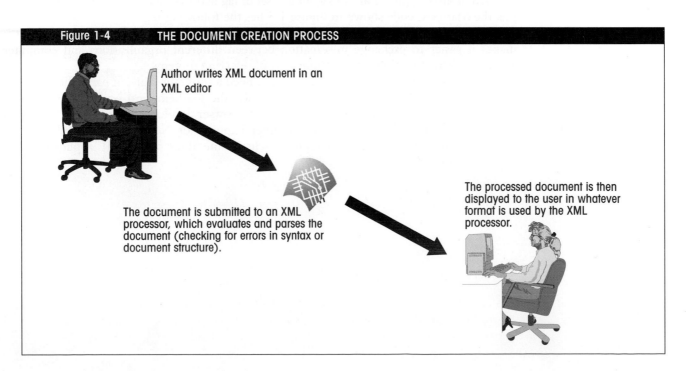

Figure 1-4   **THE DOCUMENT CREATION PROCESS**

Author writes XML document in an XML editor

The document is submitted to an XML processor, which evaluates and parses the document (checking for errors in syntax or document structure).

The processed document is then displayed to the user in whatever format is used by the XML processor.

Working with XML Applications

XML shares with SGML the ability to create markup languages, called **XML applications**. Several XML applications have been developed to work with specific types of documents. For example, a scientist may need to describe the chemical structure of a molecule, containing hundreds of atoms bonded to other atoms and molecules. That scientist could use the **Chemical Markup Language (CML)**, an XML application designed specifically to code molecular information. Another XML application, **MathML**, is used to display and evaluate mathematical equations. Figure 1-5 shows an example of MathML code and how that code might be displayed by an XML application that can interpret MathML code.

Figure 1-5   A MATHML EXAMPLE

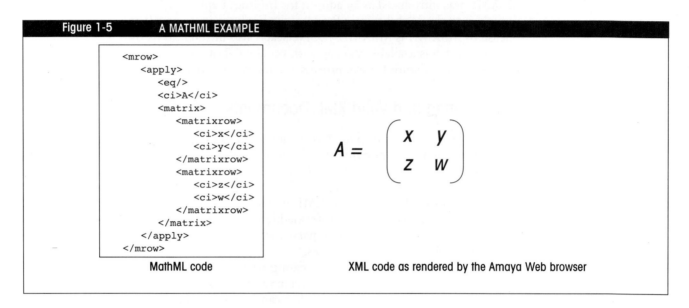

```
<mrow>
    <apply>
        <eq/>
        <ci>A</ci>
        <matrix>
            <matrixrow>
                <ci>x</ci>
                <ci>y</ci>
            </matrixrow>
            <matrixrow>
                <ci>z</ci>
                <ci>w</ci>
            </matrixrow>
        </matrix>
    </apply>
</mrow>
```

MathML code

$$A = \begin{pmatrix} x & y \\ z & w \end{pmatrix}$$

XML code as rendered by the Amaya Web browser

Each of these applications uses a defined set of tag names called a **vocabulary**. For example, the MathML code shown in Figure 1-5 has the following tag names in its vocabulary: mrow, apply, eq, ci, matrix, and matrixrow. The advantage of using a vocabulary is that it makes it easier to exchange information between different organizations and computer applications because there is a common way of referring to items.

To use one of these XML applications, you need a program that can parse the code and then display it in a useful format. For example, the mathematical equations written in MathML can be rendered using the Amaya Web browser developed by the W3C, but if you open a MathML document in either Internet Explorer or Netscape, you would see the XML code, but not the equations. Figure 1-6 lists some of the other XML applications.

Figure 1-6	XML APPLICATIONS	
XML APPLICATION	**DESCRIPTION**	**URL**
CDF	(Channel Definition Format) Permits a Web publisher to offer to automatically deliver information to PCs or other information appliances	http://www.w3.org/TR/NOTE-CDFsubmit.html
CML	(Chemical Markup Language) Used to code molecular and chemical information	http://www.xml-cml.org/
MathML	(Mathematical Markup Language) Used to present and evaluate mathematical equations	http://www.w3.org/Math/
MusicML	(Musical Markup Language) Used to display musical notation	http://www.tcf.nl/3.0/musicml/index.html
OFX	(Open Financial Exchange) Used to exchange financial data between financial institutions, businesses, and consumers via the Internet	http://www.ofx.net/
SMIL	(Synchronized Multimedia Integration Language) Used to edit interactive audiovisual presentations involving streaming audio, video, text, and any other media type	http://www.w3.org/AudioVideo/
VoiceXML	(Voice Markup Language) Used for creating audio dialogs that feature synthesized speech, digitized audio, and speech recognition	http://www.voicexml.org/

As you can see, XML can be applied to virtually any type of document. Now that you've reviewed some of the background of XML, you'll create your first XML document for the Jazz Warehouse in the next session.

Session 1.1 QUICK | CHECK

1. Define the term 'extensible.' How does the concept of extensibility relate to XML?

2. What is SGML and why was SGML not used for authoring pages on the World Wide Web?

3. What is the W3C?

4. Name three limitations of HTML that led to the development of XML.

5. Is XML a markup language? Explain your answer.

6. What is a DTD? What is a well-formed XML document, and how does it differ from a valid XML document?

7. What is an XML parser?

8. What is MathML?

Exploring the Structure of an XML Document

Now that you are familiar with the history and theory of XML, you are ready to create your first XML document. XML documents consist of three parts: the prolog, the document body, and the epilog. The **prolog** is optional, providing information about the document itself. The **document body** contains the document's content in a hierarchical tree structure. An optional **epilog** contains any final comments or processing instructions.

Creating the Prolog

A prolog consists of four parts in the following order:

1. XML declaration

2. miscellaneous statements or comments

3. document type declaration

4. miscellaneous statements or comments

The order of these parts is important. If you place the document type declaration before the XML declaration, the XML parser generates an error message. Note that none of these parts are required, but it is considered good form to include at least the XML declaration.

The XML Declaration

The XML declaration is always the first line of code in any XML document. It signals to the processor that the document is written using XML and provides information about how that code is to be interpreted by a parser. The declaration starts with the text "<?xml," which signals the parser that an XML declaration follows. The complete syntax of an XML declaration is

```
<?xml version="version number" encoding="encoding type"
standalone="yes|no" ?>
```

where *version number* is the version of the XML specification being used in the document. The default, and only, value for the version declaration is "1.0." The *encoding type* value identifies the character codes used in the document. Because different languages use different encoding schemes, this declaration allows XML to support different languages. The default encoding scheme is the English language scheme, "UTF-8." Finally, the standalone attribute indicates whether the document has any links to external files. A standalone value of "yes" indicates that the document is self-contained, and a value of "no" indicates that the XML processor must include external files when it parses the document. Note that the version number, encoding type, and standalone value must be enclosed in either double or single quotation marks. A sample XML declaration might appear as follows:

```
<?xml version="1.0" encoding="UTF-8" standalone="yes" ?>
```

This declaration indicates that the XML version is 1.0, the UTF-8 (English language) encoding scheme is being used, and the document is self-contained. You could also enter the XML declaration

```
<?xml version="1.0" ?>
```

and the processor would apply the default encoding scheme and standalone values.

It is important to remember that *XML code is case sensitive*. You cannot change the code to uppercase letters, as follows:

```
<?XML VERSION="1.0" ENCODING="UTF-8" STANDALONE="YES" ?>
```

without the parser rejecting the document. Nor can you drop the quotation marks around the values in the declaration. An XML declaration of

```
<?xml version=1.0 encoding=UTF-8 standalone=no ?>
```

also results in an error. This is a critical difference from HTML, which provides the author more latitude in entering code and does not distinguish between uppercase and lowercase letters.

REFERENCE WINDOW   **RW**

<u>Creating an XML Declaration</u>

- To create the XML declaration, enter the following code in the first line of the XML document:

  ```
  <?xml version="version number" encoding="encoding type"
  standalone="yes|no" ?>
  ```

  where *version number* is the version of the XML specification being used in the document, *encoding type* identifies the character codes used in the document, and the standalone attribute indicates whether the XML parser needs to access external files when parsing the document.

Now that you've seen how to structure an XML declaration, you can start creating your first XML document by writing the prolog.

To create the prolog:

1. Place your Data Disk in drive A (or wherever your floppy drive is located).

   TROUBLE? If you don't have a Data Disk, you need to get one. Your instructor will either give you one or ask you to make your own. See the Read This Before You Begin page at the beginning of these tutorials for instructions. Your instructor may also direct you to save your data files onto a network drive or a local hard drive.

2. Using a text editor, open a new document.

   TROUBLE? Your instructor may direct you to use an XML editor. If you don't know how to use your text or XML editor, talk to your instructor or technical resource person.

3. Type the following line of code into your document:

   ```
   <?xml version="1.0" encoding="UTF-8"
   standalone="yes" ?>
   ```

4. Save your document as **Jazz.xml** in the Tutorial.01X/Tutorial folder of your Data Disk, but do not close your text editor.

TROUBLE? Windows Notepad automatically assigns the ".txt" extension to text files. To specify the ".xml" extension, type "Jazz.xml" in the File name box, click "All Files" from the Save as Type drop-down list box, and then click the save button.

TROUBLE? If you use a word processor like Microsoft Word, you must save the document as a text file and not in the word processor's native format.

Inserting Comments

After the XML declaration, you can enter comments or miscellaneous statements that may be required by the document. You'll learn about processing instructions in the next session.

Comments may appear anywhere in the XML document. It's a good idea to insert a comment somewhere in the prolog (after the XML declaration) to provide additional information about what the document will be used for and how it was created. Comments are ignored by the processor and do not affect the document's content or structure.

The syntax for a comment is

```
<!-- comment text -->
```

where *comment text* is the text of the comment. Note that XML comments have the same syntax as HTML comments.

To add a comment to an XML document:

1. In your text editor, insert the following line *below* the XML declaration you just entered:

```
<!-- This document contains data on Jazz Warehouse
special offers -->
```

2. Save your changes to the Jazz.xml document.

You are finished working with the prolog for now. It is now time to focus your attention on the content of Richard's document.

Working with Elements and Attributes

Elements are the basic building blocks of XML files, containing the data content of the document. XML supports two kinds of elements: closed and empty (or open). A **closed element** has the following syntax:

```
<element_name>Content</element_name>
```

where *element_name* is the name given to the closed element, and *Content* represents the content of the element. For example, Richard could store the name of the artist as follows:

```
<Artist>Miles Davis</Artist>
```

There are a few important points to remember about closed elements.

- Element names are case sensitive.
- Element names must begin with a letter or the underscore character (_) and may not contain blank spaces (e.g., you cannot name an element "First Name," but you can name it "First_Name").
- Element names cannot begin with the letters "xml" because those characters are reserved for special XML commands.
- The name of the element's closing tag must match the name in the opening tag.

For example, the following element text results in an error because the starting tag is capitalized and the ending tag is not:

```
<ARTIST>Miles Davis</artist>
```

Elements can be nested within each other. Elements that are placed within other elements are called **child elements**. In the following example, the CD element contains multiple occurrences of a child element named "TRACK:"

```
<CD>Kind of Blue
      <TRACK>So What (9:22)</TRACK>
      <TRACK>Freddie Freeloader (9:46)</TRACK>
      <TRACK>Blue in Green (5:37)</TRACK>
      <TRACK>All Blues (11:33) </TRACK>
      <TRACK>Flamenco Sketches (9:26) </TRACK>
</CD>
```

Elements must either be placed side-by-side or nested. You cannot have a child element overlapping the opening and closing tags of its parent. This set of XML code

```
<CD>Kind of Blue <ARTIST>Miles Davis</CD></ARTIST>
```

results in an error message because the CD element is closed before the ARTIST element. Think of the parent element as a container that must completely contain all of its child elements.

```
<CD>Kind of Blue <ARTIST>Miles Davis</ARTIST></CD>
```

XML is much more rigorous than HTML in this regard because many Web browsers accept HTML files with improperly nested elements.

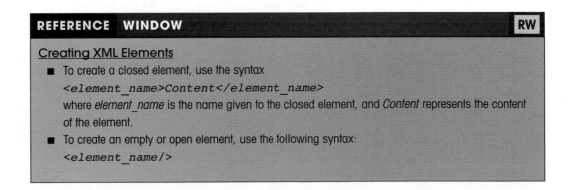

REFERENCE WINDOW   **RW**

Creating XML Elements
- To create a closed element, use the syntax
  ```
  <element_name>Content</element_name>
  ```
  where *element_name* is the name given to the closed element, and *Content* represents the content of the element.
- To create an empty or open element, use the following syntax:
  ```
  <element_name/>
  ```

The Root Element

The nesting concept applies to the entire XML document. All elements must be nested within a single **document** or **root element**. There can be only one root element. The following XML document is in error because the elements are not nested within a single root element:

```
<?xml version="1.0" ?>
<CD>Kind of Blue
      <TRACK>So What (9:22)</TRACK>
      <TRACK>Freddie Freeloader (9:46)</TRACK>
      <TRACK>Blue in Green (5:37)</TRACK>
      <TRACK>All Blues (11:33) </TRACK>
      <TRACK>Flamenco Sketches (9:26) </TRACK>
</CD>
<CD>Cookin'
      <TRACK>My Funny Valentine (5:57)</TRACK>
      <TRACK>Blues by Five (9:53)</TRACK>
      <TRACK>Airegin (4:22)</TRACK>
      <TRACK>Tune-Up (13:03)</TRACK>
</CD>
```

However, if a single root element, such as <ARTIST>, is added, the XML document is not in error.

```
<?xml version="1.0" ?>
<ARTIST>Miles Davis
   <CD>Kind of Blue
         <TRACK>So What (9:22)</TRACK>
         <TRACK>Freddie Freeloader (9:46)</TRACK>
         <TRACK>Blue in Green (5:37)</TRACK>
         <TRACK>All Blues (11:33) </TRACK>
         <TRACK>Flamenco Sketches (9:26) </TRACK>
   </CD>
   <CD>Cookin'
         <TRACK>My Funny Valentine (5:57)</TRACK>
         <TRACK>Blues by Five (9:53)</TRACK>
         <TRACK>Airegin (4:22)</TRACK>
         <TRACK>Tune-Up (13:03)</TRACK>
   </CD>
</ARTIST>
```

In addition to text and nested elements, comments can be placed within elements.

```
<CD>Cookin' <!-- Live Recording --> </CD>
```

Note that the comment must follow the same syntax used for comments placed in the document's prolog. Also, the comment must be placed entirely within the element's tags. The following code is in error because the ending </CD> tag occurs before the ending comment tag, -->:

```
<CD>Cookin' <!-- Live Recording </CD> -->
```

Empty Elements

An **open** or **empty element** is an element that contains no content. Empty element tags are comprised of the element name followed by a forward slash and ending with a right-angle bracket. The syntax for an empty element is

```
<element_name/>
```

where *element_name* is the name of the empty element. Note that empty elements consist of a single tag—there is no opening and closing tag. An equivalent way of expressing an empty element is as follows:

```
<element_name></element_name>
```

HTML supports a collection of empty elements, such as the <HR> tag for horizontal lines or the <IMG> tag used for inline graphics. In XHTML (the version of HTML based on XML specifications) these tags are represented as <HR /> and <IMG />.

Empty elements contain no content, so why use them in an XML document? One reason is to mark certain sections of the document for the XML parser. Richard might want to use an empty element to distinguish one group of CD titles from another.

Empty elements usually contain attributes that provide information to the XML parser that is not displayed in the document.

Element Attributes

An **attribute** describes a feature or characteristic of an element. The syntax for adding an attribute to an element is

```
<element_name attribute="value"> … </element_name>
```

or in the case of an empty attribute

```
<element_name attribute="value" />
```

Here, *attribute* is the name given to the attribute and *value* is the attribute's value. Attribute values are text strings and thus must always be enclosed within either single or double quotes. For example, if Richard wants to include the length of each music track as an attribute of the <TRACK> element, he could enter the following code:

```
<TRACK length="9:22">So What</TRACK>
```

Because they're considered text strings, attribute values may contain spaces and almost any character other than angle brackets (< and >). You can choose any name for the attribute subject to the following constraints:

- ■ The attribute must begin with a letter or underscore (_).
- ■ Spaces are not allowed in attribute names.
- ■ Attribute names should not begin with the text string "xml."
- ■ An attribute name can only appear once in the same starting tag.

Finally, as in all of XML, attribute names are case sensitive. Attributes are often used to provide additional information about an element to the XML parser that processes the document.

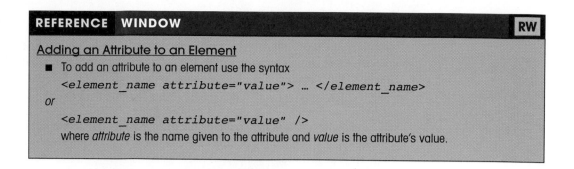

> **REFERENCE WINDOW**   `RW`
>
> **Adding an Attribute to an Element**
> - To add an attribute to an element use the syntax
>
>   `<element_name attribute="value"> … </element_name>`
>
> or
>
>   `<element_name attribute="value" />`
>
>   where *attribute* is the name given to the attribute and *value* is the attribute's value.

It's not always clear when to use attribute values instead of inserting the information within a set of element tags. Some argue that attributes should never be used because they add to the document's complexity and the information would be better placed within an element. Generally, it's best to use attributes only for that information that is processed by the XML parser and does not need to be viewed.

Adding Elements to an XML Document

Now that you've reviewed some of the features of XML elements, you'll use these elements in an XML document. Richard would like information on the CDs, shown in Figure 1-7, added to the Jazz.xml file that describes the company's monthly specials.

Figure 1-7	JAZZ WAREHOUSE CDS	
CD TITLE	**ARTIST**	**TRACKS**
Kind of Blue	Miles Davis	So What (9:22) Freddie Freeloader (9:46) Blue in Green (5:37) All Blues (11:33) Flamenco Sketches (9:26)
Cookin'	Miles Davis	My Funny Valentine (5:57) Blues by Five (9:53) Airegin (4:22) Tune-Up (13:03)
Blue Train	John Coltrane	Blue Train (10:39) Moment's Notice (9:06) Locomotion (7:11) I'm Old Fashioned (7:55) Lazy Bird (7:03)

Richard has decided to use elements named <CD>, <ARTIST>, and <TRACK> to contain the information displayed in Figure 1-7. The length of each track needs to be stored as an attribute of the <TRACK> element. He would like you to add a <TITLE> element that describes the contents of the document. Finally, all of this information is to be contained within a single root element named <SPECIALS>.

To add these elements to the XML document:

1. Open the **Jazz.xml** document from the Tutorial.01X/Tutorial folder on your Data Disk in your text editor. Figure 1-8 shows the current state of the document.

Figure 1-8	PROLOG OF RICHARD'S DOCUMENT

```
<?xml version="1.0" encoding="UTF-8" standalone="yes" ?>
<!-- This document contains data on Jazz Warehouse special offers -->
```

2. Below the comment line, insert a blank line and then the following XML code:

```
<SPECIALS>
<TITLE>Monthly Specials at the Jazz Warehouse</TITLE>
   <CD>Kind of Blue
      <ARTIST>Miles Davis</ARTIST>
      <TRACK length="9:22">So What</TRACK>
      <TRACK length="9:46">Freddie Freeloader</TRACK>
      <TRACK length="5:37">Blue in Green</TRACK>
      <TRACK length="11:33">All Blues</TRACK>
      <TRACK length="9:26">Flamenco Sketches</TRACK>
   </CD>
   <CD>Cookin'
      <ARTIST>Miles Davis</ARTIST>
      <TRACK length="5:57">My Funny Valentine</TRACK>
      <TRACK length="9:53">Blues by Five</TRACK>
      <TRACK length="4:22">Airegin</TRACK>
      <TRACK length="13:03">Tune-Up</TRACK>
   </CD>
   <CD>Blue Train
      <ARTIST>John Coltrane</ARTIST>
      <TRACK length="10:39">Blue Train</TRACK>
      <TRACK length="9:06">Moment's Notice</TRACK>
      <TRACK length="7:11">Locomotion</TRACK>
      <TRACK length="7:55">I'm Old Fashioned</TRACK>
      <TRACK length="7:03">Lazy Bird</TRACK>
   </CD>
</SPECIALS>
```

Figure 1-9 shows the revised Jazz.xml file.

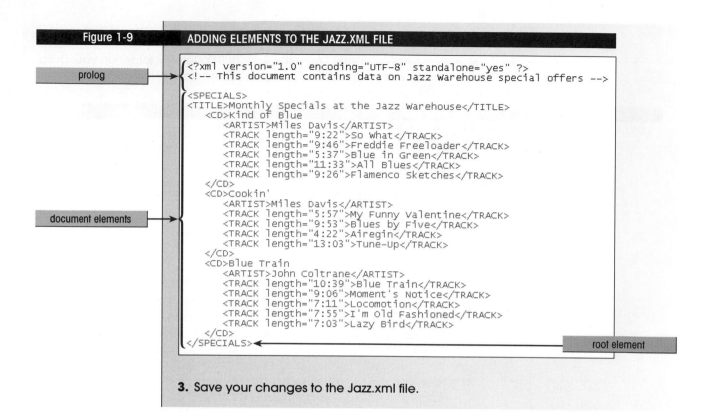

Figure 1-9   ADDING ELEMENTS TO THE JAZZ.XML FILE

prolog

```
<?xml version="1.0" encoding="UTF-8" standalone="yes" ?>
<!-- This document contains data on Jazz Warehouse special offers -->

<SPECIALS>
<TITLE>Monthly Specials at the Jazz Warehouse</TITLE>
    <CD>Kind of Blue
        <ARTIST>Miles Davis</ARTIST>
        <TRACK length="9:22">So What</TRACK>
        <TRACK length="9:46">Freddie Freeloader</TRACK>
        <TRACK length="5:37">Blue in Green</TRACK>
        <TRACK length="11:33">All Blues</TRACK>
        <TRACK length="9:26">Flamenco Sketches</TRACK>
    </CD>
    <CD>Cookin'
        <ARTIST>Miles Davis</ARTIST>
        <TRACK length="5:57">My Funny Valentine</TRACK>
        <TRACK length="9:53">Blues by Five</TRACK>
        <TRACK length="4:22">Airegin</TRACK>
        <TRACK length="13:03">Tune-Up</TRACK>
    </CD>
    <CD>Blue Train
        <ARTIST>John Coltrane</ARTIST>
        <TRACK length="10:39">Blue Train</TRACK>
        <TRACK length="9:06">Moment's Notice</TRACK>
        <TRACK length="7:11">Locomotion</TRACK>
        <TRACK length="7:55">I'm Old Fashioned</TRACK>
        <TRACK length="7:03">Lazy Bird</TRACK>
    </CD>
</SPECIALS>
```

document elements

root element

3. Save your changes to the Jazz.xml file.

You've entered the CD information that Richard has requested; but now he has some additional information for you to work with. He wants you to enter the selling price of each CD on special. Because the Jazz Warehouse has a sizable customer base in Great Britain, the XML document needs to record the selling price in both U.S. dollars ($) and British pounds (£). Figure 1-10 displays the cost of the CDs in each currency.

Figure 1-10   SALES PRICE FOR JAZZ WAREHOUSE CDS

CD TITLE	SELLING PRICE (U.S. $)	SELLING PRICE (G.B. £)
Kind of Blue	$11.99	£8.39
Cookin'	$7.99	£5.59
Blue Train	$8.99	£6.29

To accomplish this additional step, Richard needs to know how to include the £ symbol into his XML document to represent British pounds.

Using **Character References**

Sometimes, you may need to include a character not found on your keyboard, such as the copyright symbol, registered trademark symbol, or the symbol for the British pound.

REFERENCE   WINDOW   `RW`

Inserting Character References
- To insert special characters into an XML document, use the following form:

  `&#character;`

  where *character* is a character reference number or name from the ISO/IEC character set.

To insert characters into your XML document not available on a keyboard, you use a **character reference**. The syntax for a character reference is

`&#character;`

where *character* is a character reference number or name from the ISO/IEC character set. The **ISO/IEC character set** is an international numbering system for referencing characters from virtually any language. If you've used HTML, this will be familiar to you because character references in XML work the same as characters references in HTML. Figure 1-11 shows a few of the commonly used character reference numbers, and the appendix contains character reference numbers for the first 256 characters in the ISO/IEC character set. Note that not all characters have both reference numbers and names.

Figure 1-11	XML CHARACTER REFERENCES		
SYMBOL	**CHARACTER REFERENCE**	**CHARACTER NAME**	**DESCRIPTION**
©	&#169;		Copyright symbol
®	&#174;		Registered trademark
™	&#153;		Trademark symbol
<	&#60;	&lt;	Less than symbol
>	&#62;	&gt;	Greater than symbol
&	&#38;	&amp;	Ampersand
"	&#22;	&quot;	Double quote
'	&#27;	&apos;	Apostrophe (single quote)
£	&#163;		Pound sign
€	&#128;		Euro Sign
¥	&#165;		Yen sign

The character reference for the £ symbol is £. Use this character reference now to add British currency information to the Jazz.xml document.

To insert price information into the document:

1. After the first occurrence of <ARTIST>Miles Davis</ARTIST> in the Jazz.xml file, insert the following code:

```
<PRICEUS>US: $11.99</PRICEUS>
<PRICEUK>UK: &#163;8.39</PRICEUK>
```

2. After the second occurrence of `<ARTIST>Miles Davis</ARTIST>`, insert the following code:

```
<PRICEUS>US: $7.99</PRICEUS>
<PRICEUK>UK: &#163;5.59</PRICEUK>
```

3. After the `<ARTIST>John Coltrane</ARTIST>` line, insert the following code:

```
<PRICEUS>US: $8.99</PRICEUS>
<PRICEUK>UK: &#163;6.29</PRICEUK>
```

Figure 1-12 shows the revised Jazz.xml file.

Figure 1-12	INSERTING A CHARACTER REFERENCE

```
<SPECIALS>
<TITLE>Monthly Specials at the Jazz Warehouse</TITLE>
    <CD>Kind of Blue
        <ARTIST>Miles Davis</ARTIST>
        <PRICEUS>US: $11.99</PRICEUS>
        <PRICEUK>UK: &#163;8.39</PRICEUK>
        <TRACK length="9:22">So What</TRACK>
        <TRACK length="9:46">Freddie Freeloader</TRACK>
        <TRACK length="5:37">Blue in Green</TRACK>
        <TRACK length="11:33">All Blues</TRACK>
        <TRACK length="9:26">Flamenco Sketches</TRACK>
    </CD>
    <CD>Cookin'
        <ARTIST>Miles Davis</ARTIST>
        <PRICEUS>US: $7.99</PRICEUS>
        <PRICEUK>UK: &#163;5.59</PRICEUK>
        <TRACK length="5:57">My Funny Valentine</TRACK>
        <TRACK length="9:53">Blues by Five</TRACK>
        <TRACK length="4:22">Airegin</TRACK>
        <TRACK length="13:03">Tune-Up</TRACK>
    </CD>
    <CD>Blue Train
        <ARTIST>John Coltrane</ARTIST>
        <PRICEUS>US: $8.99</PRICEUS>
        <PRICEUK>UK: &#163;6.29</PRICEUK>
        <TRACK length="10:39">Blue Train</TRACK>
        <TRACK length="9:06">Moment's Notice</TRACK>
        <TRACK length="7:11">Locomotion</TRACK>
        <TRACK length="7:55">I'm Old Fashioned</TRACK>
        <TRACK length="7:03">Lazy Bird</TRACK>
    </CD>
</SPECIALS>
```

character reference

4. Save your changes to Jazz.xml.

A common mistake in XML documents is to forget that the ampersand symbol (&) is interpreted by the XML processor as a character reference and not as a character. For example, the following code

```
<ARTIST>Miles Davis & John Coltrane</ARTIST>
```

will result in an error message after the XML parser fails to find a character reference number for the & symbol. To avoid this problem, you need to use the & or & character reference for the ampersand symbol:

```
<ARTIST>Miles Davis &amp; John Coltrane</ARTIST>
```

Character references are often used to store the text of HTML code within an XML element. For example, to store the HTML tag <img src="Logo.gif"> in an element named HTMLCODE, you need to use character references to reference the < and > symbols contained in the HTML tag. The following code accomplishes this:

```
<HTMLCODE>&#60;img src="Logo.gif"&#62;</HTMLCODE>
```

Note that you can't use

```
<HTMLCODE><img src="Logo.gif"></HTMLCODE>
```

because the XML processor attempts to interpret the <IMG> tag as a tag and *not* part of the document's content.

Working with CDATA Sections

Sometimes, an XML document needs to store large blocks of text containing the < and > symbols (think of writing a tutorial about HTML in an XML document!). In that case, it would be cumbersome to replace all of the < and > symbols with < and > character references. The code itself will be difficult to read.

Instead of using character references, you can place large blocks of text into a CDATA section. A **CDATA section** is a large of block text that the XML processor interprets only as text. The syntax for creating a CDATA section is as follows:

```
<![CDATA[
     Text Block
]]>
```

A CDATA section:

- may contain most markup characters, such as <, >, and &, and those characters will be interpreted by the XML parser as text and not markup commands
- may be placed anywhere that text occurs in the document, such as between opening and closing element tags
- cannot be nested within one another
- cannot be empty

The only sequence of symbols that may not occur within a CDATA section is "]]>" because the XML parser interprets this text string as a marker ending the CDATA section.

In the following example, a CDATA section is used to store several HTML tags within an element named HTMLCODE:

```
<HTMLCODE>
   <![CDATA[
       <h1>The Jazz Warehouse</h1>
       <h2>Your Online Store for Jazz Music</h2>
   ]]>
</HTMLCODE>
```

The HTML code in this example is treated by the XML processor as simple text and not as code. In general, it is a good idea to place any large block of text within a CDATA section to protect yourself from inadvertently inserting a character that will be misinterpreted by the XML processor (such as the ampersand symbol).

Richard would like you to insert a message element into the Jazz.xml file that describes the purpose and content of the document. You decide to use a CDATA section for this task.

To create a CDATA section:

1. After the <TITLE> tag near the top of the Jazz.xml file, insert the following lines of code:

```
<MESSAGE>
<![CDATA[
    Here are some of the latest specials from the Jazz
Warehouse.
    Please note that all Miles Davis & John Coltrane CDs
will be
    on sale for the month of March.
]]>
</MESSAGE>
```

Figure 1-13 shows the updated Jazz.xml file.

Figure 1-13   **INSERTING A CDATA SECTION**

character data section

```
<?xml version="1.0" encoding="UTF-8" standalone="yes" ?>
<!-- This document contains data on Jazz Warehouse special offers -->

<SPECIALS>
<TITLE>Monthly Specials at the Jazz Warehouse</TITLE>
<MESSAGE>
<![CDATA[
    Here are some of the latest specials from the Jazz Warehouse.
    Please note that all Miles Davis & John Coltrane CDs will be on
    sale for the month of March.
]]>
</MESSAGE>
    <CD>Kind of Blue
        <ARTIST>Miles Davis</ARTIST>
        <PRICEUS>US: $11.99</PRICEUS>
        <PRICEUK>UK: &#163;8.39</PRICEUK>
        <TRACK length="9:22">So what</TRACK>
        <TRACK length="9:46">Freddie Freeloader</TRACK>
        <TRACK length="5:37">Blue in Green</TRACK>
        <TRACK length="11:33">All Blues</TRACK>
        <TRACK length="9:26">Flamenco Sketches</TRACK>
    </CD>
```

2. Save your changes to Jazz.xml.

3. Close your text editor.

Congratulations! You've completed your work on Richard's XML document. In the next session, you'll learn how to display the document in a Web browser.

Session 1.2 QUICK CHECK

1. What are the three parts of an XML document?

2. What XML declaration would you enter to specify that your XML document supports version 1.0, uses the ISO-8859-1 encoding scheme, and contains links to other documents?

3. What XML code would you enter to insert the comment "Values extracted from the JW database" into your XML document?

4. Why is the following code in error?

   `<Title>Kind of Blue</title>`

5. Why is the following code in error?

   `<CD TITLE>Kind of Blue</CD TITLE>`

6. What is the root element?

7. What is an empty element? Why would you need an empty element in your XML document?

8. Name two ways to insert the ampersand (&) symbol into the content of your XML document.

SESSION 1.3

In this session, you'll display Richard's XML document in a Web browser. You'll study how Internet Explorer and Netscape differ in displaying XML documents, and you'll learn how those browsers can "catch" syntax errors. Finally, you'll learn how to link an XML document to a cascading style sheet through the use of a processing instruction.

Displaying an XML Document in a Web Browser

You've entered all of the elements for Richard's document, and now he would like to be able to view it. Just like HTML files, XML documents can be opened in either Internet Explorer or Netscape Navigator. Both browsers contain XML parsers to verify that the document is well formed. If a syntax error is found, an error message is displayed instead of the document's contents.

If there are no syntax errors, Internet Explorer displays the document's contents including all markup tags. The various parts of the document are color coded, making it easier to read and interpret. Internet Explorer also displays the document in an expandable/collapsible outline format that allows you to hide nested elements. Netscape does not provide these options. Instead, Netscape displays the contents of the document, but not the tags. Nor does it provide the ability to hide and then redisplay nested elements.

To display the Jazz.xml file in a Web browser:

1. Start your Web browser and open the **Jazz.xml** file located in the Tutorial.01X/Tutorial folder of your Data Disk.

   Figure 1-14 shows the contents of the file in both Internet Explorer 6.0 and Netscape 6.2. Note that the character reference you used for the British pound (£) shows up as a £ when the page is processed by the browsers.

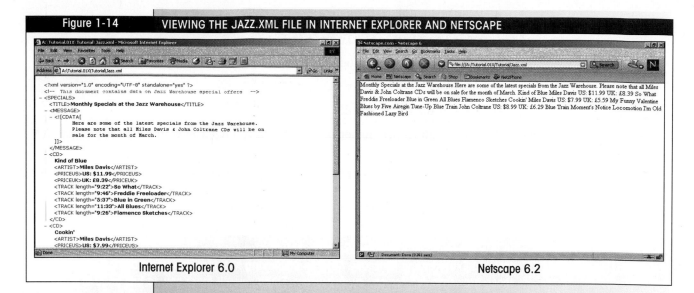

Figure 1-14 — VIEWING THE JAZZ.XML FILE IN INTERNET EXPLORER AND NETSCAPE

Internet Explorer 6.0   Netscape 6.2

2. If you are running Internet Explorer, click the **minus (–)** symbols in front of the `<CD>` tags.

Internet Explorer collapses content and the elements nested within the `<CD>` tags (see Figure 1-15).

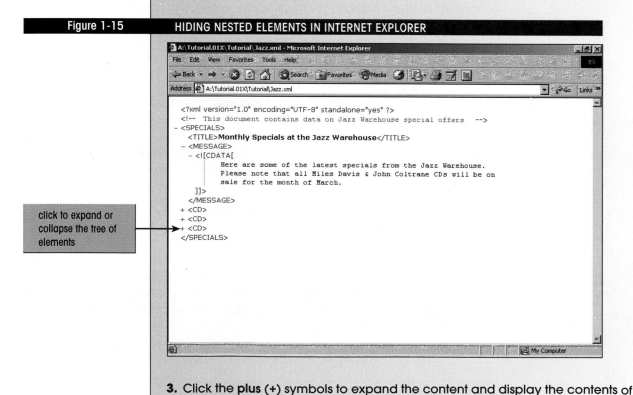

Figure 1-15 — HIDING NESTED ELEMENTS IN INTERNET EXPLORER

click to expand or collapse the tree of elements

3. Click the **plus (+)** symbols to expand the content and display the contents of the `<CD>` elements.

Having viewed the XML files with a Web browser, Richard would like to see how these browsers check for errors. He asks that you intentionally introduce an error into the Jazz.xml file to verify that the error will be identified by the browser.

To test for errors in the XML document:

1. Open the **Jazz.xml** file in your text editor.

2. Change the last line of the file from </SPECIALS> to **</Specials>**.

    This change violates the rule that all elements must have a starting and ending tag. The <SPECIALS> tag at the top of the Jazz.xml file has no corresponding ending </SPECIALS> tag because XML is case sensitive.

3. Save your changes to Jazz.xml.

4. Return to your Web browser.

5. If you are running Internet Explorer, click **View** and **Refresh** on the menu bar. If you are running Netscape, click **View** and **Reload**.

    Both browsers display error messages instead of the document's content (see Figure 1-16).

Figure 1-16	TESTING FOR ERRORS USING INTERNET EXPLORER AND NETSCAPE

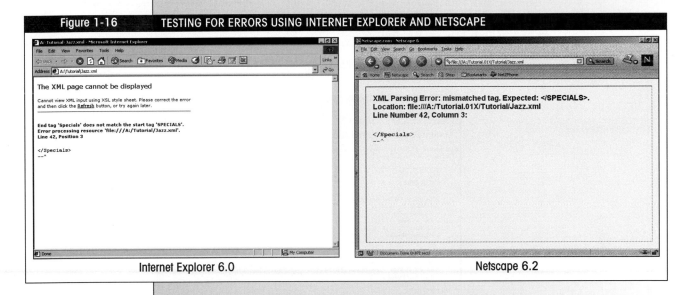

Internet Explorer 6.0   Netscape 6.2

6. Return to the Jazz.xml file in your text editor and change </Specials> back to </SPECIALS>.

Netscape does not validate XML documents, and Internet Explorer only validates XML documents against DTDs; though both test for well-formedness. If your document needs to be validated against a schema, you will need to use one of the XML editors or parsers available on the Web. This will be discussed in Tutorials 3 and 4.

Linking to a Style Sheet

Richard appreciates your work on the XML document. At this point he's concerned about the appearance of the document in the two browsers. Richard would like to share this type of information with other users and place it on the World Wide Web, but first he needs to have the data formatted—especially for users of the Netscape browser!

The easiest way to turn an XML document into a formatted document is to link the document to a style sheet. The XML document and the style sheet are then combined by the XML processor to display a single formatted document (see Figure 1-17).

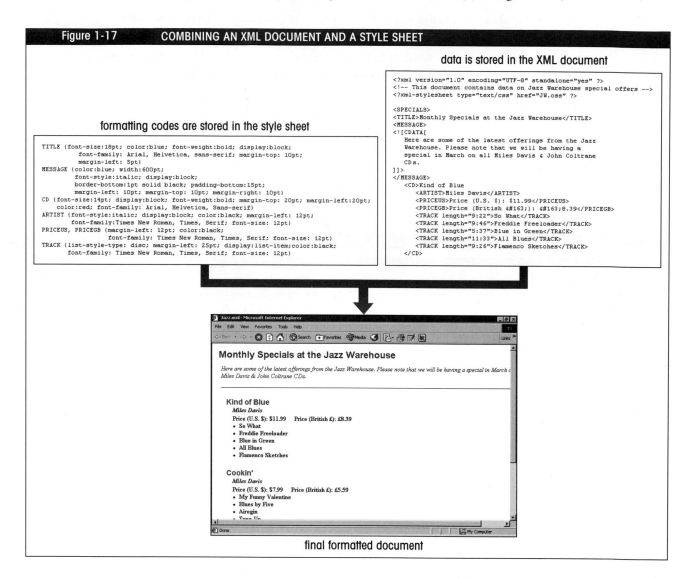

Figure 1-17 — **COMBINING AN XML DOCUMENT AND A STYLE SHEET**

final formatted document

It might seem like extra work to separate content (XML) from format (style sheets), especially when HTML combines both in a single document. However, there are some significant benefits to this approach:

- Separating content from format allows you to concentrate on the appearance of the document without having to worry about content, and to record the document's content without having to bother with the formatting questions.

- Different style sheets can be applied to the same XML document, allowing the author to tailor different style sheets for specific needs. In fact, because XML documents are device independent, the same document can be applied to different devices using the appropriate style sheet and XML processor.

- Any changes made to the style sheets are automatically reflected in any Web page based on the style sheet.

There are two main style sheet languages that are used with XML documents on the World Wide Web. **Cascading Style Sheets (CSS)** is an older standard developed for use with HTML. CSS is supported by most browsers and is relatively easy to learn and use. **Extensible Stylesheet Language (XSL)** is a newer standard. XSL is more powerful than CSS, but it is not as easy to use, nor does it have the same degree of browser support as CSS does to date.

Applying a Style to an Element

For Richard's needs, you decide to apply a cascading style sheet to the document. CSS creates styles using the following syntax:

```
selector {attribute1:value1; attribute2:value2; …}
```

where *selector* identifies an element (or a set of elements with each element separated by commas) from the XML document; and *attribute* and *value* are the style attributes and attribute values to be applied to the element. For example, to display the text of the ARTIST element in a red boldface type, you would enter the following style declaration in a cascading style sheet:

```
ARTIST {color:red; font-weight: bold}
```

CSS supports many different style attributes, and there is a great deal of flexibility in specifying to which elements a particular declaration is applied. It is not the purpose of this book to teach you CSS.

Creating Processing Instructions

Once you have created a style sheet, you create a link from the XML document to the style sheet through the use of a processing instruction. A **processing instruction** is a command that provides instructions to the XML parser. Processing instructions have the general form

```
<?target instruction ?>
```

where *target* identifies the application (or object) to which the processing instruction is directed, and *instruction* is information that the document will pass on to the parser for processing. For example, the processing instruction to access and link the contents of the XML document to a style sheet is

```
<?xml-stylesheet type="style" href="sheet" ?>
```

where *style* is the type of style sheet the XML processor will be accessing and *sheet* is the name and location of the style sheet. Here, "xml-stylesheet" is the processing instruction's target and everything else within the tag are processing instructions that identify the type and location of the style sheet. For a cascading style sheet, *style* should be "text/css".

REFERENCE WINDOW **RW**

Attaching an XML Document to a Style Sheet

■ To attach an XML document to a cascading style sheet, insert the following command within the XML document's prolog:

```
<?xml-stylesheet type="text/css" href="sheet" ?>
```

where sheet is the name and location of the style sheet file.

The Jazz Warehouse has a cascading style sheet that Richard wants you to apply to the Jazz.xml file. The style sheet, shown in Figure 1- 18, is stored in the JW.css file.

| Figure 1-18 | JW.CSS STYLE SHEET |

```
TITLE {display:block; font-size:18pt; color:blue; font-weight:bold;
       font-family: Arial, Helvetica, sans-serif;
       margin-top: 10pt; margin-left: 5pt}

MESSAGE {display:block; width:500pt; color:blue; font-style:italic;
         border-bottom:1pt solid black; padding-bottom:15pt;
         margin-left: 10pt; margin-top: 10pt; margin-right: 10pt}

CD {display:block; font-size:14pt;color:red; font-weight:bold;
    font-family: Arial, Helvetica, Sans-serif;
    margin-top: 20pt; margin-left:20pt}

ARTIST {display:block; font-size: 12pt; color:black; font-style:italic;
        font-family:Times New Roman, Times, Serif;
        margin-left: 12pt}

PRICEUS, PRICEUK {color:black; font-size: 12pt;
                  font-family: Times New Roman, Times, Serif;
                  margin-left: 12pt}

TRACK {display:list-item; font-size: 12pt; color:black; list-style-type: disc;
       font-family: Times New Roman, Times, Serif;
       margin-left: 25pt}
```

To link the JW.css style sheet to the Jazz.xml file:

1. Open **Jazz.xml** if not already open.

2. Below the comment in the prolog, insert the following processing instruction (see Figure 1-19):

   ```
   <?xml-stylesheet type="text/css" href="JW.css" ?>
   ```

| Figure 1-19 | ACCESSING A STYLE SHEET |

processing instruction to access the JW.css style sheet →

```
<?xml version="1.0" encoding="UTF-8" standalone="yes" ?>
<!-- This document contains data on Jazz Warehouse special offers -->
<?xml-stylesheet type="text/css" href="Jw.css" ?>

<SPECIALS>
<TITLE>Monthly Specials at the Jazz Warehouse</TITLE>
<MESSAGE>
<![CDATA[
   Here are some of the latest specials from the Jazz Warehouse.
   Please note that all Miles Davis & John Coltrane CDs will be on
   sale for the month of March.
]]>
</MESSAGE>
```

3. Close **Jazz.xml**, saving your changes.

4. Open **Jazz.xml** in your Web browser.

   Figure 1-20 shows the contents of the Jazz.xml file with JW.css applied to the file's contents.

   TROUBLE? If you are viewing this file using Internet Explorer 5.5 or earlier, the music tracks are not displayed in a bulleted list.

Figure 1-20	THE JAZZ.XML DOCUMENT FORMATTED WITH THE JW.CSS STYLE SHEET

Monthly Specials at the Jazz Warehouse

Here are some of the latest specials from the Jazz Warehouse. Please note that all Miles Davis & John Coltrane CDs will be on sale for the month of March.

Kind of Blue
Miles Davis
US: $11.99   UK: £8.39
- So What
- Freddie Freeloader
- Blue in Green
- All Blues
- Flamenco Sketches

Cookin'
Miles Davis
US: $7.99   UK: £5.59
- My Funny Valentine
- Blues by Five
- Airegin
- Tune-Up

Blue Train
John Coltrane
US: $8.99   UK: £6.29
- Blue Train
- Moment's Notice
- Locomotion
- I'm Old Fashioned
- Lazy Bird

You show Richard the formatted document and he tells you that it's just what he is looking for. Richard will show your work to the other members of his Web team, and they'll get back to you if they need more documents created in the future.

Session 1.3 Quick Check

1. What will happen if you try to display an XML document with syntax errors in either Internet Explorer or Netscape?

2. What will happen if you try to display an XML document that is not valid (but is well formed) in either Internet Explorer or Netscape?

3. How do Internet Explorer and Netscape differ in how they display XML documents?

4. What CSS style declaration would you enter to display the TITLE element in a bold font?

5. What is a processing instruction?

6. What XML code would you enter to display the current document using the Standard.css cascading style sheet?

REVIEW ASSIGNMENTS

Richard has returned with another document that he wants you to convert to XML. This document contains a list of hard-to-find recordings that the Jazz Warehouse has recently acquired. Richard has saved the information in a text file and needs you to edit the document and add the appropriate element tags. He also would like you to display the document using the JW2.css style sheet, which he is also providing.

To complete this task:

1. Using your text editor, open **Rare.txt**, located in the Tutorial.01X/Review folder of your Data Disk. Save the document as **Rare.xml**.

2. Create a prolog at the top of the document, indicating that this is an XML document using the UTF-8 encoding scheme and that it is a standalone document.

3. Below the XML declaration, insert the following comment: "Jazz collectibles, recently acquired."

4. Enclose the document content in a root element named "rare."

5. Create an element named "title" for the title of the document, "Rare Jazz Collectibles."

6. Create an element named "subtitle" for the subtitle "New Offerings."

7. There are five new recordings that the Jazz Warehouse needs to include in this document. Each recording contains the following information:

   - name of the artist
   - name of the album
   - year the album was released
   - album label
   - condition of the album
   - selling price of the album in dollars
   - selling price of the album in pounds

   Enter element tags for each of these items using the following element names: artist, record, year, label, condition, priceus, and priceuk.

8. Richard was not able to type the symbol for British pounds in his original text document. Instead he used a capital "L." Replace these with a character reference to the British pound, £.

Explore

9. At the bottom of the file is a message to record collectors. Enclose this message in a CDATA section and place it within an element named "message."

10. Add a processing instruction to the document's prolog, to attach the document to the JW2.css style sheet.

11. Print the contents of Rare.xml and save your changes.

12. Open **Rare.xml** in your Web browser and print the page.

13. Hand in your files and printouts to your instructor.

CASE PROBLEMS

Case 1. Jackson Electronics   Located in Santa Fe, NM, Jackson Electronics is a privately held manufacturer of consumer digital products such as scanners, printers, and digital cameras. Originally founded by Pete Jackson in 1948 as an office supply store, Jackson Electronics has thrived over the years with innovative thinking and effective use of cutting-edge technology. Alison Greely is one of the webmasters for the Jackson Electronics Web site. Her primary responsibility is to maintain information on the frequently asked questions (FAQs) section of the site. Alison would like to convert her documents into XML format and has asked for your help. She has given you a text file containing FAQs for two of Jackson Electronics' products: the ScanMaster scanner and the DigiCam digital camera. She would like this text file converted to an XML document and then linked to a cascading style sheet.

To complete this task:

1. Using your text editor, open **FAQ.txt**, located in the Tutorial.01X\Cases folder of your Data Disk. Save the document as **FAQ.xml**.

2. Create a prolog at the top of the document, indicating that this is an XML document using version 1.0 of XML.

3. After the XML declaration, insert the following comment: "ScanMaster and DigiCam FAQ."

4. Enclose the document's title, "Jackson Electronics Products," in a set of <title> tags.

5. Set the document's subtitle, "Frequently Asked Questions," as a subtitle element.

6. Set each question in the document as a question element.

7. Set each answer in the document as an answer element, and place the text of each answer within a CDATA section.

8. Set the two product name titles as product elements.

9. Enclose the entire document content within a root element named "FAQ."

10. Add a processing instruction to the prolog to direct the XML processor to access the FAQ.css style sheet when it loads this document.

11. Print your XML code and then close the FAQ.xml document, saving your changes.

12. Open the **FAQ.xml** document in your Web browser. Print the page that the browser generates. Note that FAQ text will not wrap to a new line for users of Netscape 6.21.

13. Hand in your files and printouts to your instructor.

Case 2. Midwest University   One of the original Federal Land Grant Universities, Midwest University now includes several world-class undergraduate and graduate programs. Professor David Teagarden is a member of the award-winning English department at MU. And, he is working on a Web site devoted to the work and life of William Shakespeare. He has created a document detailing the acts and scenes of *Hamlet* and has asked your help in placing this data in XML form.

To complete this task:

1. Start your text editor and open the **Hamlet.txt** file, located in the Tutorial.01X/Cases folder of your Data Disk. Save the document as **Hamlet.xml**.

2. Create a prolog at the top of the document, indicating that this is an XML document using version 1.0 of XML. You do not need to include any other information in the XML declaration.

3. Enclose the entire document content in a root element named "Play."

4. Place the title of the play in a root element named "Title".

5. Add an attribute to the Title element named "type." Set the value of the type attribute to "Tragedy."

6. Place the summary of the place in a CDATA section within an element named "Summary."

Explore ▷ 7. Place all of the information about each act of the play within an element named "Act." Place the name of each act (Act 1, Act 2, and so forth) within an element named "Act_Number."

Explore ▷ 8. Place all of the information about each scene of the play within an element named "Scene." Place the name of each scene (Scene i, Scene ii, and so forth) within an element named "Scene_Number." Place the location of each scene within an element named "Location."

9. Create a processing instruction to access the Plays.css style sheet when a Web browser accesses this document.

10. Print your XML code and save your changes.

11. Open the **Hamlet.xml** document in your Web browser. Print the pages as they are rendered by the browser.

12. Hand in your printouts and files to your instructor.

Case 3. Biotech, Inc. Located in Dallas, TX, BI was created in March of 1998 as a result of the merger of four smaller biotechnology research concerns. Linda Abrahams is a human resource representative for Biotech, Inc. Most recently, she has been entering employee data into an XML document and is running into a few problems. When she opened the document in her Web browser, the browser reported several syntax errors. Linda doesn't know how to solve the problem and has sought your help in cleaning up her code.

To complete this task:

1. Start your text editor and open the **Staff1.xml** file, located in the Tutorial.01X/Cases folder of your Data Disk. Save the document as **Staff2.xml**.

2. Open the **Staff2.xml** file in your Web browser.

Explore ▷ 3. The Web browser will report syntax errors with the document. Using the information from the browser, locate and fix the errors. (*Note*: Both Internet Explorer and Netscape will report only one error at a time. After you fix one error, the browsers will then display the next error in the file—if one exists.)

4. Once you've fixed all of the syntactical errors, link the Staff2.xml document to the Staff.css cascading style sheet.

5. Add a gender attribute to each Employee element in the document. Set the value of the gender attribute to "male" for male employees and "female" for female employees.

6. Print the final code for the Staff2.xml file.

7. Reopen the Staff2.xml file in your Web browser and print the resulting Web page. Note that Netscape 6.21 does not render this page correctly.

8. Hand in your printouts and files to your instructor.

Case 4. Delton Mutual Life Brian Carlson is an accounts manager for Delton Mutual Life and has created a text document containing personnel information for all the accounts in his portfolio. He would like your help in converting his text file to an XML document and then displaying that information in a Web page.

To complete this task:

1. Using the contents of Accounts.txt, create an XML document named **Accounts.xml** saved to the Tutorial.01X/Cases folder of your Data Disk.

2. The Accounts.xml file should contain the following items:

   ■ The root element of the document should be named "Accounts." The Accounts element should contain multiple occurrences of a child element named "Client."

   ■ The Client element should have five child elements: Name, Address, Phone, E-mail, and Account_Total.

   ■ The Client element should have a single attribute named "ID," containing the customer ID number of each person (customer ID numbers begin with the letters "CS" followed by four digits).

   ■ The Name element should contain two child elements named "First" and "Last," storing the first and last names of each person in Brian's accounts list.

   ■ The Address element should contain the following child elements: Street, City, State, and Zip, which contain the individual parts of the client's address.

   ■ The Phone element should contain the client's phone number.

   ■ The E-mail element should contain the client's e-mail address.

   ■ The Account_Total element should contain the current amount of money each client has invested with Delton Mutual Life.

3. Within the document's prolog, insert a comment describing the purpose of the document. Include your name and the date in the comment text.

4. Attach the Accounts.xml file to a cascading style sheet named "Delton.css."

5. Print the code for the Accounts.xml document.

6. Open **Accounts.xml** in your Web browser and print the page generated by the browser.

7. Hand in your printouts and files to your instructor.

QUICK | CHECK ANSWERS

Session 1.1

1. Extensible means that the language can be used to create a wide variety of document types by using elements tailored to each document. XML allows the author to create markup tags that are specific for each document type.

2. SGML stands for Standard Generalized Markup Language and was used to develop HTML, the language of the Web. However, SGML was too complicated and required too much overhead to be the language of Web page design.

3. The W3C is an organization created in 1994 to develop common protocols and standards for sharing information on the World Wide Web.

4. HTML is not "data aware," HTML does not impose rigid standards for syntax, and HTML is not easily extended to different document types.

5. No, XML is a meta-markup language used for developing other markup languages.

6. DTD stands for Document Type Definition and is used to create rules governing the structure and content of an XML document. A well-formed XML document has to satisfy the syntax of XML; a valid document has to be well formed and also satisfy the rules of the DTD or schema.

7. an application that interprets XML code, verifying that it satisfies all of the XML specifications for document structure and syntax

8. an XML application designed to work with mathematical documents

Session 1.2

1. the prolog, body, and epilog

2. `<?xml version="1.0" encoding="ISO-8859-1" standalone="yes" ?>`

3. `<!-- Values extracted from the JW database -->`

4. The case of the opening and closing tags does not match.

5. There is a blank space in the element name.

6. The element at the top of the document hierarchy; all other elements in the document are children of the root element

7. An empty element contains no content, though it might contain one or more attributes whose values might be used by the XML parser.

8. using a CDATA section or using the & or & character reference

Session 1.3

1. Both browsers will report an error.

2. The browsers will display the contents of the XML document without reporting the error.

3. Internet Explorer displays the hierarchical structure and content of the document. Netscape only displays the content of the document.

4. TITLE {font-weight:bold}

5. A processing instruction is a command that provides instructions to the XML parser.

6. `<?xml-stylesheet type="text/css" href="Standard.css" ?>`

OBJECTIVES

In this tutorial you will:

- Work with XML fields, records, and recordsets

- Create a data island in a Web page

- Bind XML elements to HTML tags

- Navigate through a collection of XML records

- Display XML data in a Web table

- Work with hierarchical recordsets

BINDING XML DATA WITH INTERNET EXPLORER

Creating a Staff Directory for Freezing Point Refrigerators

CASE

Freezing Point Refrigerators

Freezing Point is an online company that manufactures and sells refrigerators and other kitchen appliances. To make information easily accessible to its employees, the company maintains an intranet with Web pages containing a wide variety of corporate information.

Catherine Davis is a personnel manager at Freezing Point and has been assigned the job of putting the staff directory on the company's intranet. Her Web page needs to include each employee's name, department, position, phone number, years of service, and job status, as well as a picture of each employee.

Catherine has stored all of the information in an XML document, but she needs a way to put that information into her Web page. She doesn't want to re-enter all of that information into an HTML file because doing so would be time consuming and there's a possibility she would make an error in transferring the data. Catherine also doesn't want to edit the HTML file every time employee information changes, which is frequently. Catherine knows there is a way to display XML data in a formatted Web page. She finds this an attractive option because then she would only need to maintain the XML document. Catherine can format the Web page herself, but she needs your help to place XML data into the Web page.

SESSION 2.1

In this session, you'll learn how to interpret XML documents in terms of fields, records, and recordsets. You'll also examine how to reference an XML document by adding a data island to a Web page. Finally, this session explores how to bind HTML tags to specific XML elements in order to display the contents of an XML element in a Web page.

Using XML as a Data Source

So far, you've worked with XML to store your data, but you haven't used that data in an application. In this tutorial, you'll learn how to attach data from an XML document to a Web page. This technique involves **data binding** where the Web page's content is drawn from a data source (see Figure 2-1).

Figure 2-1   DATA BINDING

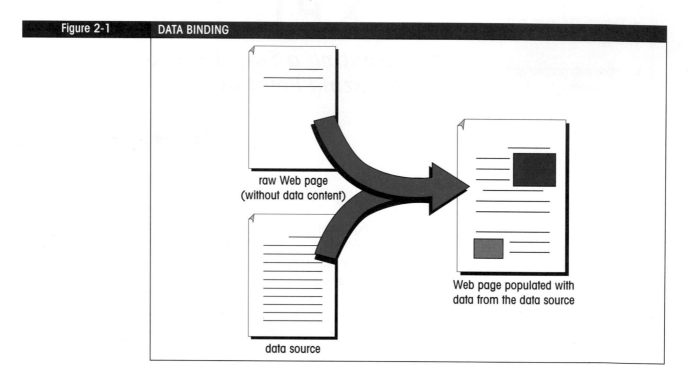

raw Web page
(without data content)

Web page populated with
data from the data source

data source

One of the advantages of data binding is that it frees the data from the format in which it is displayed. This means that the same data source can be combined with several different Web pages, without forcing the Web page designer to re-enter that data (see Figure 2-2). It also makes it easier to design the Web page because the designer only has to be concerned with the appearance of the page, not with its content.

Figure 2-2	BINDING THE SAME DATA SOURCE WITH SEVERAL WEB PAGES

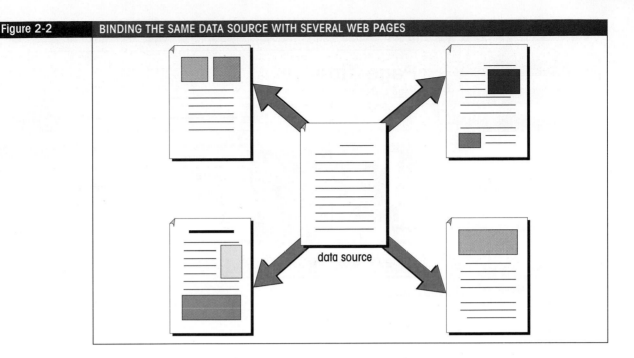

data source

Data binding can be used with a wide variety of possible data sources, from complex databases to simple text files. In Catherine's case, her data source is an XML document containing information about the employees at Freezing Point.

Catherine has already created a draft of the Web page she wants to use for the staff directory. In place of actual employee data, Catherine has inserted placeholder text that you'll replace later with actual employee data.

To open Catherine's Web page:

1. Using your text editor, open **FP1text.htm** located in the Tutorial.02X/Tutorial folder of your Data Disk.

2. Save the file as **FP1.htm**.

3. Using Internet Explorer, open and view **FP1.htm**. See Figure 2-3.

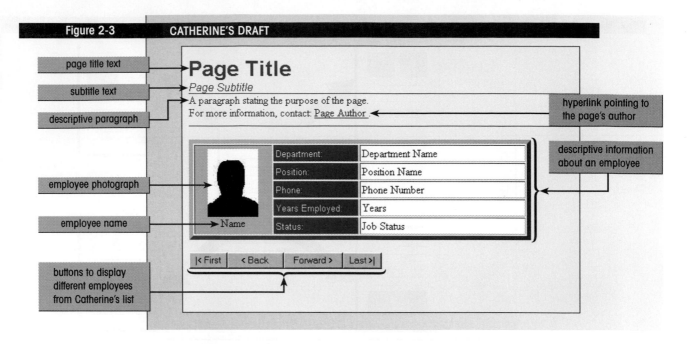

Figure 2-3   CATHERINE'S DRAFT

Catherine's Web page contains the following elements that need to be populated with data:

- page title
- page subtitle
- paragraph describing the purpose and content of the page
- hyperlink pointing to the e-mail address of the Web page designer
- table containing each employee's name, photo, department, position, phone number, years of service, and job status

The data that Catherine wants to use in this Web page comes from two XML documents: FPInfo.xml and Emp1.xml. The FPInfo.xml document contains general information about Freezing Point Refrigerators. The Emp1.xml document contains information about specific employees. Figure 2-4 shows a preview of how you'll use these documents to create a final Web page displaying information about the company and its employees.

Figure 2-4 **USING DATA BINDING TO CREATE A FINAL WEB PAGE**

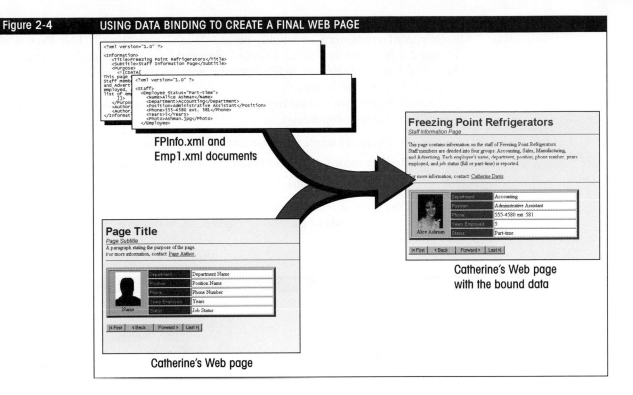

FPInfo.xml and
Emp1.xml documents

Catherine's Web page
with the bound data

Catherine's Web page

The techniques you'll use to populate these items with data work only with Internet Explorer version 5.0 and above. Netscape does not support the data-binding techniques employed by Internet Explorer.

Before we can apply data binding to Catherine's Web page, we first need to look at how data sources are organized.

Understanding Fields, Records, and Recordsets

Data in a data source is organized by fields, records, and recordsets. A **field** is an element that contains a single item of information, such as the employee's last name or age. A collection of these fields is called a **record**. Finally, a collection of records is called a **recordset**. Figure 2-5 displays the contents of an XML document in terms of fields, records, and recordsets.

Figure 2-5 **FIELDS, RECORDS, AND RECORDSETS**

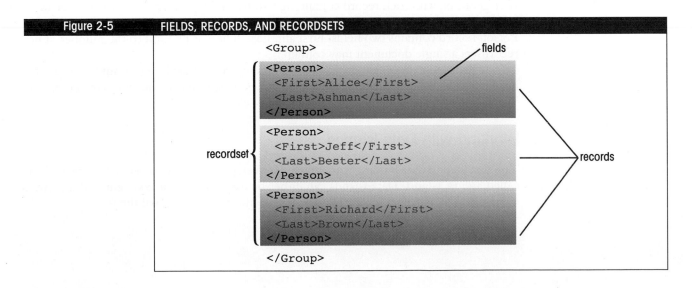

This particular document contains a single recordset, which stores three records, with each record containing two fields named "First" and "Last." The Person element in Figure 2-5 is sometimes called a **record element** because it contains a single record. The First and Last elements are **field elements** because they store field data (in this case, the person's first and last name).

Recordsets are divided into two classes: simple and hierarchical. A **simple recordset** satisfies the following properties:

- There is a single root element containing a series of records of the same type.
- Each record contains the same number of field elements.
- Each field contains character data only.

The other type of recordset is a **hierarchical recordset**, which contains a collection of recordsets nested inside of each other. Figure 2-6 shows an example of a simple and hierarchical recordset.

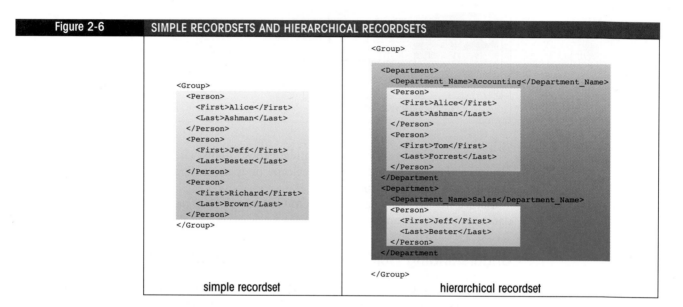

Figure 2-6	SIMPLE RECORDSETS AND HIERARCHICAL RECORDSETS

```
<Group>
   <Person>
      <First>Alice</First>
      <Last>Ashman</Last>
   </Person>
   <Person>
      <First>Jeff</First>
      <Last>Bester</Last>
   </Person>
   <Person>
      <First>Richard</First>
      <Last>Brown</Last>
   </Person>
</Group>
```
simple recordset

```
<Group>
   <Department>
      <Department_Name>Accounting</Department_Name>
      <Person>
         <First>Alice</First>
         <Last>Ashman</Last>
      </Person>
      <Person>
         <First>Tom</First>
         <Last>Forrest</Last>
      </Person>
   </Department>
   <Department>
      <Department_Name>Sales</Department_Name>
      <Person>
         <First>Jeff</First>
         <Last>Bester</Last>
      </Person>
   </Department>
</Group>
```
hierarchical recordset

The hierarchical recordset shown on the right in Figure 2-6 contains two simple recordsets. The outer recordset contains two records on the departments at Freezing Point Refrigerators, with each record containing two fields: Department_Name and Person. The inner recordset contains information on the employees within those departments. Each Person record contains two fields: First and Last. There is no limit to the number of nested recordsets a single document may contain.

The distinction between simple and hierarchical recordsets is important because Internet Explorer uses different data binding techniques depending on the form of the recordset. We'll start by using data binding with a simple recordset.

Working with Data Islands

The first step in data binding is to attach the Web page to a recordset. This attached data is called a **data island**. Data islands can either be external files or code entered directly into the HTML file. The syntax to create a data island from an external file is

```
<xml id="id" src="URL"></xml>
```

where *id* is the id name assigned to the data island, and *URL* is the filename and location of the external XML file. For example, to create a data island named "Company" attached to Company.xml, you enter the following code into your HTML file:

```
<xml id="Company" src="Company.xml"></xml>
```

To insert a data island directly into the HTML file, use the syntax

```
<xml id="id">
    xml code
</xml>
```

where *xml code* is the content of an XML document. The following code illustrates how a data island is placed directly into an HTML file:

```
<html>
<body>
    <xml id="staff">
        <?xml version="1.0"?>
        <Group>
          <Person>
             <First>Alice</First>
             <Last>Ashman</Last>
          </Person>
          <Person>
             <First>Jeff</First>
             <Last>Bester</Last>
          </Person>
          <Person>
             <First>Richard</First>
             <Last>Brown</Last>
          </Person>
        </Group>
    </xml>
    contents of the HTML file
</body>
</html>
```

Note that you have to include all of the features of a well-formed XML document, including the XML declaration and the root element.

It's generally not useful to insert the XML code directly into the HTML file. After all, the whole philosophy of XML is to separate data content from data formatting. By placing her data in a separate document, Catherine can update her staff listings and company information without editing the Web page itself. Similarly, she can edit the appearance of her Web page without having to worry about data content.

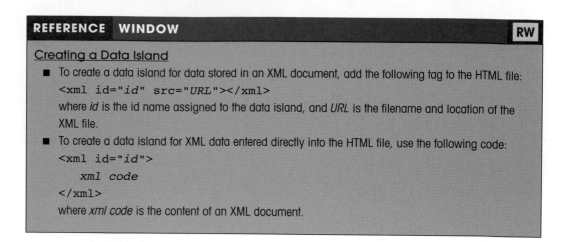

REFERENCE WINDOW · **RW**

Creating a Data Island

- To create a data island for data stored in an XML document, add the following tag to the HTML file:

  ```
  <xml id="id" src="URL"></xml>
  ```

  where *id* is the id name assigned to the data island, and *URL* is the filename and location of the XML file.

- To create a data island for XML data entered directly into the HTML file, use the following code:

  ```
  <xml id="id">
      xml code
  </xml>
  ```

  where *xml code* is the content of an XML document.

How Data Islands Are Stored

When Internet Explorer creates a data island (from an internal or external source) from an XML document, the XML parser built into Internet Explorer reads and stores the data island as a **Data Source Object** or **DSO**. The DSO handles all of the interaction between the Web page and the data island, supplying the values from the data island for each element in the Web page. More than that, one can write program code to control the actions of the DSO, such as specifying which records are displayed in the Web page at any one time. If the XML document is not well formed or valid, Internet Explorer will not create a DSO. Unfortunately, it will not report the source of the problem to the user. This differs from how Internet Explorer handles poorly formed XML documents viewed directly within the browser.

It is also important to note that the DSO is created only once for each session. If the contents of the data source are modified after Internet Explorer creates the DSO, those changes are not reflected in the Web page until the next time the page is opened or refreshed.

Creating a Data Island

You'll start your work on Catherine's Web page by creating a data island, attaching her Web page to the contents of the FPInfo.xml file. Recall that this file contains information about the company and the nature of Catherine's Web page. Figure 2-7 displays the contents of the FPInfo.xml file.

Figure 2-7   **THE CONTENTS OF THE FPINFO.XML DOCUMENT**

```
<?xml version="1.0" ?>

<Information>
    <Title>Freezing Point Refrigerators</Title>
    <Subtitle>Staff Information Page</Subtitle>
    <Purpose>
       <![CDATA[
This page contains information on the staff of Freezing Point Regrigerators.
Staff members are divided into four groups: Accounting, Sales, Manufacturing,
and Advertising. Each employee's name, department, position, phone number, years
employed, and job status (full or part-time) is reported. To move through the
list of employees, click the buttons below the table at the bottom of the page.
       ]]>
    </Purpose>
    <Author>Catherine Davis</Author>
    <Author_Email>mailto:cdavis@freezingpoint.com</Author_Email>
</Information>
```

The FPInfo.xml file contains one record and five fields: Title, Subtitle, Purpose, Author, and Author_Email. Catherine wants you to create a data island for the contents of this file named "Page_Info."

To create the data island:

1. Using your text editor, return to FP1.htm and insert a blank line following the
   <body> tag, and insert the following HTML code (see Figure 2-8):

```
<xml id="Page_Info" src="FPInfo.xml"></xml>
```

Figure 2-8   CREATING A DATA ISLAND

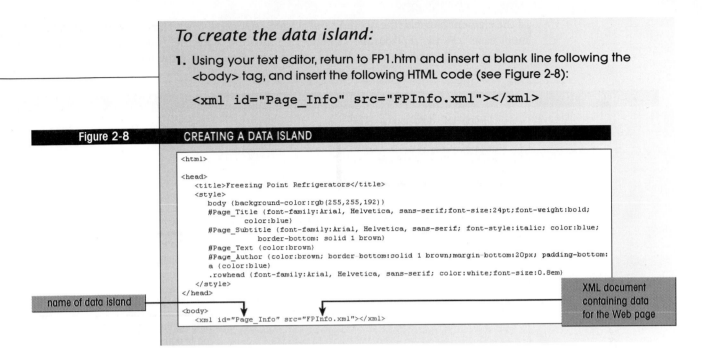

name of data island

XML document
containing data
for the Web page

The next step is to bind the elements contained in the FPInfo.xml document to specific
tags in the HTML file.

Binding XML Elements to HTML Tags

Catherine wants to bind the XML elements to HTML tags as described below (see Figure 2-9).

- Bind the Title field to the Web page title.
- Bind the Subtitle field to the Web page subtitle.
- Bind the Purpose field to the description paragraph of the Web page.
- Bind the Author field to the name of the Web page designer.
- Bind the Author_Email field to the target of the author hyperlink.

Figure 2-9   BINDING XML ELEMENTS TO THE WEB PAGE

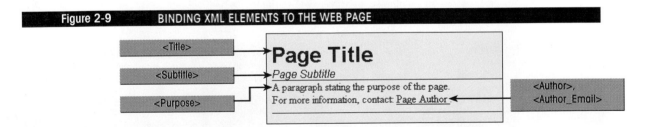

The syntax for binding an HTML tag to a data field is

```
<tag datasrc="#id" datafld="field">
```

where *tag* is the name of the HTML tag, *id* is the name of the data island, and *field* is the
name of the field in the data source. Note that the name of the data island must have the #
symbol as a prefix.

Different HTML tags employ the value of the data field in different ways. As shown in
Figure 2-10, performing data binding with the <span> tag has the effect of placing the contents

of the element between the opening and closing <span> tags. Alternately, binding an XML element to an <a> tag replaces the <a> tag's href attribute with the value of the bound element. This has the effect of changing the target of a hyperlink but not the text of the link itself.

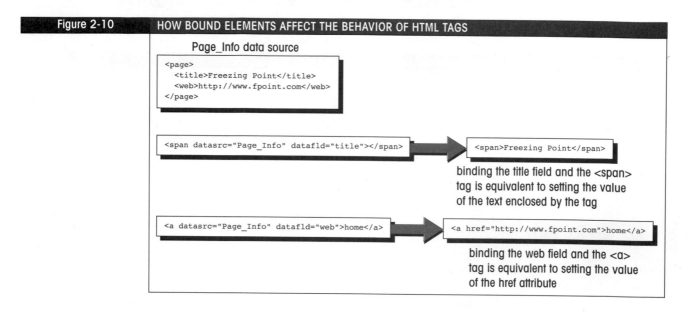

Figure 2-10   HOW BOUND ELEMENTS AFFECT THE BEHAVIOR OF HTML TAGS

Page_Info data source

```
<page>
  <title>Freezing Point</title>
  <web>http://www.fpoint.com</web>
</page>
```

```
<span datasrc="Page_Info" datafld="title"></span>
```
→
```
<span>Freezing Point</span>
```
binding the title field and the <span> tag is equivalent to setting the value of the text enclosed by the tag

```
<a datasrc="Page_Info" datafld="web">home</a>
```
→
```
<a href="http://www.fpoint.com">home</a>
```
binding the web field and the <a> tag is equivalent to setting the value of the href attribute

Not every HTML tag supports data binding. Figure 2-11 lists the HTML tags that allow for bound data and indicates how the value of the bound field is attached to the tag.

Figure 2-11   HTML TAGS THAT SUPPORT DATA BINDING IN INTERNET EXPLORER

HTML ITEM	BOUND ELEMENT
hyperlink	`<a href="bound element value">`
Java applet	`<applet param="bound element value">`
button	`<button>bound element value</button>`
div container	`<div>bound element value</div>`
frame	`<frame src="bound element value">`
internal frame	`<iframe src="bound element value">`
inline image	`<img src="bound element value">`
checkbox	`<input type="checkbox" checked="bound element value">`
hidden field	`<input type="hidden" value="bound element value">`
password field	`<input type="password" value="bound element value">`
radio button	`<input type="radio" checked="bound element value">`
text field	`<input type="text" value="bound element value">`
label	`<label>bound element value</label>`
marquee	`<marquee>bound element value</marquee>`
list box item	`<option>bound element value</option>`
span container	`<span>bound element value</span>`
text area	`<textarea>bound element value</textarea>`

Binding an HTML Tag to a Field

- To bind the contents of an HTML tag to the value of a data field, use the syntax

  `<tag datasrc="#id" datafld="field">`

  where *tag* is the name of the HTML tag, *id* is the name of the data island, and *field* is the name of the field in the data source.

- The content of the data field is interpreted as a simple text string. To force the browser to interpret the text string as HTML code, add the following attribute to *tag*:

  `dataFormatAs = "html"`

Now that you've seen how to bind HTML tags and XML elements, you are ready to bind the contents of the FPInfo document to Catherine's Web page.

To bind XML elements to HTML tags:

1. In FP1.htm, locate the <div> tag for the page title. Remove the placeholder text displayed between the opening and closing <div> tags, and add the following attributes to the <div> tag (see Figure 2-12):

   `datasrc="#Page_Info" datafld="Title"`

| Figure 2-12 | BINDING A TAG TO THE TITLE ELEMENT |

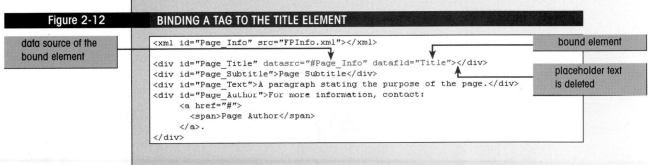

<div id="Page_Title" datasrc="#Page_Info" datafld="Title"></div> — data source of the bound element / bound element / placeholder text is deleted

```
<xml id="Page_Info" src="FPInfo.xml"></xml>

<div id="Page_Title" datasrc="#Page_Info" datafld="Title"></div>
<div id="Page_Subtitle">Page Subtitle</div>
<div id="Page_Text">A paragraph stating the purpose of the page.</div>
<div id="Page_Author">For more information, contact:
    <a href="#">
      <span>Page Author</span>
    </a>.
</div>
```

   TROUBLE? Removing the placeholder text is not strictly necessary because the bound element overwrites it. However, removing unnecessary code makes the document easier to interpret.

2. Delete the placeholder text "Page Subtitle" and add the attributes **datasrc="#Page_Info" datafld="Subtitle"** to the <div> tag.

3. Delete the placeholder text "A paragraph stating the purpose of the page." and add the attributes **datasrc="#Page_Info" datafld="Purpose"** to the <div> tag.

   Next you'll change the hyperlink that points to the e-mail address of the Web page author. Currently, this link points to "#," which represents the current file.

4. Replace the attribute href="#" with the attributes **datasrc="#Page_Info" datafld="Author_Email"**.

   Finally, bind the name of the page's author to the Author element.

5. Delete the placeholder text "Page Author" and add the attributes **datasrc="#Page_Info" datafld="Author"** to the <div> tag. Figure 2-13 shows the revised HTML code.

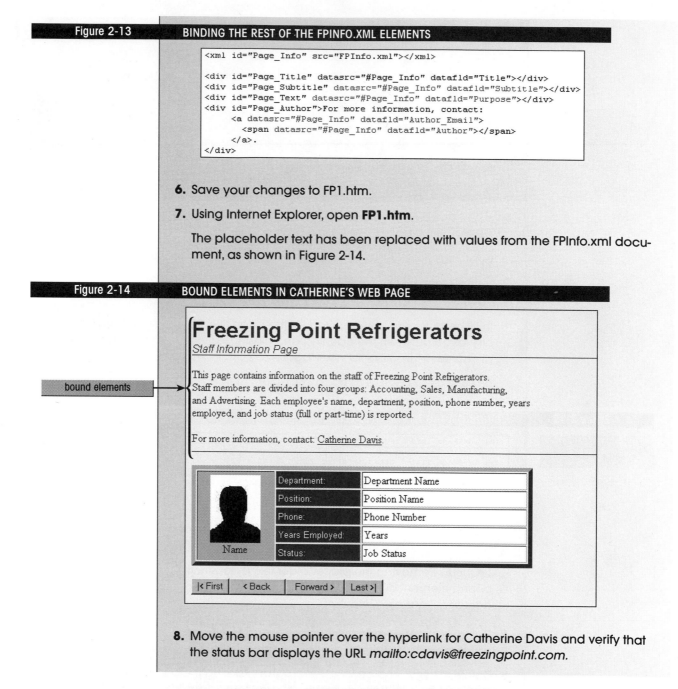

Figure 2-13   BINDING THE REST OF THE FPINFO.XML ELEMENTS

```
<xml id="Page_Info" src="FPInfo.xml"></xml>

<div id="Page_Title" datasrc="#Page_Info" datafld="Title"></div>
<div id="Page_Subtitle" datasrc="#Page_Info" datafld="Subtitle"></div>
<div id="Page_Text" datasrc="#Page_Info" datafld="Purpose"></div>
<div id="Page_Author">For more information, contact:
    <a datasrc="#Page_Info" datafld="Author_Email">
      <span datasrc="#Page_Info" datafld="Author"></span>
    </a>.
</div>
```

6. Save your changes to FP1.htm.

7. Using Internet Explorer, open **FP1.htm**.

The placeholder text has been replaced with values from the FPInfo.xml document, as shown in Figure 2-14.

Figure 2-14   BOUND ELEMENTS IN CATHERINE'S WEB PAGE

bound elements

Freezing Point Refrigerators
Staff Information Page

This page contains information on the staff of Freezing Point Refrigerators. Staff members are divided into four groups: Accounting, Sales, Manufacturing, and Advertising. Each employee's name, department, position, phone number, years employed, and job status (full or part-time) is reported.

For more information, contact: Catherine Davis

	Department:	Department Name
	Position:	Position Name
	Phone:	Phone Number
	Years Employed:	Years
Name	Status:	Job Status

| |< First | < Back | Forward > | Last >| |

8. Move the mouse pointer over the hyperlink for Catherine Davis and verify that the status bar displays the URL *mailto:cdavis@freezingpoint.com*.

Catherine's Web page still has placeholder text in the staff information table. To replace that text, you must bind those tags with the Emp1.xml document. You'll do that in the next session.

Using the dataFormatAs Attribute

By default, the contents of an XML element are interpreted by Internet Explorer as literal text. However, there may be situations where you wish to store HTML code in an XML element. For example, rather than using two elements for the author name and e-mail address, you could have included both pieces in a single element using a CDATA section:

```
<name>
  <![CDATA[
    <a href="mailto:cdavis@freezingpoint.com">
```

```
Catherine Davis</a>
  ]]>
</name>
```

However, if Catherine bound this element to an HTML tag, as follows:

```
Questions? Contact <span datasrc="#Page_Info" datafld="name">
</span>
```

Internet Explorer would still interpret contents as literal text and *not* render the text as a hyperlink. The contents would be displayed in the Web browser as follows:

```
Questions? Contact <a href="mailto:cdavis@freezingpoint.com">
Catherine Davis</a>
```

To get around this problem, you can specify that Internet Explorer interpret the content of an element as HTML code rather than literal text by using the dataFormatAs attribute. The syntax is

```
dataFormatAs="type"
```

where *type* is either "text" (the default) or "html". In Catherine's case, she would need to change her code to

```
Questions? Contact <span datasrc="#Page_Info" datafld="name"
dataFormatAs="html"></span>
```

for Internet Explorer to display the author's name as a hyperlink.

Note that only the following HTML tags support the dataFormatAs attribute: <button>, <div>, <label>, <marquee>, and <span>.

Using the $TEXT Field

Up to this point, you've used field names to reference specific elements in the XML document. The DSO also creates an pseudo field named "$Text." The **$Text** field contains the character data from all of the fields in a record, not including attribute values. For example, the value of the $Text field for the following record is "Alice Ashman", taking its value from the values of both the First and Last fields.

```
<Person>
  <First>Alice</First>
  <Last>Ashman</Last>
</Person>
```

If Catherine wanted to bind an HTML tag to the entire contents of this record, she could use an HTML tag such as:

```
The employee's name is <span datasrc="#Page_Info" datafld=
"$Text"></span>.
```

and the Web page would be rendered as

```
The employee's name is Alice Ashman.
```

The $Text field name is useful when you need to work with all of the field values as a single text string. It is also useful for binding element attributes to HTML tags, as you'll see later in the tutorial.

You've successfully completed the first stage of working with Catherine's Web page. In the next session, you'll bind more elements to her document and you'll learn how to display multiple records in a single page.

To close your work:

1. Exit Internet Explorer.

2. Close FP1.htm and exit your text editor.

Session 2.1 QUICK CHECK

1. Define the following terms:
   a. data binding
   b. field
   c. record
   d. recordset

2. What is the difference between a simple recordset and a hierarchical recordset?

3. What is a data island?

4. What HTML code would you enter to create a data island named CompInfo that is connected to the Company.xml file?

5. What HTML code would you enter to bind a <span> tag to the CName field in the CompInfo data island?

6. How is the bound element's content manifested in the <IMG> tag?

7. What is the $Text field?

SESSION 2.2

In this session, you'll learn how to use data binding with element attributes. You'll also see how to work with XML documents that contain multiple records. Finally, you'll learn to work with the recordset object in order to navigate through a collection of records within a single Web page.

Examining Multiple Records

In the last session, you learned how to bind data from a single record to a Web page. However, Catherine's staff directory involves several records, so there is some additional work that needs to be done. She has stored the data in an XML file named Emp1.xml. Take a moment to view the contents of Emp1.xml now.

To view the Emp1.xml document:

1. Using your text editor, open **Emp1.xml**.

2. Scroll through the document and examine the structure and content of the document. A portion of the file is displayed in Figure 2-15.

Figure 2-15	BOUND ELEMENTS IN CATHERINE'S WEB PAGE

```
<?xml version="1.0" ?>

<Staff>
   <Employee Status="Part-time">
      <Name>Alice Ashman</Name>
      <Department>Accounting</Department>
      <Position>Administrative Assistant</Position>
      <Phone>555-4580 ext. 581</Phone>
      <Years>5</Years>
      <Photo>Ashman.jpg</Photo>
   </Employee>
   <Employee Status="Full-time">
      <Name>Jeff Bester</Name>
      <Department>Sales</Department>
      <Position>Sales Manager</Position>
      <Phone>555-4580 ext. 411</Phone>
      <Years>3</Years>
      <Photo>Bester.jpg</Photo>
   </Employee>
   <Employee Status="Full-time">
      <Name>Richard Brown</Name>
      <Department>Manufacturing</Department>
      <Position>Shop Manager</Position>
      <Phone>555-4580 ext. 193</Phone>
      <Years>15</Years>
      <Photo>Brown.jpg</Photo>
   </Employee>
```

3. Close the file, being sure not to save any changes.

The document contains a recordset with 20 records—one for each employee. Catherine has entered the following fields for each employee record:

- **Name**: employee's full name
- **Department**: department in which the employee works
- **Position**: employee's job title
- **Phone**: employee's phone number
- **Year**: number of years the employee has worked for the company
- **Photo**: filename of an image file

In addition, the Employee record element has an attribute named "Status," indicating whether the employee works full or part time. Figure 2-16 shows how each of these items fits into the layout of Catherine's Web page.

Figure 2-16	BINDING XML ELEMENTS TO THE STAFF TABLE

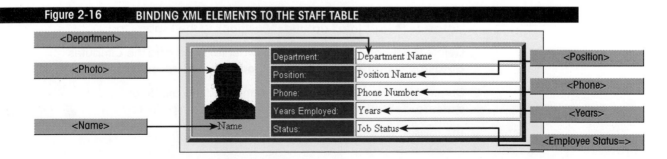

You'll start by binding the field elements, using the techniques covered in the last session.

To bind the elements to Catherine's document:

1. Using your text editor, open **FP1.htm** if it is not currently open.

2. Below the <xml> tags to create the Page_Info data island, enter the following HTML code, as shown in Figure 2-17:

```
<xml id="Staff_Info" src="Emp1.xml"></xml>
```

Figure 2-17	CREATING THE STAFF_INFO DATA ISLAND

```
<body>
    <xml id="Page_Info" src="FPInfo.xml"></xml>
    <xml id="Staff_Info" src="Emp1.xml"></xml>

    <div id="Page_Title" datasrc="#Page_Info" datafld="Title"></div>
    <div id="Page_Subtitle" datasrc="#Page_Info" datafld="Subtitle"></div>
    <div id="Page_Text" datasrc="#Page_Info" datafld="Purpose"></div>
    <div id="Page_Author">For more information, contact:
        <a datasrc="#Page_Info" datafld="Author_Email">
            <span datasrc="#Page_Info" datafld="Author"></span>
        </a>.
    </div>
```

Now bind the XML elements from the Emp1.xml file to tags in the HTML file.

3. Scroll through the HTML document to the table section and replace the src="Photo.jpg" attribute with the attributes **datasrc="#Staff_Info" datafld="Photo"**, as shown in Figure 2-18.

Figure 2-18	BINDING THE PHOTO ELEMENT TO AN <IMG> TAG

the Photo element contains the filename of a graphic file

```
<table border="6" bordercolordark="blue" bordercolorlight="#CCCCFF" cellpadding="2">
    <tr><td rowspan="5" align="center" width="110" bgcolor="#CCCCFF">
            <img datasrc="#Staff_Info" datafld="Photo"><br>
            <span>Name</span>
        </td>
        <td width="120" bgcolor="blue">
            <span class="rowhead">Department:</span>
        </td>
        <td width="240" bgcolor="white">
            <span>Department Name</span>
        </td>
    </tr>
```

4. Delete the "Name" placeholder text and add the attributes **datasrc="#Staff_Info" datafld="Name"** to the <span> tag.

5. Delete the "Department Name" placeholder text and add the attributes **datasrc="#Staff_Info" datafld="Department"** to the <span> tag.

6. Delete the "Position Name" placeholder text and add the attributes **datasrc="#Staff_Info" datafld="Position"** to the <span> tag.

7. Delete the "Phone Number" placeholder text and add the attributes **datasrc="#Staff_Info" datafld="Phone"** to the <span> tag.

8. Delete the "Years" placeholder text and add the attributes **datasrc="#Staff_Info" datafld="Years"** to the <span> tag.

The revised table is displayed in Figure 2-19.

| Figure 2-19 | BINDING THE REMAINING ELEMENTS |

```
<table border="6" bordercolordark="blue" bordercolorlight="#CCCCFF" cellpadding="2">
  <tr><td rowspan="5" align="center" width="110" bgcolor="#CCCCFF">
      <img datasrc="#Staff_Info" datafld="Photo"><br>
      <span datasrc="#Staff_Info" datafld="Name"></span>
    </td>
    <td width="120" bgcolor="blue">
      <span class="rowhead">Department:</span>
    </td>
    <td width="240" bgcolor="white">
      <span datasrc="#Staff_Info" datafld="Department"></span>
    </td>
  </tr>
  <tr><td width="120" bgcolor="blue">
      <span class="rowhead">Position:</span>
    </td>
    <td width="240" bgcolor="white">
      <span datasrc="#Staff_Info" datafld="Position"></span>
    </td>
  </tr>
  <tr><td width="120" bgcolor="blue">
      <span class="rowhead">Phone:</span>
    </td>
    <td width="240" bgcolor="white">
      <span datasrc="#Staff_Info" datafld="Phone"></span>
    </td>
  </tr>
  <tr><td width="120" bgcolor="blue">
      <span class="rowhead">Years Employed:</span>
    </td>
    <td width="240" bgcolor="white">
      <span datasrc="#Staff_Info" datafld="Years"></span>
    </td>
  </tr>
  <tr>
    <td width="120" bgcolor="blue">
      <span class="rowhead">Status:</span>
    </td>
    <td width="240" bgcolor="white">
      <span>Job Status</span>
    </td>
  </tr>
</table>
<br>
```

TROUBLE? Don't worry that we haven't created a data bind for the value of the Status attribute yet. You will accomplish that in the next set of exercises.

9. Save your changes to FP1.htm.

10. Using Internet Explorer, open and verify that your Web page matches the one shown in Figure 2-20.

| Figure 2-20 | STAFF_INFO DATA DISPLAYED IN THE WEB PAGE |

Freezing Point Refrigerators
Staff Information Page

This page contains information on the staff of Freezing Point Refrigerators.
Staff members are divided into four groups: Accounting, Sales, Manufacturing,
and Advertising. Each employee's name, department, position, phone number, years
employed, and job status (full or part-time) is reported.

For more information, contact: Catherine Davis.

bound elements →

Department:	Accounting
Position:	Administrative Assistant
Phone:	555-4580 ext. 581
Years Employed:	5
Status:	Job Status

Alice Ashman

← bound elements

| |< First | < Back | Forward > | Last >| |

After reviewing the revised Web page with Catherine, she's pleased with its appearance. However, she notices that the job status has not been included yet. You'll take on that challenge next.

Binding to an XML Attribute

Attributes, like the Status attribute of the Employee element, are treated by the DSO as fields. If the attribute is part of a record element, it's easy to bind attribute values to a Web page. For example, the following code, which has an ID attribute as part of the Employee element,

```
<Employee ID="E304">
   <Name>Alice Ashman</Name>
   <Department>Accounting</Department>
</Employee>
```

is interpreted by the DSO as

```
<Employee>
   <ID>E304</ID>
   <Name>Alice Ashman</Name>
   <Department>Accounting</Department>
</Employee>
```

Attributes become more complicated when they're part of a field element, as in the following set of code:

```
<Employee>
   <Name ID="E304">Alice Ashman</Name>
   <Department>Accounting</Department>
</Employee>
```

In this case, the attribute is still treated by the DSO as a field element, and the field element containing the attribute becomes a record element. A DSO treats the above code as follows:

```
<Employee>
   <Name>
      <ID>E304</ID>
      Alice Ashman
   </Name>
   <Department>Accounting</Department>
</Employee>
```

But, that leaves us with the text "Alice Ashman" unassociated with a field. The trick is to remember to reference all of the character data within an element using the $Text field. Therefore, the DSO interprets this code as follows:

```
<Employee>
   <Name>
      <ID>E304</ID>
      <$Text>Alice Ashman</$Text>
   </Name>
   <Department>Accounting</Department>
</Employee>
```

One possible result of DSO interpreting attribute values is that it treats a simple recordset as a hierarchical recordset, which can complicate the data binding. For this reason, it's a good idea not to use attributes in field elements if you plan to do data binding.

In Catherine's document, the Status attribute is part of the Employee record element, not one of the field elements, so you can interpret it as a separate field.

To bind the attribute value:

1. Using your text editor, open **FP1.htm** if it is not currently open.

2. Locate and delete the "Job Status" placeholder text and add the following attributes to the <span> tag: **datasrc="#Staff_Info" datafId="Status"** (see Figure 2-21).

Figure 2-21	BINDING THE <SPAN> TAG TO THE STATUS ATTRIBUTE

```
<tr>
    <td width="120" bgcolor="blue">
        <span class="rowhead">Status:</span>
    </td>
    <td width="240" bgcolor="white">
        <span datasrc="#Staff_Info" datafId="Status"></span>
    </td>
</tr>
</table>
<br>
```

3. Save your changes to FP1.htm.

4. Using Internet Explorer, refresh the contents of FP1.htm. The Web page now displays the job status information, as shown in Figure 2-22.

Figure 2-22	DATA VALUES FROM THE FIRST RECORD

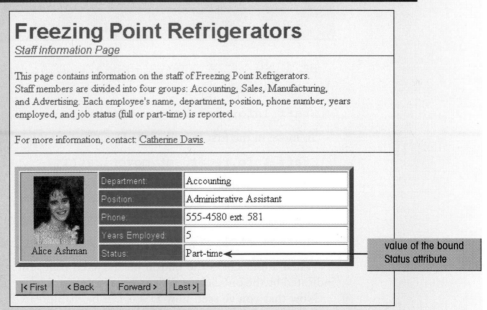

Working with the Data Source Object

Most HTML tags can only display field values one record at a time. You see an example of this in Catherine's Web page, which only displays information on the first employee. However, Catherine wants to be able to navigate through the contents of her staff directory.

To do this, you can take advantage of data-access technology supported by Microsoft called **ActiveX Data Objects** or **ADO**. ADO allows you to work with the Data Source Object by either applying a **method** (a command to perform an operation on an object) or changing one of the **properties** or characteristics of the DSO. Let's first examine how to apply a method to the Data Source Object.

Applying a Method to a Data Source Object

The syntax for applying a method to a DSO is

```
id.recordset.method
```

where *id* is the name of the data island in your Web document and *method* is the name of a method supported by ADO. There are several methods that can be applied to DSOs, but we're only going to concentrate on those that allow us to navigate through the records in the recordset. These methods are listed in Figure 2-23.

Figure 2-23	RECORDSET METHODS	

RECORDSET METHODS	DESCRIPTION
id.recordset.moveFirst()	Move to the first record in the *id* recordset
id.recordset.movePrevious()	Move to the previous record
id.recordset.moveNext()	Move to the next record
id.recordset.moveLast()	Move to the last record in the *id* recordset
id.recordset.move(*i*)	Move to record number *i* in the *id* recordset (record numbering starts with the number 0)

For example, if you want to display the last record in a DSO whose id is "Staff_Info," run the following method:

```
Staff_Info.recordset.moveLast()
```

To move to the first record in the Data Source Object, use the method

```
Staff_Info.recordset.moveFirst()
```

The other methods listed in Figure 2-23 can be applied in a similar way.

There are several ways to run these methods, but the simplest is to assign the method to the onClick event handler of a <button> element, as shown below:

```
<button onClick="Staff_Info.recordset.moveLast()">
```

When a user clicks the button on the Web page, Internet Explorer runs the command indicated by the onClick event handler, displaying the last record in the Staff_Info recordset.

Now that you've seen how DSOs can be manipulated using methods, you are ready to apply these methods to Catherine's Web page.

To assign a recordset method:

1. Using your text editor, open **FP1.htm** if it is not currently open.

2. Locate the first occurence of the <button> tag (the First button). Within the <button> tag, enter the text **onClick="Staff_Info.recordset.moveFirst()"**, as shown in Figure 2-24.

Figure 2-24   ENTERING THE MOVEFIRST() METHOD

```
<button onClick="Staff_Info.recordset.moveFirst()">
    |&lt; First
</button>
<button>
      &lt; Back   
</button>
<button>
    Forward &gt;
</button>
<button>
    Last &gt;|
</button>
</body>
</html>
```

> move to the first record in the recordset when this button is clicked

3. Locate the second occurrence of the <button> tag (the Back button). Within the <button> tag, enter the text **onClick="Staff_Info.recordset.movePrevious()"**.

4. Locate the third occurrence of the <button> tag (the Forward button). Within the <button> tag, enter the text **onClick="Staff_Info.recordset.moveNext()"**.

5. Locate the last occurrence of the <button> tag (the Last button). Within the <button> tag, enter the text **onClick="Staff_Info.recordset.moveLast()"**.

Figure 2-25 shows the completed onClick commands for all four buttons.

Figure 2-25   ENTERING THE REMAINING RECORDSET METHODS

```
<button onClick="Staff_Info.recordset.moveFirst()">
    |&lt; First
</button>
<button onClick="Staff_Info.recordset.movePrevious()">
      &lt; Back   
</button>
<button onClick="Staff_Info.recordset.moveNext()">
    Forward &gt;
</button>
<button onClick="Staff_Info.recordset.moveLast()">
    Last &gt;|
</button>
</body>
</html>
```

> move to the previous record

> move to the next record

> move to the last record

6. Save your changes to FP1.htm.

7. Using Internet Explorer, open **FP1.htm** and verify that the four buttons located below the table allow you to move through the records in the recordset. Figure 2-26 displays the contents of the last record.

Figure 2-26   **THE LAST RECORD IN THE RECORDSET**

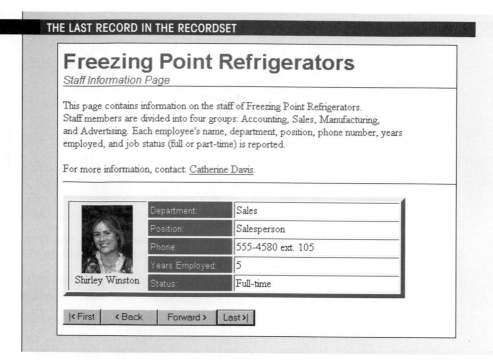

Working with Data Source Object Properties

Catherine is thrilled with your work and the button feature. However, she did discover one small problem that needs to be addressed. When she navigated to the last button and clicked the Forward button, the Web page displayed a blank record with a missing inline image.

You explain to Catherine that this is the result of the Web page trying to access a record that doesn't exist. Catherine understands your explanation but is concerned that users will find this effect disconcerting. She would like you to revise the page to prohibit users from moving outside the boundaries of the recordset.

To do this, you need to determine which record the user is currently viewing, which is accomplished by working with the properties of the Data Source Object. DSO properties are described with the syntax

    id.recordset.*property*

where *property* is one of the Data Source Object properties supported by the ADO. Just as there were DSO methods, there are many DSO properties that allow programmers to develop sophisticated data-access pages. In this tutorial, we'll concentrate on those properties that work with the location of the current record. These properties are described in Figure 2-27.

Figure 2-27   **RECORDSET PROPERTIES**

RECORDSET PROPERTIES	DESCRIPTION
id.recordset.BOF	Indicates whether the current record position is before the first record in the recordset
id.recordset.EOF	Indicates whether the current record position is after the last record in the recordset
id.recordset.Index	Returns the index number of the current record
id.recordset.RecordCount	Returns the total number of records in the recordset

Two properties are of most use to you: the BOF (beginning of file) property and the EOF (end of file) property. Both properties return a value of *true* if a user moves off the edge of the recordset. Otherwise they return the value *false*. To prevent the page from attempting to display a record before the first one in the recordset, add the following command to the Back button:

```
if (Staff_Info.recordset.BOF) Staff_Info.recordset.moveFirst()
```

The code uses the "if" command to first test whether the page is trying to display a record occurring before the first record in the recordset, which would of course be an empty record. If that is the case, the Web page displays the first record in the recordset.

Similarly, to prevent the page from attempting to display a record beyond the last record in the recordset, add the following command to the Forward button:

```
if (Staff_Info.recordset.EOF) Staff_Info.recordset.moveLast()
```

With this code, the last record is displayed if a user attempts to access a record that occurs after the last record in the recordset.

To modify the features of the Back and Forward buttons:

1. Using your text editor, open **FP1.htm** if it is not currently open.

2. Locate the <button> tag for the Back button.

3. After the movePrevious() method, type a semi-colon (;), and then type the following command, as shown in Figure 2-28:

```
if (Staff_Info.recordset.BOF) Staff_Info.recordset.move
First()
```

| Figure 2-28 | TESTING WHETHER THE CURRENT RECORD POSITION IS BEFORE THE FIRST RECORD |

```
<button onClick="Staff_Info.recordset.moveFirst()">
    |&lt; First
</button>
<button onClick="Staff_Info.recordset.movePrevious();
                 if (Staff_Info.recordset.BOF) Staff_Info.recordset.moveFirst()">
      &lt; Back   
</button>
<button onClick="Staff_Info.recordset.moveNext()">
    Forward &gt;
</button>
<button onClick="Staff_Info.recordset.moveLast()">
    Last &gt; |
</button>
</body>
</html>
```

if the current record is before the first record in the recordset...

...move back to the first record

commands must be separated by a semi-colon and the commands must be enclosed in quotes

The semicolon separates one command from another. Note also that you have to enclose both commands within the set of quotation marks.

4. After the moveNext() method in the <button> tag for the Forward button, type a semicolon followed by the command

```
if (Staff_Info.recordset.EOF) Staff_Info.recordset.moveLast()
```

See Figure 2-29.

Figure 2-29   **TESTING WHETHER THE CURRENT RECORD POSITION IS AFTER THE LAST RECORD**

```
<button onClick="Staff_Info.recordset.moveFirst()">
    |&lt; First
</button>
<button onClick="Staff_Info.recordset.movePrevious();
                if (Staff_Info.recordset.BOF) Staff_Info.recordset.moveFirst()">
      &lt; Back   
</button>
<button onClick="Staff_Info.recordset.moveNext();
                if (Staff_Info.recordset.EOF) Staff_Info.recordset.moveLast()">
    Forward &gt;
</button>
<button onClick="Staff_Info.recordset.moveLast()">
    Last &gt;|
</button>
</body>
</html>
```

5. Save your changes to FP1.htm and use Internet Explorer to refresh FP1.htm.

6. Within the browser, click the **< Back** button and verify that you cannot display a record before the first record in the recordset.

7. Click the **Last>|** button followed by the **Forward >** button to verify that you cannot display a record after the last record in the recordset.

You've completed your work on FP1.htm and Catherine is impressed with the way that you handled this latest challenge.

To complete your work:

1. Exit from Internet Explorer and your text editor.

In the next session, you'll continue to work with Catherine's employee data, learn how to display multiple records in a single table, and learn how to work with hierarchical recordsets.

Session 2.2 QUICK CHECK

1. In general, how does the DSO object treat an element attribute?

2. Describe how the DSO treats an attribute that is part of a field element.

3. What command would you use to display the last record from a data island named "Cinfo"?

4. What command would you use to display the previous record from the CInfo recordset?

5. What command would you use to display a record with the index number "5" from the CInfo recordset?

6. What recordset property indicates whether the current record is past the last record in the recordset?

7. What recordset property returns the index number of the current recordset?

SESSION 2.3

In this session, you'll display multiple records within a single table using data table binding. You'll also learn how to segment your recordset into pages and how to navigate from page to page. Finally, you'll explore how to create and work with hierarchical recordsets.

Working with Table Binding

The tags you worked with in the last session had the limitation of displaying a single value at a time. Catherine wants to create a page where she can view all of the staff records at a glance, without having to scroll through several pages of records.

As you will see in this session, this can be done using **table data binding**, in which each record is displayed in a different row of a table. The syntax for binding a recordset to a table is

```
<table datasrc="#id">
  <tr>
    <td><span datafld="field1"></span></td>
    <td><span datafld="field2"></span></td>
  </tr>
</table>
```

where *id* is the name of the data island and *field1*, *field2*, etc., are the fields from the recordset. Even though the fields are bound to a single tag in the table, the browser repeats the field value for each record in the recordset to automatically add as many rows to the table as there are records. The difference between this table and the table you worked on in the last session is that the datasrc attribute is placed in the <table> tag and the datafld attributes are placed in individual table cells. The <td> tag doesn't support data binding, so you must enclose the text of each table cell using the <span> tag, or any other tag that supports data binding (see Figure 2-11).

Catherine has put together another draft of a page she would like you to develop. As shown in Figure 2-30, she wants the table placed on the right margin of the Web page. Currently, the Web page displays a single sample row, but when you're finished, the Web page will display content from all of the records in the XML document.

Figure 2-30	CATHERINE'S NEW PAGE

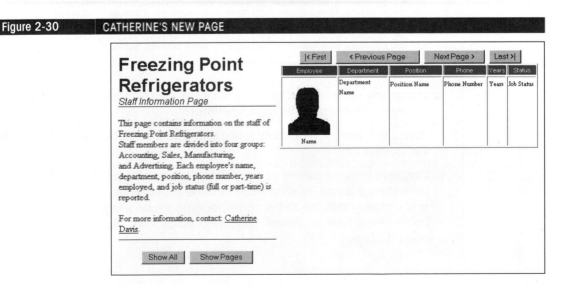

Note that the Web page also contains buttons to display the table by pages. You'll learn about pages and how to use them later in the session.

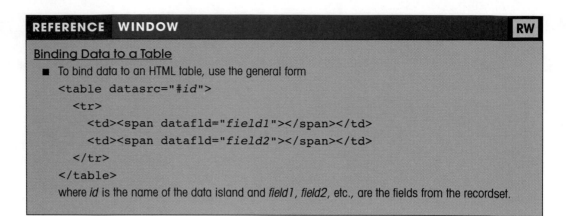

Binding Data to a Table

■ To bind data to an HTML table, use the general form

```
<table datasrc="#id">
  <tr>
    <td><span datafld="field1"></span></td>
    <td><span datafld="field2"></span></td>
  </tr>
</table>
```

where *id* is the name of the data island and *field1*, *field2*, etc., are the fields from the recordset.

Catherine has already inserted <xml> tags in her HTML file to connect the document to the FPInfo and Emp1 XML documents. Your job is to bind the cells in the table to the appropriate fields in those XML documents.

To bind the table to an XML document:

1. Using your text editor, open **FP2text.htm**, located in the Tutorial.02X/Tutorial folder of your Data Disk.

2. Save the file as **FP2.htm**.

   As before, the staff information has been placed in a data island named "Staff_Info". Reference this data island in the <table> tag.

3. Locate the <table> tag, and insert the attribute **datasrc="#Staff_Info"**, as shown in Figure 2-31.

Figure 2-31   SPECIFYING THE DATASRC FOR THE TABLE

```
<table width="460" border="1" datasrc="#Staff_Info">
  <thead>
      <th bgcolor="blue" width="100"><span class="colhead">Employee</span></th>
      <th bgcolor="blue" width="90"><span class="colhead">Department</span></th>
      <th bgcolor="blue" width="100"><span class="colhead">Position</span></th>
      <th bgcolor="blue" width="80"><span class="colhead">Phone</span></th>
      <th bgcolor="blue" wdith="30"><span class="colhead">Years</span></th>
      <th bgcolor="blue" width="50"><span class="colhead">Status</span></th>
  </thead>
```

4. Locate the <img> tag in the table's first cell and replace the src="Photo.jpg" attribute with the attribute **datafld="Photo"**.

5. Delete the "Name" placeholder text and add the attribute **datafld="Name"** to the <span> tag.

6. Continue through the rest of the table, deleting the placeholder text for Department Name, Position Name, Phone Number, Years, and Job Status, and add datafld attributes to the corresponding <span> tags that point to the Department, Position, Phone, Years, and Status fields. Figure 2-32 shows the revised code.

Figure 2-32	SPECIFYING THE DATASRC FOR THE TABLE

```
<table width="460" border="1" datasrc="#Staff_Info">
   <thead>
      <th bgcolor="blue" width="100"><span class="colhead">Employee</span></th>
      <th bgcolor="blue" width="90"><span class="colhead">Department</span></th>
      <th bgcolor="blue" width="100"><span class="colhead">Position</span></th>
      <th bgcolor="blue" width="80"><span class="colhead">Phone</span></th>
      <th bgcolor="blue" wdith="30"><span class="colhead">Years</span></th>
      <th bgcolor="blue" width="50"><span class="colhead">Status</span></th>
   </thead>
   <tr><td align="center" bgcolor="white">
      <img datafld="Photo"><br>
      <span class="celltext" datafld="Name"></span>
   </td>
   <td valign="top" bgcolor="white">
      <span  class="celltext"datafld="Department"></span>
   </td>
   <td valign="top" bgcolor="white">
      <span  class="celltext" datafld="Position"></span>
   </td>
   <td valign="top" bgcolor="white">
      <span  class="celltext" datafld="Phone"></span>
   </td>
   <td valign="top"  align="center" bgcolor="white">
      <span  class="celltext" datafld="Years"></span>
   </td>
   <td valign="top" bgcolor="white">
      <span  class="celltext" datafld="Status"></span>
   </td>
   </tr>
</table>
```

7. Save your changes to FP2.htm.

8. Using Internet Explorer, open **FP2.htm**.

   Figure 2-33 displays the completed page with all of the records from the Emp1.xml document inserted into the table.

Figure 2-33	VIEWING THE RECORDS IN A SINGLE TABLE

records from the
Staff_Info recordset

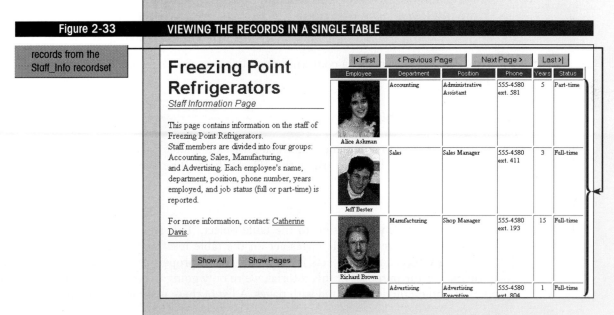

Working with Table Pages

Catherine realizes that as she adds more records to her XML document, the table in the Web page becomes increasingly long and unwieldy. With that in mind, Catherine would like to give users the option of limiting the number of records displayed at any one time to three. They could then move forward or backward through the recordset, three records at a time. This technique of breaking up the recordset into manageable chunks is called **paging**.

Specifying the Page Size

To create a table page, the first step is to add the **dataPageSize** attribute to the <table> tag. The syntax for this attribute is

```
dataPageSize="number"
```

where *number* is the number of records you want displayed in a single page. Add this attribute to the <table> tag now.

To define a page size:

1. Return to FP2.htm in your text editor.

2. Insert the attribute **dataPageSize="3"** for the <table> tag, as shown in Figure 2-34.

Figure 2-34   SPECIFYING A PAGE SIZE FOR THE TABLE

```
<table width="460" border="1" datasrc="#Staff_Info" datapagesize="3">
    <thead>
        <th bgcolor="blue" width="100"><span class="colhead">Employee</span></th>
        <th bgcolor="blue" width="90"><span class="colhead">Department</span></th>
        <th bgcolor="blue" width="100"><span class="colhead">Position</span></th>
        <th bgcolor="blue" width="80"><span class="colhead">Phone</span></th>
        <th bgcolor="blue" wdith="30"><span class="colhead">Years</span></th>
        <th bgcolor="blue" width="50"><span class="colhead">Status</span></th>
    </thead>
```

3. Save your changes to FP2.htm.

4. Using Internet Explorer, open **FP2.htm** and verify that only the first three records are displayed in the Web page.

The next step is to create a command that allows users to navigate through the pages in the table.

Navigating a Table Page

Before you can write a command to navigate through a table page, you must first assign a unique identifier to the table using the ID attribute. The syntax for assigning an ID attribute is

```
<table id="id">
```

where *id* is the name you'll assign to the table object. This step is necessary because the commands to navigate the table pages act on the table itself and not the recordset. Like Data Source Objects, table objects have   long list of properties and methods associated with them. For the purposes of this tutorial, we're only going to concern ourselves with the properties and methods associated with pages. A list of these is shown in Figure 2-35.

Figure 2-35   TABLE METHODS AND PROPERTIES

TABLE METHODS AND PROPERTIES	DESCRIPTION
id.firstPage()	Display the first page in the *id* table
id.previousPage()	Display the previous page in the table
id.nextPage()	Display the next page in the table

Figure 2-35	TABLE METHODS AND PROPERTIES (CONTINUED)

TABLE METHODS AND PROPERTIES	DESCRIPTION
id.lastPage()	Display the last page in the table
id.dataPageSize=*n*	Set the number of pages in the *id* table to *n* pages

To run these commands, you can add the command to the onClick event handler of a <button> tag as you did for the buttons in Catherine's other page. For example, to move to the last page in a data table named "StaffTable," you enter the attribute

```
onClick="StaffTable.lastPage()"
```

Complete the following steps to add the appropriate table methods to the four buttons located above the table in Catherine's Web page.

To add the table methods to Catherine's Web page:

1. Return to FP2.htm in your text editor.

2. Assign the attribute **id="StaffTable"** to the <table> tag to give an ID name to the data table.

3. Locate the <button> tag for the "First" button and insert the attribute **onClick="StaffTable.firstPage()"**.

4. Locate the <button> tag for the "Previous" button and insert the attribute **onClick="StaffTable.previousPage()"**.

5. Locate the <button> tag for the "Next" button and insert the attribute **onClick="StaffTable.nextPage()"**.

6. Finally, locate the <button> tag for the "Last" button and insert the attribute **onClick="StaffTable.lastPage()"**.

Figure 2-36 shows the revised HTML code.

Figure 2-36	ENTERING THE PAGE METHODS

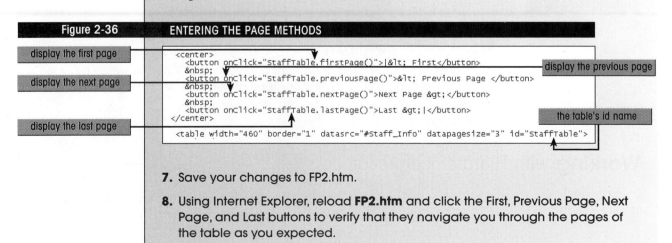

```
<center>
  <button onClick="StaffTable.firstPage()">|&lt; First</button>
   
  <button onClick="StaffTable.previousPage()">&lt; Previous Page </button>
   
  <button onClick="StaffTable.nextPage()">Next Page &gt;</button>
   
  <button onClick="StaffTable.lastPage()">Last &gt;|</button>
</center>

<table width="460" border="1" datasrc="#Staff_Info" datapagesize="3" id="StaffTable">
```

display the first page
display the previous page
display the next page
display the last page
the table's id name

7. Save your changes to FP2.htm.

8. Using Internet Explorer, reload **FP2.htm** and click the First, Previous Page, Next Page, and Last buttons to verify that they navigate you through the pages of the table as you expected.

Catherine also wants to provide users with the option of switching between a view of all records in the table and a view that displays the table by pages. To do this, you add a command to the button to change the dataPageSize attribute of the table. To show all of the records in the recordset, you must set the value of the page size to a very high value and then instruct the browser to move to the first page in the table. The complete command to accomplish this task is

```
onClick="StaffTable.dataPageSize=999999;StaffTable.firstPage()"
```

To restore the page size to three, use the command

```
onClick="StaffTable.dataPageSize=3"
```

Catherine has two buttons for this purpose located in the bottom left corner of the Web page. Modify these buttons now to solve Catherine's problem.

To modify the buttons:

1. Using your text editor, open **FP2.htm** if it is not currently open.

2. Locate the Show All <button> tag, and insert the text **onClick="StaffTable.dataPageSize=999999; StaffTable.firstPage()"**.

3. Locate the Show Pages <button> tag, and insert the attribute **onClick="StaffTable.dataPageSize=3"** with the <button tag>. Figure 2-37 shows the revised HTML code.

Figure 2-37	CHANGING THE DATAPAGESIZE

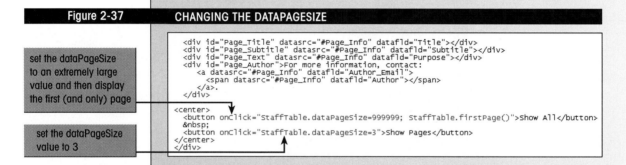

set the dataPageSize to an extremely large value and then display the first (and only) page

set the dataPageSize value to 3

```
<div id="Page_Title" datasrc="#Page_Info" datafld="Title"></div>
<div id="Page_Subtitle" datasrc="#Page_Info" datafld="Subtitle"></div>
<div id="Page_Text" datasrc="#Page_Info" datafld="Purpose"></div>
<div id="Page_Author">For more information, contact:
    <a datasrc="#Page_Info" datafld="Author_Email">
        <span datasrc="#Page_Info" datafld="Author"></span>
    </a>.
</div>

<center>
    <button onClick="StaffTable.dataPageSize=999999; StaffTable.firstPage()">Show All</button>
     
    <button onClick="StaffTable.dataPageSize=3">Show Pages</button>
</center>
</div>
```

4. Save your changes to FP2.htm.

5. Reload **FP2.htm** in Internet Explorer and verify that you can switch between a page view and a view of all records by clicking the Show Page and Show All buttons.

Working with Hierarchical Recordsets

Catherine has created another XML document, named Emp2.xml, which organizes employees by departments. Figure 2-38 shows a tree diagram of the elements in her document.

| Figure 2-38 | LAYOUT OF THE EMP2.XML DOCUMENT |

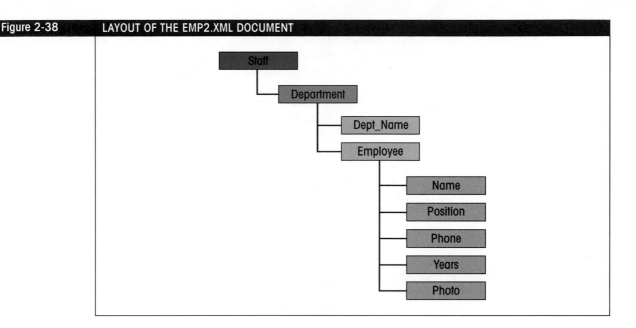

Up to this point, you've worked with simple recordsets where each record contains a fixed number of fields and is made up exclusively of character data. The layout displayed in Figure 2-38 shows a hierarchical recordset in which the Employee field contains not character data, but a record of fields describing each employee.

The syntax for binding a nested record to a table is

```
<table datasrc="#id" datafld="record">
  <tr>
    <td><span datafld="field1"></span></td>
    <td><span datafld="field2"></span></td>
  </tr>
</table>
```

where *id* is the name of the data island, *record* is the name of the field that contains the nested record, and *field1*, *field2*, etc., are fields within the nested record. Note that the main difference between this table format and the table format for a simple recordset is that you must include the name of the record element in the <table> tag. For example, to bind the Employee fields displayed in Figure 2-38 to a table, you create a table as follows:

```
<table datasrc="#Staff_Info" datafld="Employee">
  <tr>
    <td><span datafld="Name"></span></td>
    <td><span datafld="Position"></span></td>
    <td><span datafld="Phone"></span></td>
      . . .
  </tr>
</table>
```

If the recordset contains several levels of nested recordsets, you must include several levels of nested tables to match. For example, the layout shown in Figure 2-39 would be matched by the series of nested tables shown below.

```
<table datasrc="#id" datafld="record1">
  <tr>
  <td><table datasrc="#id" datafld="record2">
```

```
<tr>
  <td><table datasrc="#id" datafld="record3">
       <tr>
         <td><span datafld="field1"></span></td>
         <td><span datafld="field2"></span></td>
         <td><span datafld="field3"></span></td>
       </tr>
      </table>
  </td>
</tr>
</table>
</td>
</tr>
</table>
```

Figure 2-39	SEVERAL LAYERS OF NESTED RECORDS

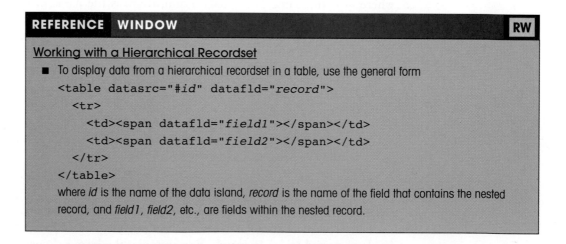

REFERENCE   WINDOW   **RW**

<u>Working with a Hierarchical Recordset</u>
■ To display data from a hierarchical recordset in a table, use the general form
```
<table datasrc="#id" datafld="record">
  <tr>
    <td><span datafld="field1"></span></td>
    <td><span datafld="field2"></span></td>
  </tr>
</table>
```
where *id* is the name of the data island, *record* is the name of the field that contains the nested record, and *field1*, *field2*, etc., are fields within the nested record.

Catherine has assembled one last draft of a Web page. This time, her Web page is based on the layout of the Emp2.xml document. Figure 2-40 shows the type of page she has in mind.

Figure 2-40	DRAFT OF CATHERINE'S FINAL WEB PAGE

employee information is grouped by department

Freezing Point Refrigerators
Staff Information Page

This page contains information on the staff of Freezing Point Refrigerators. Staff members are divided into four groups: Accounting, Sales, Manufacturing, and Advertising. Each employee's name, department, position, phone number, years employed, and job status (full or part-time) is reported.

For more information, contact: Catherine Davis.

Next Department

With this page, employee information is grouped by department. The table displays information on all employees for a given department. To navigate from the current department to the next one in the recordset, Catherine wants users to be able to click the Next Department button located in the bottom left corner of the Web page.

To bind data to Catherine's page:

1. Using your text editor, open **Emp2.xml** from the Tutorial.02X/Tutorial folder on your Data Disk. Scroll through the document, noting the document structure, the name of the various elements, and the content of each element.

2. Close the file without saving any changes.

3. Using your text editor, open **FP3text.htm** and save the file as **FP3.htm**.

4. Locate the <xml> tag that created the data island for the FPInfo.xml document. Below it insert an <xml> tag to create a data island named "Staff_Info" that connects to the Emp2.xml document:

   ```
   <xml id="Staff_Info" src="Emp2.xml"></xml>
   ```

5. Locate the placeholder text, "Department Name," and add the following attribute to its <span> tag. Delete the placeholder text.

   ```
   datasrc="#Staff_Info" datafld="Dept_Name"
   ```

6. Locate the <table> tag and insert the following attributes:

   ```
   datasrc="#Staff_Info" datafld="Employee"
   ```

7. Following the same process you used for Catherine's other Web pages, delete all of the placeholder text in the table and add datafld attributes, binding the tags to the contents of the Emp2.xml document. To assist you, Figure 2-41 shows the revised code for this file, highlighted in red.

Figure 2-41 BINDING TO A HIERARCHICAL RECORDSET

```
<body>
   <xml id="Page_Info" src="FPInfo.xml"></xml>
   <xml id="Staff_Info" src="Emp2.xml"></xml>

   <div id="Page_Data">

     <div id="Page_Title" datasrc="#Page_Info" datafld="Title"></div>
     <div id="Page_Subtitle" datasrc="#Page_Info" datafld="Subtitle"></div>
     <div id="Page_Text" datasrc="#Page_Info" datafld="Purpose"></div>
     <div id="Page_Author">For more information, contact:
        <a datasrc="#Page_Info" datafld="Author_Email">
          <span datasrc="#Page_Info" datafld="Author"></span>
        </a>.
     </div>
     <button>
       Next Department
     </button>
   </div>

   <center>
     <span id="DName" datasrc="#Staff_Info" datafld="Dept_Name"></span><br>
   </center>

   <table width="460" border="1" datasrc="#Staff_Info" datafld="Employee">
     <thead>
        <th bgcolor="blue" width="100"><span class="colhead">Employee</span></th>
        <th bgcolor="blue" width="100"><span class="colhead">Position</span></th>
        <th bgcolor="blue" width="80"><span class="colhead">Phone</span></th>
        <th bgcolor="blue" wdith="30"><span class="colhead">Years</span></th>
        <th bgcolor="blue" width="50"><span class="colhead">Status</span></th>
     </thead>
     <tr><td align="center" bgcolor="white">
          <img datafld="Photo"><br>
          <span class="celltext" datafld="Name"></span>
        </td>
        <td valign="top" bgcolor="white">
          <span  class="celltext" datafld="Position"></span>
        </td>
        <td valign="top" bgcolor="white">
          <span  class="celltext" datafld="Phone"></span>
        </td>
        <td valign="top"  align="center" bgcolor="white">
          <span  class="celltext" datafld="Years"></span>
        </td>
        <td valign="top" bgcolor="white">
          <span  class="celltext" datafld="Status"></span>
        </td>
     </tr>
   </table>

</body>
```

8. Save your changes to FP3.htm.

9. Using Internet Explorer, open **FP3.htm** and verify that it shows information on employees from the Accounting department, as shown in Figure 2-42.

Figure 2-42   EMPLOYEES FROM THE ACCOUNTING DEPARTMENT

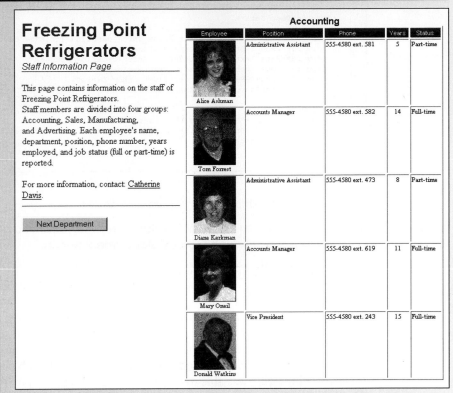

To show employee data from other departments, you move to the next record in the department recordset. Because this is the topmost recordset in the hierarchy, you can use the following command to accomplish this:

```
Staff_Info.recordset.moveNext()
```

There is only one button in Catherine's Web page to navigate through the recordset, so when users reach the last record, Catherine would like them sent back to the first record. The following code is used to add the desired functionality to the Next Department button:

```
Staff_Info.recordset.moveNext();
if (Staff_Info.recordset.EOF) Staff_Info.recordset.moveFirst()
```

To customize the Next Department button:

1. Return to FP3.htm in your text editor.

2. Locate the <button> tag for the Next Department button and insert the following code within the <button> tag (see Figure 2-43):

```
onClick="Staff_Info.recordset.moveNext();
   if (Staff_Info.recordset.EOF) Staff_Info.recordset.move
First()"
```

Figure 2-43	INSERTING A COMMAND TO MOVE TO THE NEXT DEPARTMENT

```
<div id="Page_Data">

   <div id="Page_Title" datasrc="#Page_Info" datafld="Title"></div>
   <div id="Page_Subtitle" datasrc="#Page_Info" datafld="Subtitle"></div>
   <div id="Page_Text" datasrc="#Page_Info" datafld="Purpose"></div>
   <div id="Page_Author">For more information, contact:
      <a datasrc="#Page_Info" datafld="Author_Email">
        <span datasrc="#Page_Info" datafld="Author"></span>
      </a>.
   </div>
   <button onClick="Staff_Info.recordset.moveNext();
              if (Staff_Info.recordset.EOF) Staff_Info.recordset.moveFirst()">
     Next Department
   </button>
</div>
```

3. Close the FP3.htm file, saving your changes.

4. Reload **FP3.htm** in Internet Explorer and verify that you can move through the recordset by clicking the Next Department button.

5. Close your Web browser.

Note that as you moved through the department recordset, the list of employees was automatically changed to the correct department. This is because as you moved to the next record, the Employee field, which contains the nested record, was also changed.

Catherine is pleased with the final version of her staff Web page. By using a hierarchical recordset, Catherine was able to organize the employee data in a reasonable and useful way. She'll get back to you if she needs any more work done on this issue.

Session 2.3 QUICK CHECK

1. Where should you put the datasrc attribute if you want to use table binding?

2. What is paging?

3. How do you set the size of a table to five pages?

4. A table object has the name "PTable." What command would you use to display the last page in the table?

5. What command would you use to change the page size of PTable to six?

6. How do you display a hierarchical recordset in a table?

REVIEW ASSIGNMENTS

Catherine has been using the staff page you've designed for a few weeks now. Her associates at Freezing Point Refrigerators have seen her work and would like to use data binding with some of their XML documents. Jason Lewis maintains a Web page describing the various refrigerators sold by the company. He would like to bind the contents of this page with some of his XML documents.

Jason has collected the following information on each refrigerator model: the model name, the selling price, the refrigerator's cubic capacity, the refrigerator's dimensions, whether the model is energy efficient or not, and whether the freezer unit is located above or side-by-side with the main unit. Jason has also organized the refrigerator models into two types: those that are designed to fit into cabinet spaces and those that are freestanding.

Jason has created three XML documents named SInfo.xml, Refg1.xml, and Refg2.xml. The SInfo.xml document contains information about the company that Jason wants to include in any Web page he creates. The Refg1.xml document contains data on individual refrigerator models in a simple recordset. The Refg2.xml document contains a hierarchical recordset in which the models are divided based on whether they are cabinet style or freestanding.

Jason would like to create the following three Web pages from these documents: Inv1.htm, Inv2.htm, and Inv3.htm. The purpose of these pages is similar to the three pages that Catherine created for her staff directory. The Inv1.htm Web page should display each refrigerator model in a separate page. The Inv2.htm page should display all of the refrigerator models in a single table that can be broken into individual pages. The Inv3.htm page should display the model data broken down by model type.

Jason has already created the basic format for these three pages. He needs your help in binding those pages with the contents of his XML documents and inserting commands to navigate through the records in the recordsets.

To complete this task:

1. Using your text editor, open and review the contents of the **Refg1.xml** and **Refg2.xml** documents, located in the Tutorial.02X/Review folder of your Data Disk. Take some time to become familiar with their contents and the document structure. Close the documents without saving any changes.

2. Using your text editor, open **Invtxt1.htm** from the Tutorial.02X/Review folder and save the file as **Inv1.htm**.

3. Create two data islands. The first, named "Sinfo," should point to the contents of the SInfo.xml file. The second, named "Ref_Info," should point to the contents of the Refg1.xml file.

4. Bind the text of the page's title, subtitle, and purpose with the contents of the Title, Subtitle, and Purpose fields in the SInfo data island. Bind the target of the author's hyperlink to the value of the Author_Email field of the SInfo data island. Bind the text of the author's name to the Author field.

5. Within the table describing an individual refrigerator model, bind the following items to fields in the Ref_Info data island:

   - Bind the inline image to the Photo field.
   - Bind the model type to the MType field.
   - Bind the price of the refrigerator to the Price field.
   - Bind the capacity and dimensions of the refrigerator to the Capacity and Dimensions fields.
   - Bind the energy efficiency and freezer location to the Energy and Freezer fields.

6. Add the following commands to the buttons located at the bottom of the page:

   - If the user clicks the First or Last buttons, display the first or last records in the Ref_Info recordset.

■ If the user clicks the Next button, display the next record in the Ref_Info recordset, unless this causes the Data Source Object to move off the edge of the recordset.

■ If the user clicks the Previous button, display the previous records in the Ref_Info recordset, unless this would cause the Data Source Object to move off the edge of the recordset.

7. Save your changes to Inv1.htm. Open the file in your Internet Explorer browser and verify that you can scroll though the contents of the Ref_Info data island by clicking the buttons on the Web page.

8. Using your text editor, open the **Invtxt2.htm** file from the Tutorial.02X/Review folder and save the file as **Inv2.htm**. Create data islands named "Sinfo" and "Ref_Info" for the SInfo.xml and Refg1.xml documents.

9. Bind the page's title, subtitle, purpose, author name, and author hyperlink to the appropriate fields in the SInfo data island.

10. Set the data page size for the table to 4. Bind the contents of the table to the appropriate fields in the Ref_Info data island.

11. Add the following commands to the buttons on the page:

■ If the user clicks the First, Previous Page, Next Page, or Last Page buttons, display the first, previous, next, or last page of records in the table.

■ If the user clicks the Show All button, set the data page size to an extremely high number.

■ If the user clicks the Show Pages button, set the data page size to 4.

12. Save your changes to Inv2.htm. Open the file in your Internet Explorer browser and verify that you can view the records in the Ref_Info recordset by pages.

13. Using your text editor, open **Invtxt3.htm** from the Tutorial.02X/Review folder and save the file as **Inv3.htm**. Create data islands named "Sinfo" and "Ref_Info2" for the SInfo.xml and Refg2.xml documents.

14. Bind the page's title, subtitle, purpose, author name, and author hyperlink to the appropriate fields in the SInfo data island. Bind the model type text to the MType field in the Ref_Info2 data island. Bind contents of the table to the appropriate fields in the Ref_Info2 data island.

Explore ▶ 15. Edit the Cabinet Refrigerators radio button so that it displays the first record in the Ref_Info2 data island.

Explore ▶ 16. Edit the Freestanding Refrigerators radio button so that it displays the last record in the Ref_Info2 data island.

17. Save your changes to Inv3.htm. Open the file in your Internet Explorer browser and verify that you can view the different model types in the recordset by clicking the appropriate radio button.

18. Print out the contents of Inv1.htm, Inv2.htm, and Inv3.htm. Hand in your printouts and files to your instructor.

CASE PROBLEMS

Case 1. Online Electronics, Inc. Brett Keyes is a product manager for Online Electronics (OE), an Internet superstore. He's working on a Web page that lists OE car stereo products. Brett has already created a draft of the Web page, and the product list is stored in an XML document named OE.xml. He needs your help in binding the data to the Web page.

Figure 2-44 shows the structure of Brett's XML document. The XML document is organized in the form of a hierarchical recordset. The top level indicates the car stereo type. Brett has organized the car stereos into four distinct groups: CD players/receivers for less than $200 and greater than $200, and cassette tape players selling for less than $50 and greater than $50. For each car stereo, Brett has recorded a product ID (PID), the stereo's manufacturer, the name of the product, and the product's selling price.

Figure 2-44

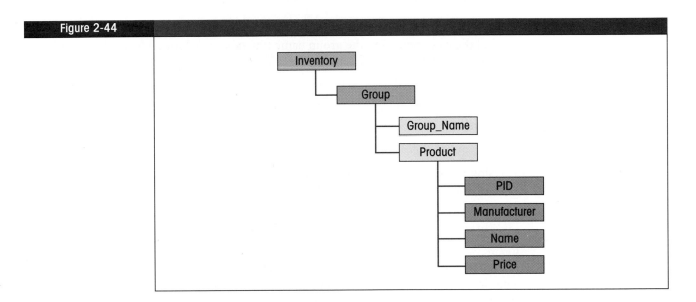

Brett would like this hierarchical recordset displayed within a single table with the information on each individual car stereo nested within that stereo's product group. Figure 2-45 shows a preview of the page you'll create.

Figure 2-45

Online Electronics
Product List

The table of products is divided into the following groups: CD Players/Receivers ($0-$200), CD Players/Receivers ($200+), Tape Players ($0-$50), and Tape Players ($50-$100).
This data has been compiled by Brett Keyes.

Product ID	Manufacturer	Product Name	Price
		CD Player/Receiver ($0-$200)	
ADX317	Addison	Addison Detachable Face CD 180 Watts Max	$119.99
ADX417	Addison	Addison Detachable Face CD Player 160 Watts Max with Steering Wheel Remote	$128.99
ADX517	Addison	Addison Detachable Face CD Player 200 Watts Max with Steering Wheel Remote	$159.99
ADCMP3	Addison	Addison Magic Flip Face CD Player 200 Watts Max with Steering Wheel Remote	$199.99
CLK216	Clarkson	Clarkson 180 Watts Max CD Player	$109.99
CLK317	Clarkson	Clarkson 180 Watts Max CD Player	$149.99
LX715K	Linax	Linax Fixed DIN CD Player with Wireless Remote	$99.99

Brett also has an XML document named OETitles.xml that contains some of the page titles and introductory text he wants to display in the document.

To complete this task:

1. Using your text editor, open **OETitles.xml** and **OE.xml** from the Tutorial.02X/Cases folder of your Data Disk. Take some time to view these documents, becoming familiar with their content and structure. Close both files without saving any changes to them.

2. Using your text editor, open **OEInvtxt.htm** located in the Tutorial.02X/Cases folder. Save the file as **OEInv.htm**.

3. Create two data islands named "Page_Info" and "Prod_Info" that point to the OETitles.xml and OE.xml files, respectively.

4. Bind the page's title, subtitle, and introduction to the Title, Subtitle, and Intro fields of the Page_Info data island.

5. Specify that the product table on this page should be bound with the Prod_Info data island.

6. Bind the row containing the group name (the table row located beneath the table heading) to the contents of the Group_Name field.

Explore 7. Bind the embedded table to the Prod_Info data island and the Product field.

8. Within the embedded table, bind each cell to the appropriate fields in the Prod_Info data island.

9. Save your changes to the file.

10. Using Internet Explorer, open **OEInv.htm** and verify that it shows information on all of the car stereo products divided into Brett's four groups.

11. Print OEInv.htm, and hand in your files and printouts to your instructor.

Case 2. Central High School Class Reunion Committee. Cindy Carlson works for Special Events, a company that promotes and organizes parties, reunions, receptions, and other special events. Cindy has been developing a class reunion Web page for Central High School. Cindy's idea is to have several computer terminals located at the class reunion site allowing participants to access online information about the party and their classmates.

Cindy has already collected information about the participants of a class reunion for Central High School, and she's stored that data in an XML document named CHList.xml. The structure of the XML document is shown in Figure 2-46.

Figure 2-46

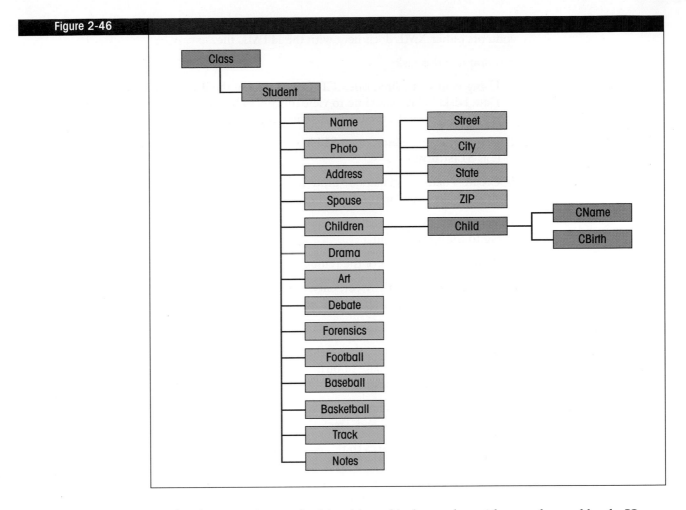

Cindy's document is organized in a hierarchical recordset with several nested levels. Her document includes information on each student's name, address, and children; activities they were involved with in school; special notes about their high school experiences; and a current photo. Figure 2-47 shows a preview of the page that Cindy wants you to create.

Figure 2-47

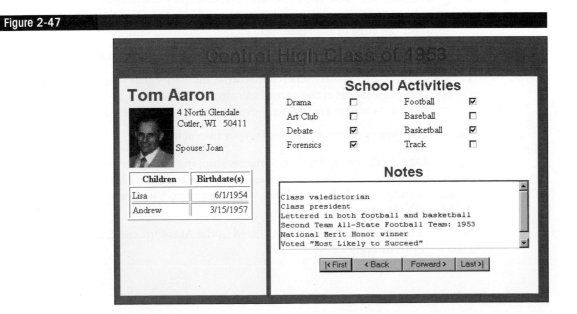

Cindy has already created a draft of the Web page, but she needs your help in binding the contents of her XML document with the HTML file.

To complete this task:

1. Using your text editor, open **CHList.xml** from the Tutorial.02X/Cases folder of your Data Disk. Take some time to view this file to become familiar with its content and structure. Close the file without saving any changes.

2. Using your text editor, open **SListtxt.htm** from the Tutorial.02X/Cases folder and save it as **SList.htm**.

3. Create a data island named "Stud_Info" that points to the CHList.xml file. Assume that all fields described in the following steps belong to this data source.

4. Locate the <div> tag that contains the participant's name and bind the contents of this tag to the SName field.

5. Bind the inline image of the reunion participant to the Photo field.

6. Bind the participant's Street, City, State, and ZIP fields to the embedded table in the SList.htm document. (*Hint*: You will have to bind this data as a hierachical recordset.)

7. Bind the Spouse field to the <span> tag containing the spouse's name.

Explore ▶ 8. Bind the CName and CBirth fields to the embedded table listing the children of each participant and their date of birth. (*Hint*: You will have to bind this data as a hierachical recordset with two nesting levels.)

Explore ▶ 9. Bind the checkboxes in the table to the Drama, Football, Art, Baseball, Debate, Basketball, Forensics, and Track fields.

Explore ▶ 10. Bind the Notes text area to the Notes field.

11. Add the following commands to the buttons at the bottom of the page:

   ■ If the user clicks the First or Last buttons, display the first or last records in the Stud_Info recordset.

   ■ If the user clicks the Next button, display the next record in the Stud_Info recordset unless this would cause the Data Source Object to move off the edge of the recordset.

   ■ If the user clicks the Previous button, display the previous records in the Stud_Info recordset unless this would cause the Data Source Object to move off the edge of the recordset.

12. Using your text editor, print the revised code, and save your changes to the SList.htm file.

13. Using Internet Explorer, open **SList.htm** and verify that you can properly scroll through the records in the recordset using the navigation buttons and that all values from the data source are properly displayed in the document.

14. Hand in your printouts and files to your instructor.

Case 3. AutoMaze, Inc. David Hansen manages shipping and receiving for AutoMaze, an auto parts superstore. The company stores shipping manifests in XML documents and then makes them accessible to employees via the company's intranet. David is exploring ways to bind the XML data to a Web page.

He has a sample shipping manifest stored in the AutoOrd.xml file. The structure of this file is shown in Figure 2-48.

Figure 2-48

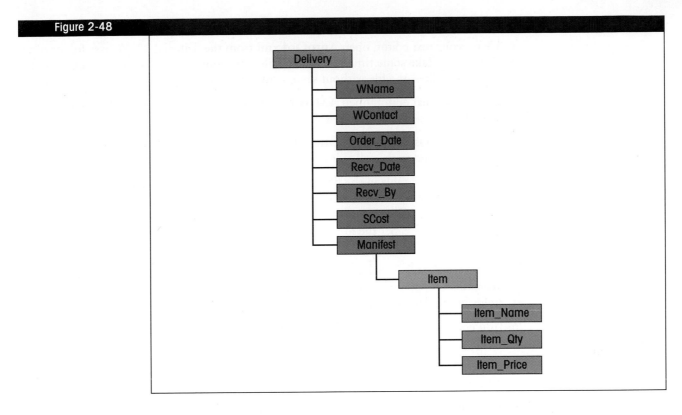

A preview of the Web page you'll create for David is shown in Figure 2-49. David has already created a draft of this page; your job will be to insert the data binding.

Figure 2-49

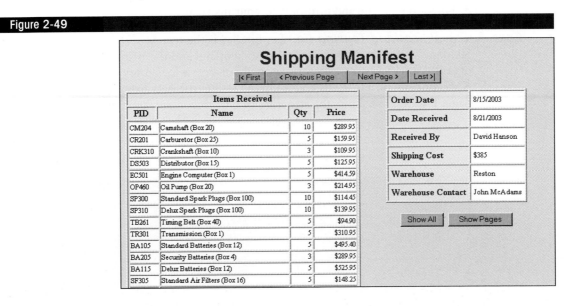

To complete this task:

1. Using your text editor, open **AutoOrd.xml** from the Tutorial.02X/Cases folder of your Data Disk. Take some time to view this file to become familiar with its content and structure. Close the file without saving any changes.

2. Using your text editor, open **AMtxt.htm** from the Tutorial.02X/Cases folder and save it as **AM.htm**.

3. Create a data island named "Order_Info" that points to the AutoOrd.xml file. All of the fields described in the following steps belong to this data source.

Explore

4. The first nested table in the file is used to display the items on the shipping manifest. Bind the outer table to the Manifest field. Bind the inner table to the Item field. Bind the cells of the inner table to the corresponding fields in the nested recordset from the AutoOrd.xml file. Set the id name of the inner table to "Orders". Set the page size of the inner table to six records.

5. The second table on the right edge of the Web page displays descriptive information about the shipping manifest. Bind each of the items in this table to the corresponding fields in the data source.

6. Add commands to the first set of four buttons to move to the first, previous, next, and last page of the Orders table.

7. Add commands to the second set of buttons to show all pages in the Orders table or to reset the page size of the Orders table back to six.

8. Print the AM.htm file, and close the file, saving your changes.

9. Using Internet Explorer, open **AM.htm** and verify that you can use the buttons on the page to navigate as you expected through the pages in the Orders table.

10. Hand in your file and printouts to your instructor.

Case 4. Travel Scotland Touring Co. Ian Findlay is the owner of the touring agency Travel Scotland, Inc., which organizes tours to Scotland and the British Isles for travelers from all over the world. He stores information about the various tours offered by his agency in an XML document. He needs your help in binding the data from his document to a Web page. Figure 2-50 shows the structure of Ian's document, tour.xml.

Figure 2-50

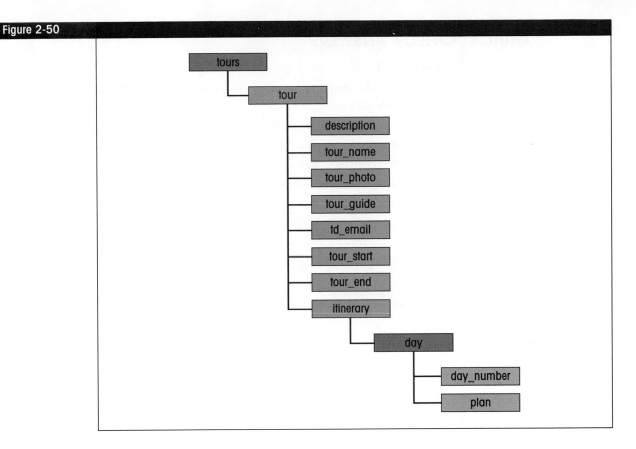

The description field contains a CDATA section of HTML code that Ian wants you to insert directly into the document. The itinerary field contains a nested recordset describing the events of each day of the tour. There are four tours in his file: the Lake District tour, the Hebrides tour, the Highland tour, and the Castles of Scotland tour. Ian has not created a Web page for his data yet. He has left the design up to you.

To complete this task:

1. Using your text editor, create a Web page named **Scotland.htm** to be stored in the Tutorial.02X/Cases folder of your Data Disk.

2. The Web page should display information about a single tour at a time, and the itinerary for each tour should be displayed as a table in the Web page.

3. The page should display an image from the selected tour (the image source file is indicated in the photo field).

4. The page should display a hyperlink to the e-mail address of the tour guide (found in the td_email field).

Explore

5. The information from the description field should be displayed in the Web page using the HTML formatting codes indicated in the tour.xml document.

6. The rest of the tour information should be displayed elsewhere in the Web page.

7. The page should include navigation buttons to move through the tours in the XML document.

8. When you are finished, print out the code for Scotland.htm and then view the page using Internet Explorer to verify that you can view information about the different Travel Scotland tours as you intended.

9. Hand in your printouts and files to your instructor.

QUICK CHECK ANSWERS

Session 2.1

1. **a.** Data binding is a technique in which the Web page's content is drawn from a data source.

   b. A field is an element that contains a single item of information.

   c. A record is a collection of fields.

   d. A recordset is a collection of records.

2. A hierarchical recordset can contain nested recordsets. A simple recordset cannot.

3. A data island is the data attached to a Web page through the process of data binding.

4. `<xml id="CompInfo" src="Company.xml"></xml>`

5. `<span datasrc="#CompInfo" datafld="CName"></span>`

6. as the value of the src attribute

7. The $Text field contains the character data from all of the fields in a record, not including attribute values.

Session 2.2

1. as a field

2. The field element becomes a record element with the attribute becoming one of the fields of the record element. The text in the field can only be accessed through the $Text field name.

3. `CInfo.recordset.moveLast()`

4. `CInfo.recordset.movePrevious()`

5. `CInfo.recordset.move(5)`

6. EOF

7. Index

Session 2.3

1. within the `<table>` tag

2. the process by which a table is divided into groups of records called pages

3. Include the dataPageSize="5" attribute in the table tag.

4. `PTable.lastPage()`

5. `PTable.dataPageSize=6`

6. If the recordset contains several levels of nested recordsets, you must include several levels of nested tables to match.

In this tutorial you will:

- Create a Document Type Definition

- Learn how to declare elements

- Work with nested elements

- Learn how to declare attributes

- Create parsed and unparsed entities

- Learn how to validate an XML document

CREATING A VALID XML DOCUMENT

Working with a Document Type Definition

CASE

Pixal Digital Products

Pixal Digital Products sells imaging hardware and software such as scanners, digital cameras, copiers, and digital tablets to individual consumers and businesses. Kristin Laughlin is the customer service manager at Pixal, and part of her job is to record information on Pixal's customers, including the individual orders they make.

Kristin is starting to use XML to record this information and has already created several XML documents containing information on customers and their orders. Eventually, Kristin wants to bind the data in the XML documents with a Web page. Kristin knows that her document needs to be well formed, following the rules of XML syntax exactly, but she would also like her document to follow certain rules regarding content. For example, every customer entered into her document must have a name, phone number, and address. Every customer order must contain a complete list of the items purchased, including the date they were ordered. In XML terms, she wants to create documents that are both well formed and valid. Kristin has asked for your help to create a valid document that adheres to both the rules of XML and the rules she has set up for the document's content and structure.

In this tutorial, you'll learn how XML can be used to create a valid document. You'll explore how to create and use internal and external document type definitions (DTDs). You'll also learn how to create element declarations to indicate which elements are valid in the document. Finally, you'll learn how to specify your document's structure, indicating which, and how many, elements are nested inside other elements.

Creating a Valid Document

In the last tutorial, you learned how to bind the contents of your XML document with an HTML file in order to publish the document to the Web or a corporate intranet in a useful way. In this and the following tutorials, you'll explore how XML documents can be validated to prevent errors in their content or structure.

You meet with Kristin to discuss the information she's collecting on Pixal's customers. To keep things to a manageable size, Kristin has limited her document to a subset of only three customers. Figure 3-1 shows the information she's entered for those customers.

Figure 3-1   CUSTOMER INFORMATION COLLECTED BY KRISTIN

Customer		Orders		Item	Qty.	Price
Name: Mr. David Lynn		OrderID: OR10311		DCT3Z	1	559.95
CustID: Cust201		Date: 8/1/2004		SM128	1	199.95
Type: home				RCL	2	29.95
Address: 211 Fox Street		OrderID: OR11424		BCE4L	1	59.95
Greenville, NH 80021		Date: 9/14/2004				
Phone: (315) 555-1812						
E-mail: dylnn@nhs.net						
Name: Mrs. Jean Kaufmann		OrderID: OR10899		WBC	1	59.99
CustID: Cust202		Date: 8/11/2004				
Type:						
Address: 411 East Oak Avenue				RCA	2	5.95
Cashton, MI 20401						
Phone: (611) 555-4033						
E-mail: JKaufmann@cshweb.com						
Name: Adservices		OrderID: OR11201		SCL4C	3	179.99
CustID: Cust203		Date: 9/15/2004				
Type: business						
Address: 55 Washburn Lane						
Creighton, UT 98712						
Phone: (811) 555-2987						
E-mail:						

For each customer, Kristin has recorded customer name, customer ID, type (home or business), address, phone number, and e-mail address. Note that she was not able to determine the customer type for Mrs. Jean Kaufmann or an e-mail address for Adservices.

Each customer has made one or more separate orders. For each order, Kristin has recorded an order ID number and the date the order was placed. Finally, within each order, Kristin has entered the items purchased, the quantity of each item, and the price.

She's already placed this information in an XML document. Open this file now.

To open Kristin's document:

1. Use your text editor to open the **Ordertxt.xml** document located in the Tutorial.03X/Tutorial folder of your Data Disk.

2. Save the file as **Orders.xml**.

Figure 3-2 displays the contents of the Orders.xml document for the first customer.

Figure 3-2	THE FIRST CUSTOMER IN THE ORDERS.XML DOCUMENT

```xml
<Customers>
    <Customer CustID="Cust201" CustType="home">
        <Name Title="Mr.">David Lynn</Name>
        <Address>
            <![CDATA[
            211 Fox Street
            Greenville, NH 80021
            ]]>
        </Address>
        <Phone>(315) 555-1812</Phone>
        <E-mail>dlynn@nhs.net</E-mail>
        <Orders>
            <Order OrderID="OR10311" OrderBy="Cust201">
                <Order_date>8/1/2004</Order_date>
                <Items>
                    <Item ItemPrice="599.95">DCT37</Item>
                    <Item ItemPrice="199.95">SM128</Item>
                    <Item ItemPrice="29.95" ItemQty="2">RCL</Item>
                </Items>
            </Order>
            <Order OrderID="OR11424" OrderBy="Cust201">
                <Order_date>9/14/2004</Order_date>
                <Items>
                    <Item ItemPrice="59.95">BCE4L</Item>
                </Items>
            </Order>
        </Orders>
    </Customer>
```

3. Examine the contents of Kristin's document. In particular, compare the elements entered in the document with the table in Figure 3-1.

Note that some of the elements in Kristin's document, like Name and Phone, can appear only once for each customer, whereas others, like Order and Item, can appear multiple times. The E-mail element appears to be optional: two customers have an e-mail address and one does not. Some of the attributes also appear to be optional. There is no need for the Title attribute when the customer is a company, nor has Kristin included an ItemQty attribute when the number of items ordered is one.

Kristin has created the diagram shown in Figure 3-3 to better illustrate the structure of the elements and attributes. Optional elements are indicated by dotted lines. Note that Kristin requires there be at least one order per customer. Also, each order needs to contain at least one item. Optional attributes are surrounded by square brackets. There are two optional attributes in the document: Title associated with the Name element and ItemQty associated with the Item element.

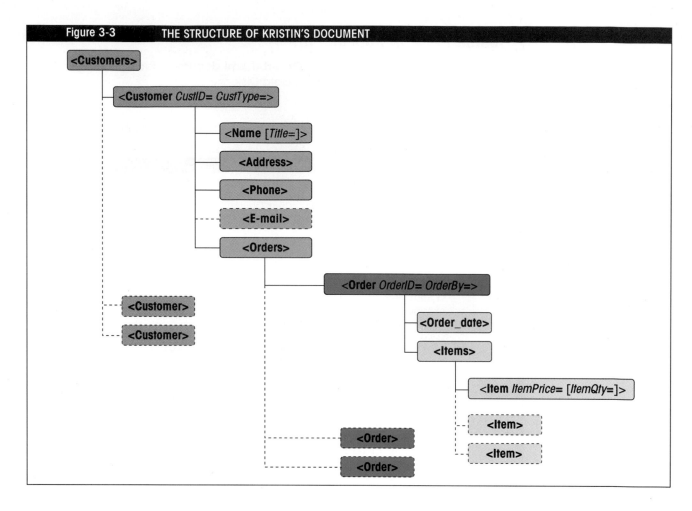

Figure 3-3 THE STRUCTURE OF KRISTIN'S DOCUMENT

The document structure is important to Kristin. As information is stored in this document, it is important that customer information include the address and phone number for each customer, the items ordered, and the date the order was placed. In XML terms, this means that her documents have to be not only well formed but also valid. XML documents can be validated using either DTDs (Document Type Definitions) or schemas. In this tutorial, we'll explore how to create and use DTDs.

Declaring a DTD

Used in conjunction with an XML parser that supports data validation, a DTD can be used to:

- ensure that all required elements are present in the document
- prevent undefined elements from being used in the document
- enforce a specific data structure on the document
- specify the use of element attributes and define their permissible values
- define default values for attributes
- describe how the parser should access non-XML or nontextual content

There can only be one DTD per XML document. To create a DTD, you must first enter a document type declaration into the XML document. Despite their similarity in names, a document type declaration is different than a document type definition. A document type definition is the collection of rules or declarations that define the content and structure of the document. A **document type declaration** attaches those rules to the document's content.

When we speak of the DTD, it should be understood that this refers to the document type definition and not the declaration. For brevity, the document type declaration is often referred to as the **DOCTYPE declaration** for reasons you'll soon understand. There can only be one DOCTYPE declaration in an XML document, and it must be placed before any document content.

Although there can also be only one DTD, the DTD can be divided into two parts: an internal subset and an external subset. The **internal subset** is a set of declarations placed in the same file as the document content, whereas the **external subset** is located in a separate file.

The DOCTYPE declaration for an internal subset is

```
<!DOCTYPE root
[
    declarations
]>
```

where *root* is the name of the document's root element, and *declarations* are the statements that comprise the DTD. If the name of the *root* attribute doesn't match the name of the document's root element, the XML parser will report an error and stop processing the document.

For external subsets, the DOCTYPE declaration takes two possible forms, one that uses a SYSTEM location and one that uses a PUBLIC location. The syntax of the declarations are

```
<!DOCTYPE root SYSTEM "URL">
```

or

```
<!DOCTYPE root PUBLIC "identifier" "URL">
```

where *root* is once again the document's root element, *identifier* is a text string that tells an application how to locate the external subset, and *URL* is the location and filename of the external subset. The PUBLIC location form is used when the DTD has to be limited to an internal system or when the XML document is part of an old SGML application. If the application can't locate the external subset from the public identifier, it uses the location and file specified by the URL. The SYSTEM location form doesn't include a public identifier; instead it simply specifies the name and location of the external subset through the "*URL*" value. In practice, unless your application requires a public identifier, you can and should use the SYSTEM location form.

Finally, a DOCTYPE declaration can indicate both an external and an internal subset. The syntax for this declaration is as follows:

```
<!DOCTYPE root SYSTEM "URL"
[
  declarations
]>
```

or

```
<!DOCTYPE root PUBLIC "identifier" "URL"
[
  declarations
]>
```

There are some advantages to using an internal DTD. By placing the DTD within the document, you can compare the DTD to the document's content without having to switch between files. However, the real power of XML comes from an external DTD that can be shared among many documents written by different authors. A common DTD forces those documents to use the same elements, attributes, and document structure.

If a document contains both an internal and external subset, the internal subset has precedence over the external subset if there is conflict between the two. This is useful when an external subset is shared among several documents. The external subset would define some basic rules for all of the documents, and the internal subset would define those rules that are specific to each document (see Figure 3-4).

| Figure 3-4 | COMBINING AN EXTERNAL AND INTERNAL DTD SUBSET |

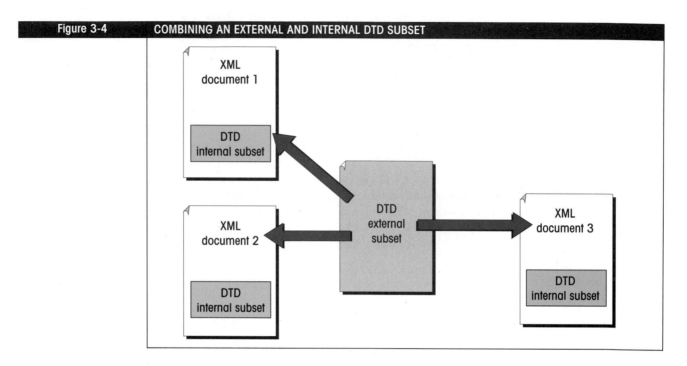

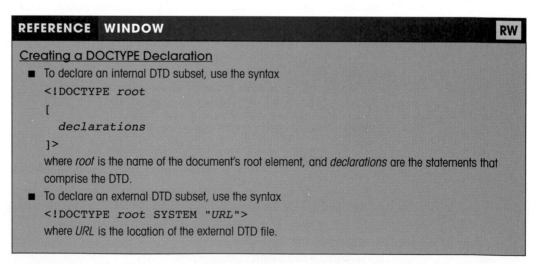

REFERENCE   WINDOW   RW

Creating a DOCTYPE Declaration
- To declare an internal DTD subset, use the syntax
  ```
  <!DOCTYPE root
  [
     declarations
  ]>
  ```
  where *root* is the name of the document's root element, and *declarations* are the statements that comprise the DTD.
- To declare an external DTD subset, use the syntax
  ```
  <!DOCTYPE root SYSTEM "URL">
  ```
  where *URL* is the location of the external DTD file.

Writing the Document Type Declaration

Kristin decides to add the DTD directly to the Orders.xml document so she can compare the DTD to the document's actual contents.

To create the document type declaration:

1. Below the XML declaration, enter the following comment line, followed by a blank line:

```
<!-- document type declaration follows -->
```

2. Next, insert the following lines below the comment:

```
<!DOCTYPE Customers
[

]>
```

Remember that "Customers" is the root element of Kristin's document and therefore must be the *root* attribute of the DOCTYPE declaration.

Figure 3-5 displays the revised code for the Orders.xml document.

Figure 3-5	INSERTING AN INTERNAL DTD SUBSET

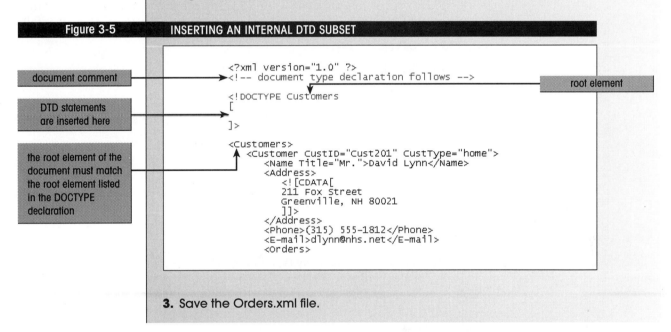

document comment

root element

DTD statements are inserted here

the root element of the document must match the root element listed in the DOCTYPE declaration

```
<?xml version="1.0" ?>
<!-- document type declaration follows -->

<!DOCTYPE Customers
[

]>

<Customers>
    <Customer CustID="Cust201" CustType="home">
        <Name Title="Mr.">David Lynn</Name>
        <Address>
            <![CDATA[
            211 Fox Street
            Greenville, NH 80021
            ]]>
        </Address>
        <Phone>(315) 555-1812</Phone>
        <E-mail>dlynn@nhs.net</E-mail>
        <Orders>
```

3. Save the Orders.xml file.

Now that you've created the document type declaration, you're ready to define the structure of Kristin's document.

Declaring **Document Elements**

In a valid document, every element used in the document must be declared in the DTD. An **element type declaration** specifies the name of the element and indicates what kind of content the element can contain. It can even specify the order in which elements appear in the document. The syntax of an element declaration is

```
<!ELEMENT element content-model>
```

where *element* is the name of the element. The element name is case sensitive, so if the element name is Products in the declaration, it must be entered as Products in the XML document. Element names cannot contain any spaces or reserved symbols such as "<" or ">."

The *content-model* specifies what type of content the element contains. Generally, elements contain either text or other elements. For example, in Kristin's document, the Name element contains a text string identifying the name of the customer. The Customer element contains five elements (Name, Address, Phone, E-mail, and Orders). We refer to the Customer element in this case as the **parent element** and the five elements it contains as **child elements**.

DTDs define five different types of element content:

- **Any elements**. There are no restrictions on the element's content.
- **Empty elements**. The element cannot store any content.
- **Character data**. The element can only contain a text string.
- **Elements**. The element can only contain child elements.
- **Mixed**. The element contains both a text string and child elements.

Let's investigate each of these types in more detail.

ANY Content

The most general type of content model is ANY, which allows the declared element to store any type of content. The syntax for declaring that an element can contain anything is as follows:

```
<!ELEMENT element ANY>
```

For example, the following declaration in the DTD

```
<!ELEMENT Products ANY>
```

would allow the Products element to take any of the following forms in the XML document:

```
<Products>SLR100 Digital Camera</Products>
<Products/>

<Products>
        <Name>SLR100</Name>
        <Type>Digital Camera</Name>
</Products>
```

Allowing an element to contain any type of content has limited use in document validation. After all, the idea behind validating a document is to enforce a particular set of rules on the elements and their content.

EMPTY Content

The EMPTY content model is reserved for elements that store no content. The syntax for an empty element declaration is as follows:

```
<!ELEMENT element EMPTY>
```

The following element declaration

```
<!ELEMENT IMG EMPTY>
```

would only allow the following forms for the IMG element:

```
<IMG></IMG>
```

or

```
<IMG />
```

Attempting to add content to any empty element results in the parser rejecting the document as invalid.

Character Content

Elements that can store only text strings are declared as follows:

```
<!ELEMENT element (#PCDATA)>
```

The keyword, #PCDATA, stands for "parsed-character data." **Parsed-character data** is any well-formed text string. Most text strings are well formed, except those that contain symbols reserved by XML, such as "<," ">," or "&."

Child elements are not allowed with this declaration. For example, if the DTD declares the Name element as follows:

```
<!ELEMENT Name (#PCDATA)>
```

this would be a valid use of the Name element:

```
<Name>Lea Ziegler</Name>
```

but this would not be:

```
<Name>
    <First>Lea</First>
    <Last>Ziegler</Last>
</Name>
```

REFERENCE   WINDOW   **RW**

Declaring Elements

- To declare that an element may contain any type of content, use
  ```
  <!ELEMENT element ANY>
  ```
  where *element* is the name of the element in the XML document.
- To declare that an element must be empty, use the following:
  ```
  <!ELEMENT element EMPTY>
  ```
- To declare that an element can only contain text, use the following:
  ```
  <!ELEMENT element (#PCDATA)>
  ```
- To declare that an element can only contain child elements, use the following:
  ```
  <!ELEMENT element (child_elements)>
  ```
  where *child_elements* is a list of the elements contained by the parent element.
- To declare that an element can contain text or child elements, use the following:
  ```
  <!ELEMENT element (#PCDATA | child1 | child2 | ...)*>
  ```
  where *child1*, *child2*, and so forth are elements contained by the parent element.

Working **with Element Content**

The most complicated element declaration is for elements that contain child elements. The syntax for declaring that an element contains only child elements is

```
<!ELEMENT element (child elements)>
```

where *child elements* is a list of child elements. The simplest content model would consist of a single child associated with a parent element. For example, the declaration

```
<!ELEMENT Customer (Phone)>
```

indicates that the Customer element can contain only one child element, named Phone. There are no exceptions. The following document is invalid because the Customer element contains two child elements:

```
<Customer>
   <Name>Lea Ziegler</Name>
   <Phone>Great 555-2819</Phone>
</Customer>
```

Additionally, you cannot repeat the same child element more than once with this declaration. The child element can only appear as many times as it is listed in the content model. The following code is invalid because it contains the Phone element twice and it's only listed once in the declaration:

```
<Customer>
   <Phone>555-3187</Phone>
   <Phone>555-8917</Phone>
</Customer>
```

For more complicated lists, DTDs allow XML authors to define sequences or choices of child elements.

Element Sequences and Choices

A **sequence** is a list of elements that follow a defined order. The syntax of the sequence model is

```
<!ELEMENT element (child1, child2, ...)>
```

where *child1*, *child2*, etc., represent the sequence of child elements within the parent element. The order of the child elements in the XML document must match the order defined in the element declaration. For example, the following element declaration defines a sequence of three child elements for the Customer parent element:

```
<!ELEMENT Customer (Name, Phone, E-mail)>
```

Under this declaration, the following document is valid:

```
<Customer>
   <Name>Lea Ziegler</Name>
   <Phone>(813) 555-8931</Phone>
   <E-mail>LZiegler@tempmail.net</E-mail>
</Customer>
```

But, the following document is not valid because the sequence doesn't match the defined order, even though the elements and their content are identical:

```
<Customer>
   <Name>Lea Ziegler</Name>
   <E-mail>LZiegler@tempmail.net</E-mail>
   <Phone>(813) 555-8931</Phone>
</Customer>
```

A sequence can also be applied to the same child element. The declaration

```
<!ELEMENT Customer (Phone, Phone, Phone)>
```

indicates that the Customer element should contain three child elements named Phone. Note that the number of child elements in the document must match the number in the element declaration. You could not use this particular declaration with only two child elements.

REFERENCE WINDOW RW

<u>Specifying a Sequence or Choice of Child Elements</u>
- To specify that child elements in an element declaration should appear in a defined order, enter the following code into an element declaration:
  ```
  <!ELEMENT element (child1, child2, ...)>
  ```
  where *child1*, *child2*, etc., represent the sequence of child elements within the parent element.
- To specify a choice of child elements for the parent element, use the element declaration
  ```
  <!ELEMENT element (child1 | child2 | ...)>
  ```
  where *child1*, *child2*, etc., are the possible child elements of the parent element.

The other way of listing child elements, **choice**, presents a set of possible child elements. The syntax of the choice model is

```
<!ELEMENT element (child1 | child2 | ...)>
```

where *child1*, *child2*, etc., are the possible child elements of the parent element. For example, the following declaration allows the Customer element to contain either the Name element or the Company element:

```
<!ELEMENT Customer (Name | Company)>
```

Therefore, either of these documents is valid:

```
<Customer>
    <Name>Lea Ziegler</Name>
</Customer>
```

or

```
<Customer>
    <Company>VTech Productions</Company>
</Customer>
```

But, you cannot have both the Name and the Company element because the choice model allows only one of the child elements.

Choice and sequence models can be combined and used together. The following declaration indicates that the Customer element must have three child elements:

```
<!ELEMENT Customer ((Name | Company), Phone, E-mail)>
```

The first must be either Name or Company, and the next two must be Phone and E-mail, in that order. With this declaration, either of the following sample documents is valid:

```
<Customer>
    <Name>Lea Ziegler</Name>
    <Phone>(813) 555-8931</Phone>
    <E-mail>LZiegler@tempmail.net</E-mail>
</Customer>
```

or

```
<Customer>
    <Company>VTech Productions</Company>
    <Phone>(813) 555-8931</Phone>
    <E-mail>LZiegler@tempmail.net</E-mail>
</Customer>
```

So far, all of the content models have limited the number of child elements to one. However, Kristin needs to be able to enter several Customer elements as child elements to the Customers element. To accomplish this, modifying symbols will be used.

Modifying Symbols

Modifying symbols are symbols appended to the content model, indicating the number of occurrences of each element. There are three modifying symbols: a question mark (?), a plus sign (+), and an asterisk (*). Figure 3-6 describes the meaning of each symbol.

Figure 3-6	MODIFYING SYMBOLS

MODIFYING SYMBOL	DESCRIPTION
?	Allow zero or one of the item
+	Allow one or more of the item
*	Allow zero or more of the item

For example, the + symbol allows the document to contain one or more of the specified item, so the following declaration allows one or more Name elements to be placed within the Customer element:

```
<!ELEMENT Customer (Name+)>
```

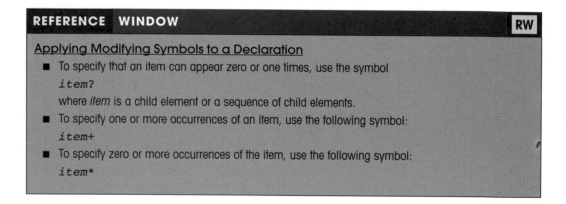

REFERENCE WINDOW | RW

Applying Modifying Symbols to a Declaration
- To specify that an item can appear zero or one times, use the symbol
  item?
  where *item* is a child element or a sequence of child elements.
- To specify one or more occurrences of an item, use the following symbol:
  item+
- To specify zero or more occurrences of the item, use the following symbol:
  item*

Modifying symbols can also be applied within sequences or choices. The following declaration allows the Customer element to contain zero or one E-mail elements, and one or more Order elements. The other child elements in the sequence (Name, Address, and Phone) can only appear once.

```
<!ELEMENT Customer (Name, Address, Phone, E-mail?, Order+)>
```

The three modifying symbols can also modify entire element sequences or choices. This is done by placing the character immediately following the closing parenthesis of the sequence or choice. When applied to a sequence, the modifying symbol is used to repeat the sequence. For example, the declaration

```
<!ELEMENT Order (Order_date, Items)+>
```

allows the child element sequence (Order_date, Items) to be included one or more times.

When applied to a choice model, the modifying symbols allow for multiple combinations of each child element. For example, the declaration

```
<!ELEMENT Customer (Name | Company)+>
```

allows any of the following lists of child elements:

```
Name
Company
Name, Company
Name, Name, Company
Name, Company, Company
```

The only requirement is that the combined total of Name and Company child elements be greater than zero.

Working with Mixed Content

As the name implies, an element with **mixed content** contains both character data and child elements. The syntax for declaring mixed content is as follows:

```
<!ELEMENT element (#PCDATA | child1 | child2 | ...)*>
```

Note that this form applies the * modifying symbol to a choice of character data or elements. This means that the parent element can contain character data or any number of the specified child elements, or it can contain no content at all. For example, the declaration

```
<!ELEMENT Title (#PCDATA | Subtitle)*>
```

allows the Title element to contain any of the following:

```
<Title>The Importance of Being Earnest</Title>
<Title>The Importance of Being Earnest
    <Subtitle>A Trivial Comedy for Serious People</Subtitle>
</Title>

<Title>The Importance of Being Earnest
    <Subtitle>A Trivial Comedy for Serious People</Subtitle>
    <Subtitle>by Oscar Wilde</Subtitle>
</Title>
```

Mixing character data and child elements restricts your ability to control the structure of your document. You can only specify the names of the child elements. You cannot constrain the order in which those child elements appear or control the number of occurrences for each element. For this reason, it is better not to work with mixed content if you want a tightly structured document.

Inserting Element Declarations into a DTD

Now that you've reviewed the syntax of element declarations, you are ready to create element declarations for all of the elements in Kristin's document. It is often best to work from the top level of the document's structure and proceed down through each child element. As we proceed through each element declaration, compare the declaration with Kristin's diagram, shown earlier in Figure 3-3.

To insert element declarations into Kristin's document:

1. The top-most element in Kristin's document is the Customers element that can contain one or more occurrences. Insert the following element declaration between the opening and closing bracket of the DOCTYPE declaration (see Figure 3-7):

```
<!ELEMENT Customers (Customer+)>
```

Figure 3-7	INSERTING THE ELEMENT DECLARATION FOR THE CUSTOMERS ELEMENT

```
<?xml version="1.0" ?>
<!-- document type declaration follows -->

<!DOCTYPE Customers
[
    <!ELEMENT Customers (Customer+)>
]>
```

the Customers element must contain one or more child elements named "Customer"

2. The Customer element has five child elements: Name, Address, Phone, E-mail, and Orders. Remember that the E-mail element is optional. Add the following element declaration directly below the Customers declaration:

```
<!ELEMENT Customer (Name, Address, Phone, E-mail?,
 Orders)>
```

3. The Name, Address, Phone, and E-mail elements can only contain character data. Add the following declarations below the Customer declaration:

```
<!ELEMENT Name (#PCDATA)>
<!ELEMENT Address (#PCDATA)>
<!ELEMENT Phone (#PCDATA)>
<!ELEMENT E-mail (#PCDATA)>
```

4. Next, add the declaration for the Orders element, which must contain at least one occurrence of the Order element:

```
<!ELEMENT Orders (Order+)>
```

5. Each Order element has two child elements: Order_date and Items. Add the following declaration below the Orders declaration:

```
<!ELEMENT Order (Order_date, Items)>
```

6. The Items element contains one or more occurrences of the Item element. Add the following declaration for the Items element:

```
<!ELEMENT Items (Item+)>
```

7. Finally, both the Order_date and Item elements contain only character data. Add the following declarations to the document.

```
<!ELEMENT Order_date (#PCDATA)>
<!ELEMENT Item (#PCDATA)>
```

Your complete list of element declarations should resemble Figure 3-8.

Figure 3-8	ELEMENT DECLARATIONS IN THE ORDERS.XML FILE

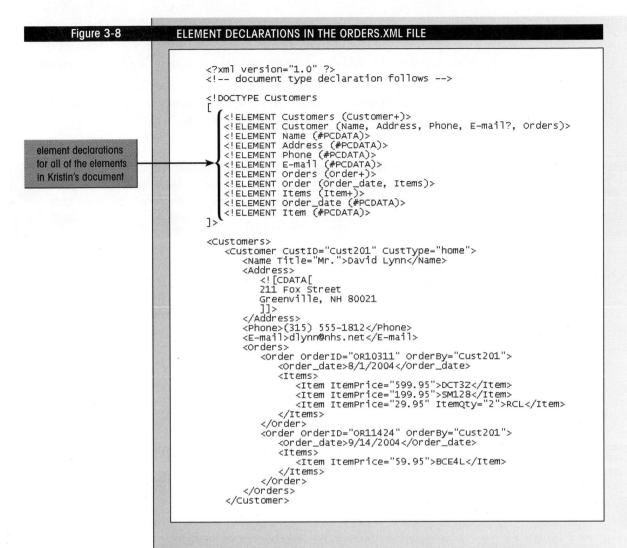

element declarations for all of the elements in Kristin's document

```
<?xml version="1.0" ?>
<!-- document type declaration follows -->

<!DOCTYPE Customers
[
    <!ELEMENT Customers (Customer+)>
    <!ELEMENT Customer (Name, Address, Phone, E-mail?, Orders)>
    <!ELEMENT Name (#PCDATA)>
    <!ELEMENT Address (#PCDATA)>
    <!ELEMENT Phone (#PCDATA)>
    <!ELEMENT E-mail (#PCDATA)>
    <!ELEMENT Orders (Order+)>
    <!ELEMENT Order (Order_date, Items)>
    <!ELEMENT Items (Item+)>
    <!ELEMENT Order_date (#PCDATA)>
    <!ELEMENT Item (#PCDATA)>
]>

<Customers>
    <Customer CustID="Cust201" CustType="home">
        <Name Title="Mr.">David Lynn</Name>
        <Address>
            <![CDATA[
            211 Fox Street
            Greenville, NH 80021
            ]]>
        </Address>
        <Phone>(315) 555-1812</Phone>
        <E-mail>dlynn@nhs.net</E-mail>
        <Orders>
            <Order OrderID="OR10311" orderBy="Cust201">
                <Order_date>8/1/2004</Order_date>
                <Items>
                    <Item ItemPrice="599.95">DCT3Z</Item>
                    <Item ItemPrice="199.95">SM128</Item>
                    <Item ItemPrice="29.95" ItemQty="2">RCL</Item>
                </Items>
            </Order>
            <Order OrderID="OR11424" orderBy="Cust201">
                <Order_date>9/14/2004</Order_date>
                <Items>
                    <Item ItemPrice="59.95">BCE4L</Item>
                </Items>
            </Order>
        </Orders>
    </Customer>
```

8. Save your changes to Orders.xml and close your text editor.

You've successfully defined a structure for Kristin's document by specifying exactly what content each element in her document can contain. In the next session, you'll learn how to do the same with the attributes in her document.

Session 3.1 QUICK CHECK

1. What code would you enter to connect your document to a DTD stored in the file "Books.dtd" (assume that the name of the root element is Inventory)?

2. What declaration would you enter for an element named "Book" that can contain any content?

3. What declaration would you enter for an empty element named "Video"?

4. What declaration would you enter for an element named "Book" that can contain only character text?

5. What declaration would you enter for an element named "Book" that contains a single child element named "Author"?

6. What declaration would you enter for an element named "Book" that contains one or more child elements named "Author"?

7. What declaration would you enter to allow the Book element to contain either character text or child elements named "Author" and "Title"?

SESSION 3.2

In this session, you'll work with element attributes. You'll learn how to declare an attribute list and how to specify the type of content that can be stored in an attribute. You'll also learn how to specify a default value for an attribute and indicate whether that attribute is required or optional.

Declaring Element Attribute

In the last session, you defined the structure of Kristin's document by declaring the names of all of the elements in her document and indicating what type of content each could contain. However, for Kristin's document to be valid, you must also declare all of the attributes associated with those elements.

In Figure 3-9, Kristin has described all of the attributes she intends to use in her document, indicating whether the attribute is required and what, if any, default values are assumed for the attribute.

Figure 3-9	ELEMENT ATTRIBUTES IN KRISTIN'S DOCUMENT			
ELEMENT	**ATTRIBUTES**	**DESCRIPTION**	**REQUIRED?**	**DEFAULT VALUE(S)**
Customer	CustID	Customer ID number	Yes	none
	CustType	Customer type	No	"home" or "business"
Name	Title	Title associated with the customer's name	No	"Mr.", "Mrs.", or "Ms."
Order	OrderID	Order ID number	Yes	none
	OrderBy	ID of the customer making the order	Yes	none
Item	ItemID	Item ID number	Yes	none
	ItemPrice	Item price	Yes	none
	ItemQty	Quantity of the item ordered	Yes	"1"

To enforce these attribution properties on Kristin's document, you must add an **attribute-list declaration** to the document's DTD. The attribute-list declaration accomplishes the following:

- lists the names of all of the attributes associated with a specific element
- specifies the data type of the attribute
- indicates whether the attribute is required or optional
- provides a default value for the attribute, if necessary

The syntax for declaring a list of attributes is

```
<!ATTLIST element attribute1 type1 default1
                  attribute2 type2 default2
                  attribute3 type3 default3 ... >
```

where *element* is the name of the element associated with the attributes, *attribute* is the name of an attribute, *type* is the attribute's data type, and *default* indicates whether the attribute is required or implied, and whether it has a fixed or a default value.

In practice, declarations for elements with multiple attributes are easier to interpret if the attribute declaration is defined separately rather than in one long declaration. An equivalent form in the DTD would be as follows:

```
<!ATTLIST element attribute1 type1 default1>
<!ATTLIST element attribute2 type2 default2>
<!ATTLIST element attribute3 type3 default3>
...
```

The XML parser combines the different statements into a single attribute declaration. If the processor encounters more than one declaration for the same attribute, it ignores the second statement. Attribute-list declarations can be located anywhere within the document type declaration, although it is easier to work with attribute declarations that are located adjacent to the declaration for the element with which they're associated.

REFERENCE WINDOW   RW

Declaring an Attribute List
- To declare an attribute, use the syntax

```
<!ATTLIST element attribute1 type1 default1
                  attribute2 type2 default2
                  attribute3 type3 default3 ... >
```

or

```
<!ATTLIST element attribute1 type1 default1>
<!ATTLIST element attribute2 type2 default2>
<!ATTLIST element attribute3 type3 default3>
...
```

where *element* is the name of the element associated with the attributes, *attribute* is the name of an attribute, *type* is the attribute's data type, and *default* indicates whether the attribute is required or implied, and whether it has a fixed value or a default value.

Working with Attribute Types

All attribute values are text strings, but you can control what type of text is used with the attribute. As shown in Figure 3-10, attribute values can be placed into three general categories: string, enumerated, and tokenized. Each of these categories gives you varying degrees of control over the attribute's content. Let's investigate these categories in greater detail.

Figure 3-10   CATEGORIES OF ATTRIBUTE VALUES

ATTRIBUTE VALUE	DESCRIPTION
String type	The attribute value can be any text string
Enumerated	The attribute value must be selected from a list of possible values
Tokenized	The attribute value must be a valid XML name

String Types

String types are the simplest form for the attribute value. The content of an attribute that is declared as a string type is ignored by the XML parser, which means that string types can contain blank spaces and any character except those reserved by XML (e.g.,<, >, and & characters), even symbols that are not part of ASCII text. To declare an attribute value as string type, use the following attribute type:

attribute CDATA

For example, the following statement indicates that the CustID attribute of the Customer element can contain simple text strings with few restrictions on its content:

Customer CustID CDATA

Any of the following attribute values are allowed under this declaration:

```
<Customer CustID="Cust259">
<Customer CustID="J. B. Browne">
<Customer CustID="β100z"
```

When Kristin needs to put more restrictions on attribute values, she can declare the attribute as either an enumerated type or a tokenized type.

Enumerated Types

One attribute whose value Kristin needs to restrict is the CustType attribute in the Customer element. Kristin uses the CustType attribute to indicate whether the customer is making purchases for business or home use. Because these are the only two possibilities, Kristin can limit the values of the CustType attribute to either "home" or "business." Attributes that are limited to a set of possible values are **enumerated types**. The general form of an enumerated type is

attribute (*value1* | *value2* | *value3* | ...)

where *value1*, *value2*, etc., are allowed values for specified attributes. Because Kristin wants to limit the value of the CustType attribute to either "home" or "business," she can include the following type in her declaration:

Customer CustType (home | business)>

Under this declaration, any document that uses a CustType value that is not "home" or "business" is rejected by the XML parser as invalid.

Another type of enumerated attribute is a **notation**. The notation associates the value of the attribute with a <!NOTATION> declaration located elsewhere in the DTD. You'll learn about <!NOTATION> declarations in the next session. Notations are primarily used when the XML document contains references to documents written in formats other than XML. The notation provides information to the XML parser as to how it should handle the non-XML data. The notation type has the following syntax:

```
NOTATION (notation1 | notation2 | notation3 | ...)
```

where *notation1*, *notation2*, etc., are valid notation values defined in a <NOTATION> declaration.

REFERENCE   WINDOW   **RW**

Declaring Attribute Types

- To declare an attribute value as a simple text string, use the type

  attribute CDATA

  where *attribute* is the name of the attribute.

- To declare the attribute as an enumerated type, use

  attribute (*value1* | *value2* | *value3* | ...)

  where *value1*, *value2*, etc., are allowed values for specified attributes.

- To declare the attribute as a tokenized type, use

  attribute token

  where *token* indicates the type of token in use. DTDs support the following token types: ID, IDREF, IDREFS, NMTOKEN, NMTOKENS, ENTITY, and ENTITIES.

Tokenized Types

Tokenized types are text strings that follow certain rules for format and content. The syntax for declaring an attribute as a tokenized type is

```
attribute token
```

where *token* is the type of token being applied to the attribute. There are seven tokenized types, described in Figure 3-11.

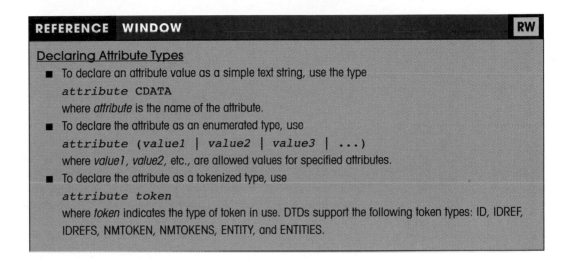

Figure 3-11	ATTRIBUTE TOKENS

TOKENIZED TYPE	DESCRIPTION
ID	Used to create a unique identifier for an attribute
IDREF	Used to allow an attribute to reference the ID attribute from another element
IDREFS	A list of ID references, separated by blank spaces
NMTOKEN	A name token whose value is restricted to a valid XML name
NMTOKENS	A list of name token references, separated by blank spaces
ENTITY	A reference to an external file, usually one containing non-XML data
ENTITIES	A list of entity references, separated by blank spaces

For example, the **ID** token is used with attributes that require unique values. In Kristin's document, the Customer element contains the CustID attribute, which stores a unique ID for each customer. For Kristin to prevent users from entering the same CustID value for different customers, she defines the attribute type for the CustID attribute as follows:

```
Customer CustID ID
```

Under this declaration, the following elements are valid:

```
<Customer CustID="Cust021"> ... </Customer>
<Customer CustID="Cust022"> ... </Customer>
```

but the following elements are not because the customer ID values are duplicated for different customers:

```
<Customer CustID="Cust021"> ... </Customer>
<Customer CustID="Cust021"> ... </Customer>
```

Once an attribute value is declared in the document, other attribute values can link to it using the IDREF token. An attribute declared as an **IDREF** type must have a value equal to the value of an ID attribute located somewhere in the same document.

The Order element in Kristin's document has an attribute named OrderBy so that Kristin can store the ID of the customer who made the order. She specifies the attribute type as follows:

```
Order OrderBy IDREF
```

When the XML parser encounters this attribute, it searches the XML document for ID values that match the value of the OrderBy attribute. For example, an Order element has the following OrderBy attribute value:

```
<Order OrderBy="Cust021">
```

unless there is another element in the document that has an ID value equal to "Cust021." Note that you cannot specify *which* attribute has the value to which the IDREF type should match.

To create a reference to multiple ID values, you use the **IDREFS** token type. Kristin might want to do this if she were to list all of the orders made by a certain customer as an attribute, as in the following sample code:

```
<Customer Orders="OR3413 OR3910 OR5310"> ... </Customer>


<Order OrderID="OR3413">...</Order>
<Order OrderID="OR3910">...</Order>
<Order OrderID="OR5310">...</Order>
```

In this case, the attribute types of the Orders and OrderID attributes are defined as follows:

```
Customer Orders IDREFS
Order OrderID ID
```

As with the IDREF token type, all of the IDs listed in an IDREFS token type must be found in an ID attribute located somewhere in the file, or the parser will reject the document as invalid.

The **NMTOKEN** type is used with character data whose values must be valid XML names. This constraint makes them less flexible than string types. The main difference between the NMTOKEN type and a simple text string defined with the CDATA type is that text strings defined as NMTOKEN attributes cannot contain blank spaces. If Kristin wants to make sure that an attribute value is always a single word, she would use the NMTOKEN type in preference to the CDATA type. An attribute that contains a list of name tokens, each separated by a blank space, can be defined using the **NMTOKENS** token type.

Finally, the **ENTITY** and **ENTITIES** token types are used for attribute values that reference unparsed entities. You'll learn more about entities in the next session.

Working with Attribute Defaults

The final part of an attribute declaration is the attribute default. There are four possible defaults: #REQUIRED, #IMPLIED, a default value, and a fixed default value. Figure 3-12 describes each of these attribute defaults.

Figure 3-12	ATTRIBUTE DEFAULTS

ATTRIBUTE DEFAULT	DESCRIPTION
#REQUIRED	The attribute must appear with every occurrence of the element.
#IMPLIED	The attribute is optional.
"default"	The attribute is optional. If an attribute value in not specified, a validating XML parser will supply the *default* value.
#FIXED *"default"*	The attribute is optional. If an attribute value is specified, it *must* match the *default* value.

Earlier, in Figure 3-9, Kristin outlined the properties for the attributes in her document. Note that the CustType attribute is required for every Customer element. That being the case, Kristin can use an attribute default as shown below:

```
<!ATTLIST Customer CustID ID #REQUIRED>
```

On the other hand, Kristin is not always able to determine whether a customer represents a home or business, so she uses the #IMPLIED attribute default for the CustType attribute. This is what the complete attribute declaration looks like:

```
<!ATTLIST Customer CustType (home | business) #IMPLIED>
```

If an XML parser encounters a Customer element without a CustType attribute, it won't invalidate the document but will instead assume a blank value for the attribute.

Another attribute from Kristin's document is the ItemQty attribute, which indicates the quantity of each item on the order. The ItemQty is optional, but Kristin wants the XML parser to assume a value of "1" for this attribute if it's missing from the Item element. The complete attribute declaration is as follows:

```
<!ATTLIST Item ItemQty CDATA "1">
```

For this attribute default to work, the XML parser must be capable of interpreting the DTD and validating the document. Not all XML parsers have this capability. This issue will be discussed later.

The last type of attribute default is the #FIXED default, which fixes the attribute to a specified value. If you omit the attribute from the element, the XML parser supplies the default value, and if you include the attribute, you must make the attribute value equal to the default or the document will be invalid. Note that you can't use the #FIXED form with an ID attribute because ID attributes need to have unique values for each element in the document.

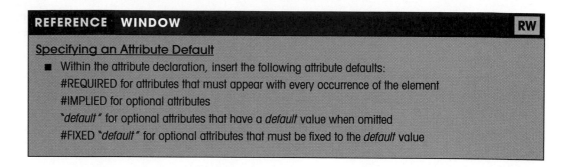

Creating and Applying Attribute Declarations

Now that you've reviewed the syntax of attribute declarations, you can create attribute-list declarations for the elements in Kristin's document. You'll place each attribute declaration into the DOCTYPE declaration right below the declaration for the element that contains the attribute.

```
<!ATTLIST Order OrderID ID #REQUIRED>
<!ATTLIST Order OrderBy IDREF #REQUIRED>
```

The attribute declarations are written as follows:

```
<!ATTLIST Item ItemPrice CDATA #REQUIRED>
<!ATTLIST Item ItemQty CDATA "1">
```

Now that you know the attribute declarations, you can add them to Kristin's document.

To insert the attribute declarations:

1. Use your text editor to open the **Orders.xml** document from the Tutorial.03X/Tutorial folder on your Data Disk.

2. Below the Customer element declaration in the DTD, insert the following attribute declarations to define the properties of the CustID and CustType attributes, which are both associated with the Customer element:

   ```
   <!ATTLIST Customer CustID ID #REQUIRED>
   <!ATTLIST Customer CustType (home | business) #IMPLIED>
   ```

   Title is the only attribute for the Name element. It's an optional element that can have one of three possible values: Mr., Mrs., or Ms.

3. Insert the following code below the element declaration:

   ```
   <!ATTLIST Name Title (Mr. | Mrs. | Ms.) #IMPLIED>
   ```

   There are two attributes associated with the Order element. The OrderID attribute assigns a required ID number to the order, and the OrderBy attribute indicates the ID of the customer who submitted the order.

4. Add the following attribute declarations below the Order element declaration:

   ```
   <!ATTLIST Order OrderID ID #REQUIRED>
   <!ATTLIST Order OrderBy IDREF #REQUIRED>
   ```

Finally, there are two attributes for the Item element: ItemPrice and ItemQty. ItemPrice is a required attribute that records the price of the item. ItemQty is an optional element that records the quantity of items ordered. The default value is "1".

5. Insert the following code beneath the Item element declaration:

```
<!ATTLIST Item ItemPrice CDATA #REQUIRED>
<!ATTLIST Item ItemQty CDATA "1">
```

Figure 3-13 shows the revised contents of the Orders.xml file.

Figure 3-13	INSERTING ATTRIBUTE-LIST DECLARATIONS

attribute declaration →

```
<?xml version="1.0" ?>
<!-- document type declaration follows -->

<!DOCTYPE Customers
[
    <!ELEMENT Customers (Customer+)>
    <!ELEMENT Customer (Name, Address, Phone, E-mail?, Orders)>
    <!ATTLIST Customer CustID ID #REQUIRED>
    <!ATTLIST Customer CustType (home | business) #IMPLIED>
    <!ELEMENT Name (#PCDATA)>
    <!ATTLIST Name Title (Mr. | Mrs. | Ms.) #IMPLIED>
    <!ELEMENT Address (#PCDATA)>
    <!ELEMENT Phone (#PCDATA)>
    <!ELEMENT E-mail (#PCDATA)>
    <!ELEMENT Orders (Order+)>
    <!ELEMENT Order (Order_date, Items)>
    <!ATTLIST Order OrderID ID #REQUIRED>
    <!ATTLIST Order OrderBy IDREF #REQUIRED>
    <!ELEMENT Items (Item+)>
    <!ELEMENT Order_date (#PCDATA)>
    <!ELEMENT Item (#PCDATA)>
    <!ATTLIST Item ItemPrice CDATA #REQUIRED>
    <!ATTLIST Item ItemQty CDATA "1">
]>
```

6. Save your changes to Orders.xml and leave the file and your text editor open.

Congratulations, you've created a DTD that declares all of the elements and attributes in the document, but how do you know that all of your hard work has resulted in a valid XML document? It's possible that you've forgotten to declare an element or attribute, or you may have made a simple typing mistake. How do you test for validity?

Validating **Documents with XML Spy**

To test for validity, your XML parser must be able to validate your XML document against the rules you set up in the DTD. The Web is an excellent source for validating parsers. A partial list is displayed in Figure 3-14.

Figure 3-14   **XML-VALIDATING PARSERS**

VALIDATING PARSER	URL
MSXML	http://msdn.microsoft.com/library/
Oracle	http://technet.oracle.com/tech/xml/content.html
ProjectX	http://java.sun.com/xml/index.html
Xerces	http://xml.apache.org/xerces-j/
XML4J	http://www.alphaworks.ibm.com/tech/xml4j
XML Spy	http://link.xmlspy.com
XP	http://jclark.com/xml/xp/index.html

The CD that accompanies this book contains an evaluation copy of XML Spy. XML Spy can test your document for being well formed as well as valid. To install XML Spy, review the material in the appendix at the end of this book. If you have any problems installing XML Spy, contact your instructor or technical resource person.

To start XML Spy:

1. Click the **Start** button on your Taskbar, point to **Programs**, point to **XML Spy Suite**, and click **XML Spy IDE** from the menu.

   TROUBLE? Your system may be configured with the XML Spy program located in a different folder or menu. Contact your instructor if you are having problems locating or starting XML Spy.

2. Click the **File** menu and then click **Open**.

3. Select the **Orders.xml** file, located in the Tutorial.03X/Tutorial folder of your Data Disk and click the **Open** button.

   With XML Spy, you can organize all of the files related to your XML document into projects. Information about the different aspects of the project is placed in separate panes in the XML Spy window. There is a pane that lists all of the files involved in your project and another pane, named Info, that provides information about the project. There are other panes that list the elements, attributes, and entities in your XML project. The contents of Orders.xml are displayed in the document pane.

   TROUBLE? By default, XML Spy verifies that your document is both well formed and valid when the document is opened. If you receive a message indicating an error in the file, you may have made a typing mistake when entering the DTD. The error message gives you a clue as to the nature of the error. Review the steps that follow to learn how to interpret and correct validation errors, and then return to Orders.xml and try to correct the mistake.

4. Click the **Maximize** button ▣ on the document pane to maximize its appearance within XML Spy. See Figure 3-15.

   TROUBLE? Your screen may appear slightly different depending on how XML Spy is configured on your computer.

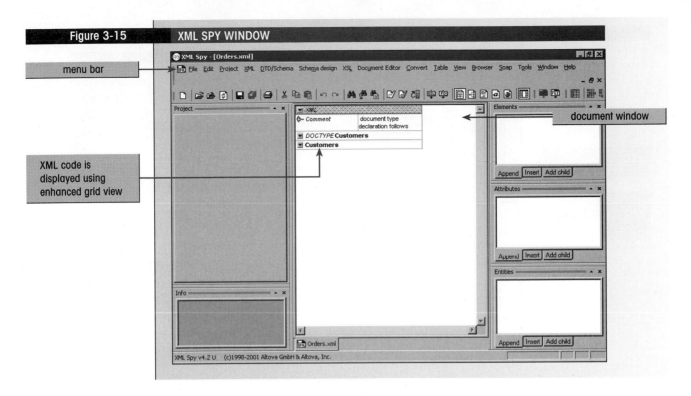

Figure 3-15   **XML SPY WINDOW**

By default, XML Spy opens documents in **enhanced grid view**, which shows the hierarchical structure of an XML document as a set of nested containers. The containers can be expanded or contracted to get a clear picture of the document's structure and content. For this example, though, we'll view the contents of the document as a text file.

To view the document as a text file:

1. Click **View** on the menu bar.

2. Click **Text view**.

   Depending on your monitor's resolution, there may be line wrap in the text, making it difficult to read. You can increase the amount of horizontal space given to the document window by dragging the borders of the document window to the left or right.

3. Move the mouse pointer over the left edge of the document pane until the pointer changes to a ↔. Drag the border to the left, increasing the width of the window (see Figure 3-16).

Figure 3-16	XML SPY WINDOW

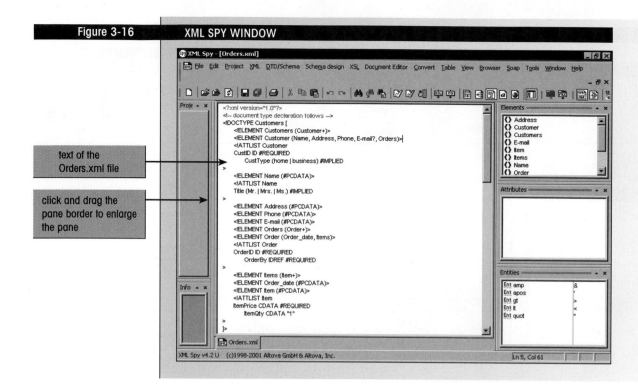

text of the
Orders.xml file

click and drag the
pane border to enlarge
the pane

Next, test the document for being both well formed and valid. Typically, XML Spy runs these tests whenever you open an XML document, but it's good practice to see how to do this manually.

To test Orders.xml:

1. Click **XML** on the menu bar, and then click **Check well-formedness**.

2. XML Spy reports that the file is well formed and indicates that you should validate the document against its DTD.

3. Click **XML** on the menu bar, and then click **Validate**.

   XML Spy returns the message that the file is valid (see Figure 3-17).

Figure 3-17	XML SPY REPORTS THAT THE FILE IS VALID

```
<?xml version="1.0"?>
<!-- document type declaration follows -->
<!DOCTYPE Customers [
    <!ELEMENT Customers (Customer+)>
    <!ELEMENT Customer (Name, Address, Phone, E-mail?, Orders)>
    <!ATTLIST Customer
    CustID ID #REQUIRED
            CustType (home | business) #IMPLIED
>
    <!ELEMENT Name (#PCDATA)>
    <!ATTLIST Name
    Title (Mr. | Mrs. | Ms.) #IMPLIED
>
    <!ELEMENT Address (#PCDATA)>
    <!ELEMENT Phone (#PCDATA)>
    <!ELEMENT E-mail (#PCDATA)>
    <!ELEMENT Orders (Order+)>
    <!ELEMENT Order (Order_date, Items)>
    <!ATTLIST Order
    OrderID ID #REQUIRED
            OrderBy IDREF #REQUIRED
>
    <!ELEMENT Items (Item+)>
    <!ELEMENT Order_date (#PCDATA)>
    <!ELEMENT Item (#PCDATA)>
    <!ATTLIST Item
    ItemPrice CDATA #REQUIRED
```

This file is valid.   OK

Orders.xml

Note that you can also run the well-formedness and validity tests by pressing the F7 and F8 keys on your keyboard or by clicking the ⊠ and ⊠ buttons on the XML Spy toolbar.

Though the file is valid, it is a good learning experience to place a few intentional errors into the XML code to see how validation errors are reported. You can edit the contents of Orders.xml directly in the document pane.

To make Orders.xml invalid:

1. Locate the element declaration for the E-mail element near the top of the document. Select the name "E-mail" and change the name in the element declaration to "Mail."

2. Click the ⊠ button to validate the file.

3. XML Spy reports that the file is not valid because the E-mail element is undefined. It also highlights the section in the document where it encountered an error. See Figure 3-18.

Figure 3-18

XML SPY REPORTS THAT THE FILE IS INVALID

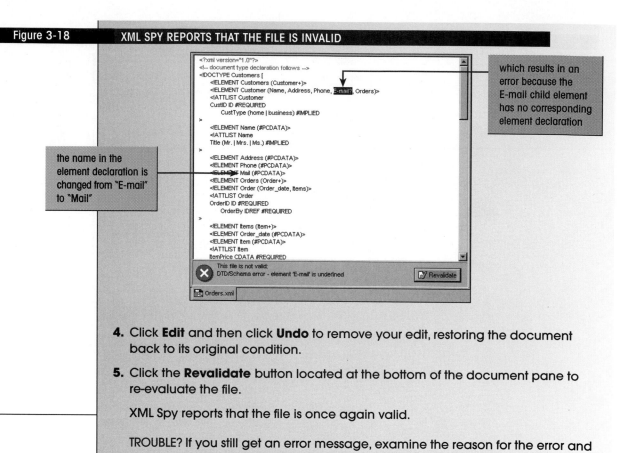

```
<?xml version="1.0"?>
<!-- document type declaration follows -->
<!DOCTYPE Customers [
   <!ELEMENT Customers (Customer+)>
   <!ELEMENT Customer (Name, Address, Phone, E-mail?, Orders)>
   <!ATTLIST Customer
   CustID ID #REQUIRED
         CustType (home | business) #IMPLIED
>
   <!ELEMENT Name (#PCDATA)>
   <!ATTLIST Name
   Title (Mr. | Mrs. | Ms.) #IMPLIED
>
   <!ELEMENT Address (#PCDATA)>
   <!ELEMENT Phone (#PCDATA)>
   <!ELEMENT Mail (#PCDATA)>
   <!ELEMENT Orders (Order+)>
   <!ELEMENT Order (Order_date, Items)>
   <!ATTLIST Order
   OrderID ID #REQUIRED
         OrderBy IDREF #REQUIRED
>
   <!ELEMENT Items (Item+)>
   <!ELEMENT Order_date (#PCDATA)>
   <!ELEMENT Item (#PCDATA)>
   <!ATTLIST Item
   ItemPrice CDATA #REQUIRED
```

the name in the element declaration is changed from "E-mail" to "Mail"

which results in an error because the E-mail child element has no corresponding element declaration

This file is not valid;
DTD/Schema error - element 'E-mail' is undefined   Revalidate

Orders.xml

4. Click **Edit** and then click **Undo** to remove your edit, restoring the document back to its original condition.

5. Click the **Revalidate** button located at the bottom of the document pane to re-evaluate the file.

   XML Spy reports that the file is once again valid.

   TROUBLE? If you still get an error message, examine the reason for the error and then make the necessary corrections.

   After confirming that Order.xml is a valid XML document, close XML Spy.

6. Click **File** and then click **Exit**. Click the **Yes** button to save your changes.

Nice work! You've completed the exercises for declaring and defining the attributes of the elements in Kristin's document. In the next session, you'll create and work with entities and binary data.

Session 3.2 QUICK CHECK

1. What attribute declaration would you enter to create an optional text string attribute named "Title" for an element named "Book"?

2. The Play element has a required attribute named "Type," which can have one of four possible values: Romance, Tragedy, History, and Comedy. Enter the appropriate attribute declaration.

3. What is the main difference between an attribute with the CDATA type and one with the NMTOKEN type?

4. The Book element has a required ID attribute named "ISBN." Enter the appropriate attribute declaration.

5. An Author element has an optional attribute named "BooksBy," which contains the ISBN numbers of the books the author has written. If ISBN is an ID attribute for another element in the document, what declaration would you use for the BooksBy attribute?

6. The Book element has an optional attribute named "InStock" that can have the value "yes" or "no." The default value is "yes." What is the declaration for the InStock attribute?

SESSION 3.3	In this session, you'll learn how to create and work with entities, and, specifically, you'll learn how to work with general entities to store long text strings containing data and elements. You'll also review how to create parameter entities to store elements and attributes. Finally, you'll learn how to use unparsed entities to include binary data, such as image files and multimedia clips, in your XML documents.

Working with Entities

Until this point, you've worked with data that has been entered directly into an XML document. As you will see, this is not always the case. In fact, one of the strengths of XML is that a document's content can be stored in multiple files and in multiple formats. These storage units are called **entities**. The most fundamental entity is the XML document itself, known as the **document entity**, but entities can refer to other items as well, including:

- a text string
- a DTD
- an element or attribute declaration
- an external file containing character or binary data

Entities can be declared in a DTD. The syntax for declaring an entity depends on how the entity is classified. There are three factors involved in classifying an entity: 1) the content of the entity, 2) how the entity is constructed, and 3) where the definition of the entity is located. Let's consider each of these factors now.

An entity that is part of an XML document's content is called a **general entity**. General entities are often used as placeholders for text strings that the author wants to repeat throughout the document or in other documents. For example, Kristin can create a general entity declaration to store the company's address and phone number. Rather than retyping this information for every document that needs it, she can reference the declarations. If this information changes, Kristin only has to change it in one location rather than several. An entity that is not part of the document's content is called a **parameter entity**. Parameter entities are used to store the various declarations found in a DTD. Those declarations can then be shared among multiple documents.

If the entity is constructed using well-formed XML text, it is a **parsed entity**. The company's address and phone number would be one such example. If the entity is constructed from non-XML data, it is an **unparsed entity**. A graphic image file would be an example of an unparsed entity.

Finally, if the entity can be defined with a text string within the document's DTD, it's an **internal entity**. If the definition relies on the content of an external file, particularly a non-XML file, it's an **external entity**. Figure 3-19 summarizes these categories.

Figure 3-19	CLASSIFYING ENTITIES		
ENTITY CLASSIFICATIONS			**DESCRIPTION**
What does the entity refer to?	General vs. Parameter		General entities are used only with the contents of an XML document. Parameter entities are used only with contents of a DTD.
How is the entity constructed?	Parsed vs. Unparsed		Parsed entities consist entirely of well-formed XML content. Unparsed entities are constructed from non-XML data, including nontext data.
Where is the entity located?	Internal vs. External		An internal entity is defined within a declaration in the document's DTD. An external entity is defined in an external file.

You'll start your work on entity declarations by learning how to declare a general parsed entity.

Working with General Parsed Entities

Like elements and attributes, general entities are declared within the DTD of a document. The syntax for declaring a general internal entity is

```
<!ENTITY entity "value">
```

where *entity* is the name you've assigned to the entity and *value* is the general entity's value. The entity name follows the same rules that apply to all XML names: there can be no blank spaces in the name and the name must begin with either a letter or underscore. The entity value itself must be well-formed XML text. This can be a simple text string, or it can be a text string containing XML tags.

For example, an entity named "Pixal" can be created to store the company's official name:

```
<!ENTITY Pixal "Pixal Digital Products">
```

Note that XML tags can be included as part of the general entity's value, as in the following declaration:

```
<!ENTITY Pixal "<Company>Pixal Digital Products</Company>" >
```

If you do include an XML tag in the entity's value, you must include both the opening and closing tag for the document to be valid.

Inserting a General Entity

Once a general entity has been declared in the DTD, it can be referenced anywhere within the XML document. The syntax for inserting a general entity reference is

```
&entity;
```

where *entity* is the name in the entity declaration. For example, to insert the Pixal entity into a document, use the following text string:

```
<Title>This is the home page of &Pixal;.</Title>
```

The XML parser interprets the contents of the Title element as

```
<Title>This is the home page of Pixal Digital Products.</Title>
```

substituting the value of the entity for the entity reference.

You may have noticed a similarity between inserting general entities and inserting character references that were discussed in the first tutorial. A character reference is actually a special case of a general entity called a **predefined entity**. The five predefined entities are: < > ' &quote; and &

Because of the way entities are inserted into XML documents, you cannot include the & symbol as part of the entity's value. The XML parser interprets the & symbol as a reference to another entity and attempts to resolve the reference. You also cannot use the % symbol, which, as you'll learn later, is the symbol used for inserting parameter entities.

Declaring a General External Entity

General entities can also refer to values located in external files. The advantage of an external entity is that it can be accessed by several XML documents, and, if the entity is modified, those documents automatically reflect that change. The syntax for declaring a general external entity is

```
<!ENTITY  entity SYSTEM "URL" >
```

where *URL* indicates the location of the file containing the entity data. For example, an author working with a collection of articles located at *www.newsflash.com* can access those external entities using the following declaration:

```
<!ENTITY  headlines SYSTEM "http://www.newsflash.com/
stories.xml" >
```

In this example, an entity named "headlines" retrieves its value from the document, stories.xml, located at *http://www.newsflash.com.* The external file can contain only text to be inserted directly into an element, such as character data or nested elements. If the stories.xml file contains the following text:

```
<Head>Stocks Surge</Head>
<Summary>The NYSE Composite Index rose 15 points yesterday in
heavy trading with 616,891,000 shares traded (details to
follow.)
</Summary>
<Head>Presidential Trip</Head>
<Summary>The President left on his European trip this
morning. He will address the British Parliament Wednesday
afternoon (details to follow.)
</Summary>
```

the news summaries could then be inserted into XML document using the following entity reference:

```
<News>
    &headlines;
</News>
```

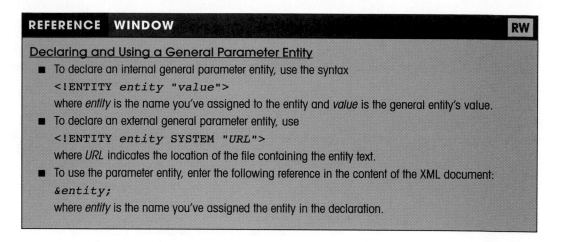

Creating and Applying General Parsed Entities

Kristin's colleagues at Pixal are developing other XML documents to be published on their web site. They decided that it will be more efficient to have certain information located in a shared document so that multiple XML authors can reference the same file. To do this, a document named Items.dtd has been created that contains entity declarations for several products. The entity names represent abbreviations for the products sold by Pixal, and the entity values are extended descriptions of the products. The contents of the file are shown in Figure 3-20.

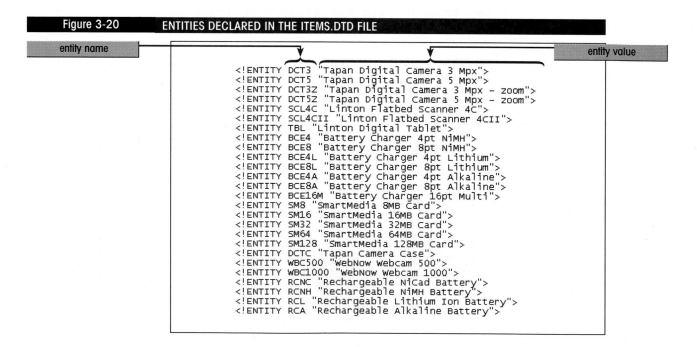

Figure 3-20   ENTITIES DECLARED IN THE ITEMS.DTD FILE

entity name   entity value

```
<!ENTITY DCT3 "Tapan Digital Camera 3 Mpx">
<!ENTITY DCT5 "Tapan Digital Camera 5 Mpx">
<!ENTITY DCT3Z "Tapan Digital Camera 3 Mpx - zoom">
<!ENTITY DCT5Z "Tapan Digital Camera 5 Mpx - zoom">
<!ENTITY SCL4C "Linton Flatbed Scanner 4C">
<!ENTITY SCL4CII "Linton Flatbed Scanner 4CII">
<!ENTITY TBL "Linton Digital Tablet">
<!ENTITY BCE4 "Battery Charger 4pt NiMH">
<!ENTITY BCE8 "Battery Charger 8pt NiMH">
<!ENTITY BCE4L "Battery Charger 4pt Lithium">
<!ENTITY BCE8L "Battery Charger 8pt Lithium">
<!ENTITY BCE4A "Battery Charger 4pt Alkaline">
<!ENTITY BCE8A "Battery Charger 8pt Alkaline">
<!ENTITY BCE16M "Battery Charger 16pt Multi">
<!ENTITY SM8 "SmartMedia 8MB Card">
<!ENTITY SM16 "SmartMedia 16MB Card">
<!ENTITY SM32 "SmartMedia 32MB Card">
<!ENTITY SM64 "SmartMedia 64MB Card">
<!ENTITY SM128 "SmartMedia 128MB Card">
<!ENTITY DCTC "Tapan Camera Case">
<!ENTITY WBC500 "WebNow Webcam 500">
<!ENTITY WBC1000 "WebNow Webcam 1000">
<!ENTITY RCNC "Rechargeable NiCad Battery">
<!ENTITY RCNH "Rechargeable NiMH Battery">
<!ENTITY RCL "Rechargeable Lithium Ion Battery">
<!ENTITY RCA "Rechargeable Alkaline Battery">
```

To use these entities in the Orders.xml file, you need to create a reference to the Items.dtd file. At this point, it may be helpful for you to review the external DTD discussion in the first session of this tutorial.

To create a reference to the Items.dtd file:

1. Using your text editor, open the **Orders.xml** document located in the Tutorial.03X/Tutorial folder of your Data Disk.

2. Locate the document type declaration at the top of the file, and insert the text **SYSTEM "Items.dtd"**, as shown in Figure 3-21.

Figure 3-21   CONNECTING TO THE ITEMS.DTD FILE

```
<?xml version="1.0"?>
<!-- edited with XML Spy v4.2 U (http://www.xmlspy.com) by Kristin Laughlin (Pixal) -->
<!-- document type declaration follows -->
<!DOCTYPE Customers SYSTEM "Items.dtd" [
  <!ELEMENT Customers (Customer+)>
  <!ELEMENT Customer (Name, Address, Phone, E-mail?, Orders)>
  <!ATTLIST Customer
  CustID ID #REQUIRED
    CustType (home | business) #IMPLIED
>
```

Note that adding the URL for the Items.dtd document changes the DTD of the Orders.xml document from a purely internal DTD to a DTD combining both internal and external subsets.

To display the entity values in her document, Kristin must replace the product abbreviations with entity references. For example, the first customer, David Lynn, purchased a DCT3Z, also known as the Tapan Digital Camera 3 Mpx - Zoom Model. To display the full product name, replace the item name with the following entity reference:

`&DCT3Z;`

The XML parser automatically inserts the entity's value. You can now add entity references for some additional Pixal products.

To add entity references:

1. Locate the first item name in the Orders.xml document, and change DCT3Z to **&DCT3Z;**

2. Locate the second item name, SM128, and change the item name to **&SM128;**

3. Continue through the rest of the document and insert an ampersand (&) before, and a semi-colon after, each item. There are a total of seven items in the document. Figure 3-22 shows the revised Orders.xml file with the modified items highlighted in red.

Figure 3-22   CHANGING PRODUCT DESCRIPTIONS TO ENTITY REFERENCES

```
<Customers>
  <Customer CustID="Cust201" CustType="home">
    <Name Title="Mr.">David Lynn</Name>
    <Address><![CDATA[
        211 Fox Street
        Greenville, NH 80021
        ]]></Address>
    <Phone>(315) 555-1812</Phone>
    <E-mail>dlynn@nhs.net</E-mail>
    <Orders>
      <Order orderID="OR10311" orderBy="Cust201">
        <Order_date>8/1/2004</Order_date>
        <Items>
          <Item ItemPrice="599.95">&DCT3Z;</Item>
          <Item ItemPrice="199.95">&SM128;</Item>
          <Item ItemPrice="29.95" ItemQty="2">&RCL;</Item>
        </Items>
      </Order>
      <Order orderID="OR11424" orderBy="Cust201">
        <Order_date>9/14/2004</Order_date>
        <Items>
          <Item ItemPrice="59.95">&BCE4L;</Item>
        </Items>
      </Order>
    </Orders>
  </Customer>
  <Customer CustID="Cust202">
    <Name Title="Mrs.">Jean Kaufmann</Name>
    <Address><![CDATA[
        411 East Oak Avenue
        Cashton, MI   20401
        ]]></Address>
    <Phone>(611) 555-4033</Phone>
    <E-mail>JKaufmann@cshweb.com</E-mail>
    <Orders>
      <Order orderID="OR10899" orderBy="Cust202">
        <Order_date>8/11/2004</Order_date>
        <Items>
          <Item ItemPrice="59.99">&WBC500;</Item>
          <Item ItemPrice="5.95" ItemQty="2">&RCA;</Item>
        </Items>
      </Order>
    </Orders>
  </Customer>
  <Customer CustID="Cust203" CustType="business">
    <Name>AdServices</Name>
    <Address><![CDATA[
        55 Washburn Lane
        Creighton, UT   98712
        ]]></Address>
    <Phone>(811) 555-2987</Phone>
    <Orders>
      <Order orderID="OR11201" orderBy="Cust203">
        <Order_date>9/15/2004</Order_date>
        <Items>
          <Item ItemPrice="179.99" ItemQty="3">&SCL4C;</Item>
        </Items>
      </Order>
    </Orders>
  </Customer>
</Customers>
```

4. Save your changes to Orders.xml.

Now, check to see whether the entity references are resolved in the entity values by an XML parser. You can check this using the Internet Explorer browser.

To view the entity values:

1. Using Internet Explorer, open **Orders.xml**. Figure 3-23 shows how Internet Explorer resolves the entity references and displays the entity values when it renders the document.

Figure 3-23	ENTITY VALUES AS RENDERED BY THE INTERNET EXPLORER BROWSER

```
<Customers>
    <Customer CustID="Cust201" CustType="home">
        <Name Title="Mr.">David Lynn</Name>
        <Address>
            <![CDATA[
            211 Fox Street
            Greenville, NH 80021
            ]]>
        </Address>
        <Phone>(315) 555-1812</Phone>
        <E-mail>dlynn@nhs.net</E-mail>
        <Orders>
            <Order OrderID="OR10311" orderBy="Cust201">
                <Order_date>8/1/2004</Order_date>
                <Items>
                    <Item ItemPrice="599.95">&DCT3Z;</Item>          entity reference
                    <Item ItemPrice="199.95">&SM128;</Item>
                    <Item ItemPrice="29.95" ItemQty="2">&RCL;</Item>
                </Items>
            </Order>
```

Orders.xml document

```
- <Customers>
  - <Customer CustID="Cust201" CustType="home">
      <Name Title="Mr.">David Lynn</Name>
    - <Address>
      - <![CDATA[
                    211 Fox Street
                    Greenville, NH 80021

        ]]>
      </Address>
      <Phone>(315) 555-1812</Phone>
      <E-mail>dlynn@nhs.net</E-mail>
    - <Orders>
      - <Order OrderID="OR10311" OrderBy="Cust201">
          <Order_date>8/1/2004</Order_date>
        - <Items>                                        resolved entity value
            <Item ItemPrice="599.95">Tapan Digital Camera 3 Mpx - zoom</Item>
            <Item ItemPrice="199.95">SmartMedia 128MB Card</Item>
            <Item ItemPrice="29.95" ItemQty="2">Rechargeable Lithium Ion Battery</Item>
          </Items>
        </Order>
```

Orders.xml document as viewed in Internet Explorer

TROUBLE? If you open the file using a Netscape browser, the entity references are not resolved.

2. Close your browser and return to your text editor.

Working with Parameter Entities

The other type of entity is the parameter entity, which is used to store the content of a DTD. Parameter entities are declared using a form similar to general entities. For internal parameter entities, the syntax is

```
<!ENTITY % entity "value">
```

where *entity* is the name of the parameter entity and *value* is a text string of the entity's value. For external parameter entities, the syntax is

```
<!ENTITY % entity SYSTEM "URL">
```

where *URL* is the URL of the file containing the entity's value.

To reference a parameter entity, you use the syntax

```
%entity;
```

where *entity* is the name assigned to the parameter entity. Parameter entity references can only be placed where a declaration would normally occur, such as an internal or external DTD. You *cannot* insert a parameter entity reference within the content of the XML document. The following example shows how to create a parameter entity for a collection of elements and attributes:

```
<!ENTITY % books
   "<!ELEMENT Book (Title, Author)>
    <!ATTLIST Book Pages CDATA #REQUIRED>
    <!ELEMENT Title (#PCDATA)>
    <!ELEMENT Author (#PCDATA)>"
>
```

The books parameter entity stores three element declarations named "Book," "Title," and "Author," and an attribute list named "Pages." To reference these declarations, you include the statement

```
%books;
```

as a separate line in a DTD.

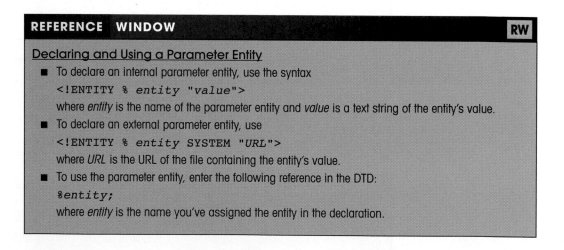

It's not a practical strategy to use parameter entities with an internal DTD because it adds an extra step without saving any time or effort.

However, an external parameter entity can overcome XML's limit of one DTD per document by combining declarations from multiple DTDs (see Figure 3-24).

Figure 3-24	USING PARAMETER ENTITIES TO COMBINE MULTIPLE DTDS

```
<!ELEMENT Book (Title, Author)>
<!ATTLIST Book Pages CDATA #REQUIRED>
<!ELEMENT Title (#PCDATA)>
<!ELEMENT Author (#PCDATA)>
```

Book.dtd

```
<!ELEMENT Magazine (Name)>
<!ATTLIST Magazine Publisher CDATA #REQUIRED>
<!ELEMENT Name (#PCDATA)>
```

Magazine.dtd

```
<!ELEMENT Book (Title, Author)>
<!ATTLIST Book Pages CDATA #REQUIRED>
<!ELEMENT Title (#PCDATA)>
<!ELEMENT Author (#PCDATA)>
<!ELEMENT Magazine (Name)>
<!ATTLIST Magazine Publisher CDATA #REQUIRED>
<!ELEMENT Name (#PCDATA)>
```

```
<!ENTITY % Books SYSTEM "Book.dtd">
<!ENTITY % Mags SYSTEM "Magazine.dtd">
%Books;
%Mags;
```

DTD contains parameter entities to two external documents

which the XML parser resolves into element and attribute declarations

Working with Unparsed Entities

So far, all of your work with Kristin has focused on character and parsed data. For an XML document to reference either binary data, such as images or video clips, or character data that is not well formed, you need to create an unparsed entity. Because the XML parser cannot work with this type of data directly, the unparsed entity includes instructions for how the unparsed entity needs be treated.

Declaring a Notation

The first step in using unparsed entities is to declare a **notation** identifying a resource that can handle the unparsed data. For example, to include a sound clip or image in the XML document, you must identify a sound- or image-editing application that can work with data in that format. The syntax for declaring a notation is

```
<!NOTATION notation SYSTEM "URL">
```

where *notation* is the notation's name and *URL* indicates the location of the resource. For example, the following declaration creates a notation named "audio" that points to the sound-editing application Recorder.exe.

```
<!NOTATION audio SYSTEM "Recorder.exe">
```

Once a notation has been declared, you declare an unparsed entity that instructs the XML parser to associate the data to the notation. The syntax of this declaration is

```
<!ENTITY entity SYSTEM "URL" NDATA notation>
```

where *entity* is the name you'll assign to the entity, *URL* is the location of the unparsed data, and *notation* is the name of the notation that handles the data. The following declaration takes unparsed data in the form of an audio file and assigns it to an unparsed entity named "Theme:"

```
<!ENTITY Theme SYSTEM "Overture.wav" NDATA audio>
```

The notation in this example is the audio notation that points to the Recorder.exe file. It's important to understand precisely what this declaration does and does not accomplish. It does *not* tell the Recorder.exe application to run the Overture.wav sound file. It merely identifies for the XML parser what resource is capable of handling the unparsed data.

REFERENCE WINDOW RW

<u>Declaring an Unparsed Entity</u>
■ To declare an unparsed entity, first you must declare a notation (a resource that the XML parser should access for the unparsed data), using the syntax
`<!NOTATION notation SYSTEM "URL">`
where *notation* is the notation's name and *URL* indicates the location of the resource.
■ To associate an unparsed entity with a notation, use
`<!ENTITY entity SYSTEM "URL" NDATA notation>`
where *entity* is the name you'll assign to the entity, *URL* is the location of the unparsed data, and *notation* is the name of the notation that handles the data.

Using Unparsed Entities in Attributes

Unparsed entities are often used as attribute values, especially for image files. The following DTD shows the structure of a very simple document. It has a root element named "Page" with a single child element named "Image." The Image element contains an entity attribute named "source." The DTD also contains a notation named "BMP" pointing to the Paint.exe file, which is an image-editing application. Finally, an unparsed entity has been declared for the Logo.bmp graphics file telling the XML processor which application can work with that particular image file.

```
<!DOCTYPE Page
[
   <!ELEMENT Page (Image)>
   <!ELEMENT Image EMPTY>
   <!ATTLIST Image Source ENTITY #REQUIRED>
   <!NOTATION BMP SYSTEM "Paint.exe">
   <!ENTITY Logo SYSTEM "Logo.bmp" NDATA BMP>
]
>
```

The XML author can put these declarations together in the following document:

```
<Page>
   <Image Source="Logo" />
</Page>
```

When this document is opened by the XML parser, the parser is able to interpret the Source attribute of the Image element to know which application is responsible for processing the unparsed data contained in the Logo.bmp file. Currently, Kristin doesn't have any unparsed data for her document, but in the future, she may want to include image files of products in the Pixal product line.

Working with Conditional Sections

When you're creating a new DTD, it's useful to be able to try out different combinations of declarations. Rather than rewriting the DTD each time a change is made, you divide the DTD into two sections. One section contains declarations that will be interpreted by the parser, and the other contains declarations that the parser will ignore. As you experiment with the structure of your DTD, you can move declarations from one section to another without losing the code.

The syntax for creating a section is

```
<![keyword
   declarations
]]>
```

where *keyword* is equal to INCLUDE (for a section of declarations that you want the parser to interpret) or IGNORE (for the declarations that you want the parser to pass over). For example, the following code creates two sections of declarations:

```
<![IGNORE
    <!ELEMENT Magazine (Name)>
    <!ATTLIST Magazine Publisher CDATA #REQUIRED>
    <!ELEMENT Name (#PCDATA)>
]]>
<![INCLUDE
    <!ELEMENT Book (Title, Author)>
    <!ATTLIST Book Pages CDATA #REQUIRED>
    <!ELEMENT Title (#PCDATA)>
    <!ELEMENT Author (#PCDATA)>
]]>
```

The parser processes the declarations involving the Book element, but it ignores the declarations involving the Magazine element.

The DTD can contain multiple IGNORE and INCLUDE sections. One effective way of handling multiple IGNORE sections is to create a parameter entity that defines whether those sections should be included or not, and use the value of the entity as the keyword for the conditional section. For example, the following UseFullDTD entity has a value of "IGNORE," which causes the conditional section that follows to be ignored by the XML parser:

```
<!ENTITY % UseFullDTD "IGNORE">
<![ %UseFullDTD [
    <!ELEMENT Magazine (Name)>
    <!ATTLIST Magazine Publisher CDATA #REQUIRED>
    <!ELEMENT Name (#PCDATA)>
]]>
```

By changing the value of the UseFullDTD from "IGNORE" to "INCLUDE," any conditional section that uses that entity reference will be added to the document's DTD. Thus, the XML author can switch multiple sections in the DTD off and on by editing a single line in the file.

You've completed your work on Kristin's document. You can close the file now.

To complete your work:

1. Return to your text editor and close Orders.xml document.

Session 3.3 QUICK CHECK

1. What is the difference between a general entity and a parameter entity?

2. What is the difference between a parsed entity and an unparsed entity?

3. What declaration would you enter to store the text string "<Title>Hamlet</Title>" as an entity named "Play"? What command would you enter to reference this entity in a document?

4. What declaration would you enter to store the contents of the Plays.xml file as an entity named "Plays"?

5. What code would you enter to store the contents of the Plays.dtd file as a parameter entity named "Works"?

6. What is a notation?

7. How would you store the image file "Shakespeare.gif" in an entity named "Portrait"? Assume that this entity is using a notation named "Paint".

Note: In the case problems that follow, some of the XML documents have intentional errors. Part of your job will be to find and correct those errors using DTDs.

REVIEW ASSIGNMENTS

Kristin has two additional documents that she needs your help on. One document describes Pixal's software products and the other describes its hardware offerings. In the software XML document, each product is contained in an element named "Software." The Software element has three child elements: Title, Company, and SPrice. The Title element has two attributes: first is SID (software ID), and second is OS, which indicates the operating system being used.

In the hardware XML file, each product is contained within an element named "Hardware." The Hardware element has three child elements: Model, Manufacturer, and MPrice. In addition, the Model element has the following attributes: MID, hardware ID, Category, and an optional attribute, SBundle, which identifies software bundled with a hardware item.

Figure 3-25 shows a diagram of the two documents.

Figure 3-25

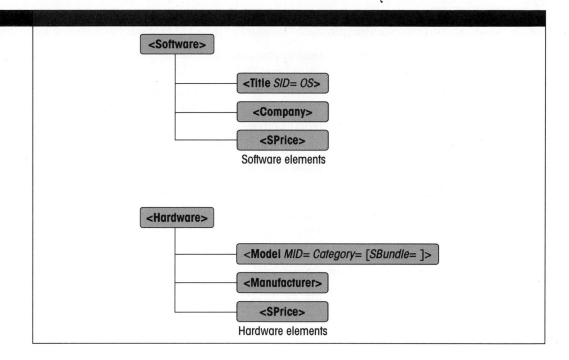

Software elements

Hardware elements

From these two documents, she wants to create a master document that contains a complete inventory of software and hardware products. As you did with the Orders document, it is important to enforce a document structure to ensure that information recorded in these documents is valid.

In the case problems that follow, some of the XML documents contain intentional errors. Part of your job is to find and correct those errors using DTDs.

To complete this task:

1. Using your text editor, open **Pixaltxt.xml**, which is located in the Tutorial.03X/Review folder of your Data Disk.

2. Save the document as **Pixal.xml**. Similarly, create a copy of the SWListtxt.xml file, saving it as **SWList.xml**, and a copy of the HWListtxt.xml file, saving it as **HWList.xml**. Review the contents of these files to get familiar with the structure of the documents involved and the type of content contained in each element and attribute.

3. Using your text editor, create a new file, name it **SW.dtd**, and save it in the Tutorial.03X/Review folder. Create element declarations for all of the software elements.

4. Within SW.dtd, create attribute list declarations for all of the attributes associated with the software elements. The SID attribute should be treated as an ID type. The OS attribute should be treated as an enumerated type, constrained to the following values: Macintosh, Windows, UNIX, or Other.

5. Using your text editor, create a file named **HW.dtd**. Create element declarations for all of the hardware elements.

6. Create attribute list declarations for all of the attributes associated with the hardware elements. Your attribute declarations should fulfill the following conditions:

   ■ The MID attribute should be declared as an ID token.

   ■ The Category attribute should be declared as an enumerated type, constrained to the following values: Camera, Scanner, or Tablet.

   ■ The SBundle attribute should be optional and treated as an ID reference token.

Explore   7. Using your text editor, open the **Pixal.xml** file and insert an internal DTD for a root element named "Inventory." The DTD should include the following declarations:

- an Inventory element that contains a choice of multiple child elements named "Hardware" and "Software" (*Hint:* Use a modifying symbol.)
- an external parameter entity named sw_decl that points to the contents of the SW.dtd file you created earlier
- an external parameter entity named hw_decl to point to the HW.dtd file
- an external general entity named sw_list to point to the SWList.xml file
- an external general entity named hw_list to point to the HWList.xml file

Explore   8. Insert the sw_decl and hw_decl entity references into the document's DTD.

Explore   9. Below the DTD, insert the body of the document. The document's body should include the Inventory root element. Within the root element, insert entity references for the sw_list and hw_list general entities.

10. Save your changes to the Pixal.xml file.

Explore   11. Use XML Spy to validate Pixal.xml. If any errors are reported, make your corrections to the SWList.xml and HWList.xml files.

12. Print the contents of all of the files you created in this project.

13. Hand in your files and printouts to your instructor.

CASE PROBLEMS

Case 1. Professional Basketball Association   Kurt Vaughn works for the Professional Basketball Association (PBL) and is responsible for coordinating information and statistics for the PBL's many developmental leagues. Part of Kurt's job is to maintain a document that lists the starting lineup for each team as well as providing individual player statistics. Kurt has asked for your help in creating XML documents that maintain a consistent document structure. He has a sample document describing six teams from the Eastern Developmental League (EDL). The document lists the five starting players on each team, including the following statistics about each player: PPG (points per game), RPG (rebounds per game), and Assists (assists per game). Figure 3-26 shows a tree diagram of the document structure. Note that PPG, RPG, and Assists attributes are all optional.

Figure 3-26

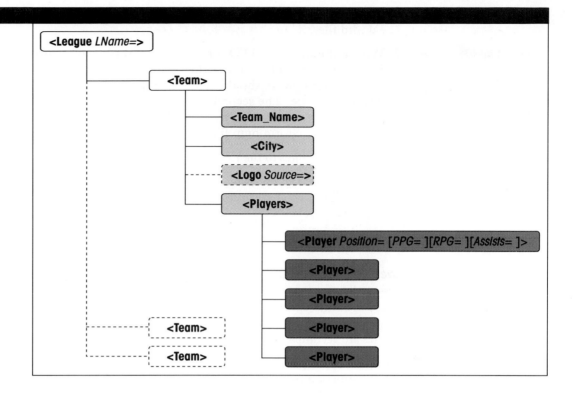

The document also contains an element that stores information about graphic files of team logos. The Logo element is optional. Any DTD that you create for this document will also need to work with the unparsed data contained in these graphic files.

To complete this task:

1. Using your text editor, open the **EDLtxt.xml** file, located in the Tutorial.03X/Cases folder of your Data Disk. Save the document as **EDL.xml**. Take some time to review the elements and attributes of the document.

2. Using your text editor, create a document named **DL.dtd**.

3. In the DL.dtd document, create a DTD, declaring elements shown in Figure 3-26. In addition to the document structure, the declarations should include the following:

   ■ The League element must contain one or more child elements named "Team."
   ■ The LName attribute must be a CDATA type.
   ■ The Team_Name and City elements must contain character data.
   ■ The optional Logo element should be empty, but it should have an entity attribute named "Source." The attribute is required.
   ■ The Players element should contain exactly five child elements named "Player."
   ■ Each Player element should contain only character data. The Player element has one required attribute named "Position," which must have the value Center, Forward, or Guard. The Player element can also have three optional elements named "PPG," "RPG," and "Assists," containing character data.

Explore   4. Also within the DTD, declare a notation named "Graphics" that references the Paint.exe application.

5. Save the DL.dtd file.

6. Within the EDL.xml file, create a mixed DTD. The DTD should reference the DL.dtd file.

Explore

7. Within the internal DTD for the EDL.xml file, create three unparsed entities. Each entity should reference the Graphics notation you created in the DL.dtd file. The first entity should be named "Tigers" and should reference the Tigers.bmp file. The second entity, named "Raiders," should reference the Raiders.bmp file. Finally, the third entity should be named "Storm" and should reference the Storm.bmp file.

8. Save your changes to the EDL.xml file.

9. Test the EDL.xml file using XML Spy. Correct any reported errors to make the document valid. If you have access to a different XML parser, you may use that as well.

10. Print out the code for the DL.dtd and EDL.xml files.

11. Hand in your files and printouts to your instructor.

Case 2. Web News Service, Inc. Alan Li works for the Web News Service, Inc. (WNS) and is responsible for entering daily news items. WNS publishes stories about national and international events, sports, entertainment, and leisure. Each news story is accompanied by a headline, a synopsis, and a reference to a file that contains the complete report. Some news stories are accompanied by image files.

Because of your growing reputation as an XML guru, Alan has asked you to help him store this information using a series of XML documents. The system that you two develop must be easy to update and maintain. Toward this objective, he has decided to place the DTDs in external files. In fact, he's already created one external DTD file for the image files, images.dtd, and another for the full text reports, full_text.dtd. Mr. Li is currently on a much-deserved vacation, and he needs you to create a DTD for the news story synopsis and for a document that displays all of the current stories.

To complete this task:

1. Using your text editor, open **newstxt.xml**, located in the Tutorial.03X/Cases folder of your Data Disk. Save the document as **news.xml**. Review the contents of this document, making careful note of the document's structure and content before proceeding.

2. Using your text editor, create a file named **stories.dtd**. The file needs to contain the following declarations:

   ■ An element named "story" containing four child elements named "headline," "synopsis," "full_text," and "image." The image child element can appear any number of times, but the rest of the child elements can appear only once.

   ■ The story element has a required attribute named "category" that must be one of the following values: national, international, sports, entertainment, leisure, or weather.

   ■ Another attribute of the story element is an optional attribute named "byline." It contains only character data.

   ■ The headline and synopsis elements should contain only character data.

   ■ The full_text and image elements should both be empty elements.

   ■ The full_text element has a entity attribute named "ref." The attribute is required.

   ■ The image element has a required entity attribute named "src."

3. Save the contents of the stories.dtd file.

4. Using your text editor, create a file named **WNS.xml**. This file will display all of the new stories from the other documents.

5. Create an internal DTD for WNS.xml. The DTD should contain the following items:

   ■ a root element named "News_Feed" that contains a single child element named "stories"

   ■ the stories element can occur zero or more times within the News_Feed element

   ■ a parameter entity declaration named "stories," pointing to the stories.dtd file

   ■ a parameter entity declaration named "images," pointing to the images.dtd file

   ■ a parameter entity declaration named "full_text," pointing to the full_text.dtd file

   ■ a general entity declaration named "news," pointing to the news.xml file

   ■ entity references for the stories, images, and full_text entities

6. Create the document body, containing a root element named "News_Feed."

7. Within the News_Feed element, insert an entity reference to the news entity.

8. Save your changes to the WNS.xml file.

9. Use XML Spy to verify that the WNS.xml document is valid. Correct any errors reported by the validator.

10. Print out the contents of all of the documents used in this project.

11. Hand in your printouts and files to your instructor.

Case 3. Freelance Programmer Linda Sanchez is a freelance programmer and is currently working on a checking account application. Having read how XML documents can be read by a wide variety of applications, she is considering using XML to store checking account records for her current project.

She's asked for your help in putting together a document of checking account transactions. She has already entered the elements and attributes, but she needs your help in making the document valid. Figure 3-27 shows the structure of her document.

Figure 3-27

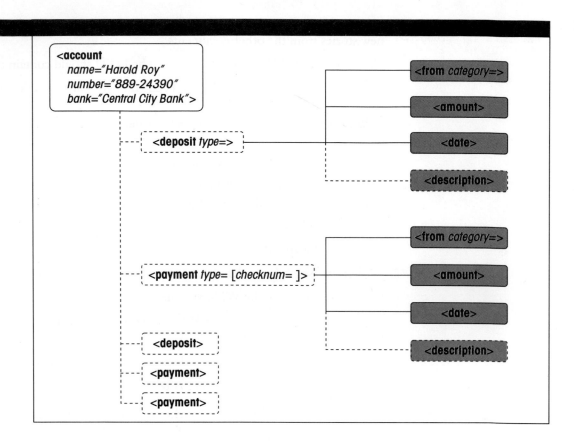

To complete this task:

1. Using your text editor, open the **accounttxt.xml** file, located in the Tutorial.03X/Cases folder of your Data Disk. Save the document as **account.xml**.

2. Take some time to review the contents of the account.xml file, noting the order of the elements and their attributes.

3. Using your text editor, create a file named **checking.dtd** in the Tutorial.03X/Cases folder.

4. Within the checking.dtd file, declare the following elements:

   ■ the account element containing two child elements named "payment" and "deposit," which can occur multiple times in any order

   ■ the deposit element that contains the child elements named "from," "amount," "date," and "description;" the description element is optional

   ■ the payment element that contains the child elements named "to," "amount," "date," and an optional description element

   ■ the from, to, amount, date, and description elements, which contain character data only

5. Add the following attributes to the DTD:

   ■ The account element should have three character data attributes: name, number, and bank. The value of the name attribute must be fixed as "Harold Roy." The value of the number attribute is fixed as "899-24390." The value of the bank attribute is fixed as "Central City Bank."

   ■ The deposit element has one required attribute named "type." The type attribute is limited to the following values: direct, cash, transfer, or check.

- The payment element has a required element named "type" limited to the values atm, check, transfer, or withdrawal. A second attribute of the payment element, named "checknum," is optional, and is treated as an ID token.
- The from element has one required attribute named "category," which must be equal to either income, savings, check, or cash.
- The to element has an optional attribute named "category" that must be equal to one of the following values: utilities, entertainment, food, clothing, cash, or other.

6. Declare a general parsed entity in the DTD named "employer" that stores the text string "Net World."

7. Save your changes to checking.dtd.

8. Return to the account.xml file in your text editor. Create an external DTD that references the checking.dtd file you just created.

9. Replace the text string "Net World" in the first checking transaction with a reference for the employer entity stored in checking.dtd.

10. Save your changes to the account.xml file.

11. Use XML Spy to validate the account.xml file for errors. Fix any errors reported.

12. Print the code of the files you created.

13. Hand in your printouts and files to your instructor.

Case 4. *The Lighthouse Charitable Trust.* Sela Voight is the Membership Coordinator for The Lighthouse, a charitable organization located in central Kentucky. One of her responsibilities is to maintain a membership list of people in the community who have contributed to The Lighthouse. Members can be in one of three categories: Platinum, Gold, and Premium. The categories assist Sela in defining her fund-raising goals and strategies to reach those goals.

Currently, most of the data that Sela has compiled resides in text files. To be a more effective fundraiser, she wants to convert this data into an XML document and wants to ensure that the resulting document follows some specific guidelines.

To complete this task:

1. Using the data stored in the Members.txt file in the Tutorial.03X/Cases folder of your Data Disk, create an XML document named **List.xml**.

2. The membership data from the Members.txt file should be organized into elements. The appearance of the document is up to you, but it should include the following features:

   - a root element named "List"
   - each member contained within an element named "Member"
   - Member containing the following child elements: Name, Address, Phone, E-mail, Contribution, and Notes; the E-mail and Notes elements are optional child elements, occurring no more than once
   - the Member element containing an attribute named "Level" to identify the level—Platinum, Gold, or Premium—for each member

3. Create a external DTD stored in LHouse.dtd. The DTD should contain declarations for the document structure you applied to List.xml.

4. Test the List.xml file and verify its validity and then print the completed code.

5. Hand in your completed assignment to your instructor.

QUICK CHECK ANSWERS

Session 3.1

1. `<!DOCTYPE Inventory SYSTEM "Books.dtd">`
2. `<!ELEMENT Book ANY>`
3. `<!ELEMENT Video EMPTY>`
4. `<!ELEMENT Book (#PCDATA)>`
5. `<!ELEMENT Book (Author)>`
6. `<!ELEMENT Book (Author+)`
7. `<!ELEMENT Book (#PCDATA | Author | Title)*>`

Session 3.2

1. `<!ATTLIST book Title CDATA #IMPLIED>`
2. `<!ATTLIST Play Type (Romance | Tragedy | History | Comedy) #REQUIRED>`
3. NMTOKEN types cannot contain blank spaces.
4. `<!ATTLIST Book ISBN ID #REQUIRED>`
5. `<!ATTLIST Author BooksBy IDREF #IMPLIED>`
6. `<!ATTLIST Book InStock (yes | no) "yes">`

Session 3.3

1. General entities are used only with the contents of an XML document. Parameter entities are used only with contents of a DTD.
2. Parsed entities consist entirely of well-formed XML content. Unparsed entities are constructed from non-XML data, including nontext data.
3. `<!ENTITY Play "<Title>Hamlet</Title>">`
   `&Play;`
4. `<!ENTITY Plays SYSTEM "Plays.xml">`
5. `<!ENTITY % Works "<!ENTITY % Works SYSTEM "Plays.dtd">`
6. A notation is a resource that an XML parser uses to handle unparsed data.
7. `<!ENTITY Portrait SYSTEM "Shakespeare.gif" NDATA Paint>`

OBJECTIVES

In this tutorial you will:

- Learn to create and apply namespaces

- Learn about schemas and schema dialects

- Create simple type declarations

- Create complex type declarations

- Learn how different schemas are structured

- Derive customized data types

- Annotate a schema and attach it to an instance document

WORKING WITH NAMESPACES AND SCHEMAS

Creating a Patient Report Document

CASE

University Hospital

Allison Grant is a project coordinator at the Clinical Cancer Center of the University Hospital. Her job is to coordinate the various research projects at the center. Allison wants to use XML to record data on the different studies and the patients enrolled in them. She then plans to use these XML documents to create Web pages for the hospital network, which investigators can use to view relevant information on patients and studies. Allison is new to XML and has sought out your help in a couple of areas.

On occasion, Allison needs to combine data from different sources into a single XML document. For example, the data from one document describing a study may need to be combined with data from another document describing individual patients. Allison would like to discuss with you how best to combine data from two XML documents.

A second issue involves data integrity. Accuracy is important to Allison. She needs to know that the data she enters is error free. For example, some of the studies have age criteria. Allison would like to be able to confirm that any patient she enters matches the age criteria for that study. Allison knows that DTDs cannot fulfill this function because they have a limited range of data types and provide no way to deal with numeric data. Allison has heard that schemas may be able to give the kind of control over data quality that she requires and would like you to help her implement them.

SESSION 4.1

In this session, you'll learn how to add namespaces to an XML document, and you'll see how namespaces can help you avoid "name collisions" when combining information from several documents. You'll also learn how namespaces can be applied to elements and attributes, and the consequences of using namespaces in the document's DTD.

Working with Namespaces

It is common practice to create several XML documents, with each document focused on one particular topic. This practice, however, can create significant challenges when information from different sources needs to be merged into a common document. One common problem is **name collision**, where elements from two or more documents share the same name. Figure 4-1 shows an example in which the Name element is used to store the name of a book in one document, while in another document, it stores the name of an author. When data from the two documents is combined, the Name element is used in two different contexts. The structure of the two Name elements is also different: in the Book document it stores text and in the Author document it contains two child elements.

Figure 4-1   NAME COLLISION

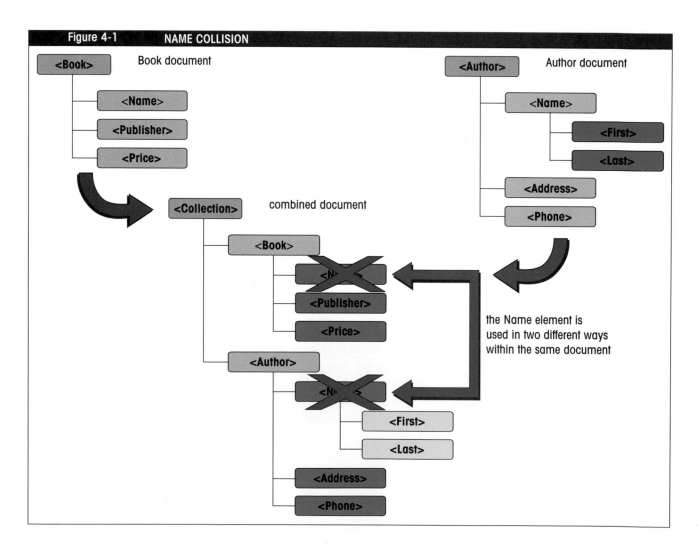

the Name element is used in two different ways within the same document

Such is the situation that Allison has with two of her XML documents. One document contains information on the clinical studies taking place at the hospital. Another document stores information on patients enrolled in those studies. Allison has combined data from both documents into a single file. Open that combined document now.

To open Allison's document:

1. Using your text editor, open **UHosptxt.xml** located in the Tutorial.04X/Tutorial folder of your Data Disk.

2. Save the file as **UHosp.xml**. Figure 4-2 shows a diagram of the structure of the UHosp.xml file. Take some time to study the document, comparing the code to the diagram.

Figure 4-2	LAYOUT OF THE UHOSP.XML DOCUMENT

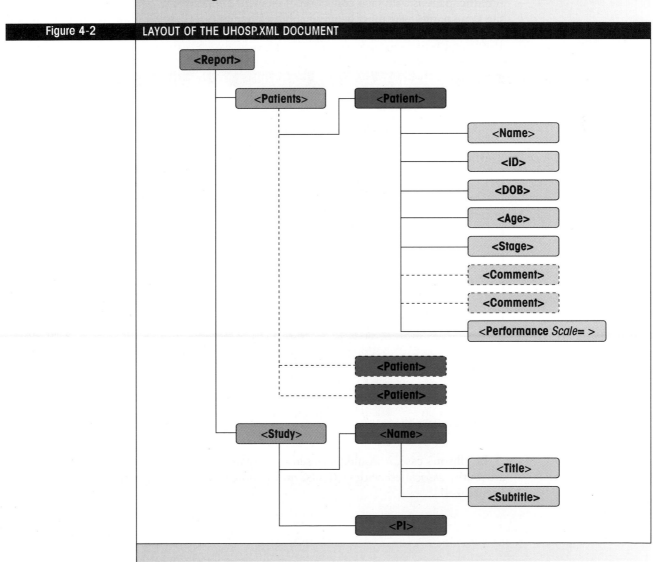

Note that there is a collision in Allison's document between the use of the Name element as a container for a patient's name and for storing information about the name of the study. As long as Allison is not concerned with validation, such collisions are not a problem. The content of her documents only needs to be well-formed. However, if she tried to validate this document, she would run into trouble because of the different ways the Name element is being used.

For a single author working on a small number of documents involving only a handful of elements, it is a relatively easy task to prevent name collisions. One simply ensures that each element has a unique name. However, in large organizations with several authors working to maintain hundreds of XML documents with thousands of element names, it is a nearly impossible job to avoid name collision. Allison doesn't have the ability to edit the original Patient and Study documents to rename their elements. Nor does she want to rename the elements in her combined document because she would then have to maintain two sets of element names: one for the individual documents and one for the combined document. There is a third way to solve this problem: namespaces.

Declaring a Namespace in the Document Prolog

A **namespace** is a defined collection of element and attribute names. Names that belong to the same namespace must be unique, but elements can share the same name as long as they reside in different namespaces (see Figure 4-3).

Figure 4-3 USING NAMESPACES TO AVOID NAME COLLISION

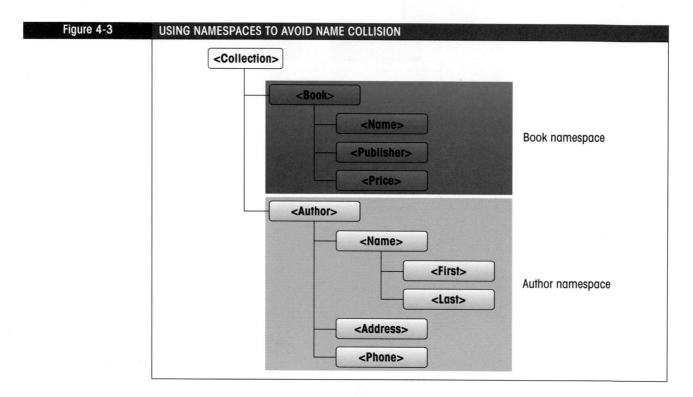

In Allison's case, it would make sense to create one namespace for all of the elements and attributes associated with patients, and another namespace for the clinical studies (see Figure 4-4).

Figure 4-4	THE PATIENT AND STUDY NAMESPACES

```
<?xml version="1.0" ?>

<Report>

    <Patients>
        <Patient>
            <Name>Cynthia Dibbs</Name>
            <ID>MR890-041-02</ID>
            <DOB>1945-05-22</DOB>
            <Age>58</Age>
            <Stage>II</Stage>
            <Performance Scale="Karnofsky">0.81</Performance>
        </Patient>
        <Patient>
            <Name>Karen Wilkes</Name>
            <ID>MR771-121-10</ID>
            <DOB>1959-02-24</DOB>
            <Age>44</Age>
            <Stage>II</Stage>
            <Comment>Dropped out of study.</Comment>
            <Performance Scale="Karnofsky">0.84</Performance>
        </Patient>
        <Patient>
            <Name>Olivia Sanchez</Name>
            <ID>MR701-891-05</ID>
            <DOB>1958-08-14</DOB>
            <Age>45</Age>
            <Stage>I</Stage>
            <Comment>Possibly Stage I/II</Comment>
            <Comment>Karnofsky performance rating unavailable.</Comment>
            <Performance Scale="Bell">0.89</Performance>
        </Patient>
        <Patient>
            <Name>Alice Russell</Name>
            <ID>MR805-891-08</ID>
            <DOB>1952-09-14</DOB>
            <Age>51</Age>
            <Stage>II</Stage>
            <Performance Scale="Karnofsky">0.76</Performance>
        </Patient>
        <Patient>
            <Name>Brenda Browne</Name>
            <ID>MR815-741-03</ID>
            <DOB>1964-04-25</DOB>
            <Age>39</Age>
            <Stage>I</Stage>
            <Performance Scale="Karnofsky">0.88</Performance>
        </Patient>
    </Patients>

    <Study>
        <Name>
            <Title>Tamoxifen Breast Cancer Study</Title>
            <Subtitle>Randomized Phase 3 Clinical Trial</Subtitle>
        </Name>
        <PI>Dr. Diane West</PI>
    </Study>

</Report>
```

patient namespace

Study namespace

Before they can be applied, namespaces must first be declared. A namespace can either be declared in the document's prolog or as an element attribute. The syntax for declaring a namespace in the prolog is

```
<?xml:namespace ns="URI" prefix="prefix"?>
```

where *URI* is a Uniform Resource Identifier that assigns a unique name to the namespace, and *prefix* is a string of letters that associates each element or attribute in the document with the declared namespace. For example, the following code declares a namespace with the prefix "pat" and the URI, "http://uhosp/patients/ns".

```
<?xml:namespace ns="http://uhosp/patients/ns" prefix="pat"?>
```

The URI looks like a Web address, but it's not. Before proceeding further with namespaces, URIs need a bit of explanation.

A Few Words About URIs, URLs, and URNs

A **Uniform Resource Identifier**, or **URI**, is a text string that identifies either a physical or an abstract resource. A physical resource would be a resource that one could access or work with, such as a file, a Web page, or an e-mail address. One type of URI is a URL, which is used to identify actual resources on the Internet. An abstract resource is a resource that doesn't have any physical existence, and the URI in this case is simply an identifier, much like an ID. Though it may look like an Internet address, an abstract resource doesn't actually reference an existing file or resource. The URI in the above sample code,

```
http://uhosp/patients/ns
```

is simply a text identifier. There is no Web page located at this address.

Actually, any unique text string can work as a namespace identifier, but there is good reason for using URIs. If the XML document is to be shared on the Web, the XML author needs to make sure that the document's namespace name will be unique. One way of doing this would be to have an organization register namespaces in the same way that Internet addresses are registered. However, because we already have a registry of unique Internet addresses, it makes sense to expand that system to encompass abstract references.

Another proposed type of URI is the URN or Universal Resource Name. A **URN** is a persistent resource identifier, which means that the user only needs to know the name of a resource, and one or more agencies retrieve the nearest copy of the resource, no matter where it is located. URNs take the following form:

```
urn:NID:NSS
```

where *NID* is the namespace identifier and *NSS* is the namespace-specific string. The *NID* tells us how to interpret the *NSS*. For example, the following URN is used to uniquely identify the ISBN number of a book:

```
urn:isbn:0-619-01969-7
```

The use of URNs with namespaces is still in its early stages, but URNs may eventually become the preferred way of expressing namespace names.

REFERENCE WINDOW   **RW**

Declaring and Applying a Namespace

- To declare a namespace in the document's prolog, use the following declaration:

  ```
  <?xml:namespace ns="URI" prefix="prefix"?>
  ```
  where *URI* is a Uniform Resource Identifier that assigns a unique name to the namespace, and *prefix* is the namespace prefix.

- To declare a namespace within an element, add the following attribute to the element:

  ```
  xmlns:prefix="URI"
  ```

- To associate an element with a namespace, insert the namespace prefix before the element name as follows:

  ```
  <prefix:element>
     content
  </prefix:element>
  ```

- To create a default namespace, do not include the *prefix* in the namespace declaration.

Applying a Namespace to an Element

Once a namespace has been declared and its URI specified, it can be applied to individual elements and attributes within the document. This is done by inserting the namespace prefix before each element name that belongs to the namespace. The general form is

```
<prefix:element>
   content
</prefix:element>
```

where *prefix* is the namespace prefix and *element* is the **local part** of the element name. Prefixed names are called **qualified names**. An element name lacking a namespace prefix is referred to as **unqualified name**.

Allison could adapt her element names to namespaces using the following code:

```
<?xml:namespace ns="http://uhosp/patients/ns" prefix="pat"?>
<?xml:namespace ns="http://uhosp/studies/ns" prefix="std"?>
<Report>
  <pat:Patients>
    <pat:Patient>
      <pat:Name>Cynthia Dibbs</pat:Name>
      <pat:ID>MR890-041-02</pat:ID>
      <pat:DOB>1945-05-22</pat:DOB>
      <pat:Age>58</pat:Age>
      <pat:Stage>II</pat:Stage>
      <pat:Performance Scale="Karnofsky">0.81</pat:
      Performance>
    </pat:Patient>

  ...

  <std:Study>
    <std:Name>Tamoxifen Breast Cancer Study</std:Name>
    <std:ID>CP2004-05-01</std:ID>
    <std:Director>Dr. Diane West</std:Director>
  </std:Study>
</Report>
```

In this sample code, there is no collision between the Name and ID elements because they belong to different namespaces. Moreover, from the prefixes, it is clear which element is associated with which namespace. In this example, each element name except Report is a qualified element name.

Declaring a Namespace as an Element Attribute

The more common way of declaring a namespace is to add the xmlns attribute to an element. The syntax is

```
xmlns:prefix="URI"
```

where *prefix* and *URI* are the prefix and URI for the namespace. Once a namespace is declared in this fashion, the namespace is made available to that element and to any of its child elements. The following code shows how to apply the namespace "http://uhosp/patients/ns namespace" to the Patient element and all of its child elements:

```
<pat:Patients xmlns:pat="http://uhosp/patients/ns">
  <Patient>
    <Name>Cynthia Dibbs</Name>
    <ID>MR890-041-02</ID>
    <DOB>1945-05-22</DOB>
    <Age>58</Age>
    <Stage>II</Stage>
    <Performance Scale="Karnofsky">0.81</Performance>
  </Patient>

...

</pat:Patients>
```

Note that the "pat" prefix was only added to the Patients element name. Even though the other elements in this sample code lack the prefix, the XML parser still considers them part of the Patients namespace because they inherit the namespace of their parent element, Patients. The lack of a namespace prefix does make them unqualified elements, however.

The most common way of declaring a namespace is to add it as an attribute of the document's root element. This method places all document elements in that namespace because all elements are children of the root element.

Declaring a Default Namespace

To avoid using namespace prefixes, you can specify a **default namespace** by omitting the prefix in the namespace declaration. The element containing the namespace attribute and all of its child elements are assumed to be part of the default namespace unless a different namespace is explicitly defined for one of those elements. The Patients namespace is applied to all of the elements in the following sample code, even though none of the elements are qualified:

```
<Patients xmlns="http://uhosp/patients/ns">
  <Patient>
    <Name>Cynthia Dibbs</Name>
    <ID>MR890-041-02</ID>
    <DOB>1945-05-22</DOB>
    <Age>58</Age>
    <Stage>II</Stage>
    <Performance Scale="Karnofsky">0.81</Performance>
```

```
    </Patient>

...

    </Patients>
```

Using Namespaces with Attributes

Like elements, attributes can become qualified by adding the namespace prefix to the attribute name as follows:

prefix:*attribute*="*value*"

There are two important rules to remember regarding attribute names:

- No element may contain two attributes with the same name, whether the attribute name is qualified or not.
- No element may contain two qualified attribute names with the same local part, pointing to identical namespaces, even if the prefixes are different.

Under these rules, the two elements in the following document would be considered invalid:

```
<Document
    xmlns:pat1="http:/uhosp/patients/ns"
    xmlns:pat2="http:/uhosp/patients/ns">

    <Name pat1:att1="1" pat1:att1="2" />
    <Name pat1:att1="1" pat2:att1="2" />
</Document>
```

The first element is invalid because the attribute names are identical and XML doesn't allow duplicate attributes within the same element. The second element is invalid because although the attribute names are different, their local parts are identical and their prefixes point to the same namespace.

A final important point to remember about attribute names is that an unqualified attribute name does not explicitly belong to any namespace, even if a default namespace has been declared for the document. This means that even if the element belongs to a namespace, the attribute does not, unless the attribute name is qualified by adding a namespace prefix. Generally, assigning a namespace to an attribute is not necessary unless you intend to use two attributes with the same name within a single element. In that case, to avoid name collision, they must be assigned to different namespaces and have different prefixes.

Creating a Namespace

After reviewing the material on namespaces, Allison decides that she needs to include namespaces in her document to avoid the problem of name collision. She has asked for your help in editing the document to ensure it is done correctly.

Allison wants to assign all of the patient data to a default namespace with the URI http://uhosp/patients/ns using the prefix "pat." She wants to assign all of the study data to a namespace with the URI "http://uhosp/studies/ns" and a namespace prefix of "std." You decide to declare the namespaces as attributes of the Patients and Study elements.

To create the two namespaces:

1. In the UHosp.xml file, add the following attribute to the Patients element: **xmlns:pat="http://uhosp/patients/ns"**.

2. Add the following attribute to the Study element: **xmlns:std="http://uhosp/studies/ns"**.

   To avoid confusion, you decide to make all of the elements in the Study namespace qualified elements. You'll leave the elements in the Patient namespace unqualified, aside from the opening and closing Patients tag.

3. Change the opening and closing tags of the Patients element from Patients to **pat:Patients**.

4. Change the opening and closing tags of the Study element from Study to **std:Study**.

5. Make all of the child elements of the std:Study element qualified elements by inserting the "std" namespace prefix.

   Figure 4-5 displays the revised XML code for UHosp.xml.

Figure 4-5   **DECLARING NAMESPACES**

```
<pat:Patients xmlns:pat="http://uhosp/patients/ns">          Patient namespace
    <Patient>                                                declaration
        <Name>Cynthia Dibbs</Name>
        <ID>MR890-041-02</ID>
        <DOB>1945-05-22</DOB>
        <Age>58</Age>
        <Stage>II</Stage>
        <Performance Scale="Karnofsky">0.81</Performance>
    </Patient>
    <Patient>
        <Name>Karen Wilkes</Name>
        <ID>MR771-121-10</ID>
        <DOB>1959-02-24</DOB>
        <Age>44</Age>
        <Stage>II</Stage>
        <Comment>Dropped out of study.</Comment>
        <Performance Scale="Karnofsky">0.84</Performance>
    </Patient>
    <Patient>
        <Name>Olivia Sanchez</Name>
        <ID>MR701-891-05</ID>
        <DOB>1958-08-14</DOB>
        <Age>45</Age>
        <Stage>I</Stage>
        <Comment>Possibly Stage I/II</Comment>
        <Comment>Karnofsky performance rating unavailable.</Comment>
        <Performance Scale="Bell">0.89</Performance>
    </Patient>
    <Patient>
        <Name>Alice Russell</Name>
        <ID>MR805-891-08</ID>
        <DOB>1952-09-14</DOB>
        <Age>51</Age>
        <Stage>II</Stage>
        <Performance Scale="Karnofsky">0.76</Performance>
    </Patient>
    <Patient>
        <Name>Brenda Browne</Name>
        <ID>MR815-741-03</ID>
        <DOB>1964-04-25</DOB>
        <Age>39</Age>
        <Stage>I</Stage>
namespace prefix                                             Study namespace
        <Performance Scale="Karnofsky">0.88</Performance>    declaration
    </Patient>
</pat:Patients>

<std:Study xmlns:std="http://uhosp/studies/ns">
    <std:Name>
        <std:Title>Tamoxifen Breast Cancer Study</std:Title>
        <std:Subtitle>Randomized Phase 3 Clinical Trial</std:Subtitle>
    </std:Name>
    <std:PI>Dr. Diane West</std:PI>
</std:Study>
```

6. Save your changes to UHosp.xml.

Now that you've inserted namespaces into the document, Allison wants to validate it with a DTD from an external subset. She has already created the DTD, but she's not sure how to modify it for use with namespaces.

Working with Namespaces and DTDs

Documents containing namespaces must adhere to the same rules for XML validity that documents without namespaces must follow. Each element and attribute appearing in the document must be included in the DTD, even if it belongs to a namespace that is not the default namespace. Namespace prefixes must also appear in the DTD for the document. For example, if a text element named "ID" becomes a qualified element with the namespace prefix "pat," it must appear in the DTD as follows:

```
<!ELEMENT pat:ID (#PCDATA)>
```

In essence, the XML parser considers the prefix, the separating colon, and the local part as a single entity.

Something else to consider is if you use the xmlns attribute to declare a namespace, you need to include this attribute in the DTD, declared as a fixed value. For example, if you have the following element in your document:

```
<pat:Patients xmlns:pat="http://uhosp/patients/ns">
```

you need to declare it in the DTD as follows:

```
<!ATTLIST pat:Patients xmlns:pat CDATA #FIXED
"http://uhosp/patients/ns">
```

Qualified attribute names also need to include the namespace prefix in any declaration in the DTD.

Allison would like you to adapt her DTD file for use with the namespaces you created.

To edit the DTD and link it to an XML document:

1. Use your text editor to open the **UHDTDtxt.dtd** document located in the Tutorial.04X/Tutorial folder of your Data Disk.

2. Save the file as **UHDTD.dtd**.

Figure 4-6 displays the current contents of UHDTD.dtd file.

| Figure 4-6 | UHDTD.DTD |

```
<!ELEMENT Report (Patients, Study)>

<!ELEMENT Patients (Patient+)>
<!ELEMENT Patient (Name, ID, DOB, Age, Stage, Comment*, Performance)>
<!ELEMENT Name (#PCDATA)>
<!ELEMENT ID (#PCDATA)>
<!ELEMENT DOB (#PCDATA)>
<!ELEMENT Age (#PCDATA)>
<!ELEMENT Stage (#PCDATA)>
<!ELEMENT Comment (#PCDATA)>
<!ELEMENT Performance (#PCDATA)>
<!ATTLIST Performance Scale (Karnofsky | Bell) #REQUIRED>

<!ELEMENT Study (Name, PI)>
<!ELEMENT Name (Title, Subtitle)>
<!ELEMENT Title (#PCDATA)>
<!ELEMENT Subtitle (#PCDATA)>
<!ELEMENT PI (#PCDATA)>
```

3. Change the name of the Patients element to **pat:Patients** wherever it appears in the DTD.

4. Change the name of the Study element to **std:Study** wherever it appears in the DTD.

5. Make all of the names of the child elements of the Study element into qualified element names by adding the "std" namespace prefix to each element name.

6. Add the attribute declarations for the two namespaces to the DTD by inserting the following two lines of code at the end of the DTD:

```
<!ATTLIST pat:Patients xmlns:pat CDATA #FIXED
"http://uhosp/patients/ns">
<!ATTLIST std:Study xmlns:std CDATA #FIXED
"http://uhosp/studies/ns">
```

Figure 4-7 displays the contents of the revised DTD. Save your changes and close the file.

| Figure 4-7 | ADDING NAMESPACE INFORMATION TO THE DTD |

namespace prefixes must be included in the DTD

the xmlns attribute that assigns the namespace must be declared as a fixed character data

```
<!ELEMENT Report (pat:Patients, std:Study)>

<!ELEMENT pat:Patients (Patient+)>
<!ELEMENT Patient (Name, ID, DOB, Age, Stage, Comment*, Performance)>
<!ELEMENT Name (#PCDATA)>
<!ELEMENT ID (#PCDATA)>
<!ELEMENT DOB (#PCDATA)>
<!ELEMENT Age (#PCDATA)>
<!ELEMENT Stage (#PCDATA)>
<!ELEMENT Comment (#PCDATA)>
<!ELEMENT Performance (#PCDATA)>
<!ATTLIST Performance Scale (Karnofsky | Bell) #REQUIRED>

<!ELEMENT std:Study (std:Name, std:PI)>
<!ELEMENT std:Name (std:Title, std:Subtitle)>
<!ELEMENT std:Title (#PCDATA)>
<!ELEMENT std:Subtitle (#PCDATA)>
<!ELEMENT std:PI (#PCDATA)>

<!ATTLIST pat:Patients xmlns:pat CDATA #FIXED "http://uhosp/patients/ns">
<!ATTLIST std:Study xmlns:std CDATA #FIXED "http://uhosp/studies/ns">
```

7. Close the UHDTD.dtd file, saving your changes, and then open **UHosp.xml** using your text editor. After the first line, insert the following document type declaration (see Figure 4-8):

```
<!DOCTYPE Report SYSTEM "UHDTD.dtd">
```

| Figure 4-8 | APPLYING THE REVISED DTD TO ALLISON'S DOCUMENT |

```
<?xml version="1.0" ?>
<!DOCTYPE Report SYSTEM "UHDTD.dtd">
<Report>
```

8. Save your changes and close UHosp.xml.

In general, there are a number of issues and practical concerns that prevent namespaces and DTDs from working particularly well together. For example, there is no way to associate a specific DTD with a namespace. What this means to XML authors is that a new DTD must be created each time two or more documents are combined into a single document. If you're in the habit of combining data from several different sources, like Allison is, this can be a frustrating use of your time. For this and other reasons, the use of namespaces is a controversial topic of discussion among some XML developers. Many developers would prefer a system where namespaces and data validation could more easily coexist.

One possible solution to this dilemma is the use of schemas, which will be discussed in the next two sessions.

Session 4.1 QUICK CHECK

1. What is a namespace and why are namespaces important?

2. What is a qualified element name?

3. How would you declare a namespace with the URI "http://ns.doc/book" and the prefix "Book" in the prolog of your document?

4. How would you declare the namespace from the previous question as an attribute of an element named "Work"?

5. How do you create a default namespace?

6. How are qualified elements represented in a DTD?

SESSION 4.2

In this session, you'll learn about schemas, their history, and their different dialects. You'll create a schema and use it to declare the features and properties of the elements and attributes in an XML document. Finally, you'll learn how to attach a schema to a document.

Introducing Schemas

Having completed your work on combining the content of the Study and Patients documents into a single XML file, Allison now wants you to look at the contents of the Patients document alone. Allison is particularly concerned that the data entered into that document is valid. Currently, she is doing validation with DTDs but feels that they are inadequate for her needs.

The use of DTDs as a validation tool is due largely to the fact that XML is an offshoot of SGML. SGML was originally designed for text-based documents such as reports and technical manuals. As long as the data content is limited to simple text, DTDs work well for validation. However, XML is being used for a wider range of document types, and there are several limitations that have prompted XML developers to explore alternatives to DTDs.

One of these limitations was discussed in the last session—the inability of DTDs to work well with namespaces. In an environment with hundreds of XML documents, it is extremely time consuming to create and manage a separate DTD for each combination of documents. Another complaint about DTDs is the lack of data types. For example, if Allison wants to record each patient's age, she can declare an Age element, but she cannot specify in the DTD that the Age element contain only numbers, or numbers within a specified range of values. She can create a Date element, but the DTD won't have the tools to ensure that only dates are entered into the document. DTDs simply do not have the control over the data that Allison requires.

A DTD is also limited in its ability to enforce a structure on mixed content. A DTD can specify that an element contain both text and child elements, but it cannot control the sequence or number of each child element. There are workarounds, but they can be complicated to implement.

Finally, DTDs use a different syntax from XML called **Extended Backus Naur Form (EBNF)**. This means that an application that validates an XML document must be able to work with not only the syntax of XML but also EBNF. XML authors also have to be conversant with both syntaxes.

Because XML stands for *Extensible* Markup Language, why not use XML itself to describe the structure of XML documents? This is the idea behind schemas.

Schemas and DTDs

A **schema** is an XML document that defines the content and structure of one or more XML documents. To avoid confusion, the XML document containing the content is called the **instance document** because it represents a specific instance of the structure defined in the schema.

Figure 4-9 outlines some of the important differences between schemas and DTDs.

Figure 4-9	COMPARING SCHEMAS AND DTDS
SCHEMAS	**DTDS**
Written in XML	Written in Extended Backus Naur Form (EBNF)
Multiple, competing schema standards	One single DTD standard
Not supported by all validating parsers	Supported by all validating parsers
Supports over 44 data types	Supports ten data types
Users can create customized data types	Users cannot create customized data types
Easily handles mixed content	Cannot easily handle mixed content
Schemas can be attached to namespaces	DTDs cannot be attached to namespaces
Does not support entities	Supports entities

Schemas have a number of advantages over DTDs. For one, the XML parser only needs to understand XML, and thus all of the tools used to create the instance document can be applied to designing the schema. Schemas also support more data types, including data types for numbers and dates. The only content supported by DTDs involves text or child elements.

So if schemas are so useful, why do we need DTDs at all? First of all, DTDs represent an older standard for XML documents and are, therefore, more widely supported. It will still be a few years before schemas entirely replace DTDs for document validation. DTDs can also do a few things that schemas cannot, such as create entities. Therefore, we need to view schemas and DTDs as complementary approaches. In some cases, an XML document might use both a schema and a DTD.

Schema Dialects

Unlike DTDs, there is not a single form of the schema. Instead, several schema "dialects" have been developed in the XML language. Each dialect has distinct advantages and disadvantages, and a few of these dialects are listed in Figure 4-10.

Figure 4-10	SCHEMA DIALECTS	
SCHEMA	**DESCRIPTION**	**URL**
DDML	DDML (Document Definition Markup Language) is a schema language for XML documents, encoding the logical (as opposed to physical) content of DTDs in an XML document. It is also known as XSchema.	http://www.w3.org/TR/NOTE-ddml
RELAX	The RELAX (Regular Language for XML) schema is based on a Japanese national schema standard.	http://www.xml.gr.jp/relax
RELAX NG	The RELAX NG schema combines the RELAX and NG schema specifications.	http://www.oasis-open.org/committees/relax-ng/
Schematron	The Schematron schema represents documents using a tree pattern, allowing support for those document structures that might be difficult to represent in more traditional schema languages.	http://www.ascc.net/xml/resource/schematron/schematron.html
TREX	The TREX (Tree Regular Expressions) schema specifies a pattern for the structure and content of an XML document, identifying a class of XML documents that match the pattern.	http://www.thaiopensource.com/trex/
XDR	The XDR (XML-Data Reduced) schema is developed and supported by Microsoft, in particular Microsoft's Internet Explorer browser. XDR is sometimes referred to as XML-Data.	http://www.ltg.ed.ac.uk/~ht/XMLData-Reduced.htm
XML-Schema	XML-Schema, created by the W3C Schema Working Group, is a large specification designed to handle a broad range of document structures. It is also referred to as XSD.	http://www.w3.org/XML/Schema

Please note that support for a particular schema depends solely on the XML parser being used for validation. Before applying any of the schemas listed in Figure 4-10, you will have to verify the level of support offered by your application for that particular schema. The two most prominent dialects are XML Schema and XDR.

XML Schema, developed by the W3C in March of 2001, represents the closest thing to a schema standard. Because the specifications for XML Schema are so new, not all applications support all of its aspects. However, due to the influence associated with the W3C and its specifications, it is certain that most XML parsers will eventually support XML Schema.

Microsoft's schema, XDR, was the first schema to be developed. As such, XDR is supported by most of Microsoft's XML-aware applications—most notably Internet Explorer. It should be noted that Microsoft is moving toward supporting both XDR and XML Schema. Internet Explorer version 5.5 and above supports both schema dialects.

The focus of this tutorial is primarily on the XML Schema dialect, though many of the concepts involved with XML Schema can be applied to the other schema dialects as well. You can convert your DTD files to XML Schema files using the dtd2xs converter, available at *http://www.w3.org/XML/Schema*. Also, for XML developers who need to work with both XML Schema and XDR, Microsoft provides a tool to convert XML Schema files into the XDR format. You can access this converter at: *http://msdn.microsoft.com/downloads/ default.asp?url=/downloads/topic.asp?url=/msdn-files/028/000/072/topic.xml*.

Starting a Schema File

DTDs can be divided into internal or external subsets. This is not the case with schemas. A schema is always placed in a separate XML document that is referenced by the instance document. A schema file written in the XML Schema dialect typically ends with the .xsd file extension. XDR schemas are usually stored in files with the .xdr file extension.

Before you start creating the schema, though, you should open and save Allison's Patients document.

> ## To open Allison's document:
>
> **1.** Using your text editor, open **Pattxt.xml** located in the Tutorial.04X/Tutorial folder of your Data Disk.
>
> **2.** Save the file as **Patient.xml**.
>
> Note that the data is this file is the same as the data in the UHosp.xml document, except that there are no study elements and the root element is now Patients rather than Report.

Allison has also created a table describing the types of rules she would like to see applied to the data in this document. For example, she wants to ensure that a number is entered for the patient's age rather than a text string. Figure 4-11 describes the contents of each element and attribute in Allison's document.

Figure 4-11	ELEMENTS AND ATTRIBUTES OF THE PATIENT DOCUMENT
ELEMENTS	**DESCRIPTION**
Patients	The root element of Allison's document
Patient	The element that stores information about each individual patient (Name, ID, DOB, Stage, and Performance)
Name	The patient's name
ID	The patient's medical record number in the format MR###-###-##
DOB	The patient's date of birth in the format YYYY-MM-DD
Age	The patient's age (must be 21 or older)
Stage	The stage of the patient's breast cancer (must be either I or II)
Performance	A measure of the patient's health (must be a number between 0 and 1)
Comment	Optional comments providing additional information about the patient
ATTRIBUTES	
Scale	A required attribute of the Performance element indicating the type of performance measure; the attribute value must be equal to either "Karnofsky" or "Bell"

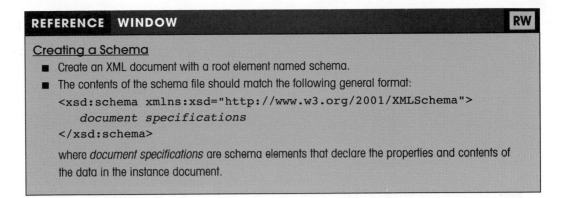

Now that you've seen the structure of Allison's document, you can begin creating the schema to match it.

To create the schema file:

1. Open a new blank file in your text editor.

   Because schemas are XML documents, they follow the same structure as other XML documents: they must have a prolog and a root element, and must begin with the xml tag.

2. Type **<?xml version="1.0" encoding="UTF-8"?>** in the first line of document.

   Add a comment to describe the purpose of this file.

3. Below the prolog, enter the following line:

   ```
   <!-- Schema for breast cancer patient data -->
   ```

   Because this file will be using the XML Schema, save it with the .xsd file extension.

4. Save the file as **PSchema1.xsd** to the Tutorial.04X/Tutorial folder of your Data Disk.

Next you insert the document's root element. In XML Schema, the root element is named "schema." Also, the schema element must contain a namespace declaration that tells the XML parser that the elements in this document are written in XML Schema form. The URI of the XML Schema namespace is *http://www.w3.org/2001/XMLSchema*. An XML Schema document is therefore constructed as follows:

```
<xsd:schema xmlns:xsd="http://www.w3.org/2001/XMLSchema">
   document specifications
</xsd:schema>
```

where *document specifications* is the XML code that we'll use to define the content of the instance document.

By convention, the prefix "xsd" or "xs" is assigned to the XML Schema namespace, though such a prefix is not required. One could define the XML Schema namespace as the default namespace for the document or use a different prefix altogether. However, the xsd prefix does serve a useful role as a visual reminder that this is an XML Schema document and not a generic XML file.

To insert the schema element in the PSchema1.xsd file:

1. Below the comment line, type the opening schema tag as shown below and press the **Enter** key.

   ```
   <xsd:schema xmlns:xsd="http://www.w3.org/2001/XMLSchema">
   ```

2. Type the closing schema tag:

   ```
   </xsd:schema>
   ```

   Figure 4-12 displays the opening tags of the PSchema1.xsd schema file.

Figure 4-12	THE SCHEMA ELEMENT

the URI for the XML Schema namespace

```
<?xml version="1.0" encoding="UTF-8"?>
<!-- Schema for breast cancer patient data -->

<xsd:schema xmlns:xsd="http://www.w3.org/2001/XMLSchema">
</xsd:schema>
```

Note that the schema tags are case sensitive. You cannot use the element name "Schema" (with an initial capital letter) in place of "schema." You are now ready to insert declarations for the elements and attributes for Allison's XML document.

Working with Simple Types

XML Schema recognizes two categories of element types: complex and simple. A **complex type** element is an element that has one or more attributes, or is the parent to one or more child elements. A **simple type** element contains only character data and has no attributes (see Figure 4-13).

Figure 4-13	TYPES OF ELEMENTS

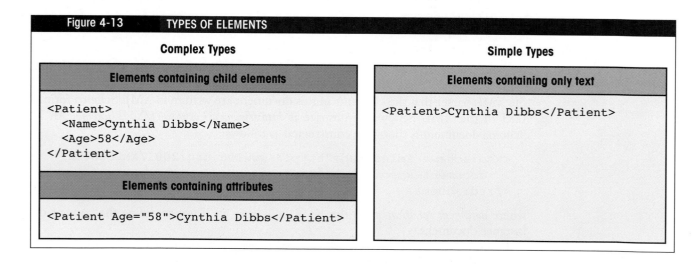

In Allison's XML document, both the Patients and Patient elements represent complex types because they contain child elements. The Performance element is also a complex type because it has the Scale attribute. All of the other elements in her XML document are simple types because they contain only text.

To declare a simple type element in XML Schema, use the general syntax

```
<element name="name" type="type"/>
```

where *name* is the name of the element in the instance document and *type* is the data type of the element. This declaration uses an empty element tag because it doesn't enclose any content in the schema file.

Note that we have not included the namespace prefix in the syntax for the element. If a namespace prefix is used with the XML Schema namespace, then any XML Schema tags must be qualified with the namespace prefix. For example, if the namespace prefix for the schema is xsd, a simple type element declaration would have to be qualified as follows:

```
<xsd:element name="name" type="xsd:type"/>
```

Note that both the tag name and the attribute name must be qualified.

The syntax for the rest of the XML Schema elements in this tutorial will not include the namespace prefix, but be aware that you will have to include the prefix in the actual schema documents you create.

Understanding Data Types

XML Schema supports two categories of data types: built-in and user-derived. A **built-in data type** is part of the XML Schema specifications and is available to all XML Schema authors. A **user-derived data type** is created by the XML Schema author for specific data values in the instance document. You'll learn how to create user-derived data types in the next session.

XML Schema divides its built-in data types into two classes: primitive and derived. A **primitive data type** or **base type** is one of 19 fundamental data types that are not defined in terms of other types. A **derived data type** is a collection of 25 data types that the XML Schema developers created based on the 19 primitive types. Figure 4-14 provides a schematic diagram of all 44 built-in data types.

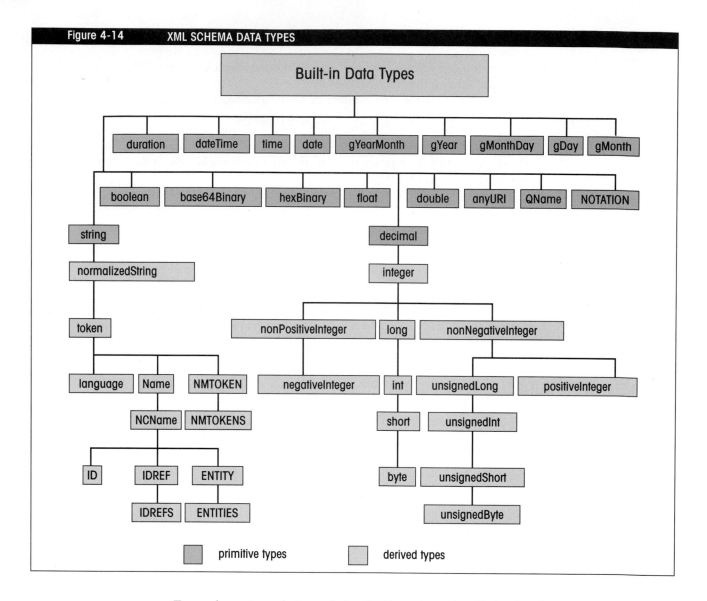

Figure 4-14   XML SCHEMA DATA TYPES

From the point of view of the XML author, the distinction between primitive and derived built-in types makes little difference because both are supported by XML Schema. Figure 4-15 describes a few of the more commonly used built-in data types.

Figure 4-15	A PARTIAL DESCRIPTION OF XML SCHEMA DATA TYPES	
DATA TYPE	**DESCRIPTION**	**EXAMPLES**
string	Any legal XML text string	Cynthia Dibbs
decimal	A decimal number of arbitrary precision	3.14, 5.9E–10, 0, 7.0
integer	An arbitrarily large or small integer	0, 10, –10
positiveInteger	An integer strictly greater than zero	10
nonNegativeInteger	An integer greater than or equal to zero	0, 10
negativeInteger	An integer strictly less than zero	–10
nonPositiveInteger	An integer less than or equal to zero	0, –10
boolean	A value representing a binary outcome (0, 1, true, or false)	0, 1, true, false
date	A date in the format CCYY-MM-DD where CC represents the century, YY represents the year, MM represents the month, and DD represents the day	2003-04-01
ID, IDREF, ENTITY, ENTITIES, NMTOKEN, NMTOKENS	Derived data types based on the original DTD data types for attribute values	

For example, Allison's XML document contains an Age element that she wants to limit to only positive integers. To do that, she could declare the Age element in her schema as follows:

```
<element name="Age" type="positiveInteger"/>
```

Note that XML Schema treats dates in a way that you might not be familiar with. In XML Schema, dates are displayed starting with the year and, reading left to right, continuing on with month and day with each unit separated by dashes. The date July 4, 1776 would be written as 1776-07-04 (leading zeroes must be included for both months and days).

Finally, all of the data types you used with your DTDs are also supported by XML Schema. The important difference is that the DTD data types are only used with attribute values, whereas XML Schema allows these data types to be applied to both attribute values and element content.

You can learn more about the wealth of built-in data types by accessing the W3 data type specifications page at *http://www.w3.org/TR/xmlschema-2/*.

REFERENCE WINDOW | **RW**

Declaring Simple and Complex Types

- To declare a simple type (an element that contains only text), use the following syntax:

  ```
  <element name="name" type="type"/>
  ```

  where *name* is the name of the element in the instance document and *type* is the data type of the element.

- To declare a complex type (an element that contains attributes and/or child elements), use the following syntax:

  ```
  <element name="name">
      <complexType>
          compositor
              element declarations
          compositor
          attribute declarations
      </complexType>
  </element>
  ```

  where *element declarations* are simple type element declarations for each child element, *compositors* define how the list of elements is to be organized, and *attribute declarations* are declarations that define any of the attributes of the element. Attribute declarations must be placed after the declarations for the child elements. XML Schema supports three kinds of compositors: sequence, choice, and all.

Working with Complex Types

A complex type element contains one or more attributes or is the parent to one or more child elements. For these types of elements, the general syntax is as follows:

```
<element name="name">
    <complexType>
        compositor
            element declarations
        compositor
        attribute declarations
    </complexType>
</element>
```

where *name* is the name of the element in the instance document, *element declarations* are simple type element declarations for each child element, *compositors* define how the list of elements is to be organized, and *attribute declarations* are declarations that define any of the attributes of the element (you'll learn about these later). Any attribute declarations, if they exist, must be placed after the declarations for the child elements.

Working with Compositors

A **compositor** is a schema tag that defines how the list is to be treated. XML Schema supports three types of compositors: sequence, choice, and all. The **sequence compositor** forces elements in the instance document to be entered in the same order as indicated in the schema. For example, the following complex type assigns the element Address four child elements—Street, City, State, and Country:

```
<element name="Address">
    <complexType>
        <sequence>
            <element name="Street" type="string"/>
            <element name="City" type="string"/>
            <element name="State" type="string"/>
            <element name="Country" type="string"/>
        </sequence>
    </complexType>
</element>
```

An instance document that doesn't display all of these child elements or displays them in a different order would be invalid.

The **choice compositor** allows any *one* of the items in the list to be used in the instance document. In the following declaration, the Sponsor element can contain either the Parent element or the Guardian element, but not both:

```
<element name="Sponsor">
    <complexType>
        <choice>
            <element name="Parent" type="string"/>
            <element name="Guardian" type="string"/>
        </choice>
    </complexType>
</element>
```

Finally, the **all compositor** allows any of the items to appear in the instance document in any order. The following declaration allows the Family element to contain an element named "Father" and/or another named "Mother" in no particular order:

```
<element name="Family">
    <complexType>
        <all>
            <element name="Father" type="string"/>
            <element name="Mother" type="string"/>
        </all>
    </complexType>
</element>
```

Compositors can be nested inside of one another. The following declaration using choice compositors allows the instance document to display the Person or Company element followed by the Cash or Credit element:

```
<element name="Account">
    <complexType>
        <sequence>
            <choice>
                <element name="Person" type="string"/>
                <element name="Company" type="string"/>
            </choice>
            <choice>
                <element name="Cash" type="string"/>
                <element name="Credit" type="string"/>
```

```
          </choice>
        </sequence>
      </complexType>
    </element>
```

The only restriction with nesting compositors is when using the all compositor type. A complex type element can only contain one all compositor and the all compositor must appear as the first child of the complex type element. You cannot combine the all compositor with either the choice or sequence compositor.

Specifying the Occurrences of an Item

In the previous code samples, it was assumed that each element in the list appeared once and only once. This will not always be the case. In Allison's document, the Comments element can appear multiple times or not at all. To specify the number of times each element appears in the instance document, you can use the **minOccurs** and **maxOccurs** attributes.

For example, the following element declaration specifies that the Phone element appears zero to three times in the instance document:

```
<element name="Phone" type="string" minOccurs="0"
maxOccurs="3"/>
```

Note that any time the minOccurs attribute is set to 0, the declared item is optional. The maxOccurs attribute can be any positive value or have a value of "unbounded," meaning that there is no upper limit to the number of occurrences of the element. If a value is specified for the minOccurs attribute, but the maxOccurs attribute is missing, the value of the maxOccurs attribute is assumed to be equal to the value of the minOccurs attribute. Finally, if both attributes are missing, their value is assumed to be 1.

The minOccurs and maxOccurs attributes can also be used with compositors to repeat entire sequences of items. In the following code, the sequence of three child elements (FirstName, MiddleName, LastName) can be repeated countless times within the Customer element:

```
<element name="Customer">
   <complexType>
      <sequence minOccurs="1" maxOccurs="unbounded">
         <element name="FirstName" type="string"/>
         <element name="MiddleName" type="string"/>
         <element name="LastName" type="string"/>
      </sequence>
   </complexType>
</element>
```

Specifying Mixed Content

As you remember, one of the limitations of using DTDs is their inability to define mixed content, which is an element that contains both text and child elements. You can specify the child elements with a DTD, but you cannot constrain their order or number. XML Schema gives you more control over mixed content. To specify that an element contains both text and child elements, add the mixed attribute to the complexType tag. When the mixed attribute is set to the value "true," XML Schema assumes that the element contains both text and child elements. The structure of the child elements can then be defined with the conventional method. For example, the following XML content:

```
<Summary>
   Patient <Name>Cynthia Davis</Name> was enrolled on
```

```
the <Study>Tamoxifen Study</Study> on 8/15/2003.
</Summary>
```

can be declared in XML Schema as

```
<element name="Summary">
   <complexType mixed="true">
      <sequence>
         <element name="Name" type="string"/>
         <element name="Study" type="string"/>
      </sequence>
   </complexType>
</element>
```

Note that XML Schema allows content text to appear before, between, and after any of the child elements.

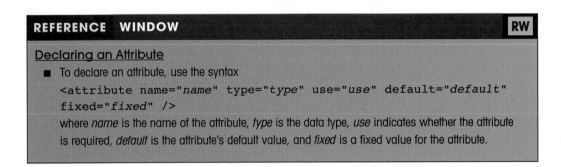

REFERENCE WINDOW **RW**

Declaring an Attribute

■ To declare an attribute, use the syntax

```
<attribute name="name" type="type" use="use" default="default"
fixed="fixed" />
```

where *name* is the name of the attribute, *type* is the data type, *use* indicates whether the attribute is required, *default* is the attribute's default value, and *fixed* is a fixed value for the attribute.

Declaring an Attribute

So far, the complex types that you've examined have involved elements that contain child elements. Remember, any element that contains an attribute is also a complex type. The syntax for declaring an attribute is

```
<attribute name="name" type="type" use="use"
default="default" fixed="fixed" />
```

where *name* is the name of the attribute, *type* is the data type, *use* indicates whether the attribute is required, *default* is the attribute's default value, and *fixed* is a fixed value for the attribute. Attributes use the same collection of data types that simple type elements do.

The use attribute has three possible values:

■ **required**: The attribute must always appear with the element.

■ **optional**: The attribute can appear once or not at all.

■ **prohibited**: The attribute cannot be used with the element.

If you fail to specify a use value in the attribute declaration, XML Schema assumes that the attribute is optional. The following attribute declaration declares the Gender attribute with a default value of female:

```
<attribute name="Gender" type="string" default="female"/>
```

An attribute must always be declared along with the element it belongs to. XML Schema will use a different structure for elements that contain content and attributes versus elements that contain only attributes. There are four possible situations:

■ The element contains only attributes but no content (an empty element).

- ■ The element contains attributes and child elements, but no text.
- ■ The element contains attributes, text, and child elements.
- ■ The element contains attributes and text, but no child elements.

Let's examine how to work with an empty element first.

Attributes with Empty Elements

If the element is empty, you declare the attributes using syntax similar to what you used for declaring child elements. The primary difference is that the order in which the attributes appear is not specified and therefore not placed within compositors. The syntax for declaring attributes within an empty element is as follows:

```
<complexType>
    attribute declarations
</complexType>
```

For example, the following element in the instance document:

```
<Patient ID="MR89-8901-25" Gender="female"/>
```

can be declared as

```
<element name="Patient">
    <complexType>
        <attribute name="ID" type="string"/>
        <attribute name="Gender" type="string"/>
    </complexType>
</element>
```

Note that you don't need a compositor with a list of attributes as you do with a list of child elements.

Attributes with Child Elements

If an element contains only child elements in addition to attributes, the attributes are placed after the element declarations. The following content:

```
<Patient ID="MR89-8901-25" Gender="female">
  <Name>Cynthia Dibbs</Name>
  <Age>58</Age>
</Patient>
```

can be declared as

```
<element name="Patient">
    <complexType>
        <sequence>
            <element name="Name" type="string"/>
            <element name="Age" type="positiveInteger"/>
        </sequence>
        <attribute name="ID" type="string"/>
        <attribute name="Gender" type="string"/>
    </complexType>
</element>
```

For content that contains text in addition to the child elements and attributes, insert the attribute mixed="true" into the complexType tag.

Attributes with Simple Content

For elements that contain attributes and text, but no child elements, XML Schema uses the following syntax:

```
<element name="name">
    <complexType>
        <simpleContent>
            <extension base="type">
                attribute declarations
            </extension>
        </simpleContent>
    </complexType>
</element>
```

where *type* is the data type of the element's content. The simpleContent and extension tags are important tools that XML Schema uses to derive new data types and design content models, although in this context we are only concerned with how they are used to declare attributes for elements that also contain text.

For example, the following content:

```
<Patient PID="MR-89-401-23">Cynthia Dibbs</Patient>
```

can be declared in XML as

```
<element name="Patient">
    <complexType>
        <simpleType>
            <extension base="string">
                <attribute name="PID" type="ID"/>
            </extension>
        </simpleType>
    </complexType>
</element>
```

Note that in this case, we use the ID data type for the attribute value and the string data type for the contents of the Patient element.

Now that you've seen how XML Schema can be used to declare simple types, complex types, and attributes, you are ready to complete the schema for Allison's XML document.

Inserting Element Declarations into a Schema

To finish a schema for Allison's document, start with the outermost element in the structure and work your way inward through all of the nested elements and attributes. The levels of element and attribute declarations in the schema correspond to the levels of parent and child elements in the instance document. With this in mind, start with the declaration for the root element of the instance document, which is Patients. As you enter the schema code, be sure to refer back to the structure of the Patients information, displayed earlier in Figure 4-2.

To create the declaration for the Patients element:

1. Verify that you are still working on the PSchema1.xsd file in your text editor.

2. Immediately following the opening schema tag, enter the opening and closing tags, as shown below, to define the element Patients. As shown in Figure 4-16, indent these lines a few spaces to offset the element tags from the surrounding schema tag. Because this is the root element, it will be defined as a complexType element.

```
<xsd:element name="Patients">
  <xsd:complexType>
    <xsd:sequence>
    </xsd:sequence>
  </xsd:complexType>
</xsd:element>
```

Figure 4-16   CREATING THE PATIENTS COMPLEX TYPE

```
<?xml version="1.0" encoding="UTF-8"?>
<!-- Schema for breast cancer patient data -->

<xsd:schema xmlns:xsd="http://www.w3.org/2001/XMLSchema">
  <xsd:element name="Patients">
    <xsd:complexType>
      <xsd:sequence>
      </xsd:sequence>
    </xsd:complexType>
  </xsd:element>
</xsd:schema>
```

Note that we must include the xsd namespace prefix for all schema tags in this document. Next, we have to insert the element declaration for the Patient element. The Patient element itself is a complexType element. Because there can be unlimited Patient elements within the root element, we have to set the value of the maxOccurs attribute to "unbounded."

3. Within the sequence tags, type the following code, once again indented a few lines (see Figure 4-17).

```
<xsd:element name="Patient" maxOccurs="unbounded">
  <xsd:complexType>
    <xsd:sequence>
    </xsd:sequence>
  </xsd:complexType>
</xsd:element>
```

Figure 4-17   CREATING THE PATIENT COMPLEX TYPE

the Patient element can appear an unlimited number of times within the Patients element

```
<?xml version="1.0" encoding="UTF-8"?>
<!-- Schema for breast cancer patient data -->

<xsd:schema xmlns:xsd="http://www.w3.org/2001/XMLSchema">
  <xsd:element name="Patients">
    <xsd:complexType>
      <xsd:sequence>
        <xsd:element name="Patient" maxOccurs="unbounded">
          <xsd:complexType>
            <xsd:sequence>
            </xsd:sequence>
          </xsd:complexType>
        </xsd:element>
      </xsd:sequence>
    </xsd:complexType>
  </xsd:element>
</xsd:schema>
```

Next, add the element declarations for the Name, ID, DOB, Age, Stage, and Comment elements. The Name, ID, Stage, and Comment elements contain text strings. The Age element should be declared as a positive integer. The DOB element should be declared using a date type. All child elements occur once, except for the Comment element, which is optional.

4. Within the sequence tags for the Patient element, enter the following schema code (see Figure 4-18):

```
<xsd:element name="Name" type="xsd:string"/>
<xsd:element name="ID" type="xsd:string"/>
<xsd:element name="DOB" type="xsd:date"/>
<xsd:element name="Age" type="xsd:positiveInteger"/>
<xsd:element name="Stage" type="xsd:string"/>
<xsd:element name="Comment" type="xsd:string"
minOccurs="0" maxOccurs="unbounded"/>
```

Figure 4-18   CREATING THE NAME, ID, DOB, AGE, STAGE, AND COMMENT ELEMENTS

```
<?xml version="1.0" encoding="UTF-8"?>
<!-- Schema for breast cancer patient data -->

<xsd:schema xmlns:xsd="http://www.w3.org/2001/XMLSchema">
  <xsd:element name="Patients">
    <xsd:complexType>
      <xsd:sequence>
        <xsd:element name="Patient" maxOccurs="unbounded">
          <xsd:complexType>
            <xsd:sequence>
              <xsd:element name="Name" type="xsd:string"/>
              <xsd:element name="ID" type="xsd:string"/>
              <xsd:element name="DOB" type="xsd:date"/>
              <xsd:element name="Age" type="xsd:positiveInteger"/>
              <xsd:element name="Stage" type="xsd:string"/>
              <xsd:element name="Comment" type="xsd:string" minOccurs="0" maxOccurs="unbounded"/>
            </xsd:sequence>
          </xsd:complexType>
        </xsd:element>
      </xsd:sequence>
    </xsd:complexType>
  </xsd:element>
</xsd:schema>
```

5. Finally, you need to declare the Performance element. Because the element has an attribute, it is also a complex type; but, it also contains decimal values, so you have to declare both the attribute type and the type of text it contains. Allison wants this to be a required attribute. To declare the Performance element and its attribute, insert the following code, as shown in Figure 4-19.

```
<xsd:element name="Performance">
  <xsd:complexType>
    <xsd:simpleContent>
      <xsd:extension base="xsd:decimal">
        <attribute name="Scale" type="xsd:string"
use="required"/>
      </xsd:extension>
    </xsd:simpleContent>
  </xsd:complexType>
</xsd:element>
```

Figure 4-19 CREATING THE PERFORMANCE ELEMENT

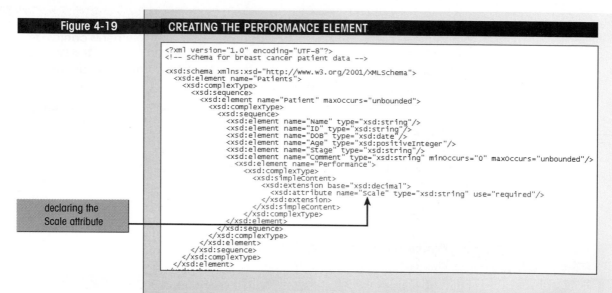

```
<?xml version="1.0" encoding="UTF-8"?>
<!-- Schema for breast cancer patient data -->

<xsd:schema xmlns:xsd="http://www.w3.org/2001/XMLSchema">
  <xsd:element name="Patients">
    <xsd:complexType>
      <xsd:sequence>
        <xsd:element name="Patient" maxOccurs="unbounded">
          <xsd:complexType>
            <xsd:sequence>
              <xsd:element name="Name" type="xsd:string"/>
              <xsd:element name="ID" type="xsd:string"/>
              <xsd:element name="DOB" type="xsd:date"/>
              <xsd:element name="Age" type="xsd:positiveInteger"/>
              <xsd:element name="Stage" type="xsd:string"/>
              <xsd:element name="Comment" type="xsd:string" minOccurs="0" maxOccurs="unbounded"/>
              <xsd:element name="Performance">
                <xsd:complexType>
                  <xsd:simpleContent>
                    <xsd:extension base="xsd:decimal">
                      <xsd:attribute name="Scale" type="xsd:string" use="required"/>
                    </xsd:extension>
                  </xsd:simpleContent>
                </xsd:complexType>
              </xsd:element>
            </xsd:sequence>
          </xsd:complexType>
        </xsd:element>
      </xsd:sequence>
    </xsd:complexType>
  </xsd:element>
</xsd:schema>
```

declaring the
Scale attribute

6. Verify that your code matches the code in Figure 4-19. Make sure that you have used the xsd namespace prefix in all of the indicated tags and that your use of upper and lower cases in the tag and attribute names match the figures.

7. Save your changes to PSchema1.xsd.

The final step in creating the schema for Allison's document is to attach the schema to a namespace.

Attaching a Schema to a Namespace

It is not required to attach a schema to a namespace, but it does have several advantages. Both the schema and the instance document can belong to the same namespace, linking the content of the document with its validation rules. This is useful when you combine several XML documents into a single file. As we've discussed with DTDs, a new DTD has to be created for each combination of XML documents. With schemas, each part of the combined document can be associated with a different namespace and, therefore, can draw upon a different schema for validation. The schemas are combined when the data is combined (see Figure 4-20).

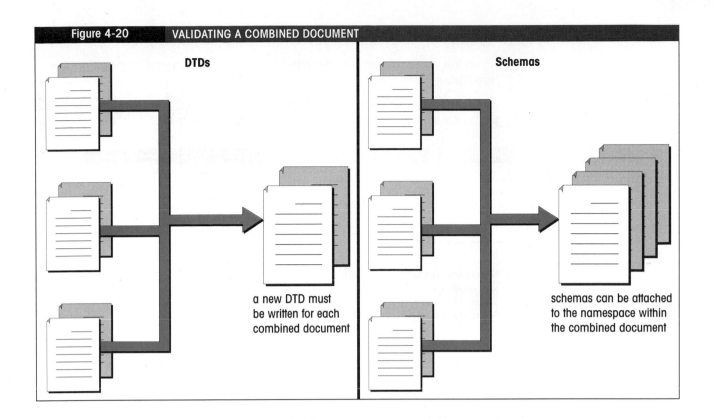

Figure 4-20 | **VALIDATING A COMBINED DOCUMENT**

DTDs

Schemas

a new DTD must be written for each combined document

schemas can be attached to the namespace within the combined document

---

REFERENCE WINDOW **RW**

Attaching a Schema to a Namespace
- To attach a schema to a namespace, add the following attributes to the schema element:

  ```
  xmlns="URI"
  targetNamespace="URI"
  ```
  where *URI* is the URI for the schema's namespace.

To associate the schema with a namespace, construct the schema element as follows:

```
<prefix:schema xmlns:prefix="http://www.w3.org/2001/
XMLSchema"
        xmlns="URI"
        targetNamespace="URI">
```

where *URI* is the URI for the schema's namespace. Note that the schema element has two namespaces. The first is the namespace for the W3C's XML Schema specifications; the second is a namespace for the validation rules declared in this particular schema file. To avoid confusion, the namespace for XML Schema is referred to as the XML Schema namespace, whereas the namespace for the schema file is referred to as the schema namespace. In a sense, every schema file is actually a combined document, combining the elements of the XML Schema namespace and the elements of the schema namespace.

To specify a namespace for the PSchema1.xsd file:

1. Within the schema element at the top of the file, insert the following attributes (see Figure 4-21):

   ```
   xmlns="http://uhosp/patients/ns"
   targetNamespace="http://uhosp/patients/ns"
   ```

Figure 4-21	SPECIFYING A NAMESPACE FOR A SCHEMA

```
<?xml version="1.0" encoding="UTF-8"?>
<!-- Schema for breast cancer patient data -->

<xsd:schema xmlns:xsd="http://www.w3.org/2001/XMLSchema"
            xmlns="http://uhosp/patients/ns"
            targetNamespace="http://uhosp/patients/ns">
```

Note that this is the same URI you used in the first session for the Patient elements in Allison's combined document. We'll use this fact later.

2. Save your changes to the document.

Now that you've completed the schema, you can return to the Patient.xml file and apply your schema to it.

Attaching an Instance Document to a Schema

The first step in attaching a schema to an instance document is to indicate which schema dialect is being used to validate the file. For the XML Schema dialect, this is accomplished by declaring the namespace "http://www.w3.org/2001/XMLSchema-instance" in the document's root element. The namespace declaration should appear as follows:

```
xmlns:xsi="http://www.w3.org/2001/XMLSchema-instance"
```

The namespace prefix xsi is commonly used, though you may specify a different one. Note that you must assign some namespace prefix or the XML parser will assume that you intend for the XML schema namespace to be used as the default namespace for the contents of the instance document.

Next, you indicate the name and location of the schema file. The attributes for doing this are

```
xmlns:prefix="URI"
xsi:schemaLocation="URI schema"
```

where *URI* is the namespace of the schema—the same URI you used in the schema file itself—*prefix* is a prefix for the namespace, and *schema* is the location and filename of the schema file. The complete form of the root element would therefore be as follows:

```
<prefix:root xmlns:xsi="http://www.w3.org/2001/
XMLSchema-instance"
            xmlns:prefix="URI"
            xsi:schemaLocation="URI schema">

document content

</prefix:root>
```

In Allison's document, the root element will appear as follows:

```
<pat:Patients
xmlns:xsi="http://www.w3.org/2001/XMLSchema-instance"
    xmlns:pat="http://uhosp/patients/ns"
    xsi:schemaLocation="http://uhosp/patients/
     ns PSchema1.xsd">


document content


</pat:Patients>
```

Apply this format to Allison's document now.

To apply a schema to Allison's document:

1. Return to the Patient.xml document in your text editor.

2. Within the Patients root element, insert the following attributes:

```
xmlns:xsi="http://www.w3.org/2001/XMLSchema-instance"
xmlns:pat="http://uhosp/patients/ns"
xsi:schemaLocation="http://uhosp/patients/ns PSchema1.xsd"
```

3. Add the **pat** namespace prefix to the opening and closing Patients tag.

Figure 4-22 shows the revised Patient.xml file.

| Figure 4-22 | ATTACHING A SCHEMA TO THE PATIENT FILE |

```
<?xml version="1.0"?>
<pat:Patients xmlns:xsi="http://www.w3.org/2001/XMLSchema-instance"
              xmlns:pat="http://uhosp/patients/ns"
              xsi:schemaLocation="http://uhosp/patients/ns PSchema1.xsd">
   <Patient>
     <Name>Cynthia Dibbs</Name>
     <ID>MR890-041-02</ID>
     <DOB>1945-05-22</DOB>
     <Age>58</Age>
     <Stage>II</Stage>
     <Performance Scale="Karnofsky">0.81</Performance>
```

```
   <Patient>
     <Name>Brenda Browne</Name>
     <ID>MR815-741-03</ID>
     <DOB>1964-04-25</DOB>
     <Age>39</Age>
     <Stage>I</Stage>
     <Performance Scale="Karnofsky">0.88</Performance>
   </Patient>
</pat:Patients>
```

4. Save your changes and close the file.

Note that a schema namespace is not necessary to validate a document. It *is* necessary if you intend on combining documents. If you don't intend to attach a schema to a namespace, use the following form for your document's root element:

```
<root xmlns:xsi="http://www.w3.org/2001/XMLSchema-instance"
      xsi:noNamespaceSchemaLocation="schema">

document content

</root>
```

where *root* is the name of the document's root element and *schema* is the name and location of the schema file.

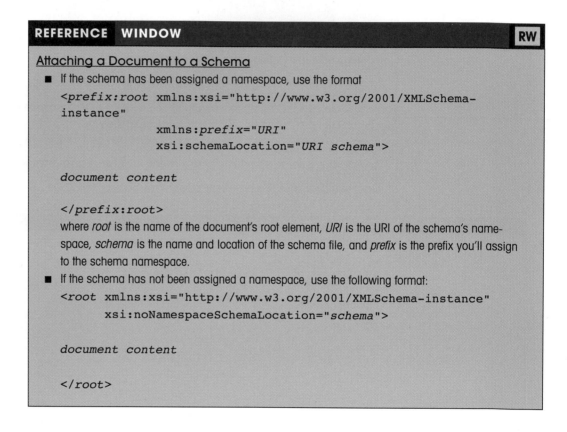

REFERENCE   WINDOW   **RW**

Attaching a Document to a Schema
- If the schema has been assigned a namespace, use the format
  ```
  <prefix:root xmlns:xsi="http://www.w3.org/2001/XMLSchema-
  instance"
                   xmlns:prefix="URI"
                   xsi:schemaLocation="URI schema">

  document content

  </prefix:root>
  ```
  where *root* is the name of the document's root element, *URI* is the URI of the schema's namespace, *schema* is the name and location of the schema file, and *prefix* is the prefix you'll assign to the schema namespace.
- If the schema has not been assigned a namespace, use the following format:
  ```
  <root xmlns:xsi="http://www.w3.org/2001/XMLSchema-instance"
        xsi:noNamespaceSchemaLocation="schema">

  document content

  </root>
  ```

Now you can validate the Patient.xml file against the PSchema1.xsd schema file to see whether the content of Allison's document actually matches the rules she set up for it.

To validate the instance document:

1. Click the **Start** button on your Taskbar, point to **Programs**, point to **XML Spy Suite**, and click **XML Spy IDE**.

2. Click **File** on the menu bar, and then click **Open**.

3. Locate and open **Patient.xml** from the Tutorial.04X/Tutorial folder on your Data Disk.

4. Maximize the contents of the document pane and then click the **Text View** button to view the text of the file.

5. Open **PSchema1.xsd** from the Tutorial.04X/Tutorial folder, and click the **Text View** button to view the contents of the file.

6. Click the **Patient.xml** tab in the document pane.

7. Click the **Validate** button 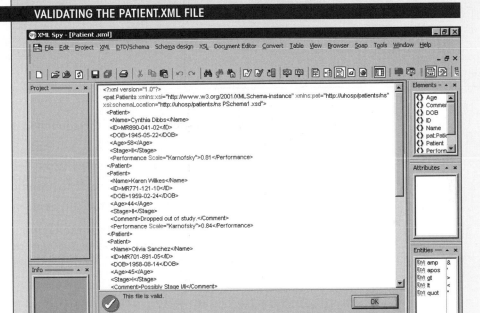 on the XML Spy toolbar.

XML Spy returns the message that Allison's document is valid with respect to the schema she designed (see Figure 4-23).

Figure 4-23	VALIDATING THE PATIENT.XML FILE

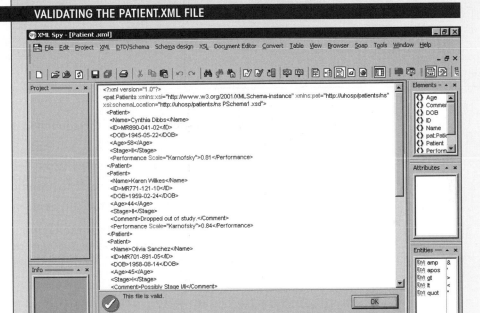

TROUBLE? If XML Spy indicates that your document is not valid, compare the code in your schema with the code shown earlier in Figure 4-19. Make sure that you have entered all of the namespaces correctly, and that namespace prefixes are used wherever necessary. Make the required changes to the PSchema1.xsd file using either your text editor, or if you prefer, the editing window in XML Spy.

TROUBLE? Based on your configuration of XML Spy, your window may look different from the one shown in Figure 4-23.

8. Once XML Spy has reported that the Patient.xml document is valid, click **File** and **Close All** to close both documents. Save any changes you may have made to the document in order to make it a valid file, but do not exit XML Spy.

Using Schemas in a Combined Document

Now that you've created a working schema for the patient data, Allison would like you to apply it to her combined document. Another schema file has already been created for you, describing the structure of the study data. The contents of this file, SSchema1.xsd, are shown in Figure 4-24. You should take some time to study the code used in this document, comparing it to the structure of the study elements shown earlier in Figure 4-2.

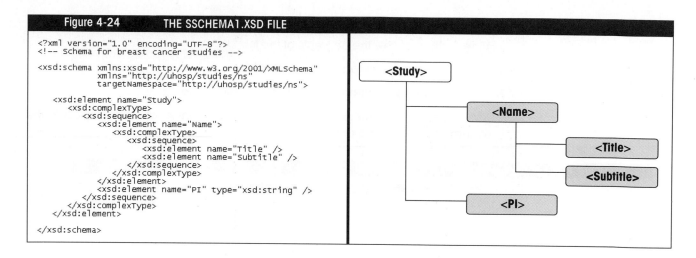

Figure 4-24   **THE SSCHEMA1.XSD FILE**

```
<?xml version="1.0" encoding="UTF-8"?>
<!-- Schema for breast cancer studies -->

<xsd:schema xmlns:xsd="http://www.w3.org/2001/XMLSchema"
            xmlns="http://uhosp/studies/ns"
            targetNamespace="http://uhosp/studies/ns">

    <xsd:element name="Study">
        <xsd:complexType>
            <xsd:sequence>
                <xsd:element name="Name">
                    <xsd:complexType>
                        <xsd:sequence>
                            <xsd:element name="Title" />
                            <xsd:element name="Subtitle" />
                        </xsd:sequence>
                    </xsd:complexType>
                </xsd:element>
                <xsd:element name="PI" type="xsd:string" />
            </xsd:sequence>
        </xsd:complexType>
    </xsd:element>

</xsd:schema>
```

To attach the schemas to the different parts of the combined document, you must do the following:

- Add the XML Schema-instance namespace to the document's root element.
- Assign namespaces to the different parts of the combined document.
- Add the schemaLocation attribute to the parent element of each part.

You assigned namespaces to the different parts of the UHosp.xml file in the last session. You only need to insert the XML Schema-instance namespace to the root element and add the schemaLocation attribute to the Patients and Study elements.

To attach the two schemas to the combined document:

1. Using your text editor, open **UHosp.xml** from the Tutorial.04X/Tutorial folder on your Data Disk.

2. Delete the DOCTYPE declaration (you won't need the DTD to validate the file anymore).

3. Insert the following attribute in the Report element:

   ```
   xmlns:xsi="http://www.w3.org/2001/XMLSchema-instance"
   ```

4. Add the following attribute to the Patients element:

   ```
   xsi:schemaLocation="http://uhosp/patients/
    ns PSchema1.xsd"
   ```

5. Add a similar attribute to the Study element:

   ```
   xsi:schemaLocation="http://uhosp/studies/
    ns SSchema1.xsd"
   ```

6. Figure 4-25 shows the revised contents of the UHosp.xml file.

Figure 4-25   ATTACHING MULTIPLE SCHEMAS

```
<?xml version="1.0" ?>
<Report xmlns:xsi="http://www.w3.org/2001/XMLSchema-instance">

   <pat:Patients xmlns:pat="http://uhosp/patients/ns"
                 xsi:schemaLocation="http://uhosp/patients/ns PSchema1.xsd">
      <Patient>
         <Name>Cynthia Dibbs</Name>
         <ID>MR890-041-02</ID>
         <DOB>1945-05-22</DOB>
         <Age>58</Age>
         <Stage>II</Stage>
         <Performance Scale="Karnofsky">0.81</Performance>
      </Patient>

      <std:Study xmlns:std="http://uhosp/studies/ns"
                 xsi:schemaLocation="http://uhosp/studies/ns SSchema1.xsd">
         <std:Name>
            <std:Title>Tamoxifen Breast Cancer Study</std:Title>
            <std:Subtitle>Randomized Phase 3 Clinical Trial</std:Subtitle>
         </std:Name>
         <std:PI>Dr. Diane West</std:PI>
      </std:Study>

</Report>
```

7. Save your changes to the file and close the text editor.

Now validate the file against the two schemas.

To validate the UHosp.xml file:

1. Using XML Spy, open **UHosp.xml**.

2. Maximize the contents of the document pane, and then click the **Text View** button 📄 to view the text of the file.

3. Click the **Validate** button 📝.

4. XML Spy reports that the file is valid (see Figure 4-26).

Figure 4-26	VALIDATING THE UHOSP.XML FILE

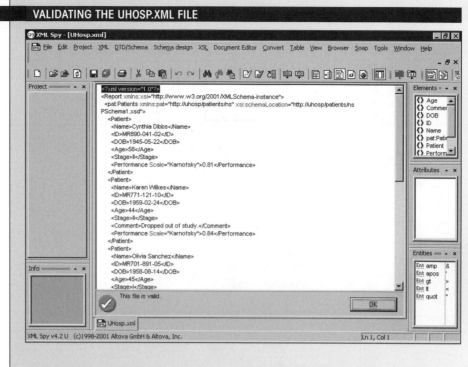

TROUBLE? If XML Spy reports that the document is invalid, check the URIs you entered for the different namespaces, and verify that you've entered the correct schema names.

5. Close XML Spy.

Allison is pleased with the work you've done applying schemas to her documents. She was particularly impressed with how she can create schemas for individual documents and then apply those schemas to a combined document.

There are still some changes that she would like to make to the XML document. For example, she would like to be able to restrict the values of some of the elements in the instance document. You'll look at this issue and some others in the next session.

Session 4.2 QUICK CHECK

1. What is a schema? What is an instance document?

2. How do schemas differ from DTDs?

3. What does the root element of an XML Schema file look like?

4. What is a simple type? What is a complex type?

5. How do you declare a simple type element named "Weight" that contains decimal data?

6. How do you declare a complex type element named "Parents" that contains two child elements named "Father" and "Mother"? (Assume that the Father and Mother elements are simple type elements containing text strings.)

7. How do you declare an attribute named "Title" that contains a text string and belongs to an element named "Book"? Assume that the Book element contains only text and no child elements.

8. What attribute would you add to the root element of an instance document to attach it to a schema file named "Schema1.xsd"? Assume that no namespace has been assigned to the schema file and that you are using the XML Schema dialect.

SESSION 4.3

In this session, you'll learn about different schema structures and the advantages and disadvantages of using them. You'll learn how to create complex types, model groups, and attribute groups. Next, you'll learn how to derive customized data types, and lists and unions of data types. You'll also work with XML Schema regular expressions to apply character patterns to element content. Finally, you'll learn how to document your completed schema file.

Structuring a Schema

There are several ways to structure a schema. The layout you applied in the last session is known as a **Russian Doll design** because it involved sets of nested declarations just like the classic Russian dolls, which are nested inside one another. Figure 4-27 illustrates the nesting of elements in PSchema1.xsd with the element levels color coded.

Figure 4-27	A RUSSIAN DOLL DESIGN

```xml
<?xml version="1.0" encoding="UTF-8"?>
<!-- Schema for breast cancer patient data -->

<xsd:schema xmlns:xsd="http://www.w3.org/2001/XMLSchema"
            xmlns="http://uhosp/patients/ns"
            targetNamespace="http://uhosp/patients/ns">
<xsd:element name="Patients">
  <xsd:complexType>
    <xsd:sequence>
      <xsd:element name="Patient" maxOccurs="unbounded">
        <xsd:complexType>
          <xsd:sequence>
            <xsd:element name="Name" type="xsd:string"/>
            <xsd:element name="ID" type="xsd:string"/>
            <xsd:element name="DOB" type="xsd:date"/>
            <xsd:element name="Age" type="xsd:positiveInteger"/>
            <xsd:element name="Stage" type="xsd:string"/>
            <xsd:element name="Comment" type="xsd:string" minOccurs="0" maxOccurs="unbounded"/>
            <xsd:element name="Performance">
              <xsd:complexType>
                <xsd:simpleContent>
                  <xsd:extension base="xsd:decimal">
                    <xsd:attribute name="Scale" type="xsd:string" use="required"/>
                  </xsd:extension>
                </xsd:simpleContent>
              </xsd:complexType>
            </xsd:element>
          </xsd:sequence>
        </xsd:complexType>
      </xsd:element>
    </xsd:sequence>
  </xsd:complexType>
</xsd:element>
</xsd:schema>
```

There are advantages and disadvantages of the Russian Doll design. On the positive side, it is easy to associate each element in the schema with the corresponding element in the instance document because the two documents are nested in the same way. However, a disadvantage is that the nesting of declarations and schema elements can be confusing and difficult to maintain. Allison's patient document has only three element levels; imagine creating a schema for an instance document with five or six levels! It would be all too easy to forget a closing tag and get lost in the maze of nested levels.

Because of this complexity, XML Schema supports other layouts that are more efficient and easier to maintain.

Working with Flat Catalogs

One of these layouts is a flat catalog. To help you understand how a flat catalog works, we first have to make a distinction between global and local components:

- **global component:** a component of the schema that is a direct child of the root schema element
- **local component:** a component nested further inside of the schema structure and not a direct child of the root schema element

The distinction is an important one. A global component can be referenced elsewhere in the schema document. A local component cannot. In a Russian Doll design, only the root element of the instance document is global, while all other element declarations are local. In the PSchema1.xsd file, only the declaration for the Patients element is global. The declarations for all the other elements are local.

In a **Flat Catalog Design**, all element declarations are made globally. The structure of the instance document is created by referencing these global element declarations at another point in the schema document. The syntax for creating a reference is

```
<element ref="name">
```

where *name* is the name of a global element.

The schema you created in the last session has been recreated in a flat catalog design. Open this new schema now.

To open the schema document:

1. Using your text editor, open **Flat.xsd** located in the Tutorial.04X/Tutorial folder of your Data Disk.

2. Scroll through the document, taking note of its structure and content (see Figure 4-28).

   The element declarations are all global; no declaration is nested inside of another. Note the use of the ref attribute to create references between one global declaration and another and between the child elements of the Patient element and their global declarations.

Figure 4-28	A FLAT CATALOG DESIGN

```
<?xml version="1.0" encoding="UTF-8"?>
<xsd:schema xmlns:xsd="http://www.w3.org/2001/XMLSchema">

    <xsd:element name="Name" type="xsd:string"/>
    <xsd:element name="ID" type="xsd:string"/>
    <xsd:element name="DOB" type="xsd:date"/>
    <xsd:element name="Age" type="xsd:positiveInteger"/>
    <xsd:element name="Stage" type="xsd:string"/>
    <xsd:element name="Comment" type="xsd:string"/>

    <xsd:element name="Performance">
        <xsd:complexType>
            <xsd:simpleContent>
                <xsd:extension base="xsd:decimal">
                    <xsd:attribute name="Scale" type="xsd:string" use="required"/>
                </xsd:extension>
            </xsd:simpleContent>
        </xsd:complexType>
    </xsd:element>

    <xsd:element name="Patient">
        <xsd:complexType>
            <xsd:sequence>
                <xsd:element ref="Name"/>
                <xsd:element ref="ID"/>
                <xsd:element ref="DOB"/>
                <xsd:element ref="Age"/>
                <xsd:element ref="Stage"/>
                <xsd:element ref="Comment" minoccurs="0" maxoccurs="unbounded"/>
                <xsd:element ref="Performance"/>
            </xsd:sequence>
        </xsd:complexType>
    </xsd:element>

    <xsd:element name="Patients">
        <xsd:complexType>
            <xsd:sequence>
                <xsd:element ref="Patient" maxoccurs="unbounded"/>
            </xsd:sequence>
        </xsd:complexType>
    </xsd:element>

</xsd:schema>
```

Name through Comment element declarations

Performance element declaration

reference to the Name through Comment declarations

Patient element declaration

reference to the Patient element declaration

Patients element declaration

3. After you are finished studying the Flat.xsd file, close it, but leave your text editor open.

There is one more important difference between local and global components. If the schema file is attached to a namespace, globally declared elements must be explicitly qualified in the instance document, but local elements do not need to be qualified. Recall that the "pat" namespace prefix was added to the Patients element in both the Patient.xml and UHosp.xml files (see Figure 4-22 and Figure 4-25). The Patients element was the only global element in the PSchema1.xsd file and thus had to be explicitly qualified. The other elements in the schema were all local elements and did not need to be qualified. On the other hand, if a Flat Catalog schema is attached to a namespace, all of the elements in the instance document have to be qualified.

If the document is large with many elements, adding namespace prefixes to all of the element names is a big chore. There's a third layout possibility: the Venetian Blind layout. This design involves creating customized types, such as the named complex type.

Working with Named Complex Types

As you learned in the last session, elements that contain attributes or child elements are known as complex types. The complex types you worked with in the last session were **anonymous complex types** because they were associated with only one element and were not given a name. In general, any schema element not assigned a name is known as an **anonymous type**. Anonymous types must be nested within another element in order to have any context within the schema design. As you saw, this could lead to several levels of nested tags. The following declaration is an example of an anonymous complex type that describes two child elements named "FirstName" and "LastName".

```
<element name="Client">
   <complexType>
      <sequence>
         <element name="FirstName" type="string"/>
         <element name="LastName" type="string" />
      </sequence>
   </complexType>
</element>
```

Upon reflection, it seems that such FirstName/LastName pairs occur frequently in XML documents, and it would be helpful if we could store this structure rather than retyping it over and over again. We can if we name the structure, creating a **named complex type** that can be used elsewhere in the schema.

To see how this is done, we'll recreate the element declaration using a named complex type with the title "fullName".

```
<complexType name="fullName">
   <sequence>
      <element name="FirstName" type="string"/>
      <element name="LastName" type="string"/>
   </sequence>
</complexType>
```

To use this complex type in an element declaration, simply apply it to the type attribute as follows:

```
<element name="Client" type="fullName"/>
<element name="Salesperson" type="fullName"/>
```

Both the Client and the Salesperson elements have the same structure: two child elements named "FirstName" and "LastName". It doesn't matter whether we create the named complex type before or after the element declaration. The only requirement is that the named complex type must be created globally (i.e., as a direct child of the schema element). If that is done, we can use the named complex type in any element declaration in the schema.

Another way of simplifying your schema structure is with a model group.

Working with Named Model Groups

As the name suggests, a **named model group** is a collection, or group, of elements. The syntax for creating a model group is

```
<group name="name">
   element declarations
</group>
```

where *name* is the name of the model group, and *element declarations* is a collection of element declarations. The element declarations must be enclosed within a sequence, choice, or all compositor. The following code creates a model group named "fullName" that contains two elements:

```
<group name="fullName">
   <sequence>
```

```
      <element name="FirstName" type="string" />
      <element name="LastName" type="string" />
   </sequence>
</group>
```

Note that because a model group is not a simple or complex type, you must use the ref attribute within the group tag to access it in your schema. Here's how you would access the fullName group for use with an element declaration:

```
<element name="Client">
   <complexType>
      <group ref="fullName"/>
   </complexType>
</element>
```

Named model groups must be globally defined so that they can be referenced anywhere within the schema. As with named complex types, model groups are useful when your document contains element declarations or code that you want to repeat throughout the schema.

Working with Named Attribute Groups

Attributes can also be placed within **named attribute groups**. This is particularly useful for attributes that you want to use with several different elements in the schema. The syntax for a named attribute group is

```
<attributeGroup name="name">
   attribute declarations
</attributeGroup>
```

where *name* is the name of the attribute group and *attribute declarations* is a collection of attributes assigned to the group. For example, one of Allison's documents might contain the following element to identify a physician:

```
<Doctor ID="DR251" Dept="Pediatrics">
   Curt Hurley
</Doctor>
```

Both the ID and Dept attributes may need to be used in other elements. To place both of these within an attribute group named "DRInfo", you can use the following code:

```
<attributeGroup name="DRInfo">
   <attribute name="ID" type="string" use="required"/>
   <attribute name="Dept" type="string" use="required"/>
</attributeGroup>
```

To use the DRInfo attribute group with the Doctor element, create a reference within an attributeGroup tag as follows:

```
<element name="Doctor" type="deptData"/>

<complexType name="deptData">
   <simpleContent>
      <extension base="string">
         <attributeGroup ref="DRInfo"/>
      </extension>
   </simpleContent>
</complexType>
```

Note that this code not only references an attribute group, but it also uses a named complex type to simplify the declaration of the Doctor element.

Working with a Venetian Blind Layout

To design your schema in **Venetian Blind layout**, declare all of the complex elements using complex types, groups, and attribute groups. The actual element declarations are still nested within one element, but they are no longer global.

The PSchema1.xsd file has been reformatted in a Venetian Blind layout. Open the new file now.

To open the schema document:

1. Using your text editor, open **Venetian.xsd** located in the Tutorial.04X/Tutorial folder of your Data Disk.

2. Save the file as **PSchema2.xsd** and leave the file open.

3. Scroll through the document, taking note of how it uses complex types in creating the various elements of the instance document (see Figure 4-29).

There are two named complex types in this document, PatType and PerfType, and one element group named Pat_Elements. The element group is used to group the elements describing each patient. PerfType is used for storing performance information, and PatType is used for storing the patient elements. The only globally declared element is the Patients element.

Figure 4-29   A VENETIAN BLIND LAYOUT

```
<?xml version="1.0" encoding="UTF-8"?>
<!-- Schema for breast cancer patient data -->

<xsd:schema xmlns:xsd="http://www.w3.org/2001/XMLSchema"
            xmlns="http://uhosp/patients/ns"
            targetNamespace="http://uhosp/patients/ns">

   <xsd:element name="Patients">
     <xsd:complexType>
       <xsd:sequence>
         <xsd:element name="Patient" type="PatType" maxOccurs="unbounded" />
       </xsd:sequence>
     </xsd:complexType>
   </xsd:element>

   <xsd:complexType name="PatType">
     <xsd:group ref="Pat_Elements" />
   </xsd:complexType>

   <xsd:group name="Pat_Elements">
     <xsd:sequence>
         <xsd:element name="Name" type="xsd:string"/>
         <xsd:element name="ID" type="xsd:string"/>
         <xsd:element name="DOB" type="xsd:date" />
         <xsd:element name="Age" type="xsd:positiveInteger"/>
         <xsd:element name="Stage" type="xsd:string"/>
         <xsd:element name="Comment" type="xsd:string" minOccurs="0" maxOccurs="unbounded"/>
         <xsd:element name="Performance" type="PerfType" />
     </xsd:sequence>
   </xsd:group>

   <xsd:complexType name="PerfType">
     <xsd:simpleContent>
       <xsd:extension base="xsd:decimal">
         <xsd:attribute name="Scale" type="xsd:string" use="required"/>
       </xsd:extension>
     </xsd:simpleContent>
   </xsd:complexType>

</xsd:schema>
```

Figure 4-30 summarizes the characteristics of the three schema designs. Because of its flexibility, you'll continue working on Allison's project using the Venetian Blind layout in the PSchema2.xsd file.

Figure 4-30	COMPARING SCHEMA DESIGNS	
RUSSIAN DOLL	**FLAT CATALOG**	**VENETIAN BLIND**
One single global element; all other elements are local	All elements are global	One single global element; all other elements are local
Element declarations are nested within a single global declaration	No nesting of element declarations	Element declarations are nested within a single global declaration, using named complex types and element groups
Element declarations can only be used once.	Element declarations can be reused throughout the schema	Complex types and element groups can be reused throughout the schema
If a namespace is attached to the schema, only the root element needs to be qualified in the instance document	If a namespace is attached to the schema, all elements need to be qualified in the instance document	If a namespace is attached to the schema, only the root element needs to be qualified in the instance document

Now that you've seen how to create types that describe complex elements, you'll look at how to create a data type.

Deriving New Data Types

In the previous session, you saw some of the variety and power of XML Schema data types, especially when compared to DTD data types. You are not limited to the 44 data types supported by XML Schema and can create your own. There are three components involved in deriving a new data type:

- **value space**: the set of values that correspond to the data type; for example, an integer data type consists of numbers such as 1, 2, 3, etc., but does not contain fractions or text strings
- **lexical space**: the set of textual representations of the value space; for example, the number 42 can be represented in several ways, such as 42, 42.0, or 4.2E01.
- **facets**: the properties of the data type that distinguish one data type from another; facets can include such properties as text string length or a range of allowable values; XML Schema uses one such facet to distinguish the integer data type from the positiveInteger data type

New data types are derived by manipulating the characteristics of these components. User-derived data types fall into three general categories:

- **list**: a list of values with each value in the list derived from a base type; for example, a list of integer values
- **union**: the combination of two or more data types; one such union might a combination of text strings and integers
- **restriction**: a limit placed on the facet of a base type; for example, the integer data type can be constrained to a range of values

Let's first examine how to derive a list data type.

Deriving a List Data Type

The syntax for deriving a list data type is

```
<simpleType name="name">
   <list itemType="type"/>
</simpleType>
```

where *name* is the name assigned to the list data type and *type* is the data type of the base. At the University Hospital, Allison often records patients' weekly white blood counts. A typical element containing a list of white blood cell counts can appear as follows:

```
<WBC>15.1 15.8 12.0 9.3 7.1 5.2 4.3 3.4</WBC>
```

To create a data type for this information, Allison first needs to define a list data type as follows:

```
<simpleType name="wbcList">
  <list itemType="decimal"/>
</simpleType>
```

and then she can use the wbcList data type in the declaration for the WBC element:

```
<element name="WBC" type="wbcList"/>
```

A list data type must always use a space as the delimiter. You cannot use commas or other characters.

Deriving a Union Data Type

A union data type is composed of the value and lexical spaces from any number of other data types. Each of the base types of a union data type is known as a **member type**. When a union data type is validated, the validator examines each member type in the order in which it is defined in the schema. The syntax for deriving a union data type is

```
<simpleType name="type">
   <union memberTypes="type1 type2 type3 …"/>
</simpleType>
```

where *type1*, *type2*, *type3*, etc., are the member types that comprise the union.

When compiling data on white blood cell counts, Allison may have precise counts as well as more narrative levels, such as high, normal, or low, to record in her research. As a result of this variety, the WBC element may look as follows:

```
<WBC>15.9 high 14.2 9.8 normal low 5.3</WBC>
```

Allison can create a data type for this information by combining a list type and union type. First, she creates a union data type for the union of the decimal and string types as follows:

```
<simpleType name="wbcType">
   <union memberTypes="decimal string"/>
<simpleType>
```

Next, she uses that data type to derive a list type and assigns the list type to the WBC element:

```
<simpleType name="wbcList">
   <list itemType="wbcType"/>
</simpleType>

<element name="WBC" type="wbcList"/>
```

Union data types are often used for multilingual documents in which the data content, expressed in different languages, must be validated based on a single schema.

Deriving a Restricted Data Type

The most common way of deriving a new data type is to restrict the properties of a base type. XML Schema provides twelve constraining facets for this purpose, listed in Figure 4-31.

Figure 4-31	CONSTRAINING FACETS
FACET	**DESCRIPTION**
length	Specifies the length of the datatype; for text strings, length measures the number of characters; for lists, length measures the number of items in the list
minLength	Specifies the minimum length of the datatype
maxLength	Specifies the maximum length of the datatype
pattern	Constrains the lexical space of the datatype to follow a specific pattern of characters
enumeration	Constrains the datatype to a specific set of values
maxInclusive	Specifies an upper bound for the datatype (can be used with datatypes that can be ordered, such as numbers); the upper boundary is included as a legitimate value
minInclusive	Specifies a lower bound for the datatype; the lower boundary is included
maxExclusive	Specifies an upper bound for the datatype, but the upper boundary is not included
minExclusive	Specifies a lower bound for the datatype, but the lower boundary is not included
whiteSpace	Controls the use of blanks in the lexical space; the whiteSpace facet has three values: preserve (no changes made to the content), replace (replace all tabs, carriage returns, and line feed characters with spaces), and collapse (replace all tabs, carriage returns, and line feeds, remove any opening or closing blanks, and collapse multiple blank spaces to a single blank space)
totalDigits	Constrains the value space to a maximum number of decimal places
fractionDigits	Constrains the value space to a maximum number of decimal places in the fractional part of the value

Constraining facets are applied to a base type using the syntax

```
<simpleType name="name">
   <restriction base="type">
      <facet1 value="value1" />
      <facet2 value="value2" />
      <facet3 value="value3" />
      ...
   </restriction>
</simpleType>
```

where *type* is the data type of the base type; *facet1, facet2, facet3*, etc., are constraining facets; and *value1, value2, value3*, etc., are values for each constraining facet. For example, white blood count values often fall between 0 and 20. A derived data type that enforces these boundaries could be derived as follows:

```
<simpleType name="wbcType">
   <restriction base="decimal">
      <minInclusive value="0"/>
```

```
        <maxInclusive value="20" />
    </restriction>
</simpleType>

<element name="WBC" type="wbcType"/>
```

With this derived data, the following content would be valid:

```
<WBC>12.8</WBC>
```

but these values would not be:

```
<WBC>22.5</WBC>
<WBC>-2.5</WBC>
<WBC>high</WBC>
```

REFERENCE WINDOW RW

Deriving New Data Types

■ To derive a list data type, use the syntax

```
<simpleType name="name">
    <list itemType="type"/>
</simpleType>
```

where *name* is the name of the derived data type and *type* is the data type of the values in the list.

■ To derive a union data type, use the syntax

```
<simpleType name="type">
    <union memberTypes="type1 type2 type3 …"/>
</simpleType>
```

where *type1, type2, type3,* etc., are the member types that comprise the union.

■ To derive a restricted data type, use

```
<simpleType name="name">
    <restriction base="type">
        <facet1 value="value1" />
        <facet2 value="value2" />
        <facet3 value="value3" />
        ...
    </restriction>
</simpleType>
```

where *facet1, facet2, facet3,* etc., are constraining facets, and *value1, value2, value3,* etc., are values for each constraining facet.

Applying a Restricted Data Type

The more Allison learns about data types, the more she sees ways that they can help her reduce the chance of erroneous data being entered into her document. Needless to say, she will require your help with this effort. She has the following restrictions she wants to apply to the elements in her document:

■ Each patient in her document must be at least 21 years of age.

■ The cancer stage for each patient in her document must be either "I" or "II".

■ The value of the Performance element must be between 0 and 1 (excluding 0 and 1).

■ Performances must be measured on either the Karnofsky or Bell scale.

To apply these restrictions, you'll derive new data types for the Age, Stage, and Performance elements, as well as for the Scale attribute. A copy of the schema has been stored in flat catalog format for you to work with.

First, you'll derive a data type for the ageType element. This derived type sets a lower value for ages at 21 but does not set an upper boundary. Because ages are represented as positive integers, the positiveInteger type is used as the base.

To derive the ageType:

1. In the PSchema.xsd file, directly below the Pat_Elements element group, insert the following text:

```
<xsd:simpleType name="ageType">
  <xsd:restriction base="xsd:positiveInteger">
    <xsd:minInclusive value="21"/>
  </xsd:restriction>
</xsd:simpleType>
```

2. Change the data type of the Age element from "xsd:positiveInteger" to **"ageType"**. See Figure 4-32.

Figure 4-32	CREATING THE AGETYPE DATATYPE

```
<xsd:group name="Pat_Elements">
    <xsd:sequence>
        <xsd:element name="Name" type="xsd:string"/>
        <xsd:element name="ID" type="xsd:string"/>
        <xsd:element name="DOB" type="xsd:date"/>
        <xsd:element name="Age" type="ageType"/>
        <xsd:element name="Stage" type="xsd:string"/>
        <xsd:element name="Comment" type="xsd:string" minOccurs="0" maxOccurs="unbounded"/>
        <xsd:element name="Performance" type="PerfType" />
    </xsd:sequence>
</xsd:group>

<xsd:simpleType name="ageType">
  <xsd:restriction base="xsd:positiveInteger">
    <xsd:minInclusive value="21"/>
  </xsd:restriction>
</xsd:simpleType>
```

The next step is to create a derived type named "stageType" that constrains the value of the Stage element to either "I" or "II" and a data type named "scaleType" for the Performance element that requires values between 0 and 1.

To create the stageType and scaleType data types:

1. Below the Pat_Elements group, insert the following text:

```
<xsd:simpleType name="stageType">
  <xsd:restriction base="xsd:string">
    <xsd:enumeration value="I"/>
    <xsd:enumeration value="II"/>
  </xsd:restriction>
</xsd:simpleType>
```

2. Change the data type of the Stage element from "xsd:string" to **"stageType"**. See Figure 4-33.

Figure 4-33   CREATING THE STAGETYPE DATATYPE

```
<xsd:group name="Pat_Elements">
   <xsd:sequence>
      <xsd:element name="Name" type="xsd:string"/>
      <xsd:element name="ID" type="xsd:string"/>
      <xsd:element name="DOB" type="xsd:date"/>
      <xsd:element name="Age" type="ageType"/>
      <xsd:element name="Stage" type="stageType"/>
      <xsd:element name="Comment" type="xsd:string" minOccurs="0" maxOccurs="unbounded"/>
      <xsd:element name="Performance" type="PerfType" />
   </xsd:sequence>
</xsd:group>

<xsd:simpleType name="stageType">
   <xsd:restriction base="xsd:string">
      <xsd:enumeration value="I"/>
      <xsd:enumeration value="II"/>
   </xsd:restriction>
</xsd:simpleType>
```

3. Insert the following code below the PerfType complex type:

```
<xsd:simpleType name="scaleType">
  <xsd:restriction base="xsd:decimal">
     <xsd:minExclusive value="0"/>
     <xsd:maxExclusive value="1"/>
  </xsd:restriction>
</xsd:simpleType>
```

4. Change the data type of PerfType from "xsd:decimal" to **"scaleType"**. See Figure 4-34.

Figure 4-34   CREATING THE SCALETYPE DATATYPE

```
<xsd:complexType name="PerfType">
   <xsd:simpleContent>
      <xsd:extension base="scaleType">
         <xsd:attribute name="Scale" type="xsd:string" use="required"/>
      </xsd:extension>
   </xsd:simpleContent>
</xsd:complexType>

<xsd:simpleType name="scaleType">
   <xsd:restriction base="xsd:decimal">
      <xsd:minExclusive value="0"/>
      <xsd:maxExclusive value="1"/>
   </xsd:restriction>
</xsd:simpleType>
```

Finally, create a data type named "psType" that requires the values of the Scale attribute to be either Karnofsky or Bell.

To create the psType data type:

1. Below the PerfType complex type, insert the following:

```
<xsd:simpleType name="psType">
  <xsd:restriction base="xsd:string">
     <xsd:enumeration value="Karnofsky"/>
     <xsd:enumeration value="Bell"/>
  </xsd:restriction>
</xsd:simpleType>
```

2. Change the Scale's data type from "xsd:string" to **"psType"**, as shown in Figure 4-35.

Figure 4-35	CREATING THE PSTYPE DATATYPE

```
<xsd:complexType name="PerfType">
   <xsd:simpleContent>
      <xsd:extension base="scaleType">
         <xsd:attribute name="Scale" type="psType" use="required"/>
      </xsd:extension>
   </xsd:simpleContent>
</xsd:complexType>

<xsd:simpleType name="psType">
   <xsd:restriction base="xsd:string">
      <xsd:enumeration value="Karnofsky"/>
      <xsd:enumeration value="Bell"/>
   </xsd:restriction>
</xsd:simpleType>
```

Finally, there is one additional restriction that Allison thinks should be made to this document. She wants to create a data type for the medical record number whose values are stored in the ID element. At the hospital, medical record numbers must follow the form MR###-###-##. The schema must enforce this format in the contents of the ID element. As you will learn, you can accomplish what Allison needs using the patterns facet.

Working with Patterns

A pattern is created with a formatted text string called a **regular expression** or **regex**. XML Schema regexes are based on the same regexes used in the Perl programming language, which in turn are descendents of regexes used in the UNIX operating system. The syntax of regular expression is capable of expressing almost any kind of string format. In this tutorial, we'll just cover the basics of the regular expression syntax. You can explore this topic in more detail and learn more about the use of regular expressions with XML Schema at *http://www.w3.org/TR/xmlschema-2/#regexs*.

The basic unit of a regex is called an **atom**, which can be a single character, a group of characters, or another regex enclosed in parentheses. Let's start with a simple example using a single character. The following pattern definition forces the value of the data type to be the text string "ABC". Any other combination of letters or the use of lowercase letters would be invalid.

```
<pattern value="ABC"/>
```

By placing a range of values within a set of square brackets, a character group is created. The following pattern allows for any letter A through Z (but not a through z!):

```
<pattern value="[A-Z]"/>
```

Similarly, the following expression allows any number from 0 to 9 to be specified:

```
<pattern value="[0-9]"/>
```

Multiple ranges can be joined together to form the values of a single, if not contiguous, range. For example, the following pattern allows for any uppercase letter followed by any lowercase letter:

```
<pattern value="[A-Z][a-z]"/>
```

or two character groups can be combined into a single group as follows:

```
<pattern value="[A-Za-z]"/>
```

To specify the number of occurrences for a particular character, a **quantifier** can be appended to an atom in the regex. XML Schema supports six quantifiers, as displayed in Figure 4-36.

| Figure 4-36 | PATTERN QUANTIFIERS |

QUANTIFIER	DESCRIPTION
?	Zero or one occurrence
*	Zero or more occurrences
+	One or more occurrences
{min, max}	Between *min* and *max* occurrences
{n}	Exactly *n* occurrences
{min, }	At least *min* occurrences

For example, to display a string of uppercase characters of any length, use the * quantifier in the following pattern:

```
<pattern value="[A-Z]*"/>
```

To allow a character string of uppercase letters no more than ten characters long, use the following pattern:

```
<pattern value="[A-Z]{0,10}"/>
```

Through the use of character ranges and quantifiers, patterns can be created for many commonly used character strings. For example, the following code creates a pattern for phone numbers, such as 555-1234:

```
<simpleType name="phoneType">
   <restriction base="string">
      <pattern value="[1-9][0-9]{2}-[0-9]{4}"/>
   </restriction>
</simpleType>
```

Note that the first digits of the phone number must be within the range of 1 through 9. This prevents phone numbers from starting with a zero in the exchange portion of the phone number.

We've only scratched the surface of what regular expressions can do. However, enough has been discussed to be able to solve Allison's request that all ID strings must be in the following format: MR###-###-##. The pattern for this expression is as follows:

```
<pattern value="MR[0-9]{3}-[0-9]{3}-[0-9]{2}"/>
```

Create a data type named "mrType" based on this expression now.

To create a data type based on a pattern:

1. Insert the following code beneath the Pat_Elements group:

```
<xsd:simpleType name="mrType">
  <xsd:restriction base="xsd:string">
    <xsd:pattern value="MR[0-9]{3}-[0-9]{3}-[0-9]{2}"/>
  </xsd:restriction>
</xsd:simpleType>
```

2. Change the type of the ID element from "xsd:string" to **"mrType"**, as shown in Figure 4-37.

Figure 4-37	CREATING THE MRTYPE DATATYPE

```
<xsd:group name="Pat_Elements">
   <xsd:sequence>
      <xsd:element name="Name" type="xsd:string"/>
      <xsd:element name="ID" type="mrType"/>
      <xsd:element name="DOB" type="xsd:date"/>
      <xsd:element name="Age" type="ageType"/>
      <xsd:element name="Stage" type="stageType"/>
      <xsd:element name="Comment" type="xsd:string" minoccurs="0" maxoccurs="unbounded"/>
      <xsd:element name="Performance" type="PerfType" />
   </xsd:sequence>
</xsd:group>

<xsd:simpleType name="mrType">
   <xsd:restriction base="xsd:string">
      <xsd:pattern value="MR[0-9]{3}-[0-9]{3}-[0-9]{2}"/>
   </xsd:restriction>
</xsd:simpleType>
```

Derived data types are a powerful and versatile feature of XML Schema. One can create a schema containing an entire library of customized data types to supplement the built-in data types supplied by XML Schema. By attaching this schema to a namespace, one can access those data types from other schema documents.

Annotating a Schema

After creating a schema, it's useful to include documentation about it. Because schemas are XML documents, you can include any information in the form of XML comments. In addition to the comments method, XML Schema provides an annotation element to store documentation regarding the schema. The syntax of the annotation element is

```
<annotation>
   <documentation>
      documentation comments
   </documentation>
   <appinfo>
      application information
   </appinfo>
</annotation>
```

The annotation element must contain at least one documentation child element or appinfo child element. The documentation element is useful for containing comments that can provide helpful information regarding the code for other XML developers.

Typically, this documentation describes the purpose and content of the schema. The appinfo element can provide information for the particular application processing the schema.

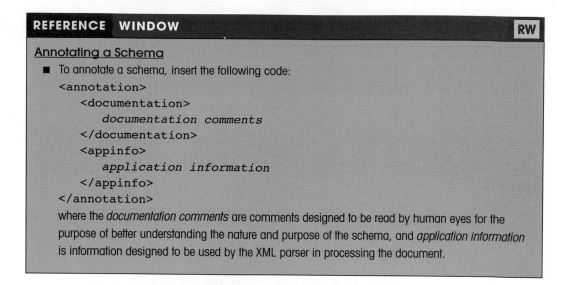

REFERENCE WINDOW RW

Annotating a Schema

■ To annotate a schema, insert the following code:

```
<annotation>
   <documentation>
      documentation comments
   </documentation>
   <appinfo>
      application information
   </appinfo>
</annotation>
```

where the *documentation comments* are comments designed to be read by human eyes for the purpose of better understanding the nature and purpose of the schema, and *application information* is information designed to be used by the XML parser in processing the document.

Why, you may be asking, should annotations be used rather than comments? The primary reason is that XML parsers ignore comments when they process XML documents. By putting information into a document or appinfo element, the information becomes available to the parser.

Annotations can appear at the beginning of the schema. You can also put annotations inside a specific element, attribute, simpleType, complexType, or group declaration. Allison appreciates the value of using annotations and would like you to insert an annotation at the beginning of the schema file to provide some documentation regarding the purpose of the file.

To create the annotation:

1. Insert the following code below the schema element:

```
<xsd:annotation>
  <xsd:documentation>
     This schema contains element and attribute declarations
     for the University Hospital's Breast Cancer study.
     Contact Allison Grant at 555-7832 for more information
     on the study and the creation of this schema.
  </xsd:documentation>
</xsd:annotation>
```

Figure 4-38 shows the code in the PSchema2.xsd file.

Figure 4-38	INSERTING AN ANNOTATION

```
<?xml version="1.0" encoding="UTF-8"?>
<!-- Schema for breast cancer patient data -->

<xsd:schema xmlns:xsd="http://www.w3.org/2001/XMLSchema"
            xmlns="http://uhosp/patients/ns"
            targetNamespace="http://uhosp/patients/ns">

  <xsd:annotation>
     <xsd:documentation>
        This schema contains element and attribute declarations
        for the Unversity Hospital's Breast Cancer study.
        Contact Allison Grant at 555-7832 for more information
        on the study and the creation of this schema.
     </xsd:documentation>
  </xsd:annotation>
```

> **2.** Save your changes and close PSchema2.xsd.

The new data types are a valuable addition to the schema. Allison suggests that you update both the Patient.xml and UHosp.xml documents to take advantage of the new schema.

To revise Allison's document:

1. Open the **Patient.xml** document in your text editor.

2. Locate the Patients element at the top of the file and change the schema location from PSchema1.xsd to **PSchema2.xsd**.

3. Close the file, saving your changes.

4. Open the UHosp.xml file in your text editor. Change the schema location for the Patients element from PSchema1.xsd to **PSchema2.xsd**.

5. Close the file and the text editor, saving your changes.

Now that you've attached a new schema to the Allison's data, she wants to validate the file. You'll do this using the Patient.xml file.

To validate the Patient.xml file:

1. Start XML Spy and open the **Patient.xml** file from the Tutorial.04X/Tutorial folder on your Data Disk. Maximize the contents of the document pane, and click the **Text View** button 📄 to view the text of the file.

2. Open **PSchema2.xsd** from the Tutorial.04X/Tutorial folder and switch to text view.

   TROUBLE? XML Spy may attempt to automatically validate your document when it opens. If an error message appears, study the error message for the reason why the validation failed. Compare the code in both the Patient.xml and PSchema2.xsd files to the figures in the text.

3. Click the **Validate** button ✅ on the XML Spy toolbar to verify that the contents of the Patient.xml file fulfill Allison's validation rules.

4. Click the **OK** button.

Allison would like to confirm that any content in the document that violates the rules she set up in the schema file will be picked up by the XML parser. She asks you to test this by changing some of the values in the Patient.xml file to obvious errors.

To test the schema validation:

1. Select the value "58"—the age of Cynthia Dibbs, the first patient in Allison's document—and change the value to "**18**".

   The schema for this document requires that patients must be 21 or older, thus the XML parser should flag this as an error.

2. Click the **Validate** button ✅.

XML Spy returns the error message shown in Figure 4-39, indicating that the change is not valid.

Figure 4-39   VALIDATING THE PATIENT DOCUMENT WITH AN AGE ERROR

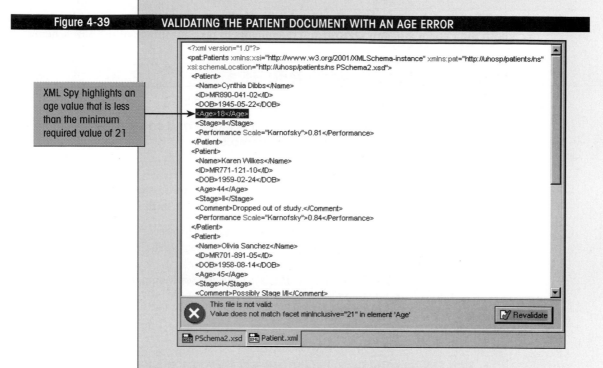

XML Spy highlights an age value that is less than the minimum required value of 21

```
<?xml version="1.0"?>
<pat:Patients xmlns:xsi="http://www.w3.org/2001/XMLSchema-instance" xmlns:pat="http://uhosp/patients/ns"
xsi:schemaLocation="http://uhosp/patients/ns PSchema2.xsd">
  <Patient>
   <Name>Cynthia Dibbs</Name>
   <ID>MR890-041-02</ID>
   <DOB>1945-05-22</DOB>
   <Age>18</Age>
   <Stage>II</Stage>
   <Performance Scale="Karnofsky">0.81</Performance>
  </Patient>
  <Patient>
   <Name>Karen Wilkes</Name>
   <ID>MR771-121-10</ID>
   <DOB>1959-02-24</DOB>
   <Age>44</Age>
   <Stage>II</Stage>
   <Comment>Dropped out of study.</Comment>
   <Performance Scale="Karnofsky">0.84</Performance>
  </Patient>
  <Patient>
   <Name>Olivia Sanchez</Name>
   <ID>MR701-891-05</ID>
   <DOB>1958-08-14</DOB>
   <Age>45</Age>
   <Stage>I</Stage>
   <Comment>Possibly Stage III</Comment>
```

(X) This file is not valid:
Value does not match facet minInclusive="21" in element 'Age'   ☑ Revalidate

🗎 PSchema2.xsd   🗎 Patient.xml

3. Click **Edit** and **Undo** to undo your change, restoring the age value to "58".

   Now test whether the pattern matching applied to the medical record number is enforced by the XML parser.

4. Change the medical record number of Cynthia Dibbs from "MR890-041-02" to **"CR890-041-02"**.

   This should be an error because the schema requires all medical record numbers to be of the form MR###-###-##.

5. Click the **Validate** button 🗹.

   XML Spy returns the error message shown in Figure 4-40, indicating that the medical record number does not match the required pattern.

Figure 4-40	VALIDATING THE PATIENT DOCUMENT WITH A PATTERN ERROR

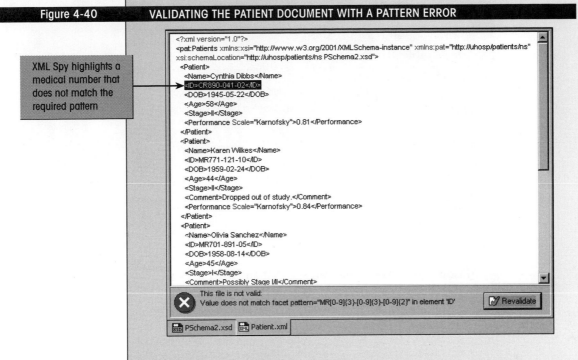

XML Spy highlights a medical number that does not match the required pattern

```
<?xml version="1.0"?>
<pat:Patients xmlns:xsi="http://www.w3.org/2001/XMLSchema-instance" xmlns:pat="http://uhosp/patients/ns"
xsi:schemaLocation="http://uhosp/patients/ns PSchema2.xsd">
  <Patient>
    <Name>Cynthia Dibbs</Name>
    <ID>CR890-041-02</ID>
    <DOB>1945-05-22</DOB>
    <Age>58</Age>
    <Stage>II</Stage>
    <Performance Scale="Karnofsky">0.81</Performance>
  </Patient>
  <Patient>
    <Name>Karen Wilkes</Name>
    <ID>MR771-121-10</ID>
    <DOB>1959-02-24</DOB>
    <Age>44</Age>
    <Stage>II</Stage>
    <Comment>Dropped out of study.</Comment>
    <Performance Scale="Karnofsky">0.84</Performance>
  </Patient>
  <Patient>
    <Name>Olivia Sanchez</Name>
    <ID>MR701-891-05</ID>
    <DOB>1958-08-14</DOB>
    <Age>45</Age>
    <Stage>I</Stage>
    <Comment>Possibly Stage I/II</Comment>
```

This file is not valid:
Value does not match facet pattern="MR[0-9]{3}-[0-9]{3}-[0-9]{2}" in element 'ID'

✗   [☑ Revalidate]

🔲 PSchema2.xsd   🔲 Patient.xml

6. Click **Edit** and **Undo** to restore the medical record number to its proper form.

7. Click the **Revalidate** button at the bottom of the document pane to confirm that the Patient.xml file is now valid.

   TROUBLE? If you still get an error message, study the message for clues to the reason why the file is invalid and take the necessary measures to correct the error.

If this were a real situation, you would probably put considerably more time into testing various possible errors in the instance document. However, having seen how to test the validation procedure against two possible errors, we'll close the document.

To close your work:

1. Click **File** and **Close All** from the XML Spy menu.

2. When prompted to save your changes, click the **Yes** button.

3. Click **File** and **Exit** to exit XML Spy.

REFERENCE WINDOW

Common Schema Syntax Errors

As you write your own schemas, you may have to deal with syntax errors. Here are some of the more common mistakes:

- failure to include the XML Schema namespace prefix before each schema tag
- failure to include a closing tag for two-sided schema elements
- failure to enter simple element declarations as empty tags
- misspelling of schema elements or improper use of upper and lowercase letters
- failure to place attributes within quotation marks
- misspelling of the XML Schema namespace in either the schema or the instance document
- when the schema is attached to a namespace, forgetting to use qualified names with all global elements in the instance document

Allison is impressed. She can see that an XML parser that can validate her documents with schemas can do a lot to reduce data entry errors. She plans to enter information on the rest of the study patients into the Patient.xml document. She feels confident that the schema you designed will help ensure the quality of her work.

Session 4.3 QUICK CHECK

1. What is a flat catalog and how does it differ from a Russian Doll design?

2. What are global elements? What are local elements?

3. How do you create a named complex type? What are the advantages of named types?

4. Define the following: value space, lexical space, and facets.

5. How would you derive a data type named "counts" that contains a list of positive integers?

6. How would you derive a data type named "Status" that can be either a decimal number or a text string?

7. How would you derive a data type named "percent" that is limited to decimal numbers between 0 and 100 (including 0 and 100)?

8. How would you create a regex for social security numbers, which have the form ###-##-####?

Note: In the case problems that follow, some of the XML documents have intentional errors. Part of your job will be to find and correct those errors using schemas.

REVIEW ASSIGNMENTS

Allison has been very pleased with your work on the patient document. She has approached you with a different file to work on. This file contains information on some of the studies being done at the hospital. As before, Allison needs you to create a schema for this document to ensure that the document contains no errors and to prevent future errors when Allison adds information about other studies to the file.

Figure 4-41 shows a diagram of the elements and structure of Allison's document.

Figure 4-41

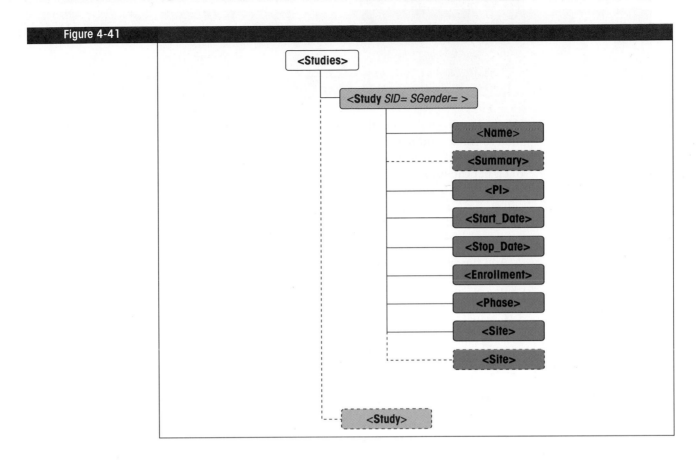

In the table in Figure 4-42, Allison has provided a description of all the elements and attributes in her document. She has also indicated which are optional and what sort of limitations she wants to place on their values.

Figure 4-42

ELEMENTS	DESCRIPTION
Studies	The root element of the document
Study	The element that stores information about each individual study
Name	The name of the study
Summary	An optional summary of the study's purpose
PI	The principal investigator on the study
Start_Date	The study's starting date
Stop_Date	The study's stopping date
Enrollment	The number of patients to be enrolled into the study
Phase	The type of study being done (Phase must be "1", "2", or "3")
Site	The hospital where the patients will be enrolled; there will be one or more sites for each study

Figure 4-42	(CONTINUED)
ATTRIBUTES	
SID	A required attribute of the Study element, providing the study's ID number; ID numbers must be in the form CCC-###-##
SGender	A required attribute of the Study element, indicating gender of patients in the study; the SGender attribute must be equal to "Female", "Male", or "All"

When you finish creating the schema, Allison wants you to attach it to her document and then to run a validity check on the document's contents. You decide to design this schema in the form of a flat catalog (you may want to refer to Figure 4-28 for guidance in laying out a flat catalog).

To complete this task:

1. Using your text editor, create a blank file named **SSchema.xsd** stored in the Tutorial.04X/Review folder of your Data Disk.

2. Add the xml declaration and root schema element to the file. Include a namespace to indicate that this is an XML Schema file. Use a namespace prefix of "xs". Do not attach the contents of the schema file to a namespace.

Explore 3. Create the following derived data types:

   ■ a data type named "PType"; limit PType values to the integers 1, 2, or 3
   ■ A data type named "SIDType", whose values must be an ID type following the pattern CCC-###-##
   ■ A data type named "SGType", whose values must be one of the following text strings: "Female", "Male", or "All"

4. Declare the following simple global elements:

   ■ the Name, Summary, PI, and Site elements, which all store a text string
   ■ the Start_Date and Stop_Date elements, which store dates
   ■ the Enrollment element, which stores a positive integer
   ■ the Phase element, which stores PType data.

5. Declare a global element named "Study", which contains a sequence of the following child elements: Name, Summary, PI, Start_Date, Stop_Date, Enrollment, Phase, and Site. Specify that the Summary element may appear 0 or 1 time, and that the Site element may appear 1 or more times. (*Hint*: Use the ref attribute to reference the elements you declared in the previous step.)

6. The Study element should also have two required attributes: SID and SGender. The data type of the SID attribute should be the SIDType. The data type of the SGender attribute should be SGType.

Explore 7. Declare a global element named "Studies", which contains one or more occurrences of the Study element.

8. Save your changes to the SSchema.xsd file.

9. Open the CCCtxt.xml file from the Tutorial.04X/Review folder on your Data Disk, using your text editor. Save the file as **CCC.xml**.

10. Attach the SSchema.xsd schema to this instance document. Do not assign a namespace to the schema.

11. Open both the CCC.xml and SSchema.xsd files in XML Spy.

12. Validate the contents of the CCC.xml document, correcting any entries you find in the CCC.xml file that violate Allison's schema. Save your changes to both files once you have a valid document that satisfies the rules set out by Allison.

13. Print a copy of both the CCC.xml and SSchema.xsd files, and hand in your files and printouts to your instructor.

CASE PROBLEMS

Case 1. The Jazz Warehouse Richard Brooks is working on an inventory of the CD collection at the Jazz Warehouse. He wants to be able to validate the information he's entering to weed out any data entry errors. The structure of his XML document is shown in Figure 4-43. Figure 4-44 describes the contents and properties of each of the attributes and elements in his document. Richard would like you to create a schema based on his document and then apply that schema to some of the data he's already entered. You'll use a Russian Doll design to create your schema.

Figure 4-43

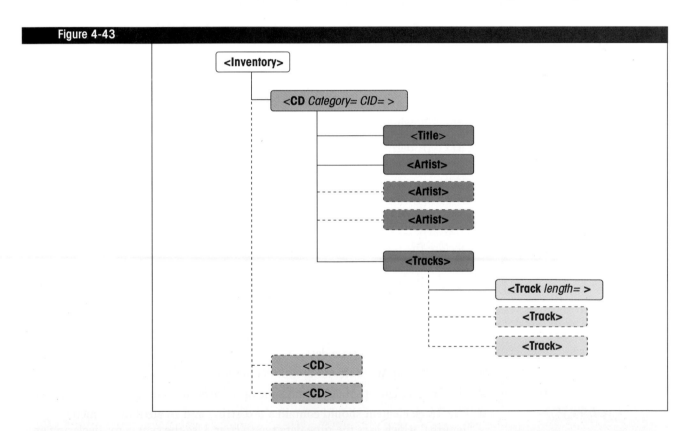

Figure 4-44

ELEMENTS	DESCRIPTION
Inventory	The root element of the document
CD	An element storing information about individual CDs
Title	The title of each CD

Figure 4-44	(CONTINUED)
ELEMENTS	**DESCRIPTION**
Artist	An element storing the name of the artist
Tracks	An element storing information about musical tracks on the CD
Track	The name of each CD track
ATTRIBUTES	
CID	A required attribute of the CD element, indicating the CD's ID number; ID numbers must be in the form JW######
Category	A required attribute of the CD element, indicating the musical category of the CD; the Category attribute must be equal to New Orleans, Swing, Bebop, or Modern

To complete this task:

1. Using your text editor, open the **JWtxt.xml file** located in the Tutorial.04X/Cases folder of your Data Disk. Save the file as **JW.xml**.

2. Using your text editor, create a blank file named **CD.xsd** in the Tutorial.04X/Cases folder of your Data Disk. Insert the initial xml declaration and opening and closing schema tags.

3. Within the opening schema tag, insert the XML Schema namespace, and assign the schema itself to the target namespace, "http://jazzwarehouse.com/schema."

Explore 4. Create the following user-derived data types as global components of your schema:

- CIDType derived from the ID data type and whose values are restricted to the pattern "JW######"
- CatType derived from the string data type, and whose values must be New Orleans, Swing, Bebop, or Modern

5. In a Russian Doll design, declare the following element attributes:

- Declare the Inventory element as a complex type containing a sequence of one or more CD elements.
- Declare the CD element to contain the following sequence of elements: Title, (one or more) Artist, and Tracks.
- The CD element should also contain two required attributes: Category and CID. The Category element should contain CatType data. The CID element should contain CIDType data.
- The Title and Artist elements should contain text strings.
- The Tracks element should contain one or more occurrences of the Track element.

Explore
- The Track element should contain a text string and an attribute named "length," which uses the time data type. (*Hint*: Use the syntax for declaring an attribute in an element with simple content.)

6. Save your changes to the CD.xsd file.

7. Return to the JW.xml file, and attach the document to the CD.xsd schema and the http://jazzwarehouse.com/schema namespace. Make sure that all global elements have qualified element names.

8. Save your changes to the JW.xml file.

9. Open JW.xml and CD.xsd in XML Spy and validate the files. Correct any entries in the JW.xml file that violate Richard's schema. Save your changes.

10. Print the contents of the JW.xml and CD.xsd files. Hand in your files and printouts to your instructor.

Case 2. Northwest Optimist Club Alicia Schaap is a board member of the Northwest Optimist Club. One of her duties is to maintain a list containing contact information for all the members. Alicia has collected information on each member's name, address, phone numbers, spouse, and children's names in an XML document. She would like to have some way of validating her data and any new data that she enters. She has asked your help in devising a schema for her document. Figure 4-45 shows a diagram of the document's structure. Figure 4-46 describes the features of each element and attribute. You decide not to attach a namespace to the schema.

Figure 4-45

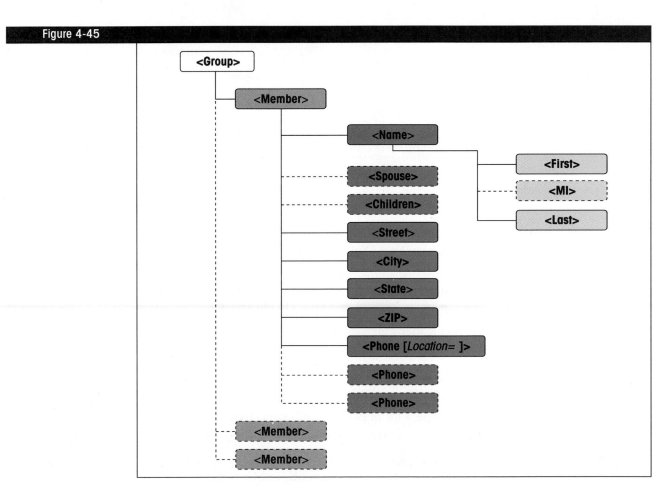

Figure 4-46

ELEMENTS	DESCRIPTION
Group	The root element of the document
Member	An element storing information about a club member
Name	An element storing information about the member's name
First	The member's first name
MI	The member's middle initial (optional)
Last	The member's last name
Spouse	The name of the member's spouse (optional)
Children	A list of the member's children (optional)
Street	The member's street address
City	The member's city of residence
State	The member's state of residence
ZIP	A 5-digit ZIP code
Phone	The member's phone number in the form ### ### - ####; a member can have one or more phone numbers
ATTRIBUTES	
Location	An optional attribute of the Phone element indicating the type of phone number; the Location attribute must be equal to home or business

To complete this task:

1. Using your text editor, open the **Listtxt.xml** file located in the Tutorial.04X/Cases folder of your Data Disk. Save the file as **List.xml**.

2. Using your text editor, create a blank file named **LSchema.xsd** in the Tutorial.04X/Cases folder of your Data Disk. Insert the initial xml declaration and opening and closing schema tags. Do not attach this schema to a target namespace.

Explore 3. Create the following user-derived data types as global items in the schema:

   - LType, a text string limited to the values "home" or "business"
   - PType, a text string that must follow the pattern ### ###-####
   - ZIPType, a text string consisting of five integers
   - CType, a list of NMTOKEN data types
   - MIType, a text string that is only one character long

Explore 4. Create a complex type with the name "FullName." FullName should contain a sequence of simple elements named First, MI, and Last. Both the First and Last elements should be NMTOKEN data types. The MI element should be an optional element and be a MIType data type.

5. Declare the following elements globally:

   - Name with a type = FullName
   - Spouse with a data type = NMTOKEN
   - Children with a data type = CType
   - Street and City with string data types

■ State with a data type = NMTOKEN

■ ZIP with a data type = ZIPType

6. Globally declare a complex element named "Phone" that contains text content with the PType data type and has an optional attribute named "Location." The Location attribute should use the LType data type.

7. Globally declare a complex element named "Member," which contains the following sequence of child elements: Name, Spouse, Children, Street, City, State, Zip, and Phone. Both the Spouse and Children elements should be optional. The Phone element can occur one or more times. (*Hint*: Use the ref attribute to create a reference between the sequence of child elements and the elements you declared in Step 5.)

8. Globally declare a complex element named "Group," which contains a single child element named "Member". The Member element can occur one or more times.

9. Save your changes to LSchema.xsd file.

Explore ➤ 10. Return to the List.xml file and attach the LSchema.xsd schema to this instance document without using a namespace. Save your changes to the file.

11. Open both the List.xml and LSchema.xsd files in XML Spy. Validate the List.xml document, correcting any errors in the file that violate the rules set up by Alicia in her schema.

12. Print out the contents of the List.xml and LSchema.xsd files. Hand in your printouts and files to your instructor.

Case 3. GrillRite Grills, Inc. James Castillo manages the inventory for GrillRite Grills, one of the leading manufacturers of grills in North America. He has been using XML to record the contents of the GrillRite warehouse. James has created two documents. One document lists all of the parts in the warehouse, including the name of each part, the cost of the part, and the number in stock. Another document describes all of the fully assembled grills in the warehouse. In this document, James has recorded the name of each grill model, the selling price of the model, the number of assembled models in stock, and the parts required to assemble each model.

James would like to create schemas for both of these documents to ensure their validity. He also plans to combine information from both documents into a single file. He would like your help in creating this combined document and validating it.

Figure 4-47 shows a diagram of the structure of both documents. Figure 4-48 lists the elements and attributes of the documents and specifies any validation rules that James would like the schemas to enforce. You decide to design these schemas using a Venetian Blinds layout.

Figure 4-47

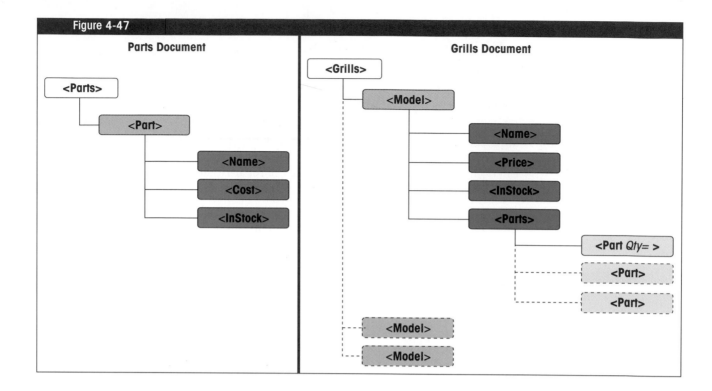

Figure 4-48

PARTS DOCUMENT ELEMENTS	DESCRIPTION
Parts	The root element of the Parts document
Part	An element storing information about a specific part
Name	The part's name
Cost	The cost of the part
InStock	The number of parts in stock
ATTRIBUTES	
None	

GRILLS DOCUMENT ELEMENTS	DESCRIPTION
Grills	The root element of the Grills document
Model	An element storing information about a specific grill model
Name	The name of the grill model
Price	The selling price of the model
InStock	The number of fully assembled grills in stock
Parts	An element storing information about the parts needed to assemble the grill model
Part	The name of each individual part (must be equal to Main Burner, Side Burner, Standard Chassis, Extended Chassis, Controls, Gas Tubing, Igniter, Main Rack, Top Rack, Side Rack, or Stand)
ATTRIBUTES	
Qty	An attribute of the Part element, indicating the number of each part used in assembling the model

To complete this task:

1. Using your text editor, open the **Partstxt.xml** file located in the Tutorial.04X/Cases folder of your Data Disk. Save the file as **Parts.xml**.

2. Use your text editor to create a blank file named **PTSchema.xsd** in your Tutorial.04X/Cases folder. Add the usual xml and schema elements to the document. Assign the schema the target namespace "http://grillrite.com/parts."

3. Create an element group named P_Elements. Within this group, create a sequence of the following elements: Name, Cost, InStock. The data type of the Name and Cost elements should be string. The InStock element should be restricted to positive integers.

4. Create a complex type named "PartType," which contains the P_Elements group.

5. Declare a global element named "Parts" that contains the child element, Part. The Part element must be present one or more times. The data type of the Part element should be PartType.

6. Save the PTSchema.xsd file and then attach the Parts.xml file to this schema and namespace. Save your changes, then open both documents in XML Spy and validate their contents.

7. With your text editor, open the Grilltxt.xml file from the Tutorial.04X/Cases folder. Save the file as **Grills.xml**.

8. Use your text editor to create a schema file named "**GRSchema.xsd**." Assign the schema to the http://grillrite.com/grills namespace.

9. Create a user-derived data type named "PartNames" that is restricted to one of the parts shown in the Grill document from Figure 4-48.

10. Create a complex type named "PartType," which is an element that contains PartNames data and has a required attribute named "Qty." The value of the Qty attribute should be a positive integer.

11. Create a complex type named "PartsType," which contains a sequence of one or more PartType elements.

12. Create a complex type named "M_Elements," which contains the following sequence of elements: Name, Price, InStock, and Parts. The Name and Price elements contain string data. The value of the InStock element should be a positive integer. The Parts element should contain the PartType complex type.

13. Declare a global element named "Grills." The Grills element should be a complex type that contains a sequence of one or more elements named "Model." The Model element should be of the type M_Elements.

14. Save the GRSchema.xsd file and then attach the Grills.xml file to this schema and namespace. Save your changes and use XML Spy to validate the contents of the file.

15. Using your text editor, create a new document named GRStock.xml that has a root element named "Stock," which contains within it the contents of both the Parts.xml and Grills.xml documents. Attach the two parts of this document to the appropriate schemas and namespaces.

16. Save the GRStock file and open it in XML Spy. Validate the contents of the file.

17. Print out the contents of the files you created for this problem. Hand in your printouts and files to your instructor.

Case 4. MediaMart Online MediaMart is an online store that specializes in selling used videos, books, and movies. Terrance Dawes, who works for MediaMart, has been given the task of putting some of their product information in XML documents. He's not very experienced with XML and would like your help in making the transfer as well as ensuring the integrity of his data. Terrance has put a small list of products into three text files named Books, Movies, and Music. Figure 4-49 describes the contents of the three files.

Figure 4-49		
BOOKS	**MOVIES**	**MUSIC**
• The name of the book • The author • The genre (fiction or nonfiction) • The format (paperback or hardcover) • The price	• The name of the movie • The genre (comedy, drama, fantasy, children, musical, or family) • A list of actors or actresses in the movie • The price • The year the movie was released • The format (VHS or DVD)	• The artist • The name of the work • The genre (rock, classical, opera, jazz, blues, rap, or pop) • The format (cassette or CD) • The price

To complete this task:

1. Create three XML documents named **Books.xml**, **Movies.xml**, and **Music.xml**, containing the data from the three text files. The structure of the XML documents is up to you.

Explore

2. Draw a schematic diagram of the three XML documents you created.

3. Create three schemas named **BSchema.xsd**, **MoSchema.xsd**, and **MuSchema.xsd** based on the document structure of your XML documents. The design of the schemas is up to you, but the schemas must ensure the integrity of Terrance's data, following the guidelines in Figure 4-49.

4. Include annotations in all three schemas describing the nature and purpose of the document.

5. Attach the schemas you created to your three XML documents. Validate both the XML documents and the schemas using XML Spy.

6. Combine the three XML documents into a single document named **MMart.xml**. Attach the three schemas to that single document and validate it in XML Spy.

7. Print out all of the files you created in this assignment and hand in your files and printouts to your instructor.

QUICK | CHECK ANSWERS

Session 4.1

1. A namespace is a defined collection of element and attribute names. Namespaces are useful in avoiding name collisions in combined documents.

2. an element name with a namespace prefix

3. `<?xml:namespace ns="http://ns.doc/book" prefix="Book"?>`

4. `<Book:Work xmlns:Book="http://ns.doc/book">`

5. Do not specify a prefix in the namespace declaration.

6. as if the namespace prefix and the local part were the complete element name

Session 4.2

1. A schema is a collection of rules and definitions, written in XML. An instance document is the XML document that the schema is written for.

2. Schemas support namespaces and work with combined documents better than DTDs. Schemas support more data types and allow the user to easily create customized data types. Schemas are also a newer standard and are not completely supported by all XML parsers.

3. `<prefix:schema`
   `xmlns:prefix="http://www.w3.org/2001/XMLSchema">`

4. A simple type element contains only text. A complex type element contains child elements and/or attributes.

5. `<element name="Weight" type="decimal" />`

6. `<element name="Parents">`

```
    <complexType>
        <sequence>
            <element name="Father" type="string" />
            <element name="Mother" type="string" />
        </sequence>
    </complexType>
</element>
```

7. `<element name="Book">`

```
    <complexType>
        <simpleType>
            <extension base="string">
                <attribute name="Title" type="string" />
            </extension>
        </simpleType>
    </complexType>
</element>
```

8. `prefix:noNamespaceSchemaLocation="Schema1.xsd"`

Session 4.3

1. A flat catalog is a schema design in which all element declarations are global. In a Russian Doll design, only one element is global and all of the rest of the elements are nested within that one global element.

2. Global elements are elements that are direct children of the schema element and can be referenced throughout the schema file. Local elements are one or more levels below global elements and cannot be referenced by other elements.

3. by assigning a name in the <complexType> declaration; a named complexType can be used to store document structures

4. the set of values that correspond to the data type; the set of textual representations of the value space; the properties of the data type that distinguish one data type from another

5. `<simpleType name="counts">`

```
    <list itemType="positiveInteger" />
</simpleType>
```

6. ```
   <simpleType name="Status">
       <union memberTypes="decimal string" />
   </simpleType>
   ```

7. ```
   <simpleType name="percent">
       <restriction base="decimal">
           <minInclusive value="0" />
           <maxInclusive value="100" />
       </restriction>
   </simpleType>
   ```

8. `[0-9]{3}-[0-9]{2}-[0-9]{3}`

New Perspectives on

X M L

Read This Before You Begin

To the Student

Data Disks

To complete the Level II tutorials, Review Assignments, and Case Problems, you need one Data Disk. Your instructor will either provide you with this Data Disk or ask you to make your own.

If you are making your own Data Disk, you will need **one** blank, formatted high-density disk. You will need to copy a set of files and/or folders from a file server, standalone computer, or the Web onto your disk. Your instructor will tell you which computer, drive letter, and folders contain the files you need. You can also download the files by going to **www.course.com** and following the instructions on the screen.

The information below shows you the Data Disk you need so that you will have enough disk space to complete all the tutorials, Review Assignments, and Case Problems:

Data Disk 1

Write this on the disk label:

Data Disk 1: XML Tutorials 5 and 6

When you begin each tutorial, Review Assignment, or Case Problem, be sure you are using the correct Data Disk. Refer to the File Finder chart at the back of this text for more detailed information on which files are used in which tutorials. See the inside front cover of this book for more information on Data Disk files, or ask your instructor or technical support person for assistance.

Using Your Own Computer

If you are going to work through this book using your own computer, you need:

- **Computer System** A text editor and a Web browser (preferably Netscape Navigator or Internet Explorer, versions 4.0 or higher) must be installed on your computer. If you are using a non-standard browser, it must support frames and HTML 4.0 or higher.

- **Data Disk** You will not be able to complete the tutorials or exercises in this book using your own computer until you have your Data Disk.

Visit Our World Wide Web Site

Additional materials designed especially for you are available on the World Wide Web.
Go to **www.course.com/NewPerspectives**.

To the Instructor

The Data Disk Files are available on the Instructor's Resource Kit for this title. Follow the instructions in the Help file on the CD-ROM to install the programs to your network or standalone computer. For information on creating Data Disks, see the "To the Student" section above.

OBJECTIVES

In this tutorial you will:

- Learn about the history and theory of Cascading Style Sheets

- Link a style sheet to an XML document

- Design a page layout using styles

- Apply styles to text and text backgrounds

- Use a style sheet to create and display background images

- Use styles with elements classified by id and class attributes

WORKING
WITH CASCADING STYLE SHEETS

Formatting Your XML Documents with CSS

CASE

Tour Nation

Tour Nation is a leading bicycle manufacturer in the country. Janet Schmidtt works in the Advertising Department, and one of her responsibilities is to maintain an XML document that describes the various models offered by Tour Nation. Janet created a test document listing a few of the bikes in the Tour Nation catalog. The document includes a descriptive paragraph and list of features for each bicycle. As Janet learns more about XML, she plans to add more information and more bicycles to her document.

In its current form, the document is not very easy for other Tour Nation employees to read. Janet wants to format the document with an interesting and readable layout, and make the document available on the Tour Nation intranet site. She knows that the Cascading Style Sheet (CSS) language is often used with HTML files to create interesting page designs, but she doesn't know if it can be used with XML. She wants your help in applying a style sheet to her document. To do this, you'll have to learn more about CSS and how it interacts with XML.

SESSION 5.1

In this session, you'll study the origins of Cascading Style Sheets (CSS) and how they can be applied to an XML document. You'll learn how to link your XML files to external style sheets. You'll also study the general syntax of a style declaration, and learn how to apply a style to a group of XML elements. Finally, you'll use CSS to set the dimensions of your XML elements, and place them on the Web page.

Exploring the History of CSS

To understand the importance of style sheets, we first must go back to the roots of HTML. Early HTML versions had minimal support for page design and layout. Part of this was intentional. HTML's original philosophy was to have basic text files that could be downloaded quickly, relying on Web browsers to format much of the document's appearance. Though efficient, this approach meant that the appearance of a document might differ slightly between different browsers and operating systems. For example, one browser might display a heading with a 20-point Arial font, while another browser uses a 24-point font.

For the basic documents that comprised much of the early history of the Web, this was fine. However, as the Web expanded in popularity, Web page designers looked for ways to improve the design and appearance of their pages. This need led to the development of a style language that could be used with HTML documents.

A **style** is a rule, or instruction, that defines the appearance of a particular element in a document. Styles cover a wide range of design features, including font types and sizes, background colors, and layout. The collection of styles for all of the elements in a document is called a **style sheet**. When the browser applies a style sheet to elements of an HTML file, the result is a formatted Web page.

Like HTML, style sheets use a common language and syntax. The accepted style sheet standard is **Cascading Style Sheets**, or **CSS**. CSS was developed by the World Wide Web Consortium (the same organization responsible for the development of HTML and XML). The first CSS standard, **CSS1**, was released in 1996, and established some of the basic styles used in CSS. The second CSS standard, **CSS2**, was released in 1998, and added support for printers, sound devices, downloadable fonts, layout, and tables. **CSS3** (in development at the time of this writing) plans to modularize the CSS standard, allowing software developers to implement the subsets of CSS that are applicable to their particular applications. CSS3 will also increase support for non-Western languages and XML namespaces.

As XML was being developed, it was natural to include support for CSS. XML would be used solely for document content, and CSS would be used to format that content. The ability to integrate XML and CSS depends upon the active Web browser. Internet Explorer 6.0 supports most of the CSS1 and CSS2 specifications when applied to an XML document. Netscape 6.0 supports most of the styles that apply to formatting text, but is less supportive with respect to styles that control page layout. Web page developers must, as usual, take into account the differences between browsers in any project they undertake.

In Janet's case, her work is seen only on Tour Nation's intranet. The company settled on Internet Explorer as its Web browser; therefore her design only needs to work with Internet Explorer. You should be aware, however, that if you intend to make your document available to a wider audience, you must test the appearance of the page on a variety of browsers and operating systems.

Attaching a Style Sheet to an XML Document

Janet created a file that contains information on Tour Nation bicycles. A list of the elements contained in Janet's document is shown in Figure 5-1.

Figure 5-1	ELEMENTS IN JANET'S DOCUMENT
ELEMENT	**ELEMENT CONTENT**
Document	The root element
Author	The author of the document
Date	The date the document was last revised
Title	The title of the document
Subtitle	The subtitle of the document
Models	A list of bikes sold by Tour Nation
Model	A record for an individual bike model
Name	The name of the bike model (the category attribute indicates the bike model category)
Description	Bike model description
IMG	An empty element used for storing an image of the bike model
Features	A list of the features of a bike model
Feature	A specific feature for a bike model
FName	The name of a feature

Her file contains a descriptive paragraph for each bicycle model, a reference to an image of the bike, and a list of features for each model. Janet also included four fields (Author, Date, Title, and Subtitle) that describe the contents of her file. Figure 5-2 illustrates the structure of the document.

Figure 5-2   THE STRUCTURE OF JANET'S DOCUMENT

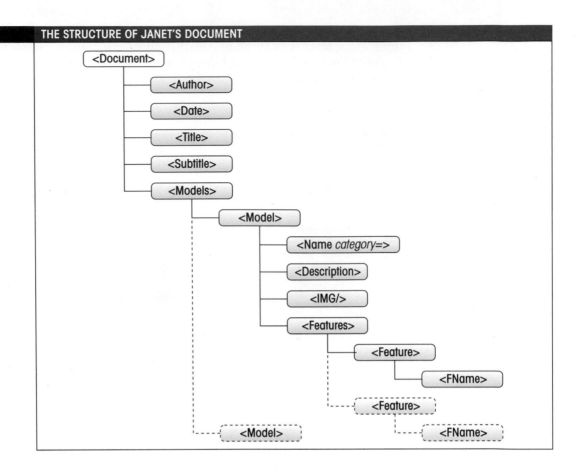

To open Janet's document:

1. Using your text editor, open **biketxt.xml** located in the tutorial.05x/tutorial folder of your Data Disk.

2. Save the file in the same location as **bike.xml**.

3. Take some time to review the contents of the document, comparing the structure to the diagram in Figure 5-2.

To attach a style sheet to this document, you must add the following processing instruction to the file:

```
<?xml-stylesheet type="text/css" href="URI" ?>
```

where *URI* is the name and location of a file containing the style sheet. You can include multiple processing instructions in a single XML document to attach several style sheets to the same document. Janet plans to store her style sheet in a file named "bike.css." Create a link to that document now in Janet's XML document.

To attach a style sheet to an XML document:

1. Insert the following processing instruction code directly below the first line (see Figure 5-3):

```
<?xml-stylesheet type="text/css" href="bike.css" ?>
```

| Figure 5-3 | ACCESSING A STYLE SHEET |

```
<?xml version="1.0"?>
<?xml-stylesheet type="text/css" href="bike.css" ?>  ◄——  style sheet
<Document>
<Author>Janet Schmidtt</Author>
<Date>8/17/2004</Date>
<Title>Tour Nation</Title>
<Subtitle>Bike Models</Subtitle>
```

2. Save your changes to bike.xml and close the file.

It is now time to create a new file, bike.css.

3. Using your text editor, create a file named **bike.css**. Be sure to save it in the tutorial.05x/tutorial folder of your Data Disk.

Next, you'll add styles to the bike.css style sheet.

Defining a Style

The syntax of CSS is relatively simple and easy to follow. Each line of the CSS file attaches a collection of styles to an element or group of elements called a **selector**. The general syntax is:

```
selector {attribute1:value1; attribute2:value2; ... }
```

where *selector* are the items in the document that receive the style; *attribute1*, *attribute2*, etc. are CSS style attributes; and *value1*, *value2*, etc. are the values applied to those attributes. For example, the following CSS style sets the font color of the Title element to red:

```
Title {color:red}
```

By default, style attributes are passed from parent elements to the descendant elements. For example, if you set the font color of the Model element to red using the following syntax:

```
Model {color:red}
```

the font color for the descendant elements of the Model element (Name, Description, Features, etc.) is also red.

You'll learn more about the different style attributes later in this tutorial. For now, let's examine the syntax used with specifying the selector.

Working with Selectors

The most common selector is simply the name of an element in the XML document. In the previous code, the font color red is applied only to the contents of the Title element. To apply a red font color to all of the elements in the document, you can use the wildcard symbol, "*", in the following style declaration:

```
* {color:red}
```

To apply a style to a group of elements, separate the element names by commas. For example, the style:

```
Author, Date, Title, Subtitle {color:red}
```

specifies the font color for only the Author, Date, Title, and Subtitle elements. If you use namespaces with your document, you must include the namespace prefix along with the element name. If the Title element belongs to a namespace with the prefix "Doc," you must enter the style as follows:

```
Doc:Title {color:red}
```

You can also define selectors based on the content of the element, or the element's location in the structure of the XML document. Figure 5-4 describes the different forms the selector can take.

Figure 5-4	CSS SELECTOR FORMS	
SELECTOR	**DESCRIPTION**	**EXAMPLE**
*	Apply the style to every element in the document	* {color:red}
element	Apply the style to the element	Title {color:red}
element1, element2, ...	Apply the style to each of the named elements	Title, Subtitle {color:red}
parent descendant	Apply the style to descendant elements of the parent element (the descendant element does not need to be a direct descendant)	Models Description {color:red}
parent > child	Apply the style to a direct descendant (child) of the parent element	Model > Name {color:red}
before + after	Apply the style only to those after elements that occur directly after the before element	Title + Subtitle {color:red}
element[attribute]	Apply the style only to an element containing specified attribute (the value of the attribute is irrelevant)	Name[category] {color:red}
element[attribute="value"]	Apply the style to an element whose attribute value is equal to "value"	Name[category="city"] {color:red}
element[attribute~="value"]	Apply the style to an element whose attribute value contains the word "value" (among other text)	Name[category~="c"] {color:red}

For example, if a document has two Title elements, the style sheet can distinguish one from the other by indicating its relation to a parent element, as in the following style declaration:

```
Document > Title {color:red}
```

In this case, only Title elements whose parent element is "Document" will have a red font color. Title elements located elsewhere in the document hierarchy will not have this style.

Unfortunately, most of the selector forms described in Figure 5-4, while supported by CSS, are not supported by browsers working in conjunction with XML. At this time, only the following selectors are reliably supported:

- *
- element
- element1, element2, ...
- parent descendant

However, future browser versions are expected to expand their support for selectors, and, in time, the complete list of CSS selectors should be supported by all browsers.

Working with Pseudo-elements and Pseudo-classes

A more general class of selectors are **pseudo-element selectors**, which specify elements based on a condition that does not involve the element's name. CSS supports the seven pseudo-elements described in Figure 5-5.

Figure 5-5	PSEUDO-ELEMENTS
PSEUDO-ELEMENT	**DESCRIPTION**
element:first-child	Apply the style to the first child of the parent *element*
element:link	Apply the style to an unvisited hypertext link named *element*
element:visited	Apply the style to a previously visited hypertext link named *element*
element:active	Apply the style to an active hypertext link named *element*
element:hover	Apply the style to a hypertext link named *element* when the mouse pointer hovers over the link
element:focus	Apply the style to an *element* that has the focus of the cursor

CSS also allows **pseudo-class selectors** for items in the document that are not elements. Figure 5-6 describes the pseudo-classes supported by CSS.

Figure 5-6	PSEUDO-CLASSES
PSEUDO-CLASS	**DESCRIPTION**
element:first-letter	Apply the style to the first letter of the content of the *element*
element:first-line	Apply the style to the first line of the content of the *element*
element:before	Apply the style directly before the content of the *element*
element:after	Apply the style directly after the content of the *element*

Currently, neither pseudo-elements nor pseudo-classes are supported by browsers through version 6.0, when they render XML documents. So you will not use them when designing a style sheet for the Tour Nation document. However, like other selectors, it is expected that future browser versions will support pseudo-elements and pseudo-classes.

Working with the Display Attribute

Janet created a proposed layout for the data in the bike.xml document, shown in Figure 5-7.

Figure 5-7   **JANET'S PROPOSED LAYOUT**

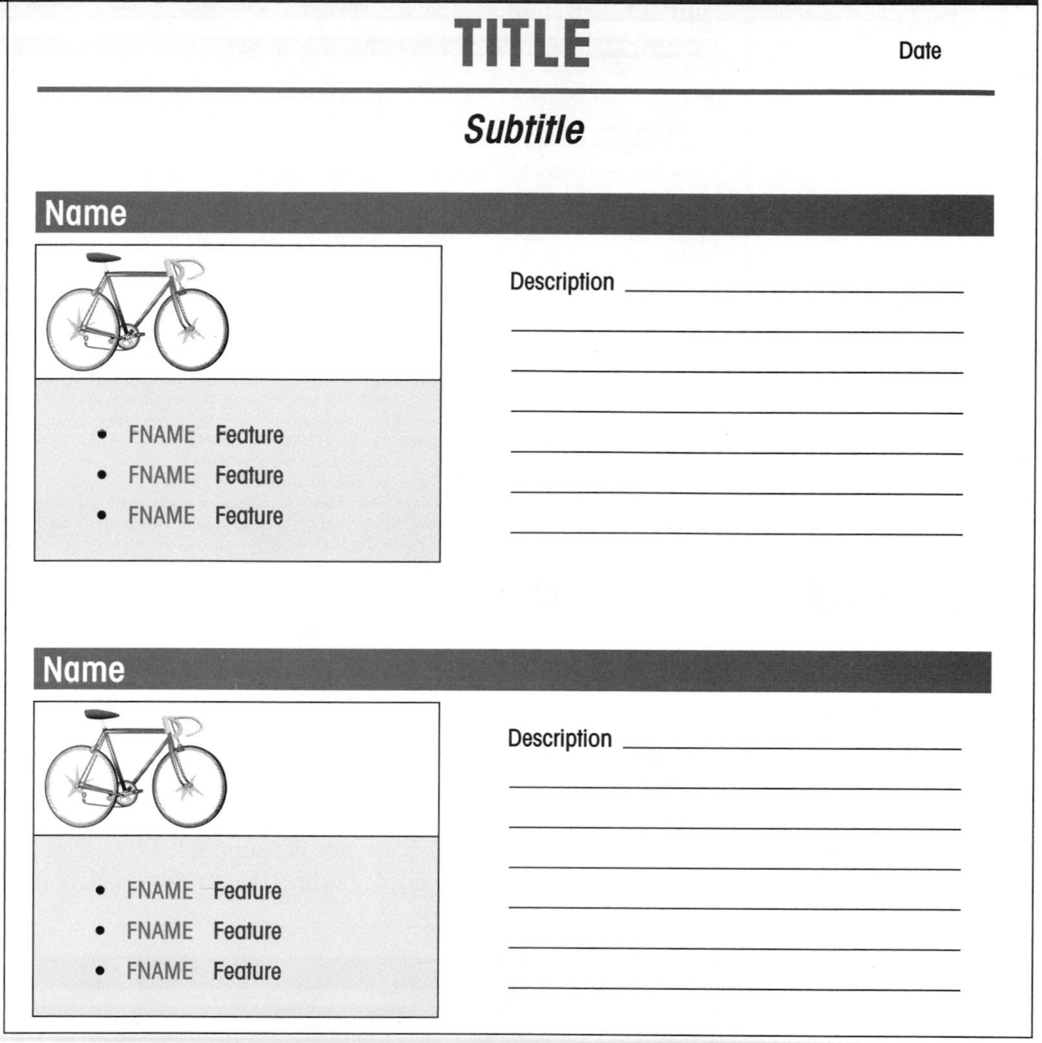

You notice that the layout she proposes places much of the information contained in bike.xml into distinct sections called **blocks** or **block-level elements**. For example, one block contains a bulleted list of bike features; another block contains a descriptive paragraph for each bike model. How does Janet's document currently appear in the browser?

To view Janet's document in your browser:

1. Using your Web browser, open **bike.xml**.

TROUBLE? The screenshots in this tutorial are based on Windows Internet Explorer 6.0. Browsers vary in their support of XML combined with CSS. If you are running a browser other than Internet Explorer 6.0, or are on a different operating system, your results may differ greatly from those presented in this tutorial.

Figure 5-8 shows the contents of the file.

| Figure 5-8 | INITIAL APPEARANCE OF BIKE.XML |

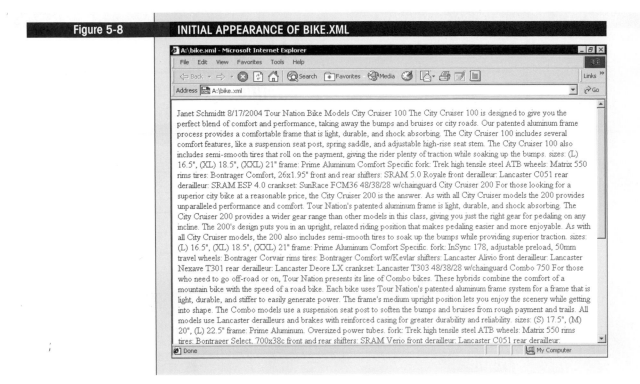

Without specifying any styles in the bike.css style sheet, the browser displays the content of each element **inline**, so that the document's content appears as a continuous text string. You can override this behavior using the **display attribute**. The display attribute has 18 possible values, most of which are not yet supported by browsers used in conjunction with XML documents. The four display values that are supported are described in Figure 5-9.

Figure 5-9	DISPLAY ATTRIBUTE VALUES

DISPLAY ATTRIBUTE	DESCRIPTION
block	Displays the contents of the element in a block, separate from other elements in the document
inline	Displays the contents of the element inline with the contents of the parent element
list-item	Displays the content of the element in a list
none	Hides the content of the element

For example, to display the Title element in its own block, separated from other elements in the document, you would use the style:

```
Title {display:block}
```

<u>Determining Display Type</u>

■ To display an element's content inline with the contents of other elements in the document, use the style:
```
display: inline
```
■ To display an element's content inline in a separate block, use the style:
```
display: block
```
■ To hide an element's content on the page, use the style:
```
display: none
```

You decide to format Janet's document so that all elements in the document appear in block format, except the Author element, which you'll hide; the FName element, which you'll display inline; and the Feature element, which you'll set up as a list item.

To specify the display attributes for Janet's document:

1. Return to **bike.css** in your text editor.

2. Enter the following styles (see Figure 5-10):

```
* {display: block}
Author {display: one}
FName {display: inline}
Feature {display: list-item}
```

Figure 5-10	ENTERING DISPLAY STYLES

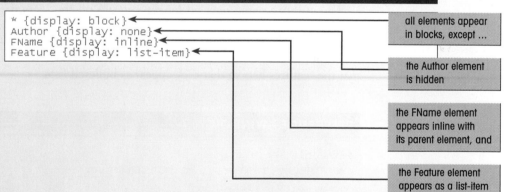

```
* {display: block}          ◄──────────────  all elements appear
Author {display: none}      ◄──────────────  in blocks, except ...
FName {display: inline}     ◄──────
Feature {display: list-item} ◄──────
```

- all elements appear in blocks, except ...
- the Author element is hidden
- the FName element appears inline with its parent element, and
- the Feature element appears as a list-item

3. Using your text editor, save your changes to bike.css and refresh **bike.xml** using your browser. Figure 5-11 shows the new layout of the page.

| Figure 5-11 | BIKE.XML LAID OUT IN BLOCKS |

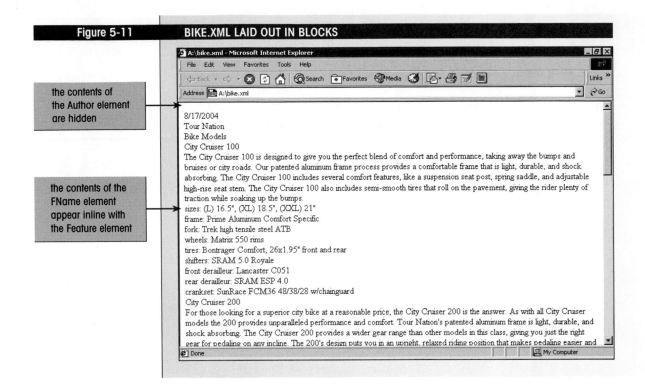

the contents of
the Author element
are hidden

the contents of the
FName element
appear inline with
the Feature element

This style sheet illustrates an important point regarding style precedence. When two styles can be applied to the same element, the one appearing later in the document overrides earlier styles. Thus, initially, every element in the document is defined as a block element, but this is overruled for the Author, FName, and Feature elements by the occurrence of additional styles later in the style sheet.

The author's name now no longer appears on the Web page, and the contents of the FName attribute (sizes, frame, fork, etc.) appear inline with the associated text for those features. However, the features lists, while formatted with the list-item style, do not look any different than the other block-level elements in the document. Your next task will be to format the features lists so that they appear as bulleted lists.

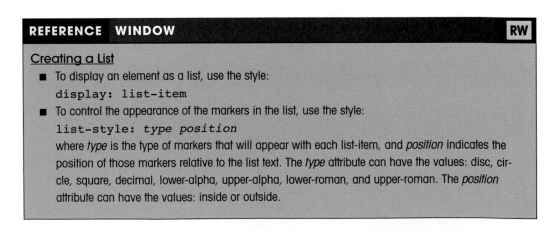

REFERENCE WINDOW | **RW**

Creating a List

■ To display an element as a list, use the style:

```
display: list-item
```

■ To control the appearance of the markers in the list, use the style:

```
list-style: type position
```

where *type* is the type of markers that will appear with each list-item, and *position* indicates the position of those markers relative to the list text. The *type* attribute can have the values: disc, circle, square, decimal, lower-alpha, upper-alpha, lower-roman, and upper-roman. The *position* attribute can have the values: inside or outside.

Working with List-items

To control the appearance of list-items, use the following style attribute:

```
list-style: type position
```

where *type* is the type of markers that appear with each list-item, and *position* indicates the position of those markers relative to the list text. Figure 5-12 describes the different *type* values supported by CSS.

Figure 5-12	LIST-ITEM TYPES

TYPE	DISPLAYED AS
disc	•
circle	○
square	■
decimal	1, 2, 3, 4, etc.
lower-alpha	a, b, c, d, etc.
upper-alpha	A, B, C, D, etc.
lower-roman	i, ii, iii, iv, etc.
upper-roman	I, II, III, IV, etc.
url(*URL*)	an image, where *URL* is the name and location of a file to use as the list marker

The *position* attribute is optional and can have two possible values:

■ inside — lines up the list item text with the list marker

■ outside — places the marker outside of the list text (see Figure 5-13)

Figure 5-13	LIST-ITEM POSITIONS

- sizes: (L) 16.5", (XL) 18.5", (XXL) 21"
- frame: Prime Aluminum Comfort Specific
- fork: Trek high tensile steel ATB
- wheels: Matrix 550 rims
- tires: Bontrager Comfort, 26x1.95" front and rear
- shifters: SRAM 5.0 Royale
- front derailleur: Lancaster C051
- rear derailleur: SRAM ESP 4.0
- crankset: SunRace FCM36 48/38/28 w/chain guard

inside

- sizes: (L) 16.5", (XL) 18.5", (XXL) 21"
- frame: Prime Aluminum Comfort Specific
- fork: Trek high tensile steel ATB
- wheels: Matrix 550 rims
- tires: Bontrager Comfort, 26x1.95" front and rear
- shifters: SRAM 5.0 Royale
- front derailleur: Lancaster C051
- rear derailleur: SRAM ESP 4.0
- crankset: SunRace FCM36 48/38/28 w/chain guard

outside

By default, bullets are placed inside, lining up with the list-item text. Some browsers do not support this style attribute, and, in some cases, an error message results. In case of an error message, you should display the Feature element as a block item, and leave off the list-style attribute.

To format the features list:

1. Return to **bike.css** in your text editor.

2. Within the style for the Feature element, insert the text **; list-style: square inside**, as shown in Figure 5-14.

Figure 5-14	ENTERING THE LIST-STYLE ATTRIBUTE

```
*       {display: block}
Author  {display: none}
FName   {display: inline}
Feature {display: list-item; list-style: square inside}
```

each feature appears with a square bullet positioned on the inside of the feature text

Remember that you *must* separate one style from another using a semicolon.

TROUBLE? If your browser does not display the features list as a bulleted item, it could be that your browser does not support this CSS style when combined with style sheets. If you receive an error message when you try to display the Web page, you should change the display style for the Feature element to a block style, and remove the list-style attribute, so that the declaration for the Feature element appears as: Feature {display: block}.

3. Using your text editor, save your changes to bike.css and refresh **bike.xml** using your browser. The features list now appears with a square bullet, as shown in Figure 5-15.

Figure 5-15	FEATURES LIST WITH SQUARE BULLETS

8/17/2004
Tour Nation
Bike Models
City Cruiser 100
The City Cruiser 100 is designed to give you the perfect blend of comfort and performance, taking away the bumps and bruises of city roads. Our patented aluminum frame process provides a comfortable frame that is light, durable, and shock absorbing. The City Cruiser 100 includes several comfort features, like a suspension seat post, spring saddle, and adjustable high-rise seat stem. The City Cruiser 100 also includes semi-smooth tires that roll on the pavement, giving the rider plenty of traction while soaking up the bumps.
- sizes: (L) 16.5", (XL) 18.5", (XXL) 21"
- frame: Prime Aluminum Comfort Specific
- fork: Trek high tensile steel ATB
- wheels: Matrix 550 rims
- tires: Bontrager Comfort, 26x1.95" front and rear
- shifters: SRAM 5.0 Royale
- front derailleur: Lancaster C051
- rear derailleur: SRAM ESP 4.0
- crankset: SunRace FCM36 48/38/28 w/chain guard

Lists are a special class of block-level elements. In the following tasks, you'll work with general properties that apply to all blocks.

Sizing **Block Elements**

One of the features of block elements is the ability to resize them and place them at particular locations on the Web page. As you refer to Janet's proposed layout, shown in Figure 5-7, you notice that she wants the Date element placed in the upper-right corner of the page, and the Description element reduced in width and placed in the right margin. Before you can start moving around these elements, you must study the methods used to resize them.

Setting the Element's Width

To set the width of a block element, use the style:

width: *value*

where *value* is expressed as a percentage of the width of the parent element, or in absolute units. CSS supports the following absolute units of measurement:

- millimeter (mm)
- centimeter (cm)
- inch (in)
- point (pt)
- pica (pc)
- pixel (px)

Therefore, to set the width of the Title element to 4 inches, use the style:

Title {width: 4in}

If you do not specify a unit of measurement, the browser assumes that the width is set in pixels. For example, the following style:

Title {width: 250}

sets the width of the Title element to 250 pixels.

Janet wants the width of the features lists and the descriptive paragraphs to be 300 pixels. She also wants the width of the entire page to be 620 pixels so that all employees see the same page layout, regardless of the resolution settings of their monitors.

To set element widths in the document:

1. Return to **bike.css** in your text editor.

2. Insert the following line of code at the top of the file:

   Document {width: 620}

3. Insert the following line of code directly above the style for the Feature element:

   Features {width: 300}

4. Insert the following line of code at the bottom of the file:

   Description {width: 300}

5. Save your changes to bike.css.

Setting the Element's Height

To set the height of an element, use the style:

```
height: value
```

where *value* is the height of the element specified as a percentage of the parent element, or in absolute units. If you do not specify a height, the browser expands the height of the block until all of the element content is visible.

If you do specify a height, you run the risk of not being able to fit the content into a defined space. In that case, you can control how the browser handles the extra content by using the style:

```
overflow: type
```

where *type* is either visible (the default), hidden, scroll, or auto. A value of "visible" instructs the browser to increase the height of the element to fit the extra content. A value of "hidden" hides the extra content. Both the "scroll" and "auto" values instruct the browser to display scroll bars to view the extra content. The "auto" option adds scroll bars only when needed, and the "scroll" option adds scroll bars whether they are needed or not (see Figure 5-16).

Figure 5-16	OVERFLOW VALUES

The City Cruiser 100 is designed to give you the perfect blend of comfort and performance, taking away the bumps and bruises of city roads. Our patented aluminum frame process provides a comfortable frame that is light, durable, and shock absorbing. The City Cruiser 100 includes several comfort features, like a suspension seat post, spring saddle, and adjustable high-rise seat stem. The City Cruiser 100 also includes semi-smooth tires that roll on the pavement, giving the rider plenty of traction while soaking up the bumps.

overflow: visible

The City Cruiser 100 is designed to give you the perfect blend of comfort and performance, taking away the bumps and bruises of city roads. Our patented aluminum frame process provides a comfortable frame that is light, durable, and shock

overflow: hidden

The City Cruiser 100 is designed to give you the perfect blend of comfort and performance, taking away the bumps and bruises of city roads. Our patented aluminum frame process

overflow: scroll

The City Cruiser 100 is designed to give you the perfect blend of comfort and performance, taking away the bumps and bruises of city roads. Our patented aluminum frame process provides a comfortable frame that is light,

overflow: auto

Related to the overflow attribute is the clip attribute. The clip attribute allows the Web designer to define a rectangular area through which the contents of an element can be viewed. Any content that falls outside of the clip area is hidden. The syntax for the clip attribute is:

```
clip: rect(top, right, bottom, left)
```

where *top*, *right*, *bottom*, and *left* define the coordinates of the rectangular region. For example, a clip value of rect (25, 250, 200, 15) defines a clip region whose top and bottom edges are 25 and 200 pixels from the top of the element, and whose right and left edges are 250 and 15 pixels from the left edge of the element (see Figure 5-17).

Figure 5-17	CLIPPING AN ELEMENT

25 pixels

250 pixels

The City Cruiser 100 is designed to give you the perfect blend of comfort and performance, taking away the bumps and bruises of city roads. Our patented aluminum frame process provides a comfortable frame that is light, durable, and shock absorbing. The City Cruiser 100 includes several comfort features, like a suspension seat post, spring saddle, and adjustable high-rise seat stem. The City Cruiser 100 also includes semi-smooth tires that roll on the pavement, giving the rider plenty of traction while soaking up the bumps.

rfect blend of comfort and performance way the bumps and bruises of city roads tented aluminum frame process provide mfortable frame that is light, durable, ar sorbing. The City Cruiser 100 includes mfort features, like a suspension seat p ring saddle, and adjustable high-rise sea e City Cruiser 100 also includes semi-s es that roll on the pavement, giving the r

200 pixels

full element

15 pixels

clip: rect(25, 250,200,15)

The *top, right, bottom,* and *left* value can also be set to "auto," which shifts the clipping region to the edge of the element. For example, a clip value of rect (10, auto, 125, 75) creates a clipping rectangle whose right edge matches the right edge of the element, while the rest of the edges are clipped.

The clip attribute can only be used with absolute position (a topic you'll learn about shortly). Janet does not need to use the height, overflow, or clip attributes with her document.

Positioning Elements

Now that you've learned how to resize a block-level element, you can focus on placing an element in a specific location on the page. To position an element with CSS, use the following style:

```
position: type; top:value; right:value; bottom:value;
left:value
```

where *type* indicates the type of positioning applied to the element, and the top, right, bottom, and left attributes indicate the coordinates of the top, right, bottom, and left edges of the element. Coordinates can be expressed as absolute units or as a percentage of the parent element. For example, to center the upper-left corner of an element within its parent, use the style:

```
top: 50%; left: 50%
```

As with the width and height attributes, pixel is the default unit of measurement.

Assuming that an element has a fixed size, only the location of the element's top or bottom edge in the vertical direction and either the left or right edge in the horizontal direction must be specified. The most common practice by Web designers is to specify only the top and left attributes.

There are four possible values for the position type: absolute, relative, fixed, and static. Let's consider each of these values in turn.

An **absolute position** places the element at defined coordinates within its parent element. In most cases, the parent element is the document window itself, so the absolute position coordinates refer to the coordinates within the window.

The coordinates are specified with respect to the upper-left corner of the parent element. A positive top value places the object down from the top edge; a negative value moves the object above the top edge of the parent. Similarly, a positive left value moves the element to the right of the left edge, while a negative value moves the element to the left of the parent.

For example, Figure 5-18 shows an object placed at the (30, 100) coordinate, that is, 30 pixels to the right and 100 pixels down from the upper-left corner of its parent.

Figure 5-18	ASSIGNING ABSOLUTE POSITION TO AN ELEMENT

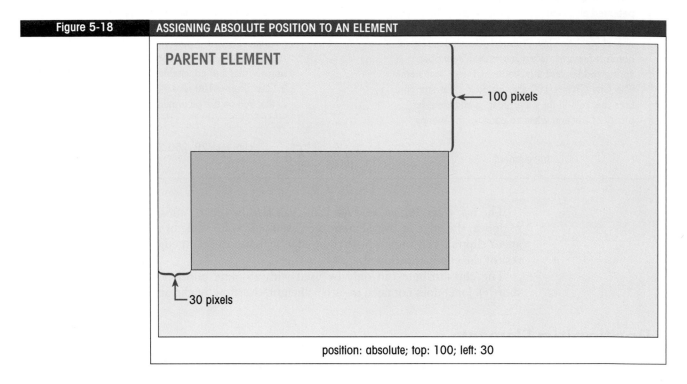

Moving an element to a new location using absolute positioning does not affect the position of other elements on the page. Those elements remain in their original locations. If you specify only one of the coordinates, such as the top coordinate, the remaining coordinate is assumed to be in the default position. For example, the style:

```
position: absolute; left: 400;
```

places the element 400 pixels to the right of the left edge of the parent element, but the top coordinate keeps its default value.

An alternate approach is to offset an element by using **relative positioning**. This approach moves element a specific distance from where the browser would place it. For example, the element shown in Figure 5-19 is offset 30 pixels to the left and 100 pixels down from the original location on the page.

Figure 5-19	ASSIGNING RELATIVE POSITION TO AN ELEMENT

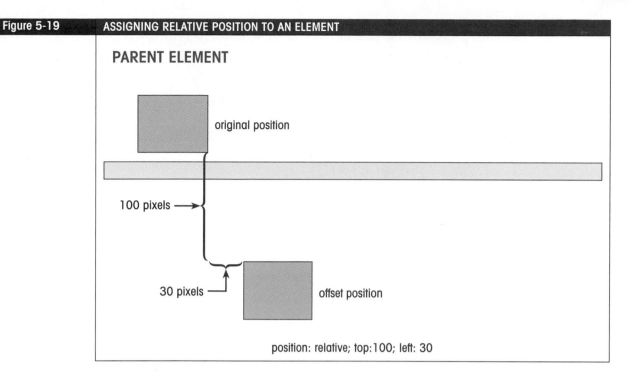

Similar to absolute positioning, relative positioning does not affect the placement of other elements. Once again, if you do not specify the offset value for one of the coordinates, it will be placed at its default location.

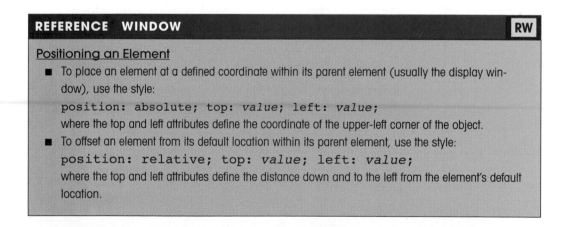

A **fixed position** places the element at a fixed location in the display window. The element remains in that location and does not scroll with other elements on the page. A **static position** places the object in its natural position in the flow of the document, as determined by the browser. In this case, you are allowing the browser, or whatever application is rendering the document, to determine the element's location. Therefore you do not specify a top, right, bottom, or left value when using static positioning.

Janet wants the contents of the Date element to be placed in the upper-right portion of the page. You decide to position it there using absolute positioning, placing it 580 pixels from the left and 0 pixels down from the edge of the display window.

To move the contents of the Date element:

1. Below the style declaration for the Author element in bike.css, insert the following line of code (see Figure 5-20):

```
Date {position: absolute; top: 0; left: 580}
```

Figure 5-20 | **POSITIONING THE DATE ELEMENT**

```
Document {width: 620}
* {display: block}
Author {display: none}
Date {position: absolute; top: 0; left: 580}
FName {display: inline}
Features {width: 300}
Feature {display: list-item; list-style: square inside}
Description {width: 300}
```

2. Save your changes to bike.css.

3. Using your browser, reload **bike.xml** and verify that the Date value was moved to its new location.

TROUBLE? Some older browsers do not support positioning with CSS. If this is the case, your Date will not move from its default location.

Floating an Element

Another way to position an element is to "float" it. When your browser renders a document, the default behavior is to stack block-level elements. **Floating** an element places it alongside the left or right margin of the page, allowing subsequent blocks to flow around it. The style to float an element is:

```
float: margin
```

where *margin* is either left or right. Figure 5-21 shows an example of a block-level element that was resized and is floating on the right margin of the page.

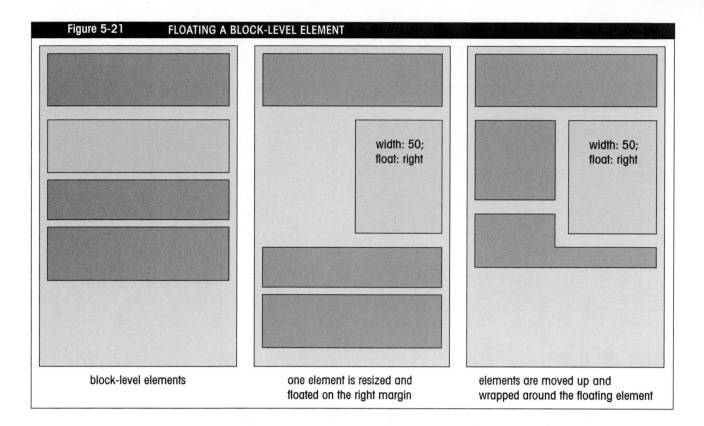

Figure 5-21   FLOATING A BLOCK-LEVEL ELEMENT

width: 50;
float: right

width: 50;
float: right

block-level elements

one element is resized and
floated on the right margin

elements are moved up and
wrapped around the floating element

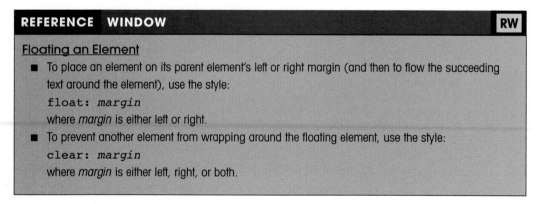

REFERENCE   WINDOW   RW

Floating an Element
- To place an element on its parent element's left or right margin (and then to flow the succeeding text around the element), use the style:

  float: *margin*

  where *margin* is either left or right.
- To prevent another element from wrapping around the floating element, use the style:

  clear: *margin*

  where *margin* is either left, right, or both.

You can prevent an element from wrapping around the floating element by using the style:

clear: *margin*

where *margin* is either left, right, or both. For example, if the value of the clear style is set to "right," the element is not rendered on the page until the right margin is clear of all floating elements. A clear value of "both" requires both margins to be clear. Figure 5-22 illustrates the flow of block-level elements when both the float and clear attributes are used.

Figure 5-22   **USING THE CLEAR ATTRIBUTE**

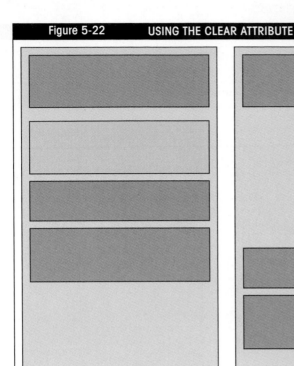

block-level elements

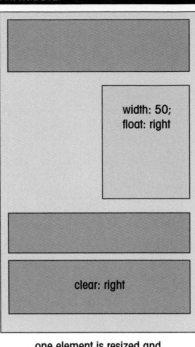

width: 50;
float: right

clear: right

one element is resized and
floated on the right margin

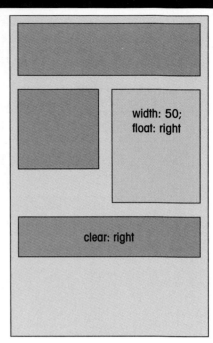

width: 50;
float: right

clear: right

the bottom element does not appear
until the right margin is clear

Janet wants the Description element to float alongside the right margin of the display window. She also wants all succeeding text to flow up to the next bike model in the list, which begins with the Name element. Finally, she wants that element to appear only when the right margin is cleared.

To modify the page layout:

1. Return to **bike.css** in your text editor.

2. Within the style declaration for the Description element, insert the style **float: right**. Be sure to separate this style from the others with a semicolon.

3. At the bottom of the file, insert the style (see Figure 5-23):

   ```
   Name {clear: right}
   ```

Figure 5-23   **FLOATING THE DESCRIPTION ELEMENT**

```
Document {width: 620}
* {display: block}
Author {display: none}
Date {position: absolute; top: 0; left: 580}
FName {display: inline}
Features {width: 300}
Feature {display: list-item; list-style: square inside}
Description {width: 300; float:right}
Name {clear: right}
```

4. Using your text editor, save your changes to bike.css.

5. Reload **bike.xml** in your Web browser. Figure 5-24 shows the revised layout of the file.

Figure 5-24	REVISED LAYOUT OF THE BIKE.XML PAGE

8/17/2004

Tour Nation
Bike Models
City Cruiser 100
- sizes: (L) 16.5", (XL) 18.5", (XXL) 21"
- frame: Prime Aluminum Comfort Specific
- fork: Trek high tensile steel ATB
- wheels: Matrix 550 rims
- tires: Bontrager Comfort, 26x1.95" front and rear
- shifters: SRAM 5.0 Royale
- front derailleur: Lancaster C051
- rear derailleur: SRAM ESP 4.0
- crankset: SunRace FCM36 48/38/28 w/chain guard

City Cruiser 200
- sizes: (L) 16.5", (XL) 18.5", (XXL) 21"
- frame: Prime Aluminum Comfort Specific.
- fork: InSync 178, adjustable preload, 50mm travel
- wheels: Bontrager Corvair rims
- tires: Bontrager Comfort w/Kevlar
- shifters: Lancaster Alivio
- front derailleur: Lancaster Nexave T301

The City Cruiser 100 is designed to give you the perfect blend of comfort and performance, taking away the bumps and bruises of city roads. Our patented aluminum frame process provides a comfortable frame that is light, durable, and shock absorbing. The City Cruiser 100 includes several comfort features, like a suspension seat post, spring saddle, and adjustable high-rise seat stem. The City Cruiser 100 also includes semi-smooth tires that roll on the pavement, giving the rider plenty of traction while soaking up the bumps.

For those looking for a superior city bike at a reasonable price, the City Cruiser 200 is the answer. As with all City Cruiser models the 200 provides unparalleled performance and comfort. Tour Nation's patented aluminum frame is light, durable, and shock absorbing. The City Cruiser 200 provides a wider gear range than other models in this class, giving you just the right gear

TROUBLE? Some older browsers do not support the float style using XML documents. If the description paragraph is not aligned with the page's right margin, this could be the reason.

6. Close your Web browser.

Stacking Elements

The ability to move elements to different locations on the page can lead to overlapping elements. By default, elements that are defined later in the XML document are placed on top of earlier elements. To specify a different stacking order, use the style:

```
z-index: value
```

where *value* is a positive or negative integer, or the value "auto." Elements are stacked based on their z-index value, with the highest z-index values placed on top. A value of "auto" uses the default stacking order. Figure 5-25 shows the effect of the z-index attribute on the stacking of several different elements.

Figure 5-25 **USING THE Z-INDEX ATTRIBUTE**

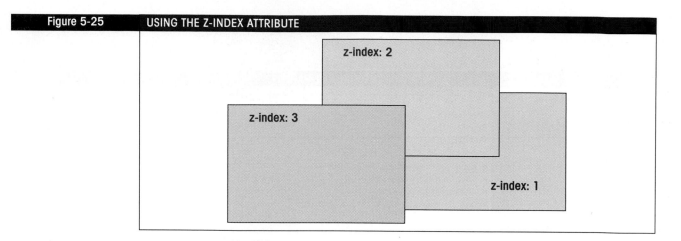

Note that the z-index attribute is applied only when elements share the same parent, but it has no effect on elements with different parents.

At this point, you've finished your work on the page layout. In the next session, you'll learn how to use CSS to modify the appearance of a page by working with fonts, background colors, borders, and margins.

Session 5.1 QUICK CHECK

1. What command would you use in an XML document to attach the document to a style sheet named "styles.css"?

2. What style declaration would you use to apply the color red to the Document element?

3. What selector would you use to select the Model element that is a direct descendant of the Models element?

4. What style declaration would you use to display the CName element as an inline item?

5. What style declaration would you use to display the Notes element as an open-circle bulleted list, with the bullet marker outside of the list text?

6. How would you set the width of the Notes element to 300 pixels?

7. What style would you use to place the Notes element at 10 pixels down and 50 pixels to the right of its parent element?

8. How would you align the Notes element with the left margin of the page?

SESSION 5.2

In this session, you'll learn how to use CSS to format the appearance of block-level elements by modifying the border, margin, and padding space for the block. You'll also learn about styles you can use to modify the appearance of fonts, including font size, color, and alignment. Finally, you'll learn how to use color in your document by creating colored backgrounds and text.

Working with Color

Janet reviewed your work from the last session and she is pleased that you were able to use CSS to control the layout of the page. At this point in the project, she wants you to make the page more readable and interesting by adding some color.

Applying a Font Color

Color can be expressed in CSS by a color name or a color value. Color names are most descriptive and perhaps easier to use, but there are a limited number of color names supported by CSS. The 16 supported color names are shown in Figure 5-26.

| Figure 5-26 | THE 16 BASIC CSS COLOR NAMES |

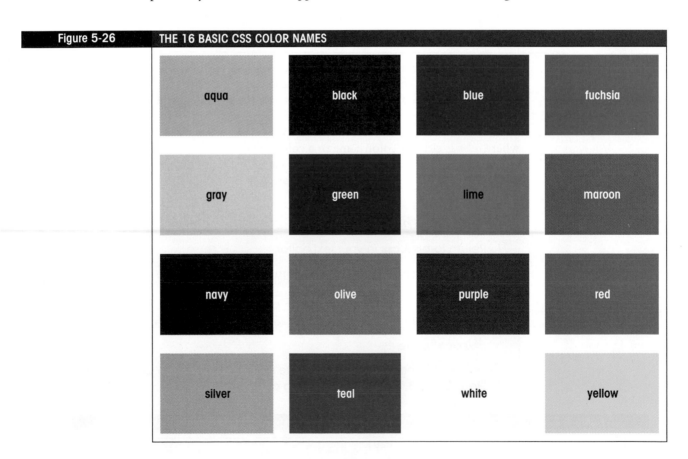

If you want to use a color name not in this list, you could use one of the 142 extended color names supported by Internet Explorer and Netscape. However, please note that these are not part of the CSS standard, and it's possible that users of other browsers will not be able to use those extended color names. You can find the complete list of extended color names at several different sites on the Web.

For a wider range of colors, you can use a color value. CSS expresses color values using the following triplet of numbers:

```
rgb(red, green, blue)
```

where *red*, *green*, and *blue* are numeric values indicating the intensity of the three primary colors: red, green, and blue. The value of each component ranges from 0 (lowest intensity) to 255 (highest intensity). As you would expect, the color red has the color value (255, 0, 0). White, being a mixture of all three primary colors at their highest intensity, has a color value of (255, 255, 255), and black, a mixture of the three primary colors at zero intensity, has a color value of (0, 0, 0). Other colors are mixtures of the three primary colors. For example, the color teal is a mixture of green and blue at moderate intensity and therefore has a color value of (0, 128, 128). Over 16 million colors, more colors than the human eye can distinguish, can be represented by the color value system. If you're not sure of a color's value, you can usually find this information in the color dialog boxes of most graphic design and image editing applications.

Color values can also be expressed as percentages as follows:

```
rgb(red%, green%, blue%)
```

where *red%*, *green%*, and *blue%* specify the percentages of red, green, and blue in the desired color. For example, the color white is defined as (100%, 100%, 100%) and the color teal is defined as (0, 50%, 50%) under this system.

Finally, color values are also often expressed in hexadecimal format as:

```
#rrggbb
```

where *rr*, *gg*, and *bb* are the hexadecimal representations of the color value. The color white, for example, has a hexadecimal representation of #FFFFFF.

To change the font color of an element, use the following style:

```
color: color
```

where *color* is either a color name or a color value.

Janet wants the features list entries for each bike to be blue, but she also wants the name of the feature (sizes, frame, fork, and so forth) to be red. Add these color styles to bike.css.

To change the font color:

1. Return to **bike.css** in your text editor.

2. In the style declaration for the FName element, enter the style:

```
color: red
```

3. In the declaration for the Feature element, enter the style:

```
color: blue
```

Figure 5-27 shows the revised file. Be sure to separate the attributes you add in Steps 2 and 3 from the others using a semicolon.

Figure 5-27	CHANGING THE FONT COLOR

```
Document {width: 620}
* {display: block}
Author {display: none}
Date {position: absolute; top: 0; left: 580}
FName {display: inline; color:red}
Features {width: 300}
Feature {display: list-item; list-style: square inside; color:blue}
Description {width: 300; float:right}
Name {clear: right}
```

4. Save your changes to bike.css.

5. Open **bike.xml** in your Web browser and verify that the feature name appears in red and the feature text appears in blue, as shown in Figure 5-28.

| Figure 5-28 | FEATURES LIST WITH NEW FONT COLORS |

8/17/2004

Tour Nation
Bike Models
City Cruiser 100
- sizes: (L) 16.5", (XL) 18.5", (XXL) 21"
- frame: Prime Aluminum Comfort Specific
- fork: Trek high tensile steel ATB
- wheels: Matrix 550 rims
- tires: Bontrager Comfort, 26x1.95" front and
rear
- shifters: SRAM 5.0 Royale
- front derailleur: Lancaster C051
- rear derailleur: SRAM ESP 4.0
- crankset: SunRace FCM36 48/38/28
w/chain guard
City Cruiser 200
- sizes: (L) 16.5", (XL) 18.5", (XXL) 21"
- frame: Prime Aluminum Comfort Specific.
- fork: InSync 178, adjustable preload, 50mm
travel
- wheels: Bontrager Corvair rims
- tires: Bontrager Comfort w/Kevlar
- shifters: Lancaster Alivio
- front derailleur: Lancaster Nexave T301

The City Cruiser 100 is designed to give you the perfect blend of comfort and performance, taking away the bumps and bruises of city roads. Our patented aluminum frame process provides a comfortable frame that is light, durable, and shock absorbing. The City Cruiser 100 includes several comfort features, like a suspension seat post, spring saddle, and adjustable high-rise seat stem. The City Cruiser 100 also includes semi-smooth tires that roll on the pavement, giving the rider plenty of traction while soaking up the bumps.

For those looking for a superior city bike at a reasonable price, the City Cruiser 200 is the answer. As with all City Cruiser models the 200 provides unparalleled performance and comfort. Tour Nation's patented aluminum frame is light, durable, and shock absorbing. The City Cruiser 200 provides a wider gear range than other models in this class, giving you just the right gear

---

| REFERENCE | WINDOW | RW |

Working with Color
- To set the font color of an element, use the style:

`color: color`

where *color* is either a color name or a color value.
- To set the background color of an element, use the style:

`background-color: color`

Applying a Background Color

The background of an element can also appear in a color using the style:

`background-color: color`

where *color* is either a color name or a color value. Janet wants you to change the background color of the features list to ivory. She also wants the name of each bike to appear as white on a background color with the color value of rgb (192,145, 192).

To add background colors to Janet's document:

1. Return to **bike.css** in your text editor.

2. Add the following style to the Features element:

   ```
   background-color: ivory
   ```

3. Add the following two styles to the Name element (see Figure 5-29):

   ```
   color: white; background-color: rgb(192, 145, 192)
   ```

Figure 5-29	SPECIFYING A BACKGROUND COLOR

```
Document {width: 620}
* {display: block}
Author {display: none}
Date {position: absolute; top: 0; left: 580}
FName {display: inline; color:red}
Features {width: 300; background-color: ivory}
Feature {display: list-item; list-style: square inside; color:blue}
Description {width: 300; float:right}
Name {clear: right; color:white; background-color: rgb(192,145,192)}
```

4. Save your changes to bike.css.

5. Refresh bike.xml in your Web browser. Figure 5-30 shows the revised format of the page.

Figure 5-30	BACKGROUND COLORS ON THE BIKE.XML PAGE

8/17/2004

Tour Nation
Bike Models

City Cruiser 100

- sizes: (L) 16.5", (XL) 18.5", (XXL) 21"
- frame: Prime Aluminum Comfort Specific
- fork: Trek high tensile steel ATB
- wheels: Matrix 550 rims
- tires: Bontrager Comfort, 26x1.95" front and rear
- shifters: SRAM 5.0 Royale
- front derailleur: Lancaster C051
- rear derailleur: SRAM ESP 4.0
- crankset: SunRace FCM36 48/38/28 w/chain guard

The City Cruiser 100 is designed to give you the perfect blend of comfort and performance, taking away the bumps and bruises of city roads. Our patented aluminum frame process provides a comfortable frame that is light, durable, and shock absorbing. The City Cruiser 100 includes several comfort features, like a suspension seat post, spring saddle, and adjustable high-rise seat stem. The City Cruiser 100 also includes semi-smooth tires that roll on the pavement, giving the rider plenty of traction while soaking up the bumps.

City Cruiser 200

- sizes: (L) 16.5", (XL) 18.5", (XXL) 21"
- frame: Prime Aluminum Comfort Specific.
- fork: InSync 178, adjustable preload, 50mm travel
- wheels: Bontrager Corvair rims
- tires: Bontrager Comfort w/Kevlar
- shifters: Lancaster Alivio
- front derailleur: Lancaster Nexave T301

For those looking for a superior city bike at a reasonable price, the City Cruiser 200 is the answer. As with all City Cruiser models the 200 provides unparalleled performance and comfort. Tour Nation's patented aluminum frame is light, durable, and shock absorbing. The City Cruiser 200 provides a wider gear range than other models in this class, giving you just the right gear

Janet likes the background colors you added to the document. To enhance the document further, she wants to see more space between information on the different bike models. To add this space, you'll work with some additional attributes of block-level elements.

Working with Borders, Margins, and Padding

Each block-level element is composed of four parts (see Figure 5-31):

- the **margin** between the box and other elements
- the **border** of the box
- the **padding** between the element's content and the border
- the **element content**

Figure 5-31	PARTS OF A BLOCK-LEVEL ELEMENT

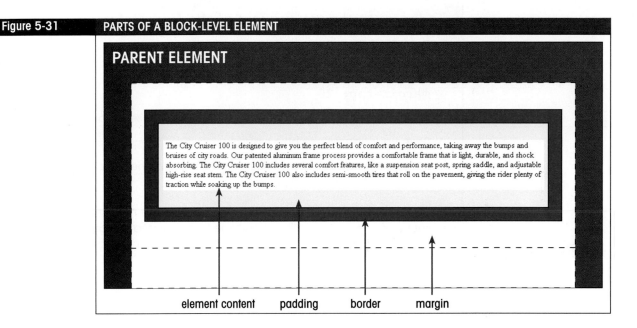

Janet wants you to increase the size of the Name element's top margin in order to offset one bike model from another on the Web page.

Working with Margins

CSS supports four attributes that can be used to control the size of the margin of a block-level element. These attributes are:

```
margin-top: value
margin-right: value
margin-bottom: value
margin-left: value
```

where *value* is the size of the margin expressed in absolute units, or as a percentage of the width of the parent element. You can also use the value "auto," which instructs the browser to determine the margin size. For example, to create margins of 10 pixels on each side and 5 pixels above and below the Title element, use the following style:

```
Title {margin-top: 5; margin-right: 10; margin-bottom:
5; margin-left: 10}
```

Margin sizes can also be negative to crowd or overlap elements on a page.
The four margin attributes can be combined into a single attribute with the style:

```
margin: top right bottom left
```

where *top*, *right*, *bottom*, and *left* are the sizes of the corresponding margins. If you include only three values in the combined attribute, they are applied in the following order: top, right, bottom, and the browser matches the size of the left and right margins. If only two values are specified, they are applied to the top and right margins, and the bottom and left margins match those two values. If only one value is entered, the browser applies that size to all four margins.

Janet suggests that you increase the size of the Name element's top margin to 20 pixels to provide more space between models and increase the readability of the page.

To increase the top margin of the Name element:

1. Return to **bike.css** in your text editor.

2. Add the following style to the Name element:

   ```
   margin-top: 20
   ```

3. Be sure to separate this style from the others by a semicolon.

4. Save your changes to bike.css.

5. Refresh **bike.xml** in your browser and verify that the space between bike models was increased by 20 pixels.

   TROUBLE? Some older browsers do not support the margin attribute for XML elements. You may not notice a change in the separation between bike models.

Working with Borders

You can create a border around any element, and define the thickness, color, and style for a border. Styles can be applied to individual borders, or all four borders at once. Figure 5-32 describes the various CSS border attributes.

Figure 5-32	BORDER ATTRIBUTES	
ATTRIBUTE	**DESCRIPTION**	**NOTES**
border-top-width: *value* border-right-width: *value* border-bottom-width: *value* border-left-width: *value* border-width: *top right bottom left*	Width of the top border Width of the right border Width of the bottom border Width of the left border Width of any or all of the borders	Where *value* is the size of the border in absolute units, as a percentage of the width of the parent element, or defined with the keywords: "thin," "medium," or "thick"
border-top-color: *color* border-right-color: *color* border-bottom-color: *color* border-left-color: *color* border-color: *top right bottom left*	Color of the top border Color of the right border Color of the bottom border Color of the left border Color of any or all of the borders	Where *color* is a color name or a color value
border-top-style: *style* border-right-style: *style* border-bottom-style: *style* border-left-style: *style* border-style: *top right bottom left*	Style of the top border Style of the right border Style of the bottom border Style of the left border Style of any or all of the borders	Where *style* is one of the nine defined border styles

Border widths can be expressed using units of length, or with the keywords "thin," "medium," or "thick." The border color is defined using a color name or value. As for the border style, CSS supports the nine different styles described in Figure 5-33.

| Figure 5-33 | BORDER STYLES |

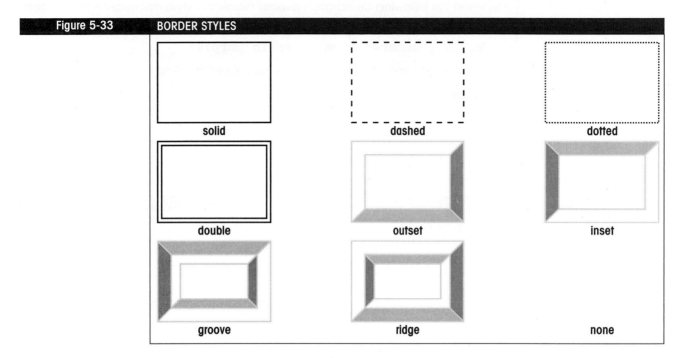

For example, to place a double border around a block-level element, use the style:

```
border-style: double
```

All of the border attributes can be combined into a single-style declaration using the style:

```
border: width style color
```

To create a 5-point blue dotted border, use the style declaration:

```
border-width: 5pt; border-style: dotted; border-color:blue
```

or

```
border: 5pt dotted blue
```

To work with individual borders, identify which border you want to format using the styles:

```
border-top: width style color
border-right: width style color
border-bottom: width style color
border-left: width style color
```

As you can see, there are several methods of formatting the border for a block element. However, browser support for all of the different methods is inconsistent across browsers and browser versions. As always, be sure that the styles you use are supported by the browsers your audience is likely to use.

Janet wants you to add the following borders to her document:

- A 2-pixel solid purple border under the Title element
- A 1-pixel solid black border under the Name element
- A 1-pixel solid black border around the Features element

To add these borders to the document:

1. Return to **bike.css** in your text editor.

2. Insert the following declaration directly below the style declaration for the Date element:

   ```
   Title {border-bottom: 2 solid purple}
   ```

3. In the Features element style declaration, insert the style:

   ```
   border: 1 solid black
   ```

4. In the Name element, insert the style:

   ```
   border-bottom: 1 solid black
   ```

   Figure 5-34 shows the revised file.

Figure 5-34   ADDING BORDER STYLES

```
Document {width: 620}
* {display: block}
Author {display: none}
Date {position: absolute; top: 0; left: 580}
Title {border-bottom: 2 solid purple}
FName {display: inline; color:red}
Features {width: 300; background-color: ivory; border: 1 solid black}
Feature {display: list-item; list-style: square inside; color:blue}
Description {width: 300; float:right}
Name {clear: right; color:white; background-color: rgb(192,145,192); margin-top:20;
      border-bottom:1 solid black}
```

5. Using your text editor, save your changes to bike.css.

6. Refresh **bike.xml** in your browser. Figure 5-35 shows the page with the new borders.

Figure 5-35   BORDERS AROUND THE BIKE.XML ELEMENTS

	8/17/2004

Tour Nation
Bike Models

City Cruiser 100

- sizes: (L) 16.5", (XL) 18.5", (XXL) 21"
- frame: Prime Aluminum Comfort Specific
- fork: Trek high tensile steel ATB
- wheels: Matrix 550 rims
- tires: Bontrager Comfort, 26x1.95" front and rear
- shifters: SRAM 5.0 Royale
- front derailleur: Lancaster C051
- rear derailleur: SRAM ESP 4.0
- crankset: SunRace FCM36 48/38/28 w/chain guard

The City Cruiser 100 is designed to give you the perfect blend of comfort and performance, taking away the bumps and bruises of city roads. Our patented aluminum frame process provides a comfortable frame that is light, durable, and shock absorbing. The City Cruiser 100 includes several comfort features, like a suspension seat post, spring saddle, and adjustable high-rise seat stem. The City Cruiser 100 also includes semi-smooth tires that roll on the pavement, giving the rider plenty of traction while soaking up the bumps.

City Cruiser 200

- sizes: (L) 16.5", (XL) 18.5", (XXL) 21"
- frame: Prime Aluminum Comfort Specific.
- fork: InSync 178, adjustable preload, 50mm travel
- wheels: Bontrager Corvair rims

For those looking for a superior city bike at a reasonable price, the City Cruiser 200 is the answer. As with all City Cruiser models the 200 provides unparalleled performance and comfort. Tour Nation's patented aluminum frame is light,

Janet likes the effect of adding borders to the different elements on the page, but feels that some of the text is too close to the borders, making the text difficult to read. She wants you to correct this situation.

Working with Padding

To increase the space between the element content and the border, you increase the size of the padding for the block. This is done using any of the following styles:

```
padding-top: value
padding-right: value
padding-bottom: value
padding-left: value
padding: top right bottom left
```

where the padding values can be expressed in absolute units, or as a percentage of the width of the block-level element. As with the combined margin style discussed earlier, you can enter less than four of the *top right bottom left* values, and the browser matches the opposite sides. For example, to set the padding of all sides to 5 millimeters, use the style:

```
padding: 5mm
```

You decide to increase the padding around the features list to 5 pixels, and the left padding space in the Name element to 10 pixels.

To add padding to Janet's document:

1. Return to **bike.css** in your text editor.

2. Add the following style to the Features element:

   ```
   padding: 5
   ```

3. Be sure to separate this style from the others with a semicolon.

4. Add the following style to the Name element:

   ```
   padding-left: 10
   ```

5. Using your text editor, save your changes to bike.css.

6. Refresh **bike.xml** in your browser and verify that the padding space was increased for both the Features and Name elements.

   TROUBLE? In some older browsers, you will not see a change in the padding space.

You've completed much of the work on the page layout for Janet. Next you'll turn your attention to formatting the content for each element.

Setting Font and Text Attributes

Browsers apply a set of default text styles to the content of XML elements. In Janet's case, the text is displayed in a 12-point Times New Roman font. She wants you to apply different fonts and font sizes to her text to make the page more readable and interesting.

Using Font Families

To change the font of an element, use the style:

```
font-family: fonts
```

where *fonts* is a list of possible fonts, separated by commas. CSS works with two types of fonts: specific and generic. A **specific font** is one that is installed on the user's computer, such as Times New Roman, Arial, or Helvetica. A **generic font** is a general description of the font, allowing the operating system to determine which installed font best matches the description. CSS supports five generic fonts: serif, sans-serif, monospace, cursive, and fantasy. Figure 5-36 shows examples of each generic font. Note that for each type, there can be a wide range of possible fonts.

Figure 5-36 **GENERIC FONTS**

Generic Names	Font Samples		
serif	defg	defg	defg
sans-serif	defg	defg	defg
monospace	defg	defg	defg
cursive	*defg*	*defg*	*defg*
fantasy	**DEFG**	**DEFG**	**defg**

with each generic font there can be a wide range of appearances

REFERENCE WINDOW **RW**

Choosing a Font Family

■ To select a font for an element, use the style:

```
font-family: font_name1, font-name2, ...
```

where *font_name1, font_name2,* and so forth are specific or generic font names. The browser attempts to use the first font name. If that fails, it goes to the second font on the list, and so forth. A generic font name must be either serif, sans-serif, monospace, cursive, or fantasy.

One issue with generic fonts is that you cannot be sure which specific font the Web browser uses to display your text. Generally speaking, it's a good idea to use specific fonts because it gives you a more accurate idea of what your audience sees. To do this effectively, you can provide the Web browser with a choice of several fonts. Browsers that don't have access to the font you specified as your first choice may have your second or third choices available. As a backup, specify a generic font as your last choice. For example, the following style provides the browser with a list of sans-serif fonts to use with the Title element.

```
Title {font-family: Arial, Helvetica, sans-serif}
```

The browser first attempts to display the Title element in an Arial font; if that is not available, it tries Helvetica; and finally, if a specific font is not found, it uses whatever generic sans-serif font is available. Janet wants you to specify the use of a sans-serif font for the following elements: Title, Subtitle, Name, and Features.

To apply the font-family style:

1. Return to the **bike.css** file in your text editor.

2. Insert the following style in the declaration for the Title element:

```
font-family: Arial, Helvetica, sans-serif
```

3. Insert the following style declaration directly below the Title element:

```
Subtitle {font-family: Arial, Helvetica, sans-serif}
```

4. Insert the following style within the declaration for the Features element and the Name element:

```
font-family: Arial, Helvetica, sans-serif
```

5. Figure 5-37 shows the revised bike.css file.

Figure 5-37	SPECIFYING THE FONT-FAMILY STYLE

```
Document {width: 620}
* {display: block}
Author {display: none}
Date {position: absolute; top: 0; left: 580}
Title {border-bottom: 2 solid purple; font-family: Arial, Helvetica, sans-serif}
Subtitle {font-family: Arial, Helvetica, sans-serif}
FName {display: inline; color:red}
Features {width: 300; background-color: ivory; border: 1 solid black; padding: 5;
         font-family: Arial, Helvetica, sans-serif}
Feature {display: list-item; list-style: square inside; color:blue}
Description {width: 300; float:right}
Name {clear: right; color:white; background-color: rgb(192,145,192); margin-top:20;
       border-bottom:1 solid black; padding-left: 10; font-family: Arial, Helvetica, sans-serif}
```

6. Using your text editor, save your changes to bike.css.

7. Refresh **bike.xml** in your browser. Figure 5-38 shows the revised file with sans-serif fonts.

Figure 5-38	SANS-SERIF FONTS ON THE BIKE.XML PAGE

8/17/2004

Tour Nation
Bike Models

City Cruiser 100

- sizes: (L) 16.5", (XL) 18.5", (XXL) 21"
- frame: Prime Aluminum Comfort Specific
- fork: Trek high tensile steel ATB
- wheels: Matrix 550 rims
- tires: Bontrager Comfort, 26x1.95" front and rear
- shifters: SRAM 5.0 Royale
- front derailleur: Lancaster C051
- rear derailleur: SRAM ESP 4.0
- crankset: SunRace FCM36 48/38/28 w/chain guard

The City Cruiser 100 is designed to give you the perfect blend of comfort and performance, taking away the bumps and bruises of city roads. Our patented aluminum frame process provides a comfortable frame that is light, durable, and shock absorbing. The City Cruiser 100 includes several comfort features, like a suspension seat post, spring saddle, and adjustable high-rise seat stem. The City Cruiser 100 also includes semi-smooth tires that roll on the pavement, giving the rider plenty of traction while soaking up the bumps.

City Cruiser 200

- sizes: (L) 16.5", (XL) 18.5", (XXL) 21"
- frame: Prime Aluminum Comfort Specific.
- fork: InSync 178, adjustable preload,

For those looking for a superior city bike at a reasonable price, the City Cruiser 200 is the answer. As with all City Cruiser models the 200 provides unparalleled performance and comfort.

Note that an element inherits the font family of its parent. For example, the Feature element is a child of the Features element in bike.xml and it uses the same font family, unless the style sheet specifies otherwise.

Managing Font Sizes

The next task Janet wants you to take on is to change the font size of some of the elements on the page. The style for setting font size is:

```
font-size: value
```

where *value* is the size of the font. Font sizes can be expressed as:

- a unit of length
- a keyword description
- a percentage of the size of the element
- a size relative to the default font size of the element

If you choose to express the font size as a unit of length, you can use an absolute unit such as millimeters (mm), centimeters (cm), points (pt), and so forth, or you can use a relative unit. A **relative unit** is one that expresses the font size relative to the size of a standard character. CSS recognizes two standard characters with which it defines relative units: em and ex. The **em unit** is equal to the width of the capital letter "M" in the browser's default font size. The **ex unit** is equal to the height of the small "x" in the default font (see Figure 5-39).

Figure 5-39   THE EM AND EX UNITS

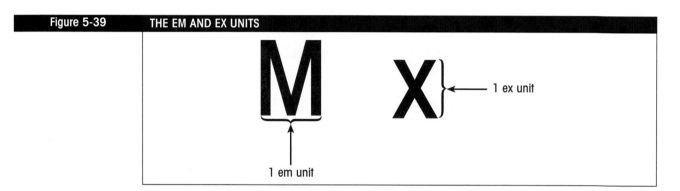

REFERENCE WINDOW   **RW**

Setting the Font Size
- To specify the font size of an element, use the style:
  ```
  font-size: value
  ```
  where *value* can either be a unit of length (specified as mm, cm, in, pt, pc, em, or ex), a keyword (xx-small, x-small, small, medium, large, x-large, xx-large), a percentage of the font size of the parent element, or a keyword describing the size relative to the font size of the parent element (larger or smaller).

Of these two units, the em unit is more useful for page design because 1 em is equal to the default font size for the browser. This is true no matter what font is used, whereas with the ex unit, the size changes depending on the font in use. For example, to set the size of the Title font at twice the "normal" size, use the style:

```
Title {font-size: 2em}
```

The default unit of measurement is pixel. Therefore a style of:

```
Title {font-size: 16}
```

assigns a font 16 pixels in height to the Title element.

If you would rather not use measurement units, you can use one of seven descriptive keywords: xx-small, x-small, small, medium, large, x-large, and xx-large. The exact meaning of these keywords depends on the browser in use, but the default font size is usually medium.

If you want the font size to be expressed relative to the size of the parent element, you can do so using percentages. In the following set of style declarations, in which the Title element is a child of the Document element, the font size of the Title element is increased by 150%, resulting in an 18-point font.

```
Document {font-size: 12pt}
Title {font-size: 150%}
```

Finally, you can use the keywords "larger" and "smaller" to relate the font size of the element to the font size of the parent element. For example, in the following style declarations, the font size of the Title element is made larger than the font size for the Document element. The exact difference in the font size is left to the browser to determine.

```
Document {font-size: 12pt}
Title {font-size: larger}
```

After reviewing this material with Janet, she decides to set the default font size of the document to 12 points, and to set the following font sizes for the Date, Title, Subtitle, Name, and Features elements:

- Date: 8pt
- Title: 32pt
- Subtitle: 14pt
- Name: 14pt
- Features: 8pt

To apply these font sizes to Janet's document:

1. Return to **bike.css** in your text editor.

2. Add the following style to the declaration for the Document element:

```
font-size: 12pt
```

3. To the style declaration for the Date element, add the style:

```
font-size: 8pt
```

4. Use the same style to set the font size of the Title element to 32 points, the Subtitle and Name elements to 14 points, and the Features element to 8 points. Figure 5-40 shows the revised file.

Figure 5-40   **SETTING FONT SIZES**

```
Document {width: 620; font-size: 12pt}
* {display: block}
Author {display: none}
Date {position: absolute; top: 0; left: 580; font-size: 8pt}
Title {border-bottom: 2 solid purple; font-family: Arial, Helvetica, sans-serif;
        font-size: 32pt}
Subtitle {font-family: Arial, Helvetica, sans-serif; font-size: 14pt}
FName {display: inline; color:red}
Features {width: 300; background-color: ivory; border: 1 solid black; padding: 5;
        font-family: Arial, Helvetica, sans-serif; font-size: 8pt}
Feature {display: list-item; list-style: square inside; color:blue}
Description {width: 300; float:right}
Name {clear: right; color:white; background-color: rgb(192,145,192); margin-top:20;
        border-bottom:1 solid black; padding-left: 10; font-family: Arial, Helvetica, sans-serif;
        font-size: 14pt}
```

5. Using your text editor, save your changes to bike.css and refresh **bike.xml** in your browser. Figure 5-41 shows the new look for Janet's page.

Figure 5-41   **THE BIKE.XML DOCUMENT WITH NEW FONT SIZES**

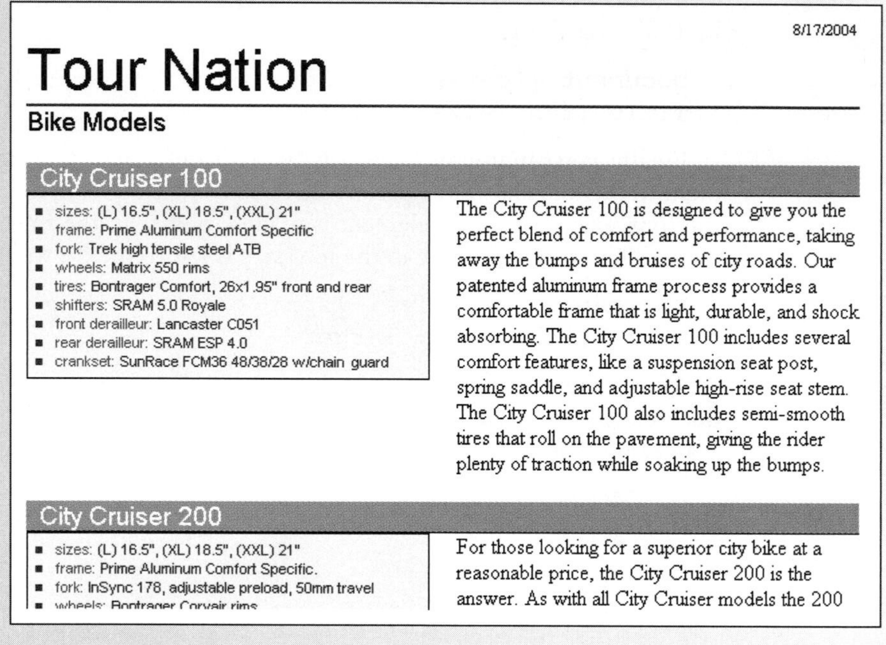

Note that because the Document element is the root element of bike.xml, setting the font size to 12 points forces all elements in the file to be 12 points, unless otherwise specified.

Controlling Word, Letter, and Line Spacing

You can also use CSS to control the spacing between letters, words, and lines of text. The styles to control letter and word spacing are:

```
letter-spacing: value
word-spacing: value
```

where *value* is the size of the space, and uses the same measurement units used to define font sizes. The letter-spacing attribute controls the amount of space between letters, or **kerning**. Changing the kerning allows you to create interesting typographical effects, and make precise typographical edits to enhance the look of your Web pages.

The word-spacing attribute controls the space between words, or **tracking**. Tracking does not have any effect on the letters within those words.

Finally, CSS supports the line-height attribute to control the amount of space between lines of text, or **leading**. The style is:

```
line-height: value
```

where *value* is either a specific length, a percentage of the font size, or a number representing the ratio of the line height to the font size. The standard ratio is 1.2, which means that the line height is typically 1.2 times the font size. If Janet wanted the text of the Description element to be double spaced, she would use the following style:

```
Description {line-height: 2}
```

A common technique is to create titles with large fonts and small line sizes in order to give the title more impact. Figure 5-42 shows how modifying the line height can change the appearance of a title.

| Figure 5-42 | TITLES WITH LARGE FONT SIZES AND VARYING LINE HEIGHTS |

Tour Nation
normal line height

Tour Nation
line height < font size

Setting Font Styles and Weights

Janet wants the subtitle of the document to be italic. To change the font style used by an element, apply the style:

```
font-style: type
```

where *type* is normal, italic, or oblique. The italic and oblique styles are similar in appearance, though there are subtle differences depending on the font.

To add italic to the subtitle:

1. Return to **bike.css** in your text editor.

2. Add the following style to the Subtitle element:

   `font-style: italic`

3. Be sure to separate this style from the others using a semicolon.

REFERENCE WINDOW   **RW**

Controlling Font Style and Weight
- To specify an appearance for an element's font, use the style:

  `font-style: type`

  where *type* is either normal, italic, or oblique.
- To specify the font's weight, use the style:

  `font-weight: value`

  where *value* is either a number ranging from 100 (lightest) to 900 (heaviest) in intervals of 100, a keyword describing the font's weight (normal or bold), or a keyword that describes the weight relative to the weight of the parent element's font (lighter or bolder).

Janet also wants the Title and Name elements to appear in a bold-faced font. To make text bold, use the style:

`font-weight: weight`

where *weight* is the level of bold formatting applied to the font. Font weights can be expressed as a value that ranges from 100 to 900, in increments of 100. While this is good in theory, most fonts do not support nine different font weights. For practical purposes, assume that a weight of 400 displays normal text, 700 displays bold text, and 900 displays "extra" bold text.

You can use the keywords "normal" and "bold" in place of a weight value, or you can express the font weight relative to the parent element by using the keywords "bolder" or "lighter."

To apply bold formatting to text in Janet's document:

1. Add the following style to the Title and Name elements:

   `font-weight: bold`

   Figure 5-43 shows the changes to the document.

Figure 5-43   **APPLYING ITALIC AND BOLD FORMATTING TO BIKE.XML**

```
Document {width: 620; font-size: 12pt}
* {display: block}
Author {display: none}
Date {position: absolute; top: 0; left: 580; font-size: 8pt}
Title {border-bottom: 2 solid purple; font-family: Arial, Helvetica, sans-serif;
       font-size: 32pt; font-weight:bold}
Subtitle {font-family: Arial, Helvetica, sans-serif; font-size: 14pt; font-style: italic}
FName {display: inline; color:red}
Features {width: 300; background-color: ivory; border: 1 solid black; padding: 5;
          font-family: Arial, Helvetica, sans-serif; font-size: 8pt}
Feature {display: list-item; list-style: square inside; color:blue}
Description {width: 300; float:right}
Name {clear: right; color:white; background-color: rgb(192,145,192); margin-top:20;
      border-bottom:1 solid black; padding-left: 10; font-family: Arial, Helvetica, sans-serif;
      font-size: 14pt; font-weight:bold}
```

2. Using your text editor, save your changes to bike.css.

3. Refresh **bike.xml** in your browser and verify that the italic and bold formatting were applied to the elements in the document.

Aligning Text Horizontally and Vertically

After examining the page you created, Janet decides that the title and subtitle would look better and have more impact if centered on the page. In addition, she wants to see the description for each bicycle justified to the left and right margins of the containing block.

To modify the horizontal alignment for text of an element, use the style:

`text-align: alignment`

where *alignment* is left, center, right, or justify. The default alignment is "left."

To align the text in Janet's document:

1. Return to **bike.css** in your text editor.

2. For the Title and Subtitle style declarations, add the style:

`text-align: center`

3. Add the following style to the Description style declaration:

`text-align: justify`

4. Save your changes to bike.css.

5. Refresh **bike.xml** in your Web browser. Figure 5-44 shows the current status of this page.

Figure 5-44   **APPLYING FULL JUSTIFICATION TO BIKE.XML**

8/17/2004

Tour Nation

Bike Models

full justification

City Cruiser 100

- sizes: (L) 16.5", (XL) 18.5", (XXL) 21"
- frame: Prime Aluminum Comfort Specific
- fork: Trek high tensile steel ATB
- wheels: Matrix 550 rims
- tires: Bontrager Comfort, 26x1.95" front and rear
- shifters: SRAM 5.0 Royale
- front derailleur: Lancaster C051
- rear derailleur: SRAM ESP 4.0
- crankset: SunRace FCM36 48/38/28 w/chain guard

The City Cruiser 100 is designed to give you the perfect blend of comfort and performance, taking away the bumps and bruises of city roads. Our patented aluminum frame process provides a comfortable frame that is light, durable, and shock absorbing. The City Cruiser 100 includes several comfort features, like a suspension seat post, spring saddle, and adjustable high-rise seat stem. The City Cruiser 100 also includes semi-smooth tires that roll on the pavement, giving the rider plenty of traction while soaking up the bumps.

City Cruiser 200

- sizes: (L) 16.5", (XL) 18.5", (XXL) 21"
- frame: Prime Aluminum Comfort Specific.
- fork: InSync 178, adjustable preload, 50mm travel
- wheels: Bontrager Corvair rims

For those looking for a superior city bike at a reasonable price, the City Cruiser 200 is the answer. As with all City Cruiser models the 200

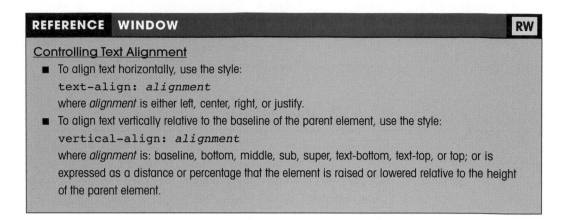

For inline elements, CSS allows you to vertically align the text of an element with the text of the parent element. The style for controlling vertical alignment for the text of an element is:

```
vertical-align: alignment
```

where *alignment* has one of the style keyword values described in Figure 5-45.

Figure 5-45	VERTICAL-ALIGN VALUES
STYLE	**DESCRIPTION**
vertical-align: baseline	Aligns the element with the baseline
vertical-align: bottom	Aligns the bottom of the element with the bottom of the lowest element (text or image) in the line
vertical-align: middle	Aligns the element with the middle of the text
vertical-align: sub	Aligns the element as a subscript
vertical-align: super	Aligns the element as a superscript
vertical-align: text-bottom	Aligns the element with the bottom of the font
vertical-align: text-top	Aligns the element with the top of the tallest letter
vertical-align: top	Aligns the element with the top of the tallest element (text or image) in the line

Instead of using keywords, you can enter a distance or percentage that an element is raised relative to the surrounding text. A positive value or percentage raises the element above the surrounding text, and a negative value lowers the element. For example, the style:

```
vertical-align: 50%
```

raises the element by half of the line height of the parent element, while the style:

```
vertical-align: -50%
```

lowers the element half of the line height.

Indenting Text

CSS allows you to indent the first line of a paragraph. The style for creating an indentation is:

```
text-indent: value
```

where *value* is the size of the indentation in either absolute or relative units, or as a percentage of the width of the element. For example, an indentation value of 5% indents the first line by 5% of the width of the element. Additionally, the length and percentage values can be negative, extending the first line to the left of the paragraph to create a **hanging indent**.

REFERENCE WINDOW   **RW**

Formatting Your Text with Special Attributes
- To decorate the element's text, use the style:
  ```
  text-decoration: type
  ```
  where *type* is: blink, line-through, overline, underline, or none.
- To change the case of the text font, use:
  ```
  text-transform: type
  ```
  where *type* is: capitalize, lowercase, uppercase, or none.
- To display a variant of the font's original appearance, use:
  ```
  font-variant: type
  ```
  where *type* is either small-caps or none.

Working with Special Text Attributes

CSS provides three attributes that can be used to apply special effects to your text. To add a line to your text, use the style:

```
text-decoration: type
```

where *type* equals none, underline, overline, or line-through (see Figure 5-46). Note that child elements do not inherit the value of the text-decoration attribute from their parent element.

Figure 5-46   **VALUES OF THE TEXT-DECORATION STYLE**

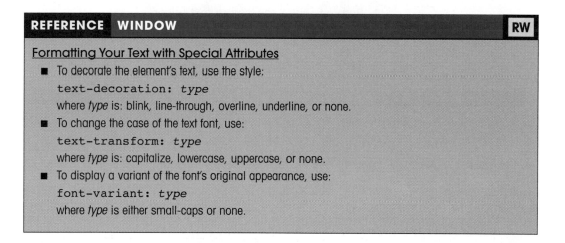

To change the case of the text in an element, use the style:

```
text-transform: case
```

where *case* equals capitalize to capitalize the first letter of each word, uppercase to capitalize all letters in a word, lowercase to display all letters of a word in lowercase, or none to make no changes to the text.

Finally, you can display the element in small capital letters using the style:

```
font-variant: small-caps
```

The values of the text-transform and the font-variant styles are passed from the parent element to the child elements.

Janet wants to see the contents of the FName element appear in small capital letters. Add this style to her style sheet.

To use the font-variant style for Janet's document:

1. Return to **bike.css** in your text editor.

2. Add the following style to the declaration for the FName element (see Figure 5-47):

   ```
   font-variant: small-caps
   ```

Figure 5-47	ADDING THE FONT-VARIANT STYLE

```
Document {width: 620; font-size: 12pt}
* {display: block}
Author {display: none}
Date {position: absolute; top: 0; left: 580; font-size: 8pt}
Title {border-bottom: 2 solid purple; font-family: Arial, Helvetica, sans-serif;
      font-size: 32pt; font-weight:bold; text-align: center}
Subtitle {font-family: Arial, Helvetica, sans-serif; font-size: 14pt; font-style: italic;
      text-align:center}
FName {display: inline; color:red; font-variant: small-caps}
Features {width: 300; background-color: ivory; border: 1 solid black; padding: 5;
      font-family: Arial, Helvetica, sans-serif; font-size: 8pt}
Feature {display: list-item; list-style: square inside; color:blue}
Description {width: 300; float:right; text-align: justify}
Name {clear: right; color:white; background-color: rgb(192,145,192); margin-top:20;
      border-bottom:1 solid black; padding-left: 10; font-family: Arial, Helvetica, sans-serif;
      font-size: 14pt; font-weight:bold}
```

3. Save your changes to **bike.css** and exit from your text editor.

4. Refresh **bike.xml** in your browser. Figure 5-48 shows the current state of the page.

Figure 5-48	DISPLAYING SMALL CAPS

small caps

5. Close your browser.

Using the Font Attribute

You can combine many of the text and font attributes discussed here into a single style as follows:

```
font: font-style font-weight font-variant font-size/
line-height font-family
```

where *font-style*, *font-weight*, and so forth are the values for the font and text style attributes. The font style provides an efficient way to define multiple attributes. For example, the following style declarations demonstrate two distinctly different approaches that yield the same results:

```
Title {font-style: italic; font-variant: small-caps;
       font-weight: bold; font-size: 3em; line-height: 0.8em;
       font-family: Times Roman}

Title {font: italic bold small-caps 3em/0.8em Times Roman}
```

The font attribute requires that you specify the font size, font weight, and font variant (in that order), while the order attributes are optional. You can only set the line height value if you've also set the font size.

At this point, you've completed your work with the layout for Janet's page. In the next session, you'll learn how to display and format images.

Session 5.2 QUICK CHECK

1. What style would you use to change the background color of the Summary element to the color value (255, 192, 255)?

2. What style would you use to set the left and right margins for an element to 3 inches?

3. What style would you use to define a dashed red border that is 5 pixels wide for the Summary element?

4. How would you increase the padding for the Summary element to 10 pixels?

5. What is the difference between a specific font and a generic font?

6. What is a relative unit? What are the two relative units supported by CSS? Which is recommended for use with Web pages and why?

7. How would you display the Summary element in a boldface Arial font?

8. How would you set the kerning of the Summary element to 0.4 points?

SESSION 5.3

In this session, you'll learn how to display images in your document using the back-ground-image style. You'll also learn how CSS can be used to select an image file, place the image within the element, and control how the image is tiled across the element space. You'll also learn how to work with the id and class attributes, and how to use these attributes to associate specific images for an element. Finally, you'll learn how to use namespaces to insert HTML tags directly into an XML document to provide even more control over your document's appearance.

Adding Background Images

The only tasks remaining from Janet's list are to add the company logo and images of all the bike models to the page. The challenge that Janet faces is that there is no way, using only CSS, to add an image to an XML document. However, you can "trick" the browser into associating an image with an element by creating a background image. The background image is specified only in the style sheet, but it appears in the browser when the XML document is opened.

Almost any element can appear with a background image, and there are four properties that can be set with a background image:

- the source of the image file
- where the image is placed in the background of the element
- how the image is repeated across the background of the element
- whether the image scrolls with the display window

To apply a background image, use the style:

```
background-image: url(URL)
```

where *URL* is the location and name of the image file. By default, background images are tiled both horizontally and vertically until they occupy the entire element space. You can control how the browser tiles the image using the style:

```
background-repeat: type
```

where *type* equals repeat, repeat-x, repeat-y, or no-repeat. A default value of "repeat" tiles the image both horizontally and vertically. The values "repeat-x" or "repeat-y" tile the image horizontally or vertically, respectively. A value of "no-repeat" displays the image once with no tiling.

Background images are placed in the upper-left corner of the element space by default, and then repeated from there, if tiling is in effect. You can place the background image in a different location using the style:

```
background-position: horizontal_postion vertical_position
```

where *horizontal_position* and *vertical_position* are the horizontal and vertical coordinates of the upper-left corner of the image. Placing a background image operates the same way as placing a block-level element inside of its parent. For example, the style:

```
background-position: 30 50
```

places the image 30 pixels to the right and 50 pixels down from the upper-left corner of the element space. If you specify one value, the browser applies it to both the horizontal and vertical coordinates.

For a more general description of the image position, you can use a combination of six keywords: left, center, right (for the horizontal position); and top, center, bottom (for the vertical position). You can also define the position of the image as a percentage of the width and height of the element. For example, the style:

```
background-position: 50% 50%
```

places the background image at the center of the element.

By default, background images move with the element as the page scrolls through the browser display window. You can change this behavior using the style:

```
background-attachment: attach
```

where *attach* is either "scroll" (the default)—to scroll the image with the page, or "fixed"—to place the image at a fixed location in the display window. Fixed background images are often used to create the illusion of a **watermark**, a translucent graphic impressed into the very fabric of the paper, often used in specialized stationary.

REFERENCE WINDOW | **RW**

Using a Background Image

- To add a background image to an element, use the style:
  ```
  background-image: url(URL)
  ```
  where *URL* is the location and filename of a graphic file to be used as the background image.
- To control how the image is tiled over the element's background, use the style:
  ```
  background-repeat: type
  ```
  where *type* is either repeat, repeat-x, repeat-y, or none.
- To place the image in a specific location in the element's background, use:
  ```
  background-position: horizontal vertical
  ```
  where *horizontal* and *vertical* are coordinates that can be expressed as the horizontal and vertical distance from the upper-left corner of the background, using either length, percentages, or one of the following keywords: top, center, bottom, right, or left.
- To specify whether the image scrolls with the background, use:
  ```
  background-attachment: type
  ```
  where *type* is "scroll," allowing the image to scroll along with the background, or "fixed," preventing the image from scrolling.
- To combine all background-image attributes into a single style, use:
  ```
  background: color image repeat attachment position
  ```
  where *color* is the color of the element background, *image* is the URL of the background image file, *repeat* specifies how the image is tiled in the background, *attachment* specifies whether the image scrolls with the page, and *position* provides the coordinates of the background image.

Like the font attribute discussed in the last session, all of the various background-image styles can be combined into a single style:

```
background: color image repeat attachment position
```

where *color* is the color of the element background, *image* is the URL of the background image file, *repeat* specifies how the image is tiled in the background, *attachment* specifies whether the image scrolls with the page, and *position* provides the coordinates of the background image. For example, the following declaration:

```
Document {background: yellow url(paper.gif) no-repeat fixed
center center}
```

specifies a non-tiled background image fixed on a yellow background, which uses the image file paper.gif. Note that you do not have to enter all of the attribute values of the background style, but the ones you do enter must follow the specified order.

Janet wants to replace the text of the Title element with a background image showing the Tour Nation logo. Janet does not want to delete the text from the XML document, so she'll reduce the font size of the Title text to 0 pixels in order to hide it. Then, she must format the Title element so that it displays the logo image file. The logo was created for you and is named "tnation.jpg." The dimensions of the image file are 620 pixels wide by 70 pixels high, so you'll need to set the size of the Title element to match these dimensions if you want the complete image to appear.

To display the Tour Nation logo:

1. Using your text editor, open **bike.css**.

2. Locate the style declaration for the Title element and change the font size from 32 point to 0 point.

3. Add the following styles to modify the size of the Title element:

   ```
   width: 620; height: 70;
   ```

4. Add the following styles to specify a background image, tnation.jpg, for the Title element (see Figure 5-49):

   ```
   background-image: url(tnation.jpg); background-
   position:center center
   ```

Figure 5-49   ADDING A BACKGROUND IMAGE TO THE TITLE ELEMENT

```
Document {width: 620; font-size: 12pt}
* {display: block}
Author {display: none}
Date {position: absolute; top: 0; left: 580; font-size: 8pt}
Title {border-bottom: 2 solid purple; font-family: Arial, Helvetica, sans-serif;
      font-size: 0pt; font-weight:bold; text-align: center;
      width: 620; height: 70;
      background-image: url(tnation.jpg); background-position: center center}
Subtitle {font-family: Arial, Helvetica, sans-serif; font-size: 14pt; font-style: italic;
      text-align:center}
FName {display: inline; color:red; font-variant: small-caps}
Features {width: 300; background-color: ivory; border: 1 solid black; padding: 5;
      font-family: Arial, Helvetica, sans-serif; font-size: 8pt}
Feature {display: list-item; list-style: square inside; color:blue}
Description {width: 300; float:right; text-align: justify}
Name {clear: right; color:white; background-color: rgb(192,145,192); margin-top:20;
      border-bottom:1 solid black; padding-left: 10; font-family: Arial, Helvetica, sans-serif;
      font-size: 14pt; font-weight:bold}
```

5. Using your text editor, save your changes to bike.css.

6. Open **bike.xml** in your Web browser and verify that the Title text was replaced by the Tour Nation logo, as shown in Figure 5-50.

Figure 5-50   **DISPLAYING THE TOUR NATION LOGO ON THE BIKE.XML PAGE**

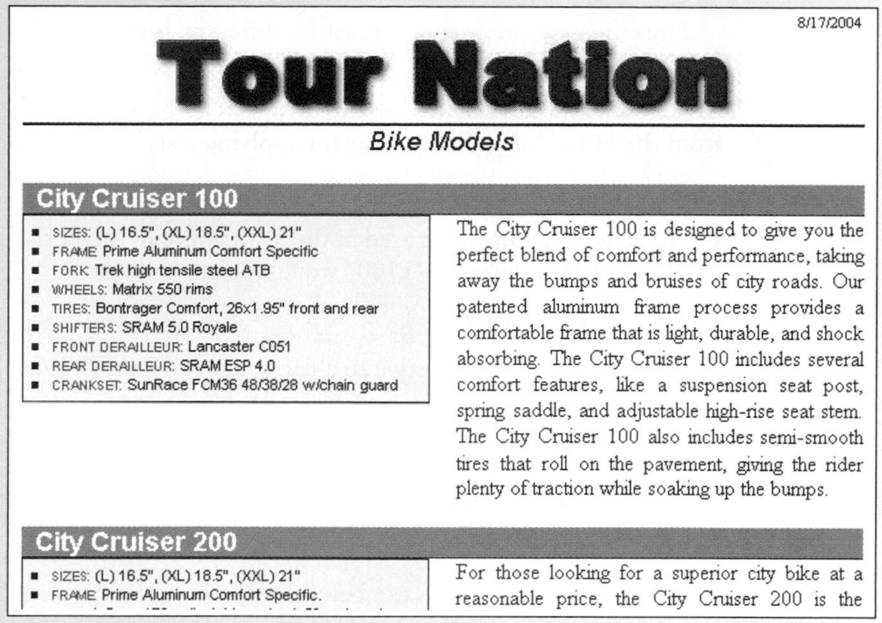

TROUBLE? Some browsers do not support the background-image style when applied to XML elements. If this is the case, you should restore the font size of the Title element to 32 points and remove the styles that create the background image. You'll learn later in the tutorial how to display images without using style sheets.

Working with Ids and Classes

The final task that Janet wants to complete for her Web page is to add images of the different bike models. Recall that Janet inserted an empty <IMG> tag in each model record (see the document structure diagram shown earlier in Figure 5-2). Janet wants to use this element to display images of those bikes. One problem is that she cannot specify different background images for the same tag. Janet needs a way of distinguishing one IMG element from another. If she can do that, she can assign a different background image to each element. Fortunately, there is a way to accomplish this using id and class attributes.

The id and class attributes are features of HTML used to distinguish one HTML tag from another. The **id** attribute identifies a unique tag in a document, while the **class** attribute identifies several tags belonging to the same group or class. In HTML, you enter the id and class attributes using the syntax:

```
<tag id="id_name">
<tag class="class_name">
```

where *tag* is the name of an HTML tag, *id_name* is the id assigned to that tag, and *class_name* is the class assigned to the tag. For example, you can add id and class attributes to the Model elements in the bike.xml file as follows:

```
<Model id="c100" class="city">
<Model id="c200" class="city">
<Model id="combo750" class="combo">
```

```
<Model id="tour250" class="road">
<Model id="tri200" class="road">
```

Note that the id attribute must be different for each tag, but tags can share the same class value.

CSS allows the Web designer to create styles based on the id and class names of the tags from the HTML file. The syntax for applying a style to a particular id element is:

```
#id_name {styles}
```

where *id_name* is the name used in the id attribute in the HTML tag. Creating a style for an id attribute with the value "c100" would look as follows:

```
#c100 {styles}
```

The syntax for applying a style to a particular class of HTML elements is:

```
.class_name {styles}
```

where *class_name* is the name used for the class attribute in those HTML tags. Creating a style for elements belonging to the "city" class would appear as:

```
.city {styles}
```

Since different elements can belong to the same class, you can distinguish different applications of the same class by including the element name. For example, the following XML elements:

```
<Model class="c100">
<Name class="c100">
```

would use the styles:

```
model.c100 {styles}
name.c100 {styles}
```

If you don't include the element name, the style is applied to all elements that use that class value.

However, the id and class attributes are not formal parts of XML. The language does not treat these attributes differently. So it doesn't appear their use will help Janet.

The good news is that Internet Explorer does recognize the existence of an id or class attribute in an XML document, and applies a style designed for a particular id or class of XML elements using the same syntax it uses for HTML documents. Admittedly, this is a violation of the spirit of XML, and not the most elegant of solutions, but until browsers support the wider range of selector types discussed, using the id and class attributes is the best workaround. This workaround only works for Internet Explorer and cannot be applied to other browsers such as Netscape. Also, this solution might not work on earlier versions of Internet Explorer.

The first thing Janet needs you to do is edit bike.xml by locating each <IMG> tag and adding an id attribute that specifies the bike model associated with that tag. Then, you can create a style for each IMG element in bike.css. Janet's document contains information on the following bike models:

- City Cruiser C100
- City Cruiser C200
- Combo 750
- Tour 250
- Triathon 200

Janet wants to associate each IMG element with a bike model by adding the following id names to those tags:

- C100
- C200
- Combo750
- Tour250
- Tri200

To add id attributes to the IMG elements:

1. Using your text editor, open **bike.xml**.
2. Locate the first occurrence of the <IMG> tag and insert the attribute:
   ```
   ID="C100"
   ```
3. Locate the second occurrence of the <IMG> tag and insert the attribute:
   ```
   ID="C200"
   ```
4. Locate the third occurrence of the <IMG> tag and insert the attribute:
   ```
   ID="Combo750"
   ```
5. Locate the fourth occurrence of the <IMG> tag and insert the attribute:
   ```
   ID="Tour250"
   ```
6. Locate the last occurrence of the <IMG> tag and insert the attribute:
   ```
   ID="Tri200"
   ```
   Figure 5-51 shows a portion of the modified bike.xml document.

Figure 5-51 ADDING ID ATTRIBUTES TO THE <IMG /> TAGS

```
The City Cruiser 100 is designed to give you the perfect blend of comfort and
performance, taking away the bumps and bruises of city roads. Our patented aluminum
frame process provides a comfortable frame that is light, durable, and shock absorbing.
The City Cruiser 100 includes several comfort features, like a suspension seat post,
spring saddle, and adjustable high-rise seat stem. The City Cruiser 100 also includes
semi-smooth tires that roll on the pavement, giving the rider plenty of traction while
soaking up the bumps.
        </Description>
        <IMG ID="C100" />
        <Features>
            <Feature><FName>sizes: </FName>(L) 16.5", (XL) 18.5", (XXL) 21"</Feature>
            <Feature><FName>frame: </FName>Prime Aluminum Comfort Specific</Feature>
            <Feature><FName>fork: </FName>Trek high tensile steel ATB</Feature>
            <Feature><FName>wheels: </FName>Matrix 550 rims</Feature>
            <Feature><FName>tires: </FName>Bontrager Comfort, 26x1.95" front and rear</Feature>
            <Feature><FName>shifters: </FName>SRAM 5.0 Royale</Feature>
            <Feature><FName>front derailleur: </FName>Lancaster C051</Feature>
            <Feature><FName>rear derailleur: </FName>SRAM ESP 4.0</Feature>
            <Feature><FName>crankset: </FName>SunRace FCM36 48/38/28 w/chain guard</Feature>
        </Features>
    </Model>

    <Model>
        <Name>City Cruiser 200</Name>
        <Description>
For those looking for a superior city bike at a reasonable price, the City
Cruiser 200 is the answer. As with all City Cruiser models the 200 provides
unparalleled performance and comfort. Tour Nation's patented aluminum frame is
light, durable, and shock absorbing. The City Cruiser 200 provides a wider gear
range than other models in this class, giving you just the right gear for pedaling
on any incline. The 200's design puts you in an upright, relaxed riding position
that makes pedaling easier and more enjoyable. As with all City Cruiser models,
the 200 also includes semi-smooth tires to soak up the bumps while providing
superior traction.
        </Description>
        <IMG ID="C200" />
        <Features>
```

7. Using your text editor, save your changes to bike.xml and close the file.

The next step is to create styles for each <IMG> element. The <IMG> element is empty, so there is no element content, but you can specify the dimensions and a background image. Janet wants the dimensions of the element set to 300 pixels wide by 78 pixels high. She wants a solid 1-pixel black border around each <IMG> element. The elements should display the following image files without tiling:

- city100.jpg
- city200.jpg
- comb750.jpg
- tour250.jpg
- tri200.jpg

To add these styles to Janet's document:

1. Return to **bike.css** in your text editor.

2. Navigate to the bottom of the file and enter the following style declarations (see Figure 5-52):

```
IMG {width: 300; height: 78; border: 1 solid black}
#C100 {background: url(c100.jpg) no-repeat}
#C200 {background: url(c200.jpg) no-repeat}
#Combo750 {background: url(combo750.jpg) no-repeat}
#Tour250 {background: url(tour250.jpg) no-repeat}
#Tri200 {background: url(tri200.jpg) no-repeat}
```

Figure 5-52 **THE COMPLETED BIKE.CSS FILE**

```
Document {width: 620; font-size: 12pt}
* {display: block}
Author {display: none}
Date {position: absolute; top: 0; left: 580; font-size: 8pt}
Title {border-bottom: 2 solid purple; font-family: Arial, Helvetica, sans-serif;
       font-size: 0pt; font-weight:bold; text-align: center;
       width: 620; height: 70;
       background-image: url(tnation.jpg); background-position: center center}
Subtitle {font-family: Arial, Helvetica, sans-serif; font-size: 14pt; font-style: italic;
          text-align:center}
FName {display: inline; color:red; font-variant: small-caps}
Features {width: 300; background-color: ivory; border: 1 solid black; padding: 5;
          font-family: Arial, Helvetica, sans-serif; font-size: 8pt}
Feature {display: list-item; list-style: square inside; color:blue}
Description {width: 300; float:right; text-align: justify}
Name {clear: right; color:white; background-color: rgb(192,145,192); margin-top:20;
      border-bottom:1 solid black; padding-left: 10; font-family: Arial, Helvetica, sans-serif;
      font-size: 14pt; font-weight:bold}
IMG {width: 300; height: 78; border: 1 solid black}
#C100 {background: url(c100.jpg) no-repeat}
#C200 {background: url(c200.jpg) no-repeat}
#Combo750 {background: url(combo750.jpg) no-repeat}
#Tour250 {background: url(tour250.jpg) no-repeat}
#Tri200 {background: url(tri200.jpg) no-repeat}
```

3. Save your changes to bike.css and close the file.

4. Refresh **bike.xml** in your browser.

   Figure 5-53 shows a portion of the completed Web page.

Figure 5-53 **THE COMPLETED WEB PAGE**

8/17/2004

Tour Nation

Bike Models

City Cruiser 100

- SIZES: (L) 16.5", (XL) 18.5", (XXL) 21"
- FRAME: Prime Aluminum Comfort Specific
- FORK: Trek high tensile steel ATB
- WHEELS: Matrix 550 rims
- TIRES: Bontrager Comfort, 26x1.95" front and rear
- SHIFTERS: SRAM 5.0 Royale
- FRONT DERAILLEUR: Lancaster C051
- REAR DERAILLEUR: SRAM ESP 4.0
- CRANKSET: SunRace FCM36 48/38/28 w/chain guard

The City Cruiser 100 is designed to give you the perfect blend of comfort and performance, taking away the bumps and bruises of city roads. Our patented aluminum frame process provides a comfortable frame that is light, durable, and shock absorbing. The City Cruiser 100 includes several comfort features, like a suspension seat post, spring saddle, and adjustable high-rise seat stem. The City Cruiser 100 also includes semi-smooth tires that roll on the pavement, giving the rider plenty of traction while soaking up the bumps.

City Cruiser 200

For those looking for a superior city bike at a reasonable price, the City Cruiser 200 is the

> TROUBLE? Depending on your browser and browser version, you might not see the bike images shown on the Web page.
>
> **5.** Close your Web browser.

Mixing HTML and XML

For browsers that do not support assigning a background image to XML elements, there are other ways of displaying graphic images. These do not involve CSS, but instead "mix" HTML tags into the XML source document. This approach involves adding the following HTML namespace to the XML document:

```
http://www.w3.org/TR/REC-html40
```

An XML processor recognizes any tag associated with this namespace as an HTML tag, and a browser like Internet Explorer or Netscape treats those HTML tags as if they came from an HTML file. For example, the following sample XML document displays Janet's bike images:

```
<?xml version="1.0">
<root xmlns:html="http://www.w3.org/TR/REC-html40">
   <html:img src="c100.jpg" />
   <html:img src="c200.jpg" />
   <html:img src="combo750.jpg" />
   <html:img src="tour250.jpg" />
   <html:img src="tri200.jpg" />
</root>
```

The browser treats this code the same as:

```
<img src="c100.jpg">
<img src="c200.jpg">
<img src="combo750.jpg">
<img src="tour250.jpg">
<img src="tri200.jpg">
```

Using the same technique, you can format the XML text, and even add hyperlinks to your XML document. In the following example, the Tour Nation title is formatted using an h3 heading, and then changed into a hyperlink, pointing to the URL *http://www.tournationbikes.com* (a fictional address).

```
<?xml version="1.0">
<root xmlns:html="http://www.w3.org/TR/REC-html40">
   <html:h3>
   <html:a href="http:/www.tournationbikes.com">
      <title>Tour Nation</title>
   </html:a>
   </html:h3>
</root>
```

This technique should work with most browsers that support XML. The downside of this approach is that it somewhat violates the spirit of XML, in which the XML document is related to content only. By adding HTML tags to the document, we are adding formatting codes, thus mixing formatting and content within a single file.

REFERENCE WINDOW | RW

Mixing HTML and XML

- To add HTML tags to an XML document, first create a namespace in the root element of the XML document using the syntax:

  `<root xmlns:prefix="http://www.w3.org/TR/REC-html40">`

  where *root* is the name of the root element, and *prefix* is the namespace prefix you'll assign to all HTML elements. One popular prefix is "html." Once the namespace prefix is assigned, simply add the HTML tags at the appropriate places in the document, with each tag associated with the HTML namespace.

- To place an inline image into an XML document, use the syntax:

  `<prefix:img src="URL" />`

  where *URL* is the filename and location of the image file.

- To create a hyperlink, use the syntax:

  ```
  <prefix:a href="URL">
     XML content
  </prefix:a>
  ```

  where *XML content* are those XML elements you want the browser to treat as hypertext.

The best approach to adding elements such as images and hypertext links to XML content may be using the Extensible Stylesheet Language, or XSL. This is a topic you'll explore in the next tutorial.

You've completed your work on combining CSS and XML. Janet is pleased with how you presented the information from her XML document in a useful and attractive layout. She plans on using CSS with future XML documents, and will certainly request your assistance again.

Session 5.3 QUICK CHECK

1. How would you display the Document element using the image file paper.gif as a background image?

2. How would you tile the paper.gif image file only in the vertical direction?

3. How would you fix the paper.gif image file in the display window so that it doesn't scroll with the rest of the page?

4. How would you apply a style to a tag with the id name "Model500"?

5. How would you apply a style to a tag with the class name "Mountain_Bikes"?

6. What are the limits to applying styles to id and class attributes in XML documents?

7. What attribute should you add to the root element of an XML document to create an HTML namespace with the namespace prefix "html"?

8. What code would you use to insert an inline image into an XML document that points to the logo.jpg file? Assume that the HTML namespace prefix is "html."

Note: The assignments that follow were created and tested on Internet Explorer 6.0 for Windows. Due to the differences in browser support for XML and CSS, other browsers or browser versions may not be able to correctly display the completed Web pages.

Janet has had time to study your document and discuss it with others at Tour Nation. She has a few changes she wants to make to the Web page, and she wants you to create a new style sheet to match her ideas. A preview of part of the page is shown in Figure 5-54.

Figure 5-54

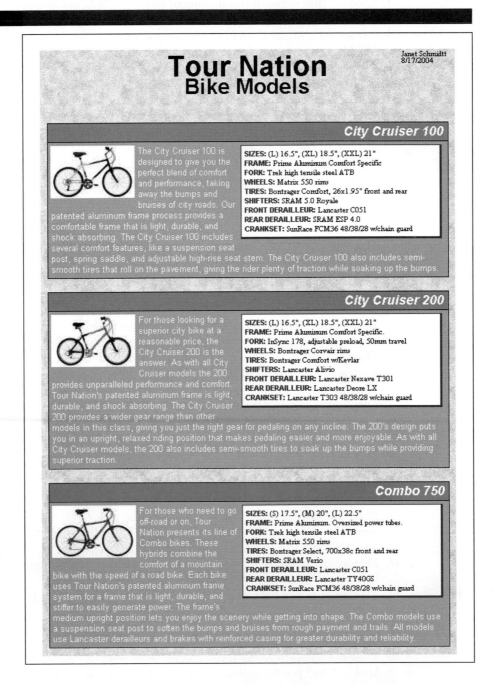

In order to insert the bike images on the page, Janet wants you to insert inline image codes directly into the XML document, not the style sheet.

To complete this task:

1. Using your text editor, open **bike2txt.xml** located in the tutorial.05x/review folder of your Data Disk and save the file as **bike2.xml**. Note that the elements in this file are the same as those used in the bike.xml file from the tutorial. The order of the elements changed slightly, and a class attribute was added to the Name element, indicating the class of the bike model.

Explore ▶ 2. Within the document's root element, insert the HTML namespace, assigning it the namespace prefix "html."

3. Create a link between this document and the bike2.css Cascading Style Sheet (a file you'll create shortly).

Explore ▶ 4. Locate each of the <IMG /> tags in the document. Assign each <IMG /> tag to the HTML namespace, adding the following attributes:

   `<IMG src="URL" align="left" hspace="5" vspace="5" />`

   where *URL* is the name of the graphic image file for each bike model. The filenames are: c100.jpg, c200.jpg, combo750.jpg, tri200.jpg, and tour250.jpg.

5. Save your changes to the bike2.xml file.

6. Using your text editor, create the text file **bike2.css** and save it in the tutorial.05x/review folder of your Data Disk.

7. Set the display type of all elements to block.

8. Set the width of the Document element to 620 pixels. Set the font size to 12 points. Display the image file paper.jpg in the Document element's background.

9. Set the position of the Author and Date elements to absolute. Make the font size of both elements 8 points. Place the Author element 550 pixels to the left. Place the Date element 550 pixels to the left and 25 pixels down from the top.

10. Display the Name, Description, FName, Title, and Subtitle elements in an Arial, Helvetica, or sans-serif font.

11. Center both the Title and Subtitle elements horizontally on the page. Display both elements in a bold font. Make the font size of the Title element 32 points. Make the subtitle 24 points. Offset the position of the Subtitle 15 pixels up from its original location. (*Hint*: Use the position:relative style, setting the top value to -15 pixels.)

12. Display the Model element only when the right margin is clear. Set the top, right, bottom, and left margins of the Model element to: 20, 10, 0, and 10 pixels.

13. Change the font color of the Name element to white and set its font size to 14 points. Display the text in a bold italic font. Align the text to the right. Set the padding space to 2 pixels. Add a 1-pixel solid black border around the element.

14. Display the Description element in a 10-point white font with a background color of rgb (255, 128, 255). Set the padding space to 5 pixels. Add a 1-pixel solid black border to the element's right, bottom, and left sides.

15. Float the Features element on the right margin of its parent element. Set the font size to 8 points. Make the element 300 pixels wide and set its background color to white. Make the border solid blue. The width of the top, right, bottom, and left borders should be 1, 3, 3, and 1 pixels, respectively. Make the margin around the element 5 pixels wide.

16. Display the FName element inline. Display the text in all uppercase letters with a blue, bold font.

Explore ▶ 17. All elements that belong to the "city" class should have a background color of rgb (128, 128, 255). All "combo" class elements should have a background color of rgb (64, 192, 64). All "road" class elements should have a background color of rgb (255, 128, 128).

18. Save your changes to the bike2.css file.

19. View the contents of the bike2.xml file in your Web browser. Verify the styles you created in bike2.css. Note that under some browsers and early browser versions, you will not see all of the styles defined in the bike2.css style sheet.

20. Hand in all relevant files to your instructor.

CASE PROBLEMS

Case 1. Hardin Financial Kevin Summers of Hardin Financial tracks stock market data for the stock exchanges, including the NASDAQ. He is interested in the NASDAQ 100, a listing of 100 representative stocks on the NASDAQ stock exchange. A server at Hardin Financial records information for each of the 100 listings every 5 minutes, and places that data into an XML document. Kevin wants to display the data from this document in an easy-to-read table. He thinks this can be accomplished using a Cascading Style Sheet, and asks for your help in creating the styles. Figure 5-55 shows a diagram of Kevin's document.

Figure 5-55

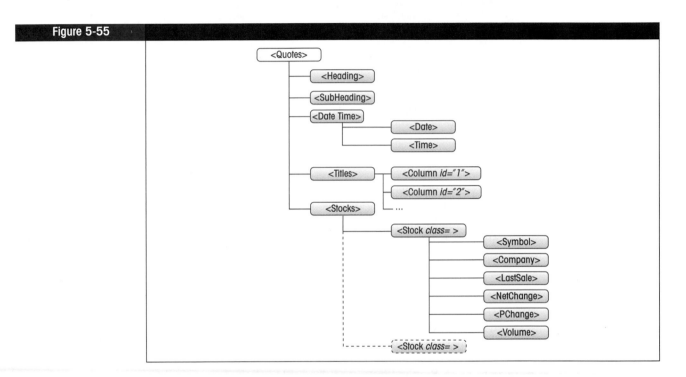

The date and time of the stock quotes are stored in the Date and Time elements, and the page headings are stored in the Heading and SubHeading elements. Kevin envisions displaying the stock data in six columns. The column titles are stored in the five Column elements. Information for each stock is stored in the Symbol, Company, LastSale, NetChange, PChange, and Volume elements. Each Stock element has a class attribute. A class value of "up" specifies an increased stock price and a class value of "down" indicates a declining stock. A class value of "unchanged" means that the stock hasn't changed in value. Kevin wants all declining stocks to appear in a red font with a down arrow graphic, and increasing stocks should appear in green with an up arrow. Stocks that haven't changed in value should appear in black with no associated graphic.

Figure 5-56 shows a preview of the page you'll create for Kevin.

Figure 5-56

11/01/2004 11:45:05

NASDAQ 100
Current Quotes

	Symbol	Name	Last Sale	Net Change	% Change	Volume
⌄	AAPL	Apple Computer, Inc.	$15.26	-0.17	-1.10%	5.548
⌃	ABGX	Abgenix, Inc.	$9.22	0.06	0.66%	1.396
⌄	ADBE	Adobe Systems Incorporated	$23.96	-0.98	-3.93%	4.432
⌄	ADCT	ADC Telecommunications, Inc.	$1.80	-0.16	-8.16%	5.980
⌃	ADRX	Andrx Group	$22.19	1.05	4.97%	2.401
⌄	ALTR	Altera Corporation	$11.83	-0.49	-3.98%	6.993
⌄	AMAT	Applied Materials, Inc.	$14.87	-0.83	-5.29%	27.627
⌄	AMCC	Applied Micro Circuits Corporation	$4.61	-0.13	-2.74%	4.126
⌃	AMGN	Amgen Inc.	$45.64	0.15	0.33%	33.644
⌄	AMZN	Amazon.com, Inc.	$14.46	-0.31	-2.11%	3.802
⌄	APOL	Apollo Group, Inc.	$39.25	-0.05	-0.13%	2.166
⌃	ATML	Atmel Corporation	$3.14	0.25	7.37%	8.349
⌄	BBBY	Bed Bath and Beyond Inc.	$31.00	-1.66	-5.08%	6.928
⌄	BEAS	BEA Systems, Inc.	$5.55	-0.52	-8.57%	14.196
⌄	BGEN	Biogen, Inc.	$35.97	-0.22	-0.61%	3.700
⌃	BMET	Biomet, Inc.	$25.93	0.42	1.65%	1.659
⌄	BRCD	Brocade Communications Systems, Inc.	$18.75	-1.14	-5.73%	10.285
⌄	BRCM	Broadcom Corporation	$18.76	-0.89	-4.53%	10.100
⌄	CDWC	CDW Computer Centers, Inc.	$47.80	-2.22	-4.44%	1.755
⌃	CEFT	Concord EFS, Inc.	$19.50	2.65	11.96%	45.162
⌃	CEPH	Cephalon, Inc.	$48.00	2.36	5.17%	3.385
	CHIR	Chiron Corporation	$33.74	0.00	0.00%	3.011

To complete this task:

1. Using your text editor, open **nasdtxt.xml** from the tutorial.05x/cases folder of your Data Disk and save the file as **nasdaq.xml**. Take some time to review the contents of the file.
2. Attach the nasdaq.css Cascading Style Sheet to this document. Save your changes to the file and close it.
3. Using your text editor, create a new file in the tutorial.05x/cases folder named **nasdaq.css**.
4. Set the width of the Quotes element to 620 pixels.
5. Display the DateTime element as a block, set the font size of the element to 8 points, and use absolute positioning to place the element 0 pixels from the top of the document window and 500 pixels to the right.
6. Display the Heading and SubHeading elements as blocks in a bold Arial or Helvetica font, and center the elements horizontally. Set the font size of the Heading element to 32 points. Set the font size of the SubHeading element to 14 points, and use relative positioning to place the SubHeading element 10 pixels up from its default position.
7. Display the Titles elements as a block and set the font size of the element to 10 points. Increase the bottom margin of the element to 10 pixels.
8. Display the Column element inline and underline the text in each column title.
9. Display the Stock element as a block with a font size of 10 points.
10. Use relative positioning to place both the Symbol and Column element with an id value of "1" 40 pixels from their default locations.
11. Use absolute positioning to place the Company and Column element with an id value of "2" 120 pixels to the right.
12. Use absolute positioning to place the LastSale and Column (id="3") elements 330 pixels to the right. Set the width of both elements to 70 pixels.
13. Use absolute positioning to place the NetChange and Column (id="4") elements 420 pixels to the right. Set the width of both elements to 65 pixels.
14. Use absolute positioning to place the PChange and Column (id="5") elements 480 pixels to the right. Set the width of both elements to 80 pixels.
15. Use absolute positioning to place the Volume and Column (id="6") elements 550 pixels to the right. Set the width of both elements to 80 pixels.
16. Right-align the text of the LastSale, NetChange, PChange, Volume, and Column (id="2" to id="6") elements.

17. For elements belonging to the "down" class, display down.gif as the background. Do not repeat the image, but place it at the left center of the element. Set the font color of the "down" elements to red.

18. For "up" class elements, display up.gif as the background. Once again, do not repeat the image, but place it at the left center of the background and set the font color to green.

19. Save your changes to nasdaq.css. Open the **nasdaq.xml** file in your Web browser and verify that the data appears in columns, and that declining stocks are shown in red and rising stocks in green. For some older browsers, the style rules will not take effect.

20. Hand in all relevant files to your instructor.

Case 2. Cutler Convention Center Karen Cho is the reservations coordinator for the Cutler Convention Center in Cutler, Indiana. Recently, the center's database began using reservation information in XML documents. Karen wants to display a table showing which convention center rooms are free at specific times during the day. A preview of the page that Karen wants to create is shown in Figure 5-57.

Figure 5-57

Cutler Convention Center

Monday, October 11th 2004

Room	7:00am	8:00am	9:00am	10:00am	11:00am	12:00pm	1:00pm	2:00pm	3:00pm	4:00pm	5:00pm
Sunrise Room	used	used	used	used	used	free	free	free	free	used	used
Granger Hall	free	free	free	free	used	used	used	used	used	used	used
Canyon View	used	used	used	used	used	used	used	used	used	used	used
Hillstadt Room	free	free	used	used	free	free	free	free	free	used	used
Alcove	free	free	free	free	free	used	used	free	free	free	free
Mountain View	used	used	free	free	free	free	used	used	used	used	used
Douglas Hall	free	free	used	used	used	free	free	free	free	free	free

To complete this task:

1. Using your text editor, open **schedtxt.xml** from the tutorial.05x/cases folder of your Data Disk and save the file as **schedule.xml**. Take some time to review the contents of the file.

2. Attach the schedule.css Cascading Style Sheet to this document. Save your changes to the file and close it.

3. Using your text editor, create a new file in the tutorial.05x/cases folder named **schedule.css**.

4. Set the width of the reservations element to 750 pixels.

5. Display the heading element as a block in a 32-point boldface Arial or Helvetica font. Center the text of the heading element horizontally and set the font color of the element to rgb (0, 128, 0).

6. Display the date element as a block and set the font size to 10 points. Right-align the element's text and set the element's margins to 20 pixels on the top and 0 pixels elsewhere.

7. Display the columns element as a block and insert a 3-pixel solid black border to the bottom of the element.

8. Display the time element inline and make each time element 55 pixels wide with a font size of 8 points. Center the time element text and display the text in an Arial or Helvetica font.

9. Display the room element as a block.

10. Display the used element inline and make the width of each element 55 pixels. Center the used element text with a font size of 8 points.

11. Make the name element 90 pixels wide with a font size of 8 points.

12. Display all elements belonging to the "yes" class in a white font with a red background.

13. Display all elements belonging to the "no" class in a green font with a white background.

14. Using your text editor, save your changes to schedule.css. Open **schedule.xml** in your Web browser and verify that the reservation schedule appears in columns with the reserved times blocked out in red. The CSS styles may not work with some older browser versions.

15. Hand in your files to your instructor.

Case 3. MidWest University Dr. Steve Karlson is a chemistry professor at MidWest University. Recently, he placed data regarding chemical elements in an XML document. Steve wants to be able to display information from this document in the classic layout of the periodic table (shown in Figure 5-58).

Figure 5-58

Periodic Chart of the Elements

1 H 1.00797																1 H 1.00797	2 He 4.0026
3 Li 6.939	4 Be 9.0122											5 B 10.811	6 C 12.0112	7 N 14.0067	8 O 15.994	9 F 18.9984	10 Ne 20.183
11 Na 22.9898	12 Mg 24.312											13 Al 26.9815	14 Si 28.086	15 P 30.9738	16 S 32.064	17 Cl 35.453	18 Ar 39.948
19 K 39.102	20 Ca 40.08	21 Sc 44.956	22 Ti 47.90	23 V 50.942	24 Cr 51.996	25 Mn 54.938	26 Fe 55.847	27 Co 58.9332	28 Ni 58.71	29 Cu 63.54	30 Zn 65.37	31 Ga 69.72	32 Ge 72.59	33 As 74.9216	34 Se 78.96	35 Br 79.909	36 Kr 83.80
37 Rb 85.47	38 Sr 87.62	39 Y 88.905	40 Zr 91.22	41 Nb 92.906	42 Mo 95.94	43 Tc 99	44 Ru 101.07	45 Rh 102.905	46 Pd 106.4	47 Ag 107.870	48 Cd 112.40	49 In 114.82	50 Sn 118.69	51 Sb 121.75	52 Te 127.60	53 I 126.904	54 Xe 131.30
55 Cs 132.905	56 Ba 137.34	57* La 138.91	72 Hf 178.49	73 Ta 180.948	74 W 183.85	75 Re 186.2	76 Os 190.2	77 Ir 192.2	78 Pt 195.09	79 Au 196.967	80 Hg 200.59	81 Tl 204.37	82 Pb 207.19	83 Bi 208.980	84 Po 210	85 At 210	86 Rn 222
87 Fr 223	88 Ra 226	89** Ac 227	104 Rf 261	105 Db 262	106 Sg 266	107 Bh 262	108 Hs 265	109 Mt 266	110 ? 271	111 ? 272	112 ? 277						

*Lanthanide Series

58 Ce 140.12	59 Pr 140.907	60 Nd 144.24	61 Pm 147	62 Sm 150.35	63 Eu 151.96	64 Gd 157.25	65 Tb 158.924	66 Dy 162.50	67 Ho 164.930	68 Er 167.26	69 Tm 168.934	70 Yb 173.04	71 Lu 174.97

**Actinide Series

90 Th 232.038	91 Pa 231	92 U 238.03	93 Np 237	94 Pu 242	95 Am 243	96 Cm 247	97 Bk 247	98 Cf 249	99 Es 254	100 Fm 253	101 Md 256	102 No 256	103 Lr 257

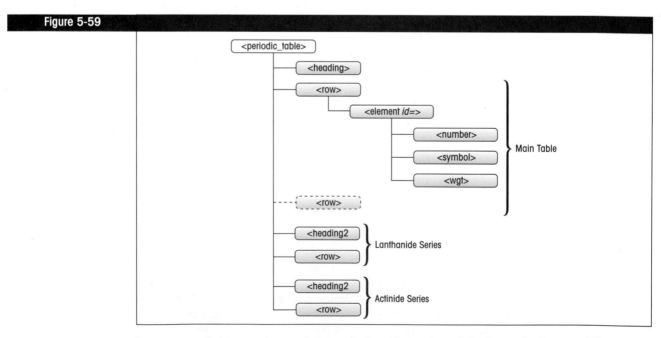

He asks for your help in creating a style sheet to display this information. The layout of his XML document is shown in Figure 5-59.

Figure 5-59

Steve entered the atomic number, symbol, and atomic weight for each element. The element tag also contains an id attribute whose value is the atomic number of the element. The elements are organized into rows that correspond to the rows of the periodic table.

Two special rows for the Lanthanide and Actinide series are offset from the main part of the table and have their own special headings stored in the heading2 element.

To complete this task:

1. Using your text editor, open **elemtxt.xml** from the tutorial.05x/cases folder of your Data Disk and save the file as **elements.xml**. Compare the contents of the file to the layout shown in Figure 5-59.
2. Attach the pchart.css CSS to this document. Save your changes to the file and close it.
3. Using your text editor, create **pchart.css** in the tutorial.05x/cases folder of your Data Disk.
4. Set the width of the periodic_table element to 750 pixels. Make Arial or Helvetica the default font for the document.
5. Display the heading element as a block in a bold 16-point font and center the heading text horizontally. Make the bottom margin 20 pixels high.
6. Display the row element as a block.
7. Display the element tag inline, center the element text, make the element tag 40 pixels wide, and add a 1-pixel solid black border around the element tag.
8. Display the number element as a block in an 8-point font.
9. Display the symbol element as a block in a 12-point bold font.
10. Display the wgt element as a block in a 6-point font.
11. Use relative positioning to move the elements with ids of "1a" and "2" 600 pixels to the right.
12. Use relative positioning to move the elements with ids of "5" through "10" and "13" through "18" 400 pixels to the right.
13. Display the heading2 element in a block with a 10-point font and set the top margin to 10 pixels.
14. Save your changes to pchart.css.
15. Open **elements.xml** using your browser and verify that it matches the periodic table. Some older browsers do not support XML and CSS. Your layout may not match the periodic table shown in Figure 5-58.
16. Hand in your files to your instructor.

Case 4. WebChef Linda Amanti works for WebChef, a Web site for recipes, cooking tips, diet advice, and articles on health and wellness. The site is moving its recipe database to XML documents. Linda placed a few Chinese recipes into an XML document. The structure of the document, mealstxt.xml, is shown in Figure 5-60.

Figure 5-60

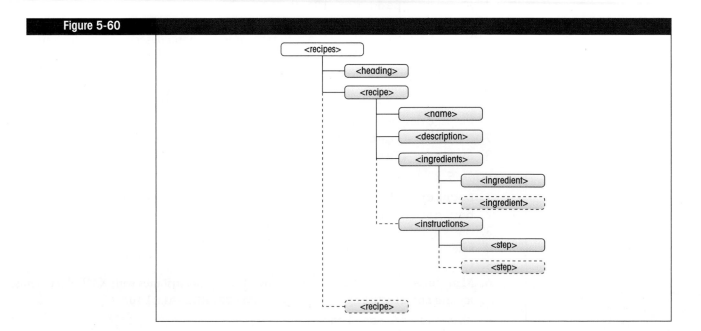

Linda wants your help in setting up a Cascading Style Sheet to display these recipes in an interesting and informative layout. The design of the Web page is up to you.
To complete this task:

1. Using your text editor, open **mealstxt.xml** from the tutorial.05x/cases folder of your Data Disk and save the file as **meals.xml**.
2. Link meals.xml to a CSS style sheet named "meal.css." Save your changes to meals.xml and close the file.
3. Using your text editor, create **meals.css**. While the design of the page is up to you, it should include at least the following style examples:
   - a selection of font faces, font sizes, font styles, and font weights
   - elements in blocks, positioned on the page by floating the element, or placing the element at defined coordinates
   - modifications of the border, padding, and margin styles for at least one element
   - application of color to the font and background of an element
4. Test your styles on a browser.
5. Hand in your completed files to your instructor.

QUICK CHECK ANSWERS

Session 5.1

1. `<?xml-stylesheet type="text/css" href="styles.css" ?>`
2. `Document {color: red}`
3. `Models > Model`
4. `CName {display: inline}`
5. `Notes {display: list-item; list-style: circle outside}`
6. `Notes {width: 300}`
7. `Notes {position: absolute; top: 10; left: 50}`
8. `Notes {float: left}`

Session 5.2

1. `Summary {background-color: rgb(255, 192, 255)}`
2. `margin-left: 3in; margin-right: 3in;`
3. `Summary {border: 5 dashed red}`
4. `Summary {padding: 10}`
5. A specific font is one that is installed on the user's computer such as Times New Roman, Arial, or Helvetica. A generic font is a general description of the font, allowing the operating system to determine which installed font best matches the description.
6. A relative unit is one that expresses the font size relative to the size of a standard character. CSS supports two relative units: em and ex. The em unit is more useful for page design because 1 em is equal to the default font size for the browser.
7. `Summary {font-family: Arial; font-weight: bold}`
8. `Summary {letter-spacing: 0.4pt}`

Session 5.3

1. `Document {background-image: url(paper.gif) }`
2. `background-repeat: repeat-y`
3. `background-attach: fixed`
4. Use the selector #Model500
5. Use the selector .Mountain_Bikes
6. Many browsers do not yet support using id and class attributes with XML documents.
7. `xmlns:html="http://www.w3.org/TR/REC-html40"`
8. `<html:img src="logo.jpg" />`

In this tutorial you will:

- Learn about the history and theory of XSL

- Create an XSLT style sheet

- Be introduced to syntax of the XPath language

- Transform an XML document into an HTML file

- Create templates to format sections of the XML document

- Sort the contents of an XML document

- Create conditional nodes to generate different HTML code

- Use predicates to select subsets of an XML document

- Insert new elements and attributes in the transformed document

WORKING WITH XSLT

Transforming an XML Document

CASE

Hardin Financial

Hardin Financial is a brokerage firm with headquarters in Chicago, Illinois. Founded by Alan Hardin, the company has provided financial planning and investment services to Chicago-area corporations and individuals for 25 years. As part of its investment services business, the company advises clients on investment portfolios, so it needs to have a variety of stock market information available for its employees.

Kevin Summers, a Hardin Financial analyst, is investigating the possibility of storing stock data in XML format. He created a small test document describing the financial status of 14 stocks listed on the New York Stock Exchange. Kevin is especially interested in the different ways this data can be presented in Web documents.

Kevin heard that the content of an XML document can be transformed into a variety of publishing formats, including HTML, and he asks for your help in creating prototype documents that showcase this feature of XML.

SESSION 6 .1

In this session, you'll be introduced to XSL. You'll learn about the family of XSL languages, including XSLT and XPath. You'll create an XSLT style sheet and write HTML code to generate a result document. You'll also learn how to use XPath to navigate the hierarchical structure of an XML document. Finally, you'll transform an XML document into an HTML file.

Working with XSL

One of the challenges of working with an XML document is presenting the XML data in a useful format, particularly for users of the Web. As you've seen, one method of accomplishing this is with CSS. However, CSS has several limitations, including:

- CSS displays element content as it appears in the XML document. While you can apply a style, such as the font size, to the content, you can't change the format of the content itself. For example, you can't display a date entered in the XML document as "June 28, 2004" as "6/28/2004."
- CSS does not allow you to insert additional text to the element content. There are some CSS3 styles that provide some capability to do this, but they are not well supported by current browsers.
- CSS doesn't provide easy methods to display images or insert hypertext links.
- CSS displays only element content, not element attributes.
- It's difficult to display content from several documents with CSS.
- An element can be formatted only one way in a document. For example, you cannot display an element as a heading on one part of the page and as a table cell on another.

In 1998, in an effort to overcome limitations of CSS and provide a more robust method of displaying XML data, the W3C began developing the **Extensible Style sheet Language** or **XSL**. XSL allows you to transform your XML data into a variety of formats, including HTML, the portable document format (PDF), the rich text format (RTF), and even a new XML document.

Introducing XSL-FO, XSLT, and XPath

XSL is actually composed of three parts, with each part acting as a separate language. These three languages are:

- **XSL-FO (Extensible Style sheet Language – Formatting Objects)** is used to implement page layout and design.
- **XSLT (Extensible Style sheet Language Transformations)** is used to transform XML content into another presentation format.
- **XPath** is used to locate information from an XML document and perform operations and calculations upon that content.

At the time of this writing, XSL-FO is in development and, consequently, has few applications and minimal support. Therefore, this tutorial focuses on XSLT, though it will, by necessity, involve some aspects of XPath.

Introducing XSLT Style Sheets and Processors

To use XSLT, you must create an **XSLT style sheet** that contains instructions for transforming the contents of an XML document into another format. An XSLT style sheet is itself an XML document, with elements, attributes, and processing instructions that correspond to the XSLT style sheet language. It is customary to distinguish an XSLT style sheet document from other XML documents by using the file extension .xsl.

An XSLT style sheet converts a **source document** of XML content into a **result document** containing the markup codes and other instructions for formatting. The result document may be an actual physical document that is stored as a separate file on your computer, or it may simply be the source document as it is displayed by an application, such as a Web browser that employs the style sheet. Later in this tutorial, you'll be able to choose between creating a separate file for your result document, or viewing the results of the transformation in your Web browser.

To perform this transformation, you need an **XSLT processor** that takes the source document and uses the style sheet to generate the result document (see Figure 6-1).

Figure 6-1	GENERATING A RESULT DOCUMENT

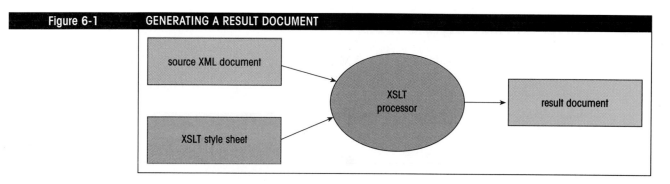

This transformation can be performed by a server or a client. In a **server-side transformation**, the server receives a request from a client to generate the result document. The server applies the style sheet to the source document, and returns the result document to the client—often as a new file. In a server-side transformation, the client does not need an XSLT processor because all of the work is done on the server. A disadvantage to server-side transformations is the heavy load they can place on the server as it attempts to handle all the transformation requests from clients.

In a **client-side transformation**, a client requests retrieval of both the source document and the style sheet from the server. The client then performs the transformation and generates its own result document. There are several client-side XSLT processors available, including:

- MSXML — available from Microsoft at *www.msdn.microsoft.com*. MSXML is included with Internet Explorer 5.0 and above

- xt — an open source XSLT processor developed by James Clark and available at *www.jclark.com/xml/xt.hmtl*

- Saxon — an open source XSLT processor developed by Michael Kay and available at *http://saxon.sourceforge.net*

- Xalan Apache available at *http://xml.apache.org/xalan-j/*

At the time of this writing, there are few browsers that have built-in support for XSLT. The current browser support is as follows:

- Internet Explorer 5.0 and 5.5, which support the original XSLT working draft. However, since the final version of XSLT is different from the working draft, IE 5.0 and 5.5 are not 100% compatible with the official XSLT standard. MSXML 2.0 is provided with Internet Explorer 5.0. MSXML 2.5 is provided with Internet Explorer 5.5.

- Internet Explorer 6.0 fully supports the official W3C XSLT specifications. MSXML 3.0 is provided with Internet Explorer 6.0.
- Netscape 6.0 does not fully support the W3C XSLT specifications.

The advantage of having a browser with a built-in XSLT processor is that you can view the transformation of the source document without having to create a separate file. However, creating a separate document does allow browsers without XSLT processors to view the results.

At Hardin Financial Services, Kevin Summers plans to display the contents of his XML documents on the company intranet using Internet Explorer 6.0. Because this release of Internet Explorer is fully compliant with XSLT, he feels comfortable using the browser as his XSLT processor. He will also create a separate file for browsers without XSLT processors.

Creating an XSLT Style Sheet

Kevin already created the XML document containing the desired stock market information. Figure 6-2 describes the contents of Kevin's document.

Figure 6-2	CONTENTS OF KEVIN'S DOCUMENT
ELEMENT	DESCRIPTION
portfolio	The root element
author	The author of the document
date	The date of the document contents
time	The 24 hour time the document was last updated
stock	Information for an individual stock
name	The name of the stock, containing an attribute named "symbol" that stores the stock abbreviation
description	A description of the stock
category	The category for the stock: Industrials, Transportation, or Utilities
link	The URL of the stock's Web page
year_high	The high value of the stock during the past year
year_low	The low value of the stock during the past year
pe_ratio	The price/earnings ratio for a stock
earnings	The earnings per share for a stock
yield	The yield percentage for a stock
today	The current values of the stock, stored in the following attributes: open, high, low, current, and vol
five_day	Stock activity information for the last five days
day	Stock value for each day, stored in the following attributes: open, high, low, close, vol, and date

Kevin's file contains information on 14 different stocks, including the opening value of the stock on the New York Stock Exchange, its low and high values for the day, its current value, and the number of shares traded for the day. Kevin also included several financial indicators, such as the stock's yearly high and low values, its price/earnings ratio, yield, and earnings per share. Finally, Kevin recorded the previous five days of activity for each stock. Figure 6-3 shows the structure of the file.

Figure 6-3	STRUCTURE OF KEVIN'S DOCUMENT

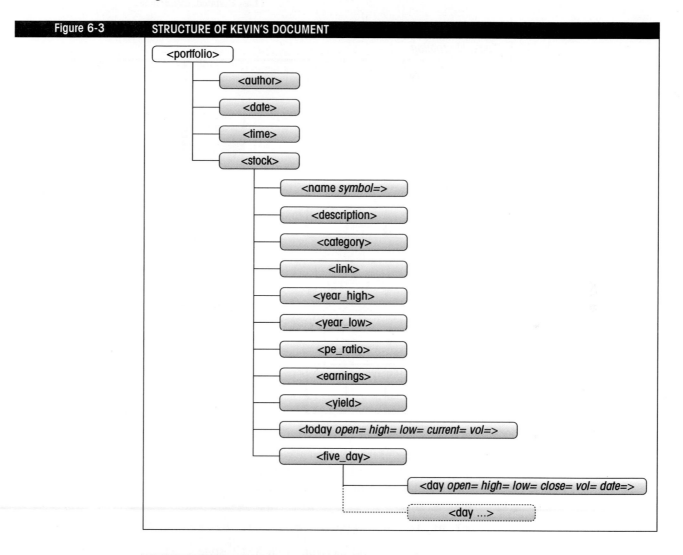

To open Kevin's document:

1. Using your text editor, open **stocktxt.xml** located in the tutorial.06x/tutorial folder of your Data Disk.

2. Save the file as **stock.xml** in the same location.

3. Take a few minutes to review the file. Refer to Figure 6-2 and Figure 6-3 so that you fully understand the document's structure and content.

Kevin created a sketch to illustrate how he wants the data in the stock.xml document to appear on his Web page. See Figure 6-4.

Figure 6-4   **KEVIN'S PROPOSED DOCUMENT**

Last Updated: date at time

Hardin Financial
Stock Information

Stock Category

Stock Name
Today's Values

———— ———— ———— ———— ————

Stock Description ————————————
————————————
————————————
————————————

Recent History			

Summary Information

Stock Name
Today's Values

———— ———— ———— ———— ————

Stock Description ————————————
————————————
————————————
————————————

Recent History			

Summary Information

All of the features of this Web page will be defined in the style sheet. The actual content of the page already exists in the stock.xml file. The processing instruction to link the stock.xml file to the style sheet is similar to what is used to create a link to a CSS style sheet. The syntax is:

```
<?xml-stylesheet type="text/xsl" href="URI" ?>
```

where *URI* is the name and location of an XSLT style sheet. You decide to create a style sheet named "stock.xsl."

To attach Kevin's document to an XSLT style sheet:

1. Insert the following code immediately following the first line in the document (see Figure 6-5):

```
<?xml-stylesheet type="text/xsl" href="stock.xsl" ?>
```

Figure 6-5   **ATTACHING THE STOCK.XML DOCUMENT TO THE STOCK.XSL STYLE SHEET**

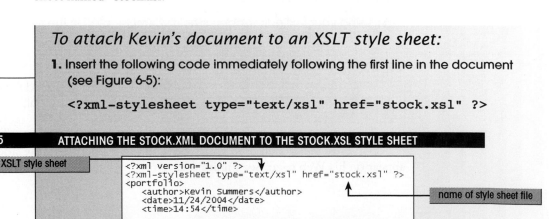

XSLT style sheet

```
<?xml version="1.0" ?>
<?xml-stylesheet type="text/xsl" href="stock.xsl" ?>
<portfolio>
    <author>Kevin Summers</author>
    <date>11/24/2004</date>
    <time>14:54</time>
```

name of style sheet file

2. Save your changes to stock.xml and close the file.

The next step is to create stock.xsl.

3. Using your text editor, create a new file named **stock.xsl** in the tutorial.06/ tutorial folder of your Data Disk.

Since an XSLT style sheet is an XML document, it must follow the general structure of all XML documents. The root element of an XSLT style sheet is either <stylesheet> or <transform> (they are synonymous). You should include the version attribute in the <stylesheet> or <transform> element to indicate the version of XSLT in use. Currently, the default (and only) version number is 1.0.

Finally, in order for the document to be recognized by your XML processor as an XSLT style sheet, it must be placed in the following namespace:

```
http://www.w3.org/1999/XSL/Transform
```

Note that if you're using Internet Explorer 5.0 as your XSLT processor, you must use the following namespace:

```
http://www.w3.org/TR/WD-xsl
```

This is because Internet Explorer 5.0 was based on an early draft of the XSLT specifications. An error will result if you attempt to use the http://www.w3.org/1999/XSL/Transform namespace with IE 5.0. Given that IE 5.0 is based on a draft version of XSLT, it is a good idea to upgrade to version 6.0, or use an XSLT processor that supports the final specification. Attempting to base your style sheet on the draft specification can lead to unpredictable results. Typically, the XSLT namespace is associated with a namespace prefix of "xsl." Any XSLT-specific elements must be associated with the XSLT namespace.

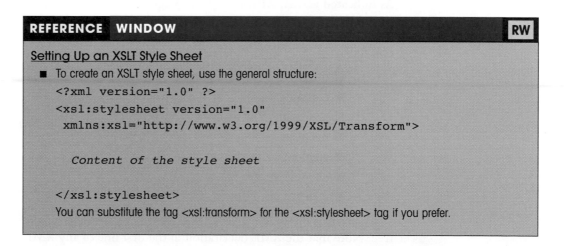

REFERENCE WINDOW   RW

Setting Up an XSLT Style Sheet
■ To create an XSLT style sheet, use the general structure:

```
<?xml version="1.0" ?>
<xsl:stylesheet version="1.0"
 xmlns:xsl="http://www.w3.org/1999/XSL/Transform">

   Content of the style sheet

</xsl:stylesheet>
```
You can substitute the tag <xsl:transform> for the <xsl:stylesheet> tag if you prefer.

Putting all of this together, the general structure of an XSLT style sheet is:

```
<?xml version="1.0" ?>
<xsl:stylesheet version="1.0"
 xmlns:xsl="http://www.w3.org/1999/XSL/Transform">

   Content of the style sheet

</xsl:stylesheet>
```

Use this structure to begin creating the XSLT style sheet.

To create the XSLT style sheet:

1. Using your text editor, enter the following code into stock.xsl (see Figure 6-6):

```
<?xml version='1.0' ?>
<xsl:stylesheet version='1.0'
  xmlns:xsl="http://www.w3.org/1999/XSL/Transform">

</xsl:stylesheet>
```

Figure 6-6   BEGINNING THE XSLT STYLE SHEET

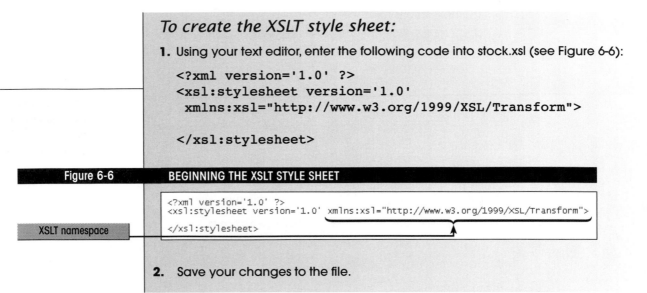

```
<?xml version='1.0' ?>
<xsl:stylesheet version='1.0' xmlns:xsl="http://www.w3.org/1999/XSL/Transform">

</xsl:stylesheet>
```

XSLT namespace

2. Save your changes to the file.

With the basic structure of the XSLT style sheet file set, you can begin working on the design of Kevin's Web page. First, however, let's examine how to reference the contents of the source document.

Working with Document Nodes

As indicated earlier, XPath is the language for referencing the contents of an XML document. Under XPath, each component in the document is referred to as a **node**, and the entire structure of the document is a **node tree**. The node tree consists of the following objects:

- the XML document itself
- comments
- processing instructions
- namespaces
- elements
- element text
- element attributes

Figure 6-7 shows how part of the stock.xml document would appear as an XPath node tree. Note that the XML declaration in the first line of any XML document is not counted as part of the node tree.

Figure 6-7 **PART OF THE STOCK.XML NODE TREE**

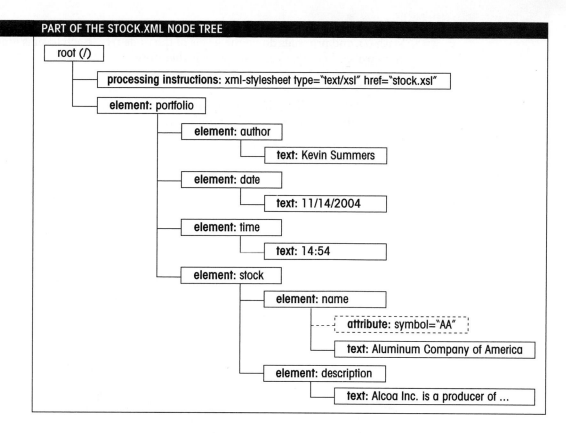

At the top of the node tree is the **root node**. This is not the same as the root element of the XML document, which in the case of the stock.xml file is the portfolio element. The root node refers to the XML document itself. Below the root node is the processing instruction that links the stock.xml file with the XSLT style sheet and the root element, portfolio.

The relationship between the nodes in the node tree follows a familial structure. A node that contains other nodes is called a **parent node**, and the nodes contained in the parent are called **child nodes**. Nodes that share a common parent are called **sibling nodes**. Note that a node can have only one parent. As we progress further down the tree, any node found at a level below another node is referred to as a **descendant** of that node. The node at the top of the branch is referred to as the **ancestor** of all nodes that lie beneath it.

For example, in Kevin's document, the portfolio node is the parent of these child nodes: author, date, time, and stock. Further down the node tree, elements such as name, description, and category are descendants of the portfolio element.

Nodes are distinguished based on the object they refer to in the document. A node for an element is called an **element node**; the node that stores element attributes is called an **attribute node**, and so forth.

Using XPath to Reference a Node

XPath provides the syntax to refer to the various nodes in the node tree. The syntax is used by UNIX or DOS to specify file pathnames. The location of a node can be expressed in either absolute or relative terms.

In describing an absolute path, XPath begins with the root node, identified by a forward slash (/), and proceeds down the levels of the node tree. Each level is identified by additional forward slashes. The general syntax is therefore:

`/child1/child2/child3/…`

where *child1*, *child2*, *child3*, and so forth are the descendants from the root node. For example, the absolute path to the description element node from Kevin's document is:

`/portfolio/stock/description`

You can avoid listing all of the levels of the node tree by using a double forward slash (//) with the syntax:

`//descendant`

where *descendant* is the name of the descendant node. For example, the path:

`//yield`

refers to all yield elements in the document, no matter where they are located in the node tree.

With a relative path, the location of the node is indicated relative to a specific node in the tree called the **context node** (you'll see how to select the context node later in the tutorial). Figure 6-8 describes some of the common constructions for relative paths.

Figure 6-8   **RELATIVE PATHS**

PATH	DESCRIPTION
.	Refers to the context node
..	Refers to the parent of the context node
child	Refers to the child of the context node with the node name *child*
child1/child2	Refers to the *child2* node, a child of the *child1* node beneath the context node
../sibling	Refers to a sibling of the context node
//name	Refers to a descendant of the context node with the name *name*

For example, if the stock element is the context node, Figure 6-9 provides examples of relative paths to other nodes in Kevin's document.

Figure 6-9   **RELATIVE PATHS BETWEEN THE STOCK ELEMENT AND OTHER NODES**

PATH	DESCRIPTION *
.	Refers to the stock element
..	Refers to the portfolio element
category	Refers to the category element, a child of the stock element
five_day/day	Refers to the day element, a child of the five_day element, which is itself a child of the stock element
../time	Refers to the time element, a sibling of the stock element
//day	Refers to the day element, a descendant of the stock element
* Assumes that the stock element is the context node	

An easy way to distinguish between an absolute path and a relative path is by recognizing that any path beginning with a forward slash (/) is an absolute path.

REFERENCE WINDOW   **RW**

<u>Using XPath to Match Element Nodes</u>
- To create an absolute reference to an element node, use the path:
  `/child1/child2/child3/…`
  where *child1*, *child2*, *child3*, and so forth are the descendants from the root node.
- To reference an element node without regard for its location in the node tree, use the expression:
  `//descendant`
  where *descendant* is the name of the descendant node.

Referencing Groups of Elements

XPath also allows you to refer to groups of nodes by using the wildcard character (*). For example, the path:

`/portfolio/stock/*`

matches all of the children of the stock element. To select all of the nodes in the node tree, you can use the path:

`//*`

In this case, the * symbol matches any node, and the // symbol matches any level of the node tree.

XPath allows you to combine different paths into a single expression by using the | operator. For example, the expression:

`/portfolio/date | /portfolio/time`

matches both the date and time child elements of the portfolio element. Similarly, the following expression:

`//name | //description`

selects all of the name and description node elements in the node tree.

Referencing Attribute Nodes

Because attribute nodes are not strictly considered children of their parent elements, XPath uses different notation to refer to them. The syntax for an attribute node is:

`@attribute`

where *attribute* is the name of the attribute. For example, the absolute path to the symbol attribute in Kevin's stock.xml document is:

`/portfolio/stock/name/@symbol`

If the stock element is the context node, this would be:

`name/@symbol`

and if name is the context node, the relative path is:

`@symbol`

To select all attribute nodes named "symbol" from the node tree, use the expression:

```
//@symbol
```

Finally, to select all attribute nodes in the tree, use the path:

```
//@*
```

Working with Text Nodes

The text contained in an element node is treated as a **text node**. The syntax for selecting a text node is:

```
text()
```

For example, to reference the text node of the name element, you can use the absolute path:

```
/portfolio/stock/name/text()
```

or

```
//name/text()
```

To match all text nodes in the document, use:

```
//text()
```

By accessing the text nodes, you can use XSLT to create result documents that act upon the actual text content of the elements in the source document. This is something that we will not cover in this tutorial.

At this point, we've barely scratched the surface of all that XPath can do, but it's enough to begin work on designing an XSLT style sheet for Kevin's document.

Creating the Root Template

The first task in designing the stock.xsl style sheet is to create a template for the root node. A **template** is a collection of elements that define how a particular section of the source document should be transformed in the result document. Since the root node refers to the entire document, the **root template** sets up the initial code for the result document. The general syntax of a template is:

```
<xsl:template match="node">
    XSLT and Literal Result Elements
</xsl:template>
```

where *node* is either the name of a node from the source document's node tree, or an XPath expression that points to a specific node in the tree. For the root node, the form of the root template is:

```
<xsl:template match="/">
    XSLT and Literal Result Elements
</xsl:template>
```

Note that we included the namespace prefix "xsl" in this syntax to indicate that these elements are part of the XSLT namespace. You could choose a different namespace prefix, but it is customary to use "xsl."

Creating a Template

- To create a template, use the syntax:

```
<xsl:template match="node">
   XSLT and Literal Result Elements
</xsl:template>
```

where *node* is either the name of a node from the source document's node tree, or an XPath expression that points to a specific node in the tree.

- To create the root node *template,* use the expression:

```
<xsl:template match="/">
   XSLT and Literal Result Elements
</xsl:template>
```

The root template can be located anywhere between the opening and closing <xsl:stylesheet> tags of the XSLT document. However, it is common practice to put the root template at the top of the document, directly after the opening <xsl:stylesheet> tag.

A template contains two types of content: XSLT elements and literal result elements. **XSLT elements** are those elements that are part of the XSLT namespace and are used to send commands to the XSLT processor. A **literal result element** is text sent to the result document, but not acted upon by the XSLT processor. If you use XSLT to create an HTML file, any HTML tags in the style sheet are considered literal result elements because they are ignored by the XSLT processor and sent directly to the result document.

In this case, Kevin wants to create a Web page based on the contents of the stock.xml file. He shows you the initial code for the HTML file that he wants to generate:

```
<html>
<head>
<title>Stock Information</title>
<link href="stock.css" rel="stylesheet" type="text/css">
</head>
<body>
<h1 class="title">Hardin Financial</h1>
<h2 class="title">Stock Information</h2>
</body>
</html>
```

Note that Kevin created an external CSS style sheet named "stock.css" to format some of the tags of his HTML file. HTML uses the <link> tag to attach the HTML file to the external style sheet. Kevin also created a class attribute named "title" to apply specific styles to the h1 and h2 headings. If you would like to review your CSS, you can examine the contents of stock.css to see how these headings are formatted by the browser.

All of these tags are examples of literal result elements because they do not involve any of the elements associated with XSLT. To place these tags in the result document, we need only to add the text of the HTML file to the root template as follows:

```
<xsl:template match="/">
<html>
<head>
<title>Stock Information</title>
<link href="stock.css" rel="stylesheet" type="text/css" />
</head>
```

```
<body>
<h1 class="title">Hardin Financial</h1>
<h2 class="title">Stock Information</h2>
</body>
</html>
</xsl:template>
```

There are a few points worth mentioning here. First, note how the use of the "xsl" namespace prefix instructs the XSLT processor which tags are XSLT elements and which are literal result elements. Any tag that *doesn't* contain the "xsl" namespace prefix is treated by the XSLT processor as text, and is passed to the result document without modification.

Another important point to remember is that even though the HTML tags are treated as text, they must still follow basic XML syntax. That means all empty tags must be entered as *<tag_name />* and not *<tag_name>*. For this reason, the code for <link> tag in the root templates was changed from:

```
<link href="stock.css" rel="stylesheet" type="text/css">
```

to

```
<link href="stock.css" rel="stylesheet" type="text/css" />
```

Similarly, if you wanted the result document to include one-sided HTML tags such as <img> or <br>, they would have to be written as <img /> and <br /> in the style sheet. In addition, all HTML attribute values must be enclosed in single or double quotes. Failure to follow XML syntax will result in an error message from the XML processor.

To create the root template:

1. If necessary, return to **stock.xsl** in your text editor.

2. Insert the root template code immediately before the closing </xsl:stylesheet> tag (see Figure 6-10):

```
<xsl:template match="/">
<html>
<head>
<title>Stock Information</title>
<link href="stock.css" rel="stylesheet" type="text/css" />
</head>
<body>
<h1 class="title">Hardin Financial</h1>
<h2 class="title">Stock Information</h2>
</body>
</html>
</xsl:template>
```

Figure 6-10	CREATING THE ROOT TEMPLATE

```
<?xml version='1.0' ?>
<xsl:stylesheet version='1.0' xmlns:xsl="http://www.w3.org/1999/XSL/Transform">

<xsl:template match="/">
<html>
<head>
<title>Stock Information</title>
<link href="stock.css" rel="stylesheet" type="text/css" />
</head>
<body>
<h1 class="title">Hardin Financial</h1>
<h2 class="title">Stock Information</h2>
</body>
</html>
</xsl:template>

</xsl:stylesheet>
```

template matches the root node

literal result elements

So far we've sent the text of an HTML file to the result document. How does the XSLT processor know to treat this text as HTML code rather than simple text? One way is to indicate the output method in the XSLT style sheet.

Specifying the Output Method

By default, the XSLT processor will render the result document as an XML file. There are exceptions to this rule. Most processors will create an HTML file if the <html> tag is included as a literal result element in the root template. However, this is a convention followed by the programmers of XSLT processors and is not part of the XSLT specifications. To have complete control over how the processor formats the source document, you can specify the output method using the XSLT element:

```
<xsl:output attributes />
```

where *attributes* are the attributes that define the output format of the result document. Figure 6-11 describes the different attributes associated with the <xsl:output /> element.

Figure 6-11	ATTRIBUTES OF THE <XSL:OUTPUT /> ELEMENT

ATTRIBUTE	DESCRIPTION
method	Defines the output format using one of the following values: "xml," "html," or "text"
version	Specifies the version of the output
encoding	Specifies the character encoding
omit-xml-declaration	Specifies whether to omit an xml declaration in the first line of the result document ("yes") or to include it ("no")
standalone	Specifies whether a standalone attribute should be included in the output and sets its value ("yes" or "no")
doctype-public	Sets the URI for the public identifier in the <!DOCTYPE> declaration
doctype-system	Sets the system identifier in the <!DOCTYPE> declaration
cdata-section-elements	A list of element names whose content should be output in CDATA sections
indent	Specifies whether the output should be indented to better display its structure. Note that indentations are automatically added to HTML files
media-type	Sets the MIME type of output

For example, to instruct the XSLT processor to create an HTML 4.0 file, you would insert the following tag directly after the opening <xsl:stylesheet> tag:

```
<xsl:output method="html" version="4.0" />
```

On the other hand, if your style sheet is used to transform one XML document into another, you would add this tag to the style sheet file:

```
<xsl:output method="xml" version="1.0" />
```

Sometimes programmers need only a piece of an XML document consisting of a few elements or attributes. These documents, called **XML fragments**, do not include an opening XML declaration:

```
<?xml version="1.0" ?>
```

To remove this declaration from the result document, you would use the following open method:

```
<xsl:output method="xml" version="1.0"
omit-xml-declaration="yes" />
```

Finally, to create a plain text file, the open method is:

```
<xsl:output method="text" />
```

Text files are used in cases where the code of the result document follows neither the HTML nor the XML syntax. One such format is the Rich Text Format (RTF), supported by most word processors. To create an RTF file, you insert the RTF code as literal result elements into the style sheet, and the XSLT processor passes those codes through as text, without checking the document for well-formedness or validity.

The other attributes of the <xsl:output> element provide additional control over the format of the text and content of any XML elements that may be placed in the file. For example, you can control the content of the <!DOCTYPE> declaration using the doctype-public and doctype-system attributes. Naturally this would only be applicable if the result document is an XML file. For international documents, you may need to set the encoding attribute to match the character encoding used by the reader.

After discussing the importance of specifying an open method, Kevin agrees that you should add the <xsl:output> element to the stock.xsl style sheet.

To specify the output method:

1. Insert the following code immediately before the opening <xsl:template> element located at the top of the stock.xsl file:

```
<xsl:output method="html" version="4.0" />
```

2. Save your changes to stock.xsl and close your text editor.

Now that you've specified an open method, you can create the result document.

Transforming a Document

There are two ways to view the result document. One way is to use a browser that contains an XSLT processor to view the source document. Since the source document includes a processing instruction that applies the stock.xsl style sheet, the browser will transform the source document itself. Alternately, if your browser does not contain an XSLT processor, you can use XML Spy to create the result document as a separate file on your computer, and then view that file in your browser.

Viewing the Result Document in a Browser

Internet Explorer 6.0 contains an XSLT processor so you can view the transformed document by simply opening stock.xml in the browser. Other browsers, like Netscape 6.2, contain XSLT processors that might render the result document with some formatting errors. In the end, you may have to test several browsers to determine which ones can reliably transform your source documents. The steps that follow assume that you are using Internet Explorer 6.0 for Windows.

If you are not running a browser with a built-in XSLT processor, you do not have to complete the steps in the section, and can proceed to the next section to learn how to create a separate file using XML Spy.

To view Kevin's transformed document:

1. Use your browser to open **stock.xml** from the tutorial.06x/tutorial folder of your Data Disk.
Figure 6-12 shows the transformed page.

Figure 6-12	THE RESULT DOCUMENT

Hardin Financial
Stock Information

TROUBLE? If your browser doesn't display the page shown in Figure 6-12, it could be that your browser does not contain a built-in XSLT processor. If this is case, you may need to generate the result document as a separate file using the instructions described in the next section.

2. Close your browser.

Internet Explorer 6.0 allows you to quickly view the results of the transformation. However, if you don't have access to Internet Explorer, or you are concerned that your audience does not have access to this browser, you can create the transformed document as a separate file to be viewed in any browser. You'll do this now using XML Spy.

Creating an HTML File in XML Spy

Most XSLT processors provide the capability to create the result document as a separate file. In this tutorial, you'll use XML Spy, but you can use other processors such as Saxon, xt, or MSXML. If you have not already installed XML Spy, the appendix includes installation instructions and an overview of how to work with the program.

One advantage of creating a separate HTML file is that it can then be viewed in any Web browser, whether or not that browser contains an XSLT processor. However, this also means that every time you make a change to the source document, or the style sheet, you have to regenerate the HTML file.

To create an HTML file:

1. Start the XML Spy application.

2. Using XML Spy, open **stock.xml** and **stock.xsl** from the tutorial.06x/tutorial folder of your Data Disk.

3. Click the **stock.xml** tab to make this document the active pane in the window.

4. Click **XSL Transformation** from the XSL menu (or press the **F10** key on your keyboard). XML Spy creates a new pane named "XSL Output.html" displaying the HTML file (see Figure 6-13).

Figure 6-13	TRANSFORMING THE SOURCE DOCUMENT IN XML SPY

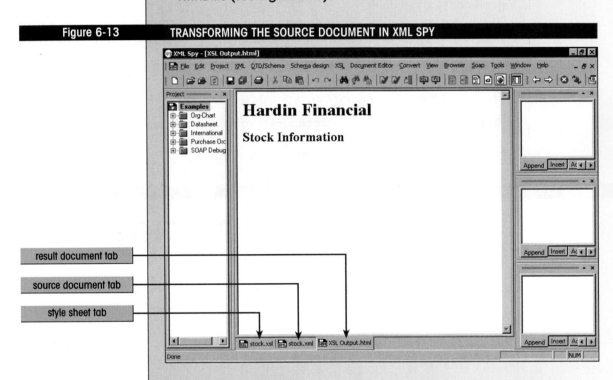

result document tab
source document tab
style sheet tab

TROUBLE? XML Spy does not apply the styles defined in the style.css style sheet to this pane. This is not a problem when the file is saved in a permanent form to your Data Disk.

5. With the XSL Output.html pane active, select **Save As** from the **File** menu.

6. Save the XSL Output.html pane as **stock.htm** in the tutorial.06x/tutorial folder of your Data Disk.

7. Choose **Exit** from the **File** menu to close XML Spy, without saving any other changes to the three documents.

8. Open **stock.htm** in your Web browser and verify that its appearance matches the page shown earlier in Figure 6-12, and then close your Web browser.

If you open stock.htm using your text editor, you should see the complete HTML code, indicating that it is a fully functioning HTML file, which can be used by any Web browser that supports CSS. The XSLT processor added one extra line to the document:

```
<META http-equiv="Content-Type" content="text/html;
charset=UTF-16">
```

that provides additional information to the browser about the content of the document and its encoding.

At this point, we have not placed any content of the XML file into the result document. What we did create so far are the literal result elements, specifically the h1 and h2 headings, formatted using styles from the stock.css style sheet. In the next session, you'll learn how to insert values from the stock.xml source document into the result document.

Session 6.1 QUICK CHECK

1. What are XSLT, XPath, and XSL-FO?

2. What processing instruction would link an XML document to an XSLT style sheet named "styles.xsl"?

3. In an XML document, the root element is named "books" and it contains one child element named "book." The book element contains two child elements named "author" and "title." What is the absolute path for the title element?

4. In the above example, what is the relative path from the author to the title element, assuming that the author element is the context node?

5. If, in the above examples, the title element contains an attribute named "isbn," what is the absolute path to this attribute?

6. What XPath expression would you use to reference the author element, regardless of where it is located in the node tree?

7. Does the root template refer to the root element of the source document? Explain your answer.

8. What are literal result elements?

9. What XSLT element would you use to specify that the result document should be a text file? Under what circumstances might you wish to create a text file and not an HTML or XML document?

SESSION 6.2

In this session, you'll learn how to display values from the source document in the result document. This session also focuses on how to create and use templates in order to write code that is easy to develop and maintain. You'll also learn about XSLT's built-in templates and how to use them in your style sheets. The session concludes by examining how to display attribute values in the result document.

Inserting a Node Value

To insert a node's value into the result document, use the XSLT element:

```
<xsl:value-of select="XPath Expression" />
```

where *XPath Expression* is an expression that identifies the node from the source document's node tree. To see how this works, we'll go back to Kevin's proposed sketch of his Web page, shown earlier in Figure 6-4. At the top of the page, Kevin wants to display the date and time of the source document as follows:

```
Last Updated: date at time
```

where *date* and *time* are values taken from the source document. In the case of the stock.xml file, this is:

```
Last Updated: 11/24/2004 at 14:54
```

To create this output string, you would add the following code to the root template of stock.xsl:

```
Last Updated:
<xsl:value-of select="portfolio/date" />
at
<xsl:value-of select="portfolio/time" />
```

You may wonder why the XPath expression is "portfolio/date" rather than "/portfolio/date". This is because we're using a relative path. The context node, in this case, is the root node because the code is added to the root template.

REFERENCE WINDOW   **RW**

Inserting a Node's Value

■ To insert a node's value into the result document, use the XSLT element:

```
<xsl:value-of select="XPath Expression" />
```

where *XPath Expression* is an expression that identifies the node from the source document's node tree.

Typically, the string value of the node is the text that the node contains. If the node contains child elements in addition to text content, the text in those child nodes appears as well.

To display the date and time values in Kevin's document:

1. Using your text editor, open **stock.xsl**.

2. Insert the following code immediately after the <body> tag in the root template (see Figure 6-14):

```
<div id="datetime"><b>Last Updated: </b>
   <xsl:value-of select="portfolio/date" /> at
   <xsl:value-of select="portfolio/time" />
</div>
```

Figure 6-14   **USING THE <XSL:VALUE-OF> ELEMENT**

date and time values
appear in the document

```
<xsl:template match="/">
<html>
<head>
<title>Stock Information</title>
<link href="stock.css" rel="stylesheet" type="text/css" />
</head>
<body>
<div id="datetime"><b>Last Updated: </b>
   <xsl:value-of select="portfolio/date" /> at
   <xsl:value-of select="portfolio/time" />
</div>
<h1 class="title">Hardin Financial</h1>
<h2 class="title">Stock Information</h2>
</body>
</html>
</xsl:template>
```

Note that the <div id="datetime"> tag was added to format the date and time
text string using a style from the stock.css style sheet, which places this text in
the upper-right corner of the Web page.

3. Save your changes to stock.xsl.

4. Using either your browser (if it contains a built-in XSLT processor) or XML Spy,
generate the revised result document. If you use XML Spy, follow the techniques
described in the last session to create a file named "stock.htm" containing the
transformed document. Figure 6-15 shows the new Web page.

Figure 6-15   **THE DATE AND TIME VALUES IN THE RESULT DOCUMENT**

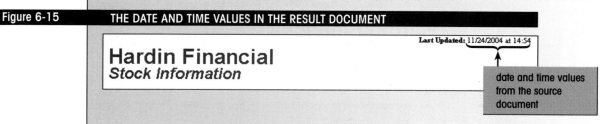

Last Updated: 11/24/2004 at 14:54

Hardin Financial
Stock Information

date and time values
from the source
document

The next step is to add the names of the stocks in Kevin's document, displaying them as
h3 headings. The XSLT code to insert the stock names is:

```
<h3><xsl:value-of select="portfolio/stock/name" /></h3>
```

Add this code now to the stock.xsl style sheet.

To add the stock names:

1. Return to the **stock.xsl** style sheet in your text editor.

2. Insert the following code immediately before the </body> tag (see
Figure 6-16):

```
<h3 class="name">
   <xsl:value-of select="portfolio/stock/name" />
</h3>
```

| Figure 6-16 | DISPLAYING THE STOCK NAME VALUE |

```
<xsl:template match="/">
<html>
<head>
<title>Stock Information</title>
<link href="stock.css" rel="stylesheet" type="text/css" />
</head>
<body>
<div id="datetime"><b>Last Updated: </b>
    <xsl:value-of select="portfolio/date" /> at
    <xsl:value-of select="portfolio/time" />
</div>
<h1 class="title">Hardin Financial</h1>
<h2 class="title">Stock Information</h2>
<h3 class="name">
    <xsl:value-of select="portfolio/stock/name" />
</h3>
</body>
</html>
</xsl:template>
```

Note that, once again, we're applying a class name to this h3 heading to format it using a style defined in the style.css style sheet.

3. Save your changes to stock.xsl.

4. Regenerate the result document by opening **stock.xml** with your browser, or by using XML Spy to recreate stock.htm. Figure 6-17 shows the resulting page.

| Figure 6-17 | THE FIRST STOCK NAME |

Last Updated: 11/24/2004 at 14:54

Hardin Financial
Stock Information

Aluminum Company of America

The first stock name appears in the document, but where are the others? While the <xsl:value-of> element does display the node's value, if there are multiple nodes that match the XPath expression, only the value of the first node appears.

Processing a Batch of Nodes

When there are several nodes that match an XPath expression, we specify that each node should be formatted using the <xsl:for-each> element as follows:

```
<xsl:for-each select="XPath Expression">
    XSLT and Literal Result Elements
</xsl:for-each>
```

where *XPath Expression* is an XPath expression that defines the group of nodes to which the XSLT and literal result elements are applied.

Processing a Batch of Nodes

■ To process a batch of nodes, use:

```
<xsl:for-each select="XPath Expression">
   XSLT and Literal Result Elements
</xsl:for-each>
```

where *XPath Expression* is an XPath expression that defines the group of nodes to which the XSLT and literal result elements are applied.

For example, to format each stock name in Kevin's document, you would use the code:

```
<xsl:for-each select="portfolio/stock">
<h3 class="name">
   <xsl:value-of select="name" />
</h3>
</xsl:for-each>
```

For each stock node, display the value of the name element formatted with an <h3> heading. Note that in this code, the context node changed from the root node / to "portfolio/stock". So the value of the select attribute in the <xsl:value-of> element changed from "portfolio/stock/name" to simply "name". One of the challenges for new XSLT programmers is to keep track of the context node. A common source of errors is to assume an incorrect context node for a given expression.

To use the <xsl:for-each> element in Kevin's style sheet:

1. Return to the **stock.xsl** style sheet in your text editor.

2. Replace the three lines of code located above the </body> tag with the following code:

```
<xsl:for-each select="portfolio/stock">
<h3 class="name">
   <xsl:value-of select="name" />
</h3>
</xsl:for-each>
```

See Figure 6-18.

| Figure 6-18 | DISPLAYING THE COLLECTION OF STOCK NAMES |

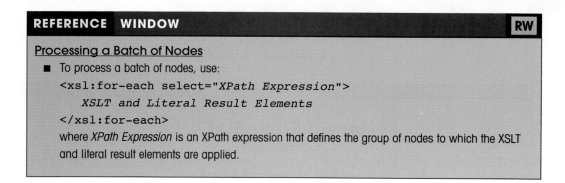

```
<xsl:template match="/">
<html>
<head>
<title>Stock Information</title>
<link href="stock.css" rel="stylesheet" type="text/css" />
</head>
<body>
<div id="datetime"><b>Last Updated: </b>
   <xsl:value-of select="portfolio/date" /> at
   <xsl:value-of select="portfolio/time" />
</div>
<h1 class="title">Hardin Financial</h1>
<h2 class="title">Stock Information</h2>
<xsl:for-each select="portfolio/stock">
<h3 class="name">
   <xsl:value-of select="name" />
</h3>
</xsl:for-each>
</body>
</html>
</xsl:template>
```

3. Save your changes to stock.xsl and then view the result document by opening **stock.xml** with Internet Explorer 6.0, or by updating stock.htm using XML Spy. Figure 6-19 shows the updated result document.

Figure 6-19	THE FIRST SEVERAL STOCK NAMES

Last Updated: 11/24/2004 at 14:54

Hardin Financial
Stock Information

Aluminum Company of America

Unocal Corporation

General Motors Corporation

Eastman Kodak Company

Ryder Systems Inc.

Airborne Freight Corporation

Southwest Airlines Co.

The <xsl:for-each> element is one way of displaying multiple values. A more versatile approach is to create a template for nodes that are repeated throughout the document.

Working with Templates

Rather than using the <xsl:for-each> construction, we can create a template for the name element. The template would appear as follows:

```
<xsl:template match="name">
<h3 class="name">
   <xsl:value-of select="." />
</h3>
</xsl:template>
```

where the match attribute now matches the name of the element node, "name". Thus, each name element in the node tree is associated with this template. Once again, the context node shifted—this time from "portfolio/stock" to "name". Therefore the value of the select attribute changed from "name" to ".". Recall that the . symbol is used to refer to the context node (see Figure 6-8).

Simply creating the template does not cause the processor to use it in the result document. You also must indicate where you want the template applied.

Applying a Template

To apply a template, use the XSLT element:

```
<xsl:apply-templates select="XPath Expression" />
```

where *XPath Expression* indicates the node template to be applied. For relative paths, the XPath expression depends on the context node. For example, if the context node is the root node, the code appears as:

```
<xsl:template match="/">
    <xsl:apply-templates select="portfolio/stock/name" />
</xsl:template>
```

but if the context node is the stock element, the code is:

```
<xsl:template match="stock">
    <xsl:apply-templates select="name" />
</xsl:template>
```

In both cases, the XSLT processor searches the node tree of the source document, starting with the context node and working down. If the specified path is repeated several times (as is the name node), the template is applied for each occurrence. This is why templates can be used in place of the <xsl:for-each> element.

REFERENCE   WINDOW   **RW**

Applying a Template

- To apply a template in the result document, use the XSLT element:

  `<xsl:apply-templates select="XPath Expression" />`

  where *XPath Expression* indicates the node template to be applied.

To see how this works, let's replace the <xsl:for-each> construct with a template.

To revise stock.xsl to use templates:

1. Return to **stock.xsl** in your text editor.

2. Delete the <xsl:for-each> construction from the root template (all of the lines in red, as shown in Figure 6-18).

3. Insert the following code immediately before the </body> tag:

   ```
   <xsl:apply-templates select="portfolio/stock/name" />
   ```

4. Insert the following code immediately above the closing </xsl:stylesheet> tag:

   ```
   <xsl:template match="name">
   <h3 class="name">
       <xsl:value-of select="." />
   </h3>
   </xsl:template>
   ```

   Figure 6-20 shows the revised file.

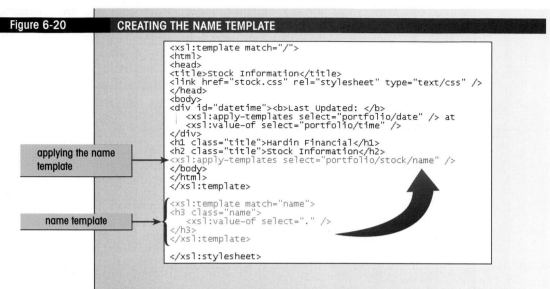

Figure 6-20   CREATING THE NAME TEMPLATE

```
<xsl:template match="/">
<html>
<head>
<title>Stock Information</title>
<link href="stock.css" rel="stylesheet" type="text/css" />
</head>
<body>
<div id="datetime"><b>Last Updated: </b>
   <xsl:apply-templates select="portfolio/date" /> at
   <xsl:value-of select="portfolio/time" />
</div>
<h1 class="title">Hardin Financial</h1>
<h2 class="title">Stock Information</h2>
<xsl:apply-templates select="portfolio/stock/name" />
</body>
</html>
</xsl:template>

<xsl:template match="name">
<h3 class="name">
   <xsl:value-of select="." />
</h3>
</xsl:template>

</xsl:stylesheet>
```

applying the name template

name template

5. Save your changes to the file.

6. Use your browser or XML Spy to regenerate the result document and verify that the appearance of the page is unchanged with this new code.

One of the advantages of using templates instead of the <xsl:for-each> element is that you can break up the nodes of the source document into manageable chunks. A template can also be called from other templates in the style sheet, making it very easy to reuse the same code in different locations in the result document.

Using the Built-In Templates

It is not necessary to include the select attribute with the <xsl:apply-templates> element. If you use the <xsl:apply-templates> element without the select attribute, the XSLT processor will apply whatever templates exist for the context node and all descendants of the context node.

What happens if no template has been defined for the context node or a descendant? In that case, the XSLT processor applies one of the **built-in templates** to the node. Each node type has its own built-in template. For example, the built-in template for element nodes is:

```
<xsl:template match="*|/">
   <xsl:apply-templates />
<xsl:template>
```

This template matches the document root and all elements, and thus instructs the processor to navigate the entire node tree and apply templates to all elements in the node tree. If you have a template matching an element located deep in the node tree, the default template continues processing until that template is applied.

For text nodes, the built-in template is:

```
<xsl:template match="text()">
   <xsl:value-of select="." />
</xsl:template>
```

This template matches all text nodes and causes their values to appear in the result document. The combination of built-in templates for element and text nodes causes: 1) all elements in the node tree to be processed, and 2) all element text to appear in the result document.

XSLT also provides built-in templates for comments, namespaces, and processing instructions. These templates, however, do not affect the content of the result document at all.

To see how the built-in templates work, we'll modify the stock.xsl style sheet to process the built-in templates instead of only the name template.

To use the built-in templates:

1. Return to **stock.xsl** in your text editor.

2. Locate the <xsl:apply-templates> element in the root template and delete the select attribute from the element so that the element is now:

   ```
   <xsl:apply-templates />
   ```

3. Save your changes to the file.

4. Use your browser or XML Spy to regenerate the result document (Figure 6-21).

Figure 6-21   **RESULTS OF THE BUILT-IN TEMPLATES**

Last Updated: 11/24/2004 at 14:54

Hardin Financial
Stock Information

Kevin Summers 11/14/2004 14:54

Aluminum Company of America

Alcoa Inc. is a producer of primary aluminum, fabricated aluminum, and alumina, and is active in all major aspects of the industry, including technology, mining, refining, smelting, fabricating, and recycling. Alcoa serves customers worldwide in the packaging, consumer, automotive, aerospace and other transportation, building and construction, industrial products and distribution markets. Related businesses include packaging machinery, precision castings, vinyl siding, plastic bottles and closures, fiber-optic cables, and electrical distribution systems for cars and trucks. Alcoa's operations consist of five worldwide segments: Alumina and Chemicals, Primary Metals, Flat-Rolled Products, Engineered Products, and Packaging and Consumer Goods. Industrialshttp://www.alcoa.com42.0027.3639.400.732.0912345

Unocal Corporation

Unocal Corporation operates as the parent of Union Oil Company of California. Virtually all operations are conducted by Union Oil and its subsidiaries. Unocal is an independent oil and gas exploration and production company, with principal operations in North America and Asia. Unocal is also a producer of geothermal energy and a provider of electrical power in Asia. Other activities include ownership in proprietary and common carrier pipelines, natural gas storage facilities and the marketing and trading of hydrocarbon commodities. Industrialshttp://www.unocal.com39.7029.5124.571.342.4312345

The result document now shows the text contained in all elements of the source document's node tree. Except for the stock name, the text in these elements is unformatted text. The stock name text is formatted because the processor located the template you designed for this element and applied it, instead of the built-in text node template.

You can also use the select attribute for templates that don't yet exist. Because of how the processor works with the built-in templates, the following elements are equivalent when no date template has been defined:

```
<xsl:value-of select="/portfolio/date" />
<xsl:apply-templates select="/portfolio/date" />
```

If the processor searches for the date template and doesn't find it, the built-in template is used, and the text of the date element appears. There is an advantage to using the <xsl:apply-templates> element rather than the <xsl:value-of> element. If, at a later time in the development process, you decide to create the date template, you do not have to modify the section of the style sheet that displays the date value to access the new template.

Creating **the Stock Template**

Now that you've seen the flexibility that templates can provide, you can continue working with Kevin's style sheet. The next template you want to add to the style sheet displays more descriptive information about the stock. Kevin wants the following HTML code to be applied to each stock:

```
<div class="stock_info">
<h3 class="name">Stock Name</h3>
<p>Stock Description</p>
</div>
```

where *Stock Name* is the name of each stock (drawn the name element) and *Stock Description* is the description of the stock (taken from the description element). The template to create this looks as follows:

```
<xsl:template match="stock">
<div class="stock_info">
<xsl:apply-templates select="name" />
<p><xsl:value-of select="description" /></p>
</div>
</xsl:template>
```

Note that to create the h3 heading, we simply reference the name template that was already created. The code for the name template is inserted into the stock template, creating the code that Kevin wants.

To add the stock template to the style sheet:

1. Return to **stock.xsl** in your text editor.

2. Insert the following stock template between the root and name templates:

```
<xsl:template match="stock">
<div class="stock_info">
  <xsl:apply-templates select="name" />
  <p><xsl:value-of select="description" /></p>
</div>
</xsl:template>
```

3. Change the <xsl:apply-templates /> in the root template to:

```
<xsl:apply-templates select="portfolio/stock" />
```

Figure 6-22 shows the revised code.

Figure 6-22

Figure 6-22   CREATING THE STOCK TEMPLATE

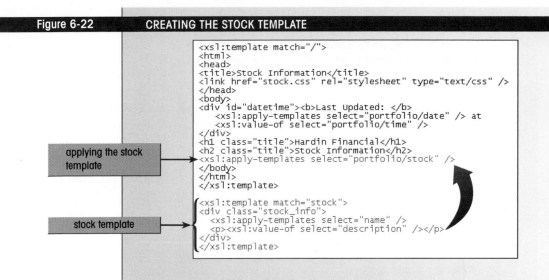

applying the stock template

stock template

```
<xsl:template match="/">
<html>
<head>
<title>Stock Information</title>
<link href="stock.css" rel="stylesheet" type="text/css" />
</head>
<body>
<div id="datetime"><b>Last Updated: </b>
    <xsl:apply-templates select="portfolio/date" /> at
    <xsl:value-of select="portfolio/time" />
</div>
<h1 class="title">Hardin Financial</h1>
<h2 class="title">Stock Information</h2>
<xsl:apply-templates select="portfolio/stock" />
</body>
</html>
</xsl:template>

<xsl:template match="stock">
<div class="stock_info">
    <xsl:apply-templates select="name" />
    <p><xsl:value-of select="description" /></p>
</div>
</xsl:template>
```

4. Save your changes to stock.xsl.

5. Use your browser or XML Spy to regenerate the result document. Figure 6-23 shows the revised layout of the result page.

Figure 6-23   RESULTS OF THE STOCK TEMPLATE

Last Updated: 11/24/2004 at 14:54

Hardin Financial
Stock Information

Aluminum Company of America

Alcoa Inc. is a producer of primary aluminum, fabricated aluminum, and alumina, and is active in all major aspects of the industry, including technology, mining, refining, smelting, fabricating, and recycling. Alcoa serves customers worldwide in the packaging, consumer, automotive, aerospace and other transportation, building and construction, industrial products and distribution markets. Related businesses include packaging machinery, precision castings, vinyl siding, plastic bottles and closures, fiber-optic cables, and electrical distribution systems for cars and trucks. Alcoa's operations consist of five worldwide segments: Alumina and Chemicals, Primary Metals, Flat-Rolled Products, Engineered Products, and Packaging and Consumer Goods.

Unocal Corporation

Unocal Corporation operates as the parent of Union Oil Company of California. Virtually all operations are conducted by Union Oil and its subsidiaries. Unocal is an independent oil and gas exploration and production company, with principal operations in North America and Asia. Unocal is also a producer of geothermal energy and a provider of electrical power in Asia. Other activities include ownership in proprietary and

---

Kevin wants summary information for each stock to appear in a table that is aligned with the right margin of the Web page. The HTML code to create this table is:

```
<table class="summary" border="1">
<tr>
    <th colspan="2" class="summtitle">Summary Information</th>
</tr>
<tr>
    <th class="summary">Year High</th>
    <td class="number">year_high</td>
```

```
   </tr>
   <tr>
      <th class="summary">Year Low</th>
      <td class="number">year_low</td>
   </tr>
   <tr>
      <th class="summary">Price/Earnings Ratio</th>
      <td class="number">pe_ratio</td>
   </tr>
   <tr>
      <th class="summary">Earnings per Share</th>
      <td class="number">earnings</td>
   </tr>
   <tr>
      <th class="summary">Yield</th>
      <td class="number">yield</td>
   </tr>
</table>
```

where *year_high*, *year_low*, *pe_ratio*, *earnings*, and *yield* are stock values for each stock from the source document. Add this table to the stock template in the stock.xsl style sheet.

To add the summary table to the style sheet:

1. Return to **stock.xsl** in your text editor.

2. Insert the following code immediately before the <div> tag in the stock template (see Figure 6-24):

```
<table class="summary" border="1">
<tr>
   <th colspan="2" class="summtitle">
Summary Information</th>
</tr>
<tr>
   <th class="summary">Year High</th>
   <td class="number">
   <xsl:value-of select="year_high" /></td>
</tr>
<tr>
   <th class="summary">Year Low</th>
   <td class="number">
   <xsl:value-of select="year_low" /></td>
</tr>
<tr>
   <th class="summary">Price/Earnings Ratio</th>
   <td class="number">
   <xsl:value-of select="pe_ratio" /></td>
</tr>
<tr>
   <th class="summary">Earnings per Share</th>
   <td class="number">
   <xsl:value-of select="
earnings" /></td>
</tr>
```

```
<tr>
   <th class="summary">Yield</th>
   <td class="number"><xsl:value-
of select="yield" /></td>
</tr>
</table>
```

Figure 6-24 ADDING THE SUMMARY TABLE TO THE STOCK TEMPLATE

```
<xsl:template match="stock">
<table class="summary" border="1">
<tr>
   <th colspan="2" class="summtitle">Summary Information</th>
</tr>
<tr>
   <th class="summary">Year High</th>
   <td class="number"><xsl:value-of select="year_high" /></td>
</tr>
<tr>
   <th class="summary">Year Low</th>
   <td class="number"><xsl:value-of select="year_low" /></td>
</tr>
<tr>
   <th class="summary">Price/Earnings Ratio</th>
   <td class="number"><xsl:value-of select="pe_ratio" /></td>
</tr>
<tr>
   <th class="summary">Earnings per Share</th>
   <td class="number"><xsl:value-of select="earnings" /></td>
</tr>
<tr>
   <th class="summary">Yield</th>
   <td class="number"><xsl:value-of select-"yield" /></td>
</tr>
</table>
<div class="stock_info">
   <xsl:apply-templates select="name" />
   <p><xsl:value-of select="description" /></p>
</div>
</xsl:template>
```

3. Save your changes to stock.xsl.

4. Use your browser or XML Spy to regenerate the result document (shown in Figure 6-25).

Figure 6-25 REVISED RESULT DOCUMENT

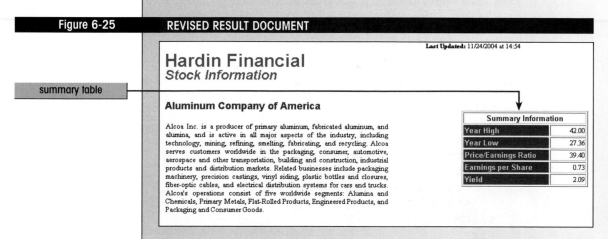

summary table

Now that the result document contains descriptive and summary information on each stock, Kevin wants you to add information regarding the current and recent value of the stock. You'll accomplish this by displaying the values of attribute nodes in the result document.

Working with Attribute Nodes

The first attribute that Kevin wants to add to the result document is the stock's NYSE symbol, and he wants it to appear after the stock name, as follows:

Aluminum Company of America (AA)

Recall that the XPath syntax for attribute values is *@attribute*, where *attribute* is the attribute's name. Since symbol is an attribute of the name element, you can modify the name template to display the symbol text using the following code:

```
<xsl:template match="name">
<h3 class="name">
   <xsl:value-of select="." />
   (<xsl:value-of select="@symbol" />)
</h3>
</xsl:template>
```

Modify the name template now.

To modify the name template:

1. Return to **stock.xsl** in your text editor.

2. Insert the following code immediately above the </h3> tag in the name template:

   ```
   (<xsl:value-of select="@symbol" />)
   ```

3. Save your changes to the file.

4. Use your browser or XML Spy to regenerate the result document and verify that the symbol for each stock appears in parentheses after the stock name.

Kevin entered stock values for each stock as attributes of the today element. For example, the stock values of the ALCOA stock are:

```
<today open="29.60" high="29.94" low="28.59" current="29.20"
 vol="2.94" />
```

Kevin wants this data to appear in a table that appears directly below each stock's name in the result document. The HTML code he wants you to use for this task is:

```
<table class="today">
<tr>
   <th class="today">Current</th>
   <th class="today">Open</th>
   <th class="today">High</th>
   <th class="today">Low</th>
   <th class="today">Volume</th>
</tr>
<tr>
   <td class="number">current</td>
   <td class="number">open</td>
   <td class="number">high</td>
   <td class="number">low</td>
   <td class="number">volume</td>
```

```
</tr>
</table>
```

where *current*, *open*, *high*, *low*, and *volume* are the attribute values from the today element. You'll insert this code by creating a template for the today element and then applying that template directly below the h3 heading that displays the stock's name.

To add this table to the style sheet:

1. Return to **stock.xsl** in your text editor.

2. Insert the today template immediately below the name template using the following code:

```
<xsl:template match="today">
<table class="today">
<tr>
    <th class="today">Current</th>
    <th class="today">Open</th>
    <th class="today">High</th>
    <th class="today">Low</th>
    <th class="today">Volume</th>
</tr>
<tr>
    <td class="number"><xsl:value-of select="@current" /></td>
    <td class="number"><xsl:value-of select="@open" /></td>
    <td class="number"><xsl:value-of select="@high" /></td>
    <td class="number"><xsl:value-of select="@low" /></td>
    <td class="number"><xsl:value-of select="@vol" /></td>
</tr>
</table>
</xsl:template>
```

The next step is to call this template from within the stock template, placing the table below the stock name.

3. Insert the following code immediately below <xsl:apply-templates select="name" />:

```
<xsl:apply-templates select="today" />
```

Figure 6-26 shows the revised code.

Figure 6-26 | CREATING THE TODAY TEMPLATE

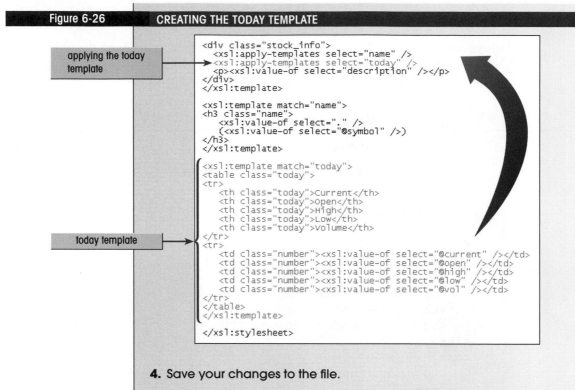

applying the today template

today template

```
<div class="stock_info">
  <xsl:apply-templates select="name" />
  <xsl:apply-templates select="today" />
  <p><xsl:value-of select="description" /></p>
</div>
</xsl:template>

<xsl:template match="name">
<h3 class="name">
  <xsl:value-of select="." />
  (<xsl:value-of select="@symbol" />)
</h3>
</xsl:template>

<xsl:template match="today">
<table class="today">
<tr>
  <th class="today">Current</th>
  <th class="today">Open</th>
  <th class="today">High</th>
  <th class="today">Low</th>
  <th class="today">Volume</th>
</tr>
<tr>
  <td class="number"><xsl:value-of select="@current" /></td>
  <td class="number"><xsl:value-of select="@open" /></td>
  <td class="number"><xsl:value-of select="@high" /></td>
  <td class="number"><xsl:value-of select="@low" /></td>
  <td class="number"><xsl:value-of select="@vol" /></td>
</tr>
</table>
</xsl:template>

</xsl:stylesheet>
```

4. Save your changes to the file.

5. Use your browser or XML Spy to regenerate the result document. Figure 6-27 shows the revised file.

Figure 6-27 | APPLYING THE TODAY TEMPLATE

table generated by the today template

The final item that Kevin wants you to add to the result document is a table that displays the values for each stock for the previous five days. Kevin stored this information in his XML document as attributes of the day element. For example, the five day stock values for the ALCOA stock are:

```
<five_day>
  <day open="31.20" high="32.61" low="30.15" close="30.51"
    vol="6.70" date="11/17/2004">1</day>
```

```
<day open="30.51" high="30.90" low="28.76" close="29.20"
     vol="4.84" date="11/18/2004">2</day>
<day open="29.20" high="30.33" low="27.12" close="28.53"
     vol="5.24" date="11/19/2004">3</day>
<day open="28.53" high="31.32" low="28.24" close="30.92"
     vol="5.91" date="11/22/2004">4</day>
<day open="30.92" high="31.12" low="28.84" close="29.60"
     vol="3.44" date="11/23/2004">5</day>
</five_day>
```

Kevin suggests that you display these values following the format of the table shown in Figure 6-28.

Figure 6-28   **THE RECENT HISTORY TABLE**

Recent History					
Day	Open	High	Low	Close	Volume
11/17/2004	31.20	32.61	30.15	30.51	6.70
11/18/2004	30.51	30.90	28.76	29.20	4.84
11/19/2004	29.20	30.33	27.12	28.53	5.24
11/22/2004	28.53	31.32	28.24	30.92	5.91
11/23/2004	30.92	31.12	28.84	29.60	3.44

Kevin wants the table placed below each stock description. To create the table, you'll use two templates. The first template sets up the HTML code for the entire table, formatting the table's size, border, and headings. The code is:

```
<table border="1" width="620" class="history">
<tr>
    <th class="histtitle" colspan="6">Recent History</th>
</tr>
<tr>
    <th class="history">Day</th>
    <th class="history">Open</th>
    <th class="history">High</th>
    <th class="history">Low</th>
    <th class="history">Close</th>
    <th class="history">Volume</th>
</tr>
    stocks values
</table>
```

where *stocks values* are five rows of values for the stock. To create this code, you'll use the following template for the five_day element:

```
<xsl:template match="five_day">
<table border="1" width="620" class="history">
<tr>
    <th class="histtitle" colspan="6">Recent History</th>
</tr>
<tr>
```

```
        <th class="history">Day</th>
        <th class="history">Open</th>
        <th class="history">High</th>
        <th class="history">Low</th>
        <th class="history">Close</th>
        <th class="history">Volume</th>
    </tr>
    <xsl:apply-templates select="day" />
    </table>
    </xsl:template>
```

The second template defines the HTML code for each row of the table. The HTML code for each table row is:

```
<tr>
    <td class="number">day</td>
    <td class="number">open</td>
    <td class="number">high</td>
    <td class="number">low</td>
    <td class="number">close</td>
    <td class="number">volume</td>
</tr>
```

where *day*, *open*, *high*, *low*, *close*, and *volume* are the values and attribute values of the day element. The day template would therefore appear as:

```
<xsl:template match="day">
<tr>
    <td class="number"><xsl:value-of select="@date" /></td>
    <td class="number"><xsl:value-of select="@open"/></td>
    <td class="number"><xsl:value-of select="@high"/></td>
    <td class="number"><xsl:value-of select="@low"/></td>
    <td class="number"><xsl:value-of select="@close"/></td>
    <td class="number"><xsl:value-of select="@vol"/></td>
</tr>
</xsl:template>
```

The combination of the five_day and day templates would then create the table shown in Figure 6-28.

To create the Recent History table:

1. Return to **stock.xsl** in your text editor.

2. Insert the five_day template immediately below the today template as follows:

```
<xsl:template match="five_day">
<table border="1" width="620" class="history">
<tr>
    <th class="histtitle" colspan="6">Recent History</th>
</tr>
<tr>
    <th class="history">Day</th>
    <th class="history">Open</th>
    <th class="history">High</th>
    <th class="history">Low</th>
    <th class="history">Close</th>
```

```
    <th class="history">Volume</th>
</tr>
<xsl:apply-templates select="day" />
</table>
</xsl:template>
```

3. Insert the following code for the day template immediately below the five_day template:

```
<xsl:template match="day">
<tr>
    <td class="number"><xsl:value-
of select="@date" /></td>
    <td class="number"><xsl:value-of select="@open"/></td>
    <td class="number"><xsl:value-of select="@high"/></td>
    <td class="number"><xsl:value-of select="@low"/></td>
    <td class="number"><xsl:value-
of select="@close"/></td>
    <td class="number"><xsl:value-of select="@vol"/></td>
</tr>
</xsl:template>
```

Figure 6-29 shows the revised code for the style sheet.

Figure 6-29   CREATING THE FIVE_DAY AND DAY TEMPLATES

```
<xsl:template match="five_day">
<table border="1" width="620" class="history">
<tr>
    <th class="histtitle" colspan="6">Recent History</th>
</tr>
<tr>
    <th class="history">Day</th>
    <th class="history">Open</th>
    <th class="history">High</th>
    <th class="history">Low</th>
    <th class="history">Close</th>
    <th class="history">Volume</th>
</tr>
<xsl:apply-templates select="day" />
</table>
</xsl:template>

<xsl:template match="day">
<tr>
    <td class="number"><xsl:value-of select="@date" /></td>
    <td class="number"><xsl:value-of select="@open" /></td>
    <td class="number"><xsl:value-of select="@high"/></td>
    <td class="number"><xsl:value-of select="@low"/></td>
    <td class="number"><xsl:value-of select="@close"/></td>
    <td class="number"><xsl:value-of select="@vol"/></td>
</tr>
</xsl:template>

</xsl:stylesheet>
```

five_day template

day template

Next you have to apply the five_day template.

4. Navigate to the stock template, and below the paragraph that contains the stock description, insert the following code (see Figure 6-30):

```
<xsl:apply-templates select="five_day" />
```

Figure 6-30 APPLYING THE FIVE_DAY TEMPLATE

```
<div class="stock_info">
  <xsl:apply-templates select="name" />
  <xsl:apply-templates select="today" />
  <p><xsl:value-of select="description" /></p>
  <xsl:apply-templates select="five_day" />
</div>
</xsl:template>
```

5. Save your changes to stock.xsl and close the file and your text editor.

6. Use your browser or XML Spy to regenerate the result document. Figure 6-31 shows the result document for the Alcoa stock.

Figure 6-31 VIEWING THE RECENT HISTORY TABLE

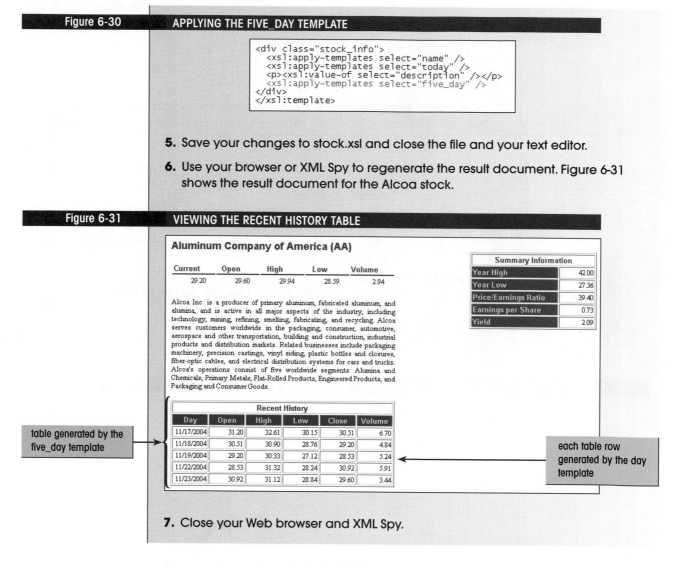

table generated by the five_day template

Aluminum Company of America (AA)

Current	Open	High	Low	Volume
29.20	29.60	29.94	28.59	2.94

Alcoa Inc. is a producer of primary aluminum, fabricated aluminum, and alumina, and is active in all major aspects of the industry, including technology, mining, refining, smelting, fabricating, and recycling. Alcoa serves customers worldwide in the packaging, consumer, automotive, aerospace and other transportation, building and construction, industrial products and distribution markets. Related businesses include packaging machinery, precision castings, vinyl siding, plastic bottles and closures, fiber-optic cables, and electrical distribution systems for cars and trucks. Alcoa's operations consist of five worldwide segments: Alumina and Chemicals, Primary Metals, Flat-Rolled Products, Engineered Products, and Packaging and Consumer Goods.

Summary Information	
Year High	42.00
Year Low	27.36
Price/Earnings Ratio	39.40
Earnings per Share	0.73
Yield	2.09

Recent History

Day	Open	High	Low	Close	Volume
11/17/2004	31.20	32.61	30.15	30.51	6.70
11/18/2004	30.51	30.90	28.76	29.20	4.84
11/19/2004	29.20	30.33	27.12	28.53	5.24
11/22/2004	28.53	31.32	28.24	30.92	5.91
11/23/2004	30.92	31.12	28.84	29.60	3.44

each table row generated by the day template

7. Close your Web browser and XML Spy.

At this point, you've added all of the stock data that Kevin wants to show in the result document. In the next session, you'll learn how to modify the appearance of the document by sorting the nodes of the node tree and creating conditional nodes.

Session 6.2 QUICK CHECK

1. In an XML document, the root element is named "books" and it has one child named "book." There are several book nodes in the node tree. Within each book element there are two child elements named "title" and "author." What XSLT command would you use to display the book's title formatted with an h1 heading? Assume that the context node is "book."

2. In the previous question, if the context node is "books," what code would you use to display all of the book titles in the source document?

3. What does the command:

```
<xsl:apply-templates />
```

in the root template display in the result document?

4. What command would you use to access the category template?

5. If isbn is an attribute of the book element, what command would you use to display the value of the attribute from within the book template?

SESSION 6.3

In this session, you'll learn how to sort nodes in either alphabetical or numerical order. You'll also learn how to create and use comparison elements that allow you to change the contents of the result document based on the values of the nodes in the source document. You'll learn how to use predicates to create subsets of the source document's node tree. Finally, you'll use XSLT to create elements and attributes in the result document.

Sorting Nodes

Kevin carefully examined the document you created and he has a few suggestions to improve its appearance. The first change involves the table of recent stock history. Kevin notices that the most recent stock values are at the bottom of the table. He wants the most recent values to appear at the top of the table.

By default, nodes are processed in **document order**, the order in which they appear in the document. To specify a different order, XSLT provides the <xsl:sort> element. This element can be used with either the <xsl:apply-templates> or the <xsl:for-each> element. The general form is:

```
<xsl:apply-templates select="expression">
    <xsl:sort attributes />
<xsl:apply-templates>
```

or

```
<xsl:for-each select="expression">
    <xsl:sort attributes />
</xsl:for-each>
```

Note that when you sort with the <xsl:apply-templates> element, the <xsl:apply-templates> element changes from an empty element into a two-sided element. If you sort with the <xsl:for-each> method, you must place the <xsl:sort> element with any other XSLT and literal result elements.

REFERENCE WINDOW   **RW**

Sorting a Node

- To sort a node, use the expression:

```
<xsl:apply-templates select="expression">
   <xsl:sort attributes />
<xsl:apply-templates>
```
or
```
<xsl:for-each select="expression">
   <xsl:sort attributes />
</xsl:for-each>
```
where *attributes* are attributes that define how the nodes should be sorted.

- To specify the item by which to sort, use the attribute:

```
<xsl:sort select="expression" />
```
where *expression* is a node in the node tree by which you want to sort the element.

- To specify that the sorting should be done numerically or alphabetically, use the attribute:

```
<xsl:sort data-type="type"
```
where *type* is "text" or "qname" for alphabetical sorting, or "number" for numerical sorting.

- To sort in ascending or descending order, use the attribute:

```
<xsl:sort order="type" />
```
where *type* equals "ascending" or "descending."

- In the case of text, to sort by either lowercase or uppercase letters first, use the attribute:

```
<xsl:sort case-order="type" />
```
where *type* equals either "upper-first" or "lower-first."

The <xsl:sort> element contains several attributes to control how the XSLT processor sorts the nodes in the source document. The syntax of the <xsl:sort> element is:

```
<xsl:sort select="expression" data-type="type" order="type"
          case-order="type" />
```

where the select attribute determines the criteria under which the context node is sorted, the data-type attribute indicates the type of data (text, number, or qname), the order attribute indicates the direction of the sorting (ascending or descending), and the case-order attribute indicates how to handle the sorting of uppercase and lowercase letters (upper-first or lower-first).

For example, if you want to sort the stocks by the stock name, you would use the following code in the root template:

```
<xsl:apply-templates select="portfolio/stock">
   <xsl:sort select="name" />
</xsl:apply-templates>
```

or equivalently:

```
<xsl:for-each select="portfolio/stock">
   <xsl:sort select="name" />
</xsl:for-each>
```

If you don't include the select attribute, the XSLT processor assumes that you wish to sort the values of the context node. Thus the following code can also be used to sort the stocks by stock name:

```
<xsl:for-each select="portfolio/stock/name">
    <xsl:sort />
</xsl:for-each>
```

By default, the <xsl:sort> element assumes that the data is in text form and that it should be sorted in ascending order. To sort by descending order, add the order attribute to the <xsl:sort> element as follows:

```
<xsl:sort select="name" order="descending" />
```

You must show caution when using the <xsl:sort> element with numeric values. For example, if you try to sort the numbers 1 through 100, you'll end up with the sort order: 1, 10, 100, 11, 12, and so forth since the default is to treat the element content as text. To sort numerically, you must include the data-type attribute as follows:

```
<xsl:sort select="expression" data-type="number" />
```

If you need to sort by more than one factor, you must place one <xsl:sort> element after another. For example, to sort the stocks first by category and then by name within each category, enter the following code into the root templates:

```
<xsl:apply-templates select="portfolio/stock">
    <xsl:sort select="category" />
    <xsl:sort select="name" />
</xsl:apply-templates>
```

Kevin wants to sort the Recent History table in descending order by date. Unfortunately there is no "date" data-type. To get around this problem, each of the five day values has been assigned a number, with "1" assigned to the first day in the five-day period and "5" assigned to the last day. Kevin wants the fifth day to appear first, followed by the fourth day, and so forth. To sort these values, you'll modify the <xsl:apply-templates> element in the five_day template, changing it from:

```
<xsl:apply-templates select="day" />
```

to

```
<xsl:apply-templates select="day">
    <xsl:sort data-type="number" order="descending" />
</xsl:apply-templates>
```

Remember that since we did not include the select attribute, the sorting is applied to the context node, in this case the day element.

To sort the dates in the Recent History table:

1. Using your text editor, open **stock.xsl**.

2. Locate the five_day template near the bottom of the file, and replace the <xsl:apply-templates> element that applies the day template with:

```
<xsl:apply-templates select="day">
    <xsl:sort data-type="number" order="descending" />
</xsl:apply-templates>
```

> TROUBLE? Make sure that you change the <xsl:apply-template> from an empty tag to a two-sided tag by removing the / character at the end of the opening tag.
>
> **3.** Save your changes to the file.
>
> **4.** Use your browser or XML Spy to regenerate the result document and verify that the Recent History tables contain the most recent date (11/23/2004) at the top.

Creating **Conditional Nodes**

Kevin also wants to be able to tell, at a glance, whether a particular stock is increasing or decreasing from its opening value. Kevin created three graphics for you to use to identify a stock as increasing, decreasing, or unchanged:

- **up.gif** — a green triangle pointing up indicating the stock's value has increased since the market opened
- **down.gif** — a red triangle pointing down indicating the stock's value has declined
- **same.gif** — a blue line indicating that the stock's value is unchanged

To use these graphics, the style sheet must apply different HTML code based on the performance of the stock. If the stock increased in value, the HTML code is:

```
<td class="number">
   <img src="up.gif"> Stock Value
</td>
```

If it decreased in value, the HTML code is:

```
<td class="number">
   <img src="down.gif"> Stock Value
</td>
```

and if the value is unchanged, the HTML code is:

```
<td class="number">
   <img src="same.gif"> Stock Value
</td>
```

To create this code, you need to use a conditional element. XSLT supports two kinds: <xsl:if> and <xsl:choose>.

Using the <xsl:if> Element

The syntax for the <xsl:if> element is:

```
<xsl:if test="expression">
   XSLT and Literal Result Elements
</xsl:if>
```

where *expression* is an XPath expression that is either true or false. If the expression is true, the XSLT and literal result elements are generated by the processor, otherwise nothing is done. For example, the following code displays the stock name, but only if the value of the symbol attribute is equal to 'AA'.

```
<xsl:if test="@symbol = 'AA'">
   <h3><xsl:value-of select="name" /></h3>
</xsl:if>
```

Note that the text string must be enclosed in either double or single quotes. Like other aspects of XML, comparisons are case sensitive.

Be careful when comparing node sets and single values. When there are multiple nodes involved, the expression is true if *any* of the nodes satisfies the test condition. For example, the following expression:

```
/portfolio/stock/name/@symbol = "AA"
```

is true as long as there is at least one symbol attribute in the node set that is equal to "AA". This means that the following <xsl:if> condition:

```
<xsl:if test="/portfolio/stock/name/@symbol = 'AA'">
   <xsl:value-of select="/portfolio/stock/name" />
</xsl:if>
```

will display a stock name even for those stock names whose attribute values are *not* equal to "AA", just as long as there is one stock that has a symbol equal to "AA".

REFERENCE   WINDOW   **RW**

Applying a Conditional Node

■ To apply a format only if a particular condition is met, use the XSLT element:

```
<xsl:if test="expression">
   XSLT and Literal Result Elements
</xsl:if>
```

where *expression* is an XPath expression that is either true or false.

■ To apply formats under several possible conditions, use the syntax:

```
<xsl:choose>
    <xsl:when test="expression1">
       XSLT and Literal Result Elements
    </xsl:when>
    <xsl:when test="expression2">
       XSLT and Literal Result Elements
    </xsl:when>


    • • •


    <xsl:otherwise>
       XSLT and Literal Result Elements
    </xsl:otherwise>
</xsl:choose>
```

where *expression1*, *expression2*, and so forth are expressions that are either true or false. If none of the expressions is true, then the code in the <xsl:otherwise> element is used in the result document.

Using Comparison Operators and Functions

The = symbol in the test is an example of a **comparison operator** used to compare one value to another. Comparisons can be made between numbers, text strings, attribute nodes, element nodes, or text nodes.

Figure 6-32 shows other comparison operators supported by XPath.

Figure 6-32	COMPARISON OPERATORS	
OPERATOR	**DESCRIPTION**	**EXAMPLE**
=	Tests whether two values are equal to each other	@symbol = "AA"
!=	Tests whether two values are unequal	@symbol != "AA"
&lt;	Tests whether one value is less than another	day < 5
<=	Tests whether one value is less than or equal to another	day <= 5
>	Tests whether one value is greater than another	day > 1
>=	Tests whether one value is greater than or equal to another	day >= 1

Because XML treats the < character as the opening character for a tag, you must use the text string < for less-than comparisons. XML doesn't have a problem with the > character. As a result, one way to avoid using the < expression is to reverse the order of the comparison. For example, instead of writing the comparison as:

```
day &lt; 5
```

write it as:

```
5 > day
```

Comparison tests can be combined using the "and" and "or" operators. For example, the following expression:

```
day > 2 and day &lt; 5
```

tests whether the value of the day element lies between 2 and 5. Similarly, the expression:

```
@symbol = "AA" or @symbol = "UCL"
```

tests whether the value of the symbol attribute is equal to "AA" or "UCL".

You can reverse the true/false value of an expression using the not() function. The expression:

```
not(@symbol = "AA")
```

returns a value of false if the value of the symbol attribute is equal to "AA", and true if the symbol attribute is *not* equal to "AA".

Using the <xsl:choose> Element

Unlike other programming languages, XSLT does not support an else-if construction, thus the <xsl:if> element tests for only one condition and allows for only one outcome. If you want to test for multiple conditions and display different outcomes, use the <xsl:choose> element. The syntax of the <xsl:choose> element is:

```
<xsl:choose>
    <xsl:when test="expression1">
```

```
        XSLT and Literal Result Elements
    </xsl:when>
    <xsl:when test="expression2">
        XSLT and Literal Result Elements
    </xsl:when>

...

    <xsl:otherwise>
        XSLT and Literal Result Elements
    </xsl:otherwise>
</xsl:choose>
```

where *expression1*, *expression2*, and so forth are expressions that are either true or false. The XSLT processor proceeds through the list of <xsl:when> elements one at a time. When it encounters an expression that is true, it processes the corresponding XSLT and literal result elements and ignores the rest of the <xsl:when> elements. If no expressions are true, the XSLT and literal result elements contained in the <xsl:otherwise> element are processed.

Since Kevin needs you to test for three possible conditions, you will use the <xsl:choose> element rather than <xsl:if>. Kevin needs the code to test whether the value of the current attribute is greater than, less than, or equal to the opening value of the stock, and display the appropriate image file. The code to accomplish this is:

```
<xsl:choose>
    <xsl:when test="@current &lt; @open">
        <img src="down.gif" />
    </xsl:when>
    <xsl:when test="@current > @open">
        <img src="up.gif" />
    </xsl:when>
    <xsl:otherwise>
        <img src="same.gif" />
    </xsl:otherwise>
</xsl:choose>
<xsl:value-of select="@current">
```

To add a conditional node to the style sheet:

1. Return to **stock.xsl** in your text editor.

2. Navigate to the today template located in the middle of the file.

3. Insert the following code immediately after the <td class="number"> tag for the @current node (see Figure 6-33):

```
<xsl:choose>
    <xsl:when test="@current &lt; @open">
        <img src="down.gif" />
    </xsl:when>
    <xsl:when test="@current > @open">
        <img src="up.gif" />
    </xsl:when>
    <xsl:otherwise>
        <img src="same.gif" />
    </xsl:otherwise>
</xsl:choose>
```

Figure 6-33   **ADDING THE <XSL:CHOOSE> ELEMENT TO THE TODAY TEMPLATE**

```
<xsl:template match="today">
<table class="today">
<tr>
   <th class="today">Current</th>
   <th class="today">Open</th>
   <th class="today">High</th>
   <th class="today">Low</th>
   <th class="today">Volume</th>
</tr>
<tr>
   <td class="number">
   <xsl:choose>
     <xsl:when test="@current &lt; @open">
       <img src="down.gif" />
     </xsl:when>
     <xsl:when test="@current > @open">
       <img src="up.gif" />
     </xsl:when>
     <xsl:otherwise>
       <img src="same.gif" />
     </xsl:otherwise>
   </xsl:choose>
       <xsl:value-of select="@current" />
   </td>
   <td class="number"><xsl:value-of select="@open" /></td>
   <td class="number"><xsl:value-of select="@high" /></td>
   <td class="number"><xsl:value-of select="@low" /></td>
   <td class="number"><xsl:value-of select="@vol" /></td>
</tr>
</table>
</xsl:template>
```

code when the stock value declines

code when the stock value increases

code when the stock value stays the same

Kevin also wants these graphics added to the Recent History table. In this case, you'll test whether the closing value is greater than, less than, or equal to the opening value.

4. Navigate to the day template located at the bottom of the file.

5. Insert the following code immediately after the <td class="number"> tag for the @date attribute node (see Figure 6-34):

```
<xsl:choose>
    <xsl:when test="@close &lt; @open">
        <img src="down.gif" />
    </xsl:when>
    <xsl:when test="@close > @open">
        <img src="up.gif" />
    </xsl:when>
    <xsl:otherwise>
        <img src="same.gif" />
    </xsl:otherwise>
</xsl:choose>
```

Figure 6-34 ADDING THE <XSL:CHOOSE> ELEMENT TO THE DAY TEMPLATE

```
<xsl:template match="day">
<tr>
   <td class="number">
   <xsl:choose>
      <xsl:when test="@close &lt; @open">
         <img src="down.gif" />
      </xsl:when>
      <xsl:when test="@close > @open">
         <img src="up.gif" />
      </xsl:when>
      <xsl:otherwise>
         <img src="same.gif" />
      </xsl:otherwise>
   </xsl:choose>
      <xsl:value-of select="@date" />
   </td>
   <td class="number"><xsl:value-of select="@open"/></td>
   <td class="number"><xsl:value-of select="@high"/></td>
   <td class="number"><xsl:value-of select="@low"/></td>
   <td class="number"><xsl:value-of select="@close"/></td>
   <td class="number"><xsl:value-of select="@vol"/></td>
</tr>
</xsl:template>
```

6. Save your changes to stock.xsl.

7. Use your browser or XML Spy to regenerate the result document. Figure 6-35 shows the revised result document for the Alcoa stock.

Figure 6-35 UP AND DOWN GRAPHICS

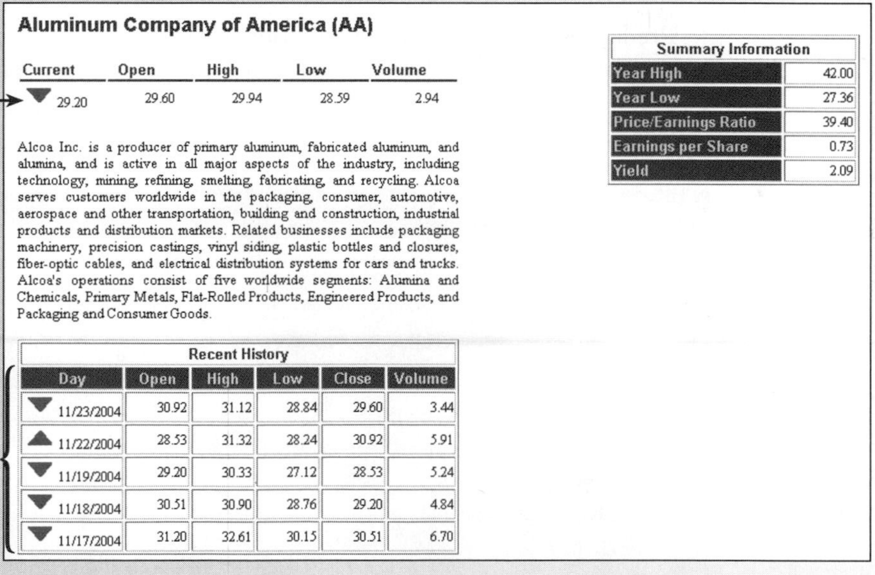

graphic changes depending on whether the stock value increases, decreases, or stays the same

Working with Predicates

The stocks in Kevin's document are grouped into three categories: industrials, utilities, and transportation, and he wants the result document to organize the stocks in a similar fashion. One way to accomplish this is to use predicates.

Predicates are XPath expressions that test for a condition and create subsets of nodes that fulfill that condition. The general syntax for a predicate is:

node[*expression*]

where *node* is a node from the source document's node tree, and *expression* is an expression for the condition that the node must fulfill. For example, the following predicate

```
name[@symbol = "AA"]
```

matches the name elements whose symbol attribute is equal to "AA". If you do not include a value for the attribute, you can select only those nodes that contain the attribute. For example, the expression:

```
name[@symbol]
```

selects only those name elements that have a symbol attribute.

The predicate can also indicate the position of the node in the node tree. The following expression:

```
stock[1]
```

selects the first stock element in the source document. To select the last stock element from the node tree, use the last() function as follows:

```
stock[last()]
```

To select a specific position in the node tree, use the position() function combined with an XPath expression. The following predicate selects the second stock element in the node tree:

```
stock[position()=2]
```

Predicates can be used in combination with any XPath expression. The following example uses a predicate to return the name of the second stock element:

```
<xsl:value-of select="stock[position()=2]/name" />
```

REFERENCE WINDOW   RW

Using Node Predicates

- To select a subset of nodes from the node tree, use the XPath expression:

  node[*expression*]

  where *node* is a node from the source document's node tree, and *expression* is an expression for the condition that the node must fulfill.

- To process only the first node from a branch of the node tree, use the expression:

  node[1]

- To process only the last node from a branch of the node tree, use the expression:

  node[last()]

- To process a node from a specific location in the node's tree branch, use the expression:

  node[position()=*value*]

  where *value* is an integer indicating the node's location in the branch.

Kevin wants to display the name of each stock category using an h2 heading. Under each heading, Kevin wants to display the stocks that belong to that category. He also wants the stocks sorted in alphabetical order within each category. The code to display the industrial stocks would look as follows:

```
<h2 class="category">Industrials</h2>
<xsl:apply-templates
```

```
  select="portfolio/stock[category='Industrials']">
    <xsl:sort select="name" />
</xsl:apply-templates>
```

Add code to the style sheet to display the stocks in categories.

To use predicates in the root templates:

1. Return to **stock.xsl** in your text editor.

2. Go to the root template and replace the line:

```
<xsl:apply-templates select="portfolio/stock" />
```

with the following code (see Figure 6-36):

```
<h2 class="category">Industrials</h2>
<xsl:apply-templates
 select="portfolio/stock[category='Industrials']">
    <xsl:sort select="name" />
</xsl:apply-templates>

<h2 class="category">Utilities</h2>
<xsl:apply-templates
 select="portfolio/stock[category='Utilities']">
    <xsl:sort select="name" />
</xsl:apply-templates>

<h2 class="category">Transportation</h2>
<xsl:apply-templates
 select="portfolio/stock[category='Transportation']">
    <xsl:sort select="name" />
</xsl:apply-templates>
```

Figure 6-36	ADDING PREDICATES TO THE ROOT TEMPLATE

```
<xsl:template match="/">
<html>
<head>
<title>Stock Information</title>
<link href="stock.css" rel="stylesheet" type="text/css" />
</head>
<body>
<div id="datetime"><b>Last Updated: </b>
    <xsl:apply-templates select="portfolio/date" /> at
    <xsl:value-of select="portfolio/time" />
</div>
<h1 class="title">Hardin Financial</h1>
<h2 class="title">Stock Information</h2>
<h2 class="category">Industrials</h2>
<xsl:apply-templates select="portfolio/stock[category='Industrials']">
    <xsl:sort select="name" />
</xsl:apply-templates>

<h2 class="category">Utilities</h2>
<xsl:apply-templates select="portfolio/stock[category='Utilities']">
    <xsl:sort select="name" />
</xsl:apply-templates>

<h2 class="category">Transportation</h2>
<xsl:apply-templates select="portfolio/stock[category='Transportation']">
    <xsl:sort select="name" />
</xsl:apply-templates>
</body>
</html>
</xsl:template>
```

industrial stocks

utility stocks

transportation stocks

3. Save your changes to stock.xsl.

4. Use your browser or XML Spy to regenerate the result document and verify that the stocks are now grouped into categories, and that within each category, stocks are listed alphabetically (see Figure 6-37).

| Figure 6-37 | DISPLAYING THE STOCK DATA BY CATEGORIES |

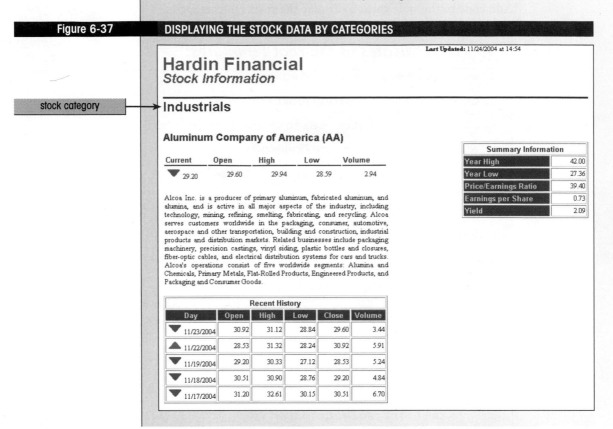

Creating Elements and Attributes

As a final task, Kevin thinks it would be useful to change the name of each stock in the result document to a hypertext link, connected to the company's home page. Using the Alcoa stock as an example, the HTML code Kevin wants added to the result document would look as follows:

```
<a href="http://www.alcoa.com">
<h3 class="name">
   Aluminum Company of America
</h3>
</a>
```

Kevin included the URL for the company's home page in the link element of the source document (see Figure 6-2). He thinks it is a simple matter to place this link in the document. Kevin's first attempt looks something like the following:

```
<xsl:template match="name">
<a href=" <xsl:value-of select="../link" /> ">
<h3 class="name">
   <xsl:value-of select="." />
```

```
</h3>
</a>
</xsl:template>
```

However, the XSLT processor returned an error message and the reason is not surprising. Because Kevin's style sheet is an XML document, it must follow the syntax rules for all XML documents. One such rule is that tags must be well formed, but because there is no closing bracket for the tag:

```
<a href="< ...
```

it is rejected by the processor.

Kevin turns to you for help with inserting the value of the link element as an attribute of HTML's <a> tag. One way of solving Kevin's problem is to create the <a> element in the result document, providing that element with all attributes it needs to create a hypertext link. The ability to create an element is often used to transform one XML document into another. In this case, we'll use XML to create HTML tags in the result document.

Creating an Element

To create an element, XSLT uses the <xsl:element> tag as follows:

```
<xsl:element name="name" namespace="URI"
 use-attribute-sets="namelist">
   XSLT and Literal Result Elements
</xsl:element>
```

where the name attribute assigns a name to the element, the namespace attribute provides a namespace, and use-attribute-sets provides a list of attribute-sets (more on this later). For example, to create an element with the name "stock_name" that contains the name of each stock in Kevin's document, you could use the following code:

```
<xsl:element name="stock_name">
   <xsl:value-of select="name" />
</xsl:element>
```

For the Alcoa stock, the code generated for the result document would be:

```
<stock_name>
   Aluminum Company of America
</stock_name>
```

To see how a style sheet can be used to create a new XML document, the following set of code generates a result document that lists the symbols of all of the transportation stocks in Kevin's portfolio in alphabetical order.

```
<?xml version="1.0" ?>
<xsl:stylesheet version="1.0"
 xmlns:xsl="http://www.w3.org/1999/XSL/Transform">
<xsl:output method="xml" version="1.0" indent="yes" />

<xsl:template match="/">
<xsl:apply-templates select="portfolio" />
</xsl:template>

<xsl:template match="portfolio">
<xsl:element name="Transportation">
```

```
      <xsl:for-each select="stock[category='Transportation']">
      <xsl:sort select="name" />
      <xsl:element name="stock">
         <xsl:value-of select="name/@symbol" />
      </xsl:element>
      </xsl:for-each>
   </xsl:element>
   </xsl:template>

   </xsl:stylesheet>
```

After transforming the stock.xml document, the XSLT processor would create the following XML document:

```
<?xml version="1.0" encoding="UTF-16"?>
<Transportation>
   <stock>ABF</stock>
   <stock>CNI</stock>
   <stock>R</stock>
   <stock>LUV</stock>
   <stock>UNP</stock>
</Transportation>
```

If we need to create a one-sided element, we simply use a one-sided <xsl:element> tag. For example:

```
<xsl:element name="stocks" />
```

creates the following empty element in the result document:

```
<stocks />
```

To experiment with the <xsl:element> tag, we'll use it to create the <a> tag for Kevin's result document. As you know, you could accomplish the same result by using a literal result element, as we did for the other HTML tags in the style sheet, but this is good practice for using the tag.

To create an element using the <xsl:element> tag:

1. Return to **stock.xsl** in your text editor.

2. Navigate to the name template located near the middle of the file.

3. Insert the following code immediately before the <h3 class="name"> tag:

```
<xsl:element name="a">
```

4. Insert the following code immediately after the closing </h3> tag:

```
</xsl:element>
```

5. Figure 6-38 shows the revised template code.

Figure 6-38   CREATING AN ELEMENT

used to create the <a>
tag in the result
document

```
<xsl:template match="name">
<xsl:element name="a">
<h3 class="name">
   <xsl:value-of select="." />
   (<xsl:value-of select="@symbol" />)
</h3>
</xsl:element>
</xsl:template>
```

Next we need to add attributes to this element to turn the stock name into a hypertext link.

REFERENCE WINDOW | **RW**

Creating Elements and Attributes

- To create an element, use the command:
  ```
  <xsl:element name="name" namespace="URI"
   use-attribute-sets="namelist">
     XSLT and Literal Result Elements
  </xsl:element>
  ```
  where the name attribute assigns a name to the element, the namespace attribute provides a namespace, and use-attribute-sets provides a list of attribute-sets.

- To create a one-sided or empty element, use:
  ```
  <xsl:element attributes />
  ```

- To create an attribute, use:
  ```
  <xsl:attribute name="name" namespace="URI">
     XSLT and Literal Result Elements
  </xsl:attribute>
  ```
  where the name attribute specifies the name of the attribute and the namespace attribute indicates the namespace.

- To create a set of attributes, use:
  ```
  <xsl:attribute-set name="name" use-attribute-sets="name-list">
      <xsl:attribute name="name1">elements</xsl:attribute>
      <xsl:attribute name="name2">elements</xsl:attribute>


  </xsl:attribute-set>
  ```
  where the name attribute is the name of the set and use-attribute-sets can refer to the contents of another attribute set.

Creating an Attribute

Attributes are created in XSLT by using the <xsl:attribute> element as follows:

```
<xsl:attribute name="name" namespace="URI">
   XSLT and Literal Result Elements
</xsl:attribute>
```

where the name attribute specifies the name of the attribute and the namespace attribute indicates the namespace. One use of the attribute tag is to create inline images in the result document. For example, if an element named "source" contains the value "logo.jpg", then the code:

```
<xsl:element name="img">
<xsl:attribute name="src">
   <xsl:value-of select="source" />
</xsl:attribute>
</xsl:element>
```

creates the following tag in the result document:

```
<img src="logo.jpg">
```

If Kevin wanted to create an XML document that included each Transportation stock's current value as an attribute of the stock element, he could use the following style sheet:

```
<?xml version="1.0" ?>
<xsl:stylesheet version="1.0"
 xmlns:xsl="http://www.w3.org/1999/XSL/Transform">
<xsl:output method="xml" version="1.0" indent="yes" />

<xsl:template match="/">
<xsl:apply-templates select="portfolio" />
</xsl:template>

<xsl:template match="portfolio">
<xsl:element name="Transportation">
   <xsl:for-each select="stock[category='Transportation']">
   <xsl:sort select="name" />
   <xsl:element name="stock ">
   <xsl:attribute name="current">
      <xsl:value-of select="today/@current" />
   </xsl:attribute>
      <xsl:value-of select="name/@symbol" />
   </xsl:element>
   </xsl:for-each>
</xsl:element>
</xsl:template>

</xsl:stylesheet>
```

The resulting XML document would contain the following code:

```
<?xml version="1.0" encoding="UTF-16"?>
<Transportation>
   <stock current="13.00">ABF</stock>
   <stock current="47.19">CNI</stock>
   <stock current="25.23">R</stock>
   <stock current="14.00">LUV</stock>
   <stock current="59.32">UNP</stock>
</Transportation>
```

Related to the <xsl:attribute> element is the <xsl:attribute-set> element that is used to create sets of attributes to be applied to different elements within the style sheet. The syntax of the <xsl:attribute-set> element is:

```
<xsl:attribute-set name="name" use-attribute-sets="name-
list">
   <xsl:attribute name="name1">elements</xsl:attribute>
   <xsl:attribute name="name2">elements</xsl:attribute>

...

</xsl:attribute-set>
```

where the name attribute is the name of the set and use-attribute-sets can refer to the contents of another attribute set. You can create a hierarchy of attribute-sets by referencing one attribute-set from another.

Note that the <xsl:attribute-set> element can only have <xsl:attribute> elements as children, though those elements can contain other XSLT and literal result elements.

An area where attribute-sets can be useful is formatting. On some Web pages, Kevin may want to use the HTML <font> tag to format text on the page. The <font> tag is an early HTML tag, compatible with older browsers. For example, to create text in size 4, red, Arial font, the following attribute-set can be used:

```
<xsl:attribute-set name="font1">
    <xsl:attribute name="face">Arial</xsl:attribute>
    <xsl:attribute name="size">4</xsl:attribute>
    <xsl:attribute name="color">red</xsl:attribute>
</xsl:attribute-set>
```

To apply this attribute-set to the <font> tag, use the following code:

```
<xsl:element name="font" attribute-set="font1">
    sample text
</xsl:element>
```

which results in the following HTML code:

```
<font face="Arial" size="4" color="red">
    sample text
</font>
```

Creating Comments and Processing Instructions

XSLT can also include elements to create comments and processing instructions in the result document. To create a comment, use the code:

```
<xsl:comment>
    Comment Text
</xsl:comment>
```

For example, the following code:

```
<xsl:comment>
    Kevin Summers Stock Portfolio
</xsl:comment>
```

creates the comment:

```
<!-- Kevin Summers Stock Portfolio -->
```

REFERENCE WINDOW   **RW**

Creating Comments and Processing Instructions
- To add a comment to the result document, use:
```
<xsl:comment>
    Comment Text
</xsl:comment>
```
- To add a processing instruction to the result document, use:
```
<xsl:processing-instruction name="name">
    Processing instruction attributes
</xsl:processing-instruction>
```

To create a processing instruction, use the syntax:

```
<xsl:processing-instruction name="name">
    Processing instruction attributes
</xsl:processing-instruction>
```

If you want to add a processing instruction in order to attach the result document to the styles.css style sheet, use the following code:

```
<xsl:processing-instruction name="xml-style sheet">
    href="styles.css" type="text/css"
</xsl:processing-instruction>
```

which generates the following tag in the result document:

```
<?xml-stylesheet href="styles.css" type="text.css"?>
```

Note that the content of the processing instruction is treating the processor as a string of text to be added to the processing instruction. Do not use the <xsl:attribute> element.

Now that you've seen how to use XSLT to create different types of nodes in the result document, you can add the href attribute to the <a> tag of Kevin's Web page.

To add an attribute to the <a> tag:

1. Insert the following code immediately after the <xsl:element> tag in the name template (see Figure 6-39):

```
<xsl:attribute name="href">
    <xsl:value-of select="../link" />
</xsl:attribute>
```

Note that because the name and link elements are siblings, you must travel up the node tree, using the .. character in the XPath expression.

Figure 6-39	CREATING AN ATTRIBUTE

used to add the href attribute to the <a> tag →

```
<xsl:template match="name">
<xsl:element name="a">
<xsl:attribute name="href">
    <xsl:value-of select="../link" />
</xsl:attribute>
<h3 class="name">
    <xsl:value-of select="." />
    (<xsl:value-of select="@symbol" />)
</h3>
</xsl:element>
</xsl:template>
```

2. Save your changes to stock.xsl and close the file and your text editor.

3. Use your browser or XML Spy to generate the result document.

4. Click the heading **Aluminum Company of America** from the first stock listed and verify that this heading now acts as a hypertext link and opens the Web page at *www.alcoa.com*.

5. Close your Web browser.

If you view the source of the result document (assuming that you created it as a separate file), you'll notice that the HTML code for the Alcoa heading is now:

```
<a href="http://www.alcoa.com">
<h3 class="name">
    Aluminum Company of America(AA)
</h3>
</a>
```

You've completed your work. Kevin will examine the document and discuss the results with his colleagues. If he needs to make changes, he'll contact you.

Session 6.3 QUICK CHECK

1. An XML document contains the root element named "books," which has a single child element named "book." Each book element has two child elements named "title" and "author." Using the <xsl:for-each> construction, sort the book elements in alphabetical order based on the title.

2. By default, does the <xsl:sort> element sort items numerically or alphabetically?

3. The book element has a single attribute named "category." The value of category can be either Fiction or Non-fiction. Write an <xsl:if> construction that displays the book title only if it is a non-fiction book.

4. Use a <xsl:choose> construction that displays book titles in an h3 heading if they're fiction and an h2 heading if they're non-fiction.

5. What is wrong with the following test expression? Correct the expression so that it doesn't result in an error.

   ```
   test="sales < 20000"
   ```

6. Redo Question 3, but this time solve the problem using a predicate expression rather than an <xsl:if> construction.

7. What code would you use to select the first book from the XML document described in Question 1? What would you use to select the last book?

8. What code would you use to create an element named "inventory" that contains the value 15000?

9. What code would you use to create an empty element named "inventory" that contains a single attribute named "amount" with the value 15000?

10. What code would you use to create a processing instruction in the result document linking the result document to an XSLT style sheet with the name "styles.xsl"?

REVIEW ASSIGNMENTS

Kevin Summers has worked with the Web page you created. He wants to try a new design, in which the current stock values appear prominently in a table at the top of the page, and summary information about each stock appears lower on the page. Figure 6-40 shows a preview of the page you'll create.

Figure 6-40

As of 11/24/2004 at 14:54

Stock Values

Stock	Current	Open	High	Low	Volume
▼ AA	29.20	29.60	29.94	28.59	2.94
▲ ABF	13.00	12.80	13.18	11.90	1.00
▼ AEP	34.45	36.10	36.42	34.35	2.67
▼ AZO	67.19	68.00	69.30	65.80	1.59
▼ CNI	47.19	47.70	48.14	46.63	0.35
▼ ED	37.05	37.17	37.50	36.43	1.22
▲ EK	29.84	29.40	29.84	27.83	3.16
─ GM	46.67	46.67	47.00	44.53	6.08
─ LUV	14.00	14.00	14.59	13.53	4.03
▼ MRO	24.08	24.15	24.63	23.70	1.84
▲ PPL	30.50	30.05	30.62	29.40	0.84
▼ R	25.23	25.62	26.29	24.93	0.26
▲ UCL	33.80	33.35	34.00	32.66	1.01
▲ UNP	59.32	59.00	59.70	58.20	1.81

Summary Information

Aluminum Company of America

Category	Industrials
Year High	42.00
Year Low	27.36
P/E Ratio	39.40
Earnings	0.73
Yield	2.09

Alcoa Inc. is a producer of primary aluminum, fabricated aluminum, and alumina, and is active in all major aspects of the industry, including technology, mining, refining, smelting, fabricating, and recycling. Alcoa serves customers worldwide in the packaging, consumer, automotive, aerospace, and other transportation, building and construction, industrial products and distribution markets. Related businesses include packaging machinery, precision castings, vinyl siding, plastic bottles and closures, fiber-optic cables, and electrical distribution systems for cars and trucks. Alcoa's operations consist of five worldwide segments: Alumina and Chemicals, Primary Metals, Flat-Rolled Products, Engineered Products, and Packaging and Consumer Goods.

Airborne Freight Corporation

Category	Transportation
Year High	23.34
Year Low	7.00
P/E Ratio	207.67
Earnings	0.06
Yield	1.28

Airborne Freight Corporation is an air express company and air freight forwarder that expedites shipments of all sizes to destinations throughout the United States and most foreign countries. ABX Air, Inc., the Company's principal wholly owned subsidiary, provides domestic express cargo service and cargo service to Canada. The Company is the sole customer of ABX for this service. ABX also offers limited charter service. Airborne Express provides door-to-door express delivery of small packages and documents throughout the United States and to and from most foreign countries. The Company also acts as an international and domestic freight forwarder for shipments of any size.

In addition to placing the current stock values at the top of the page, Kevin wants to create hypertext links between each stock's entry and the summary paragraph for that stock, located further down the page. He created a CSS style sheet named "stock2.css" to help you format the HTML tags on the Web page. Kevin decided not to include any five day information in this page version.

Note that creating a style sheet can be complicated. It is *strongly recommended* that you save your changes and generate the result document as you complete each step below to check on your progress and detect any problems early.

To complete this assignment:

1. Using your text editor, open **stocktxt.xml** located in the tutorial.06x/review folder of your Data Disk. Save the file as **stock2.xml**.

2. Add a processing instruction after the XML declaration that attaches this XML document to an XSLT style sheet file named "stock2.xsl." Save your changes to the document and close it.

3. Use your text editor to create a blank document named **stock2.xsl** and save the file in the tutorial.06x/review folder of your Data Disk. Set up this document as an XSLT style sheet by creating the required XML declaration, stylesheet root element, and XSLT namespace.

4. Add an output method that tells the XSLT processor to create an HTML version 4.0 file.

5. Create a root template that sends the following output to the result document:

```
<html>
<head>
<title>Stock Information</title>
<link href="stock2.css" rel="stylesheet" type="text/css" />
</head>
<body>
<div id="datetime">
As of
    date
at
    time
</div>
<h2>Stock Values</h2>
<h2 id="summary">Summary Information</h2>
</body>
</html>
```

where *date* and *time* are the values of the date and time element from the stock2.xml file.

6. Between the Stock Values and Summary Information headings in the root template, insert the following HTML code:

```
<table width="350" border="1" align="center" id="stocktable">
<tr>
    <th class="head1">Stock</th>
    <th class="head1">Current</th>
    <th class="head1">Open</th>
    <th class="head1">High</th>
    <th class="head1">Low</th>
    <th class="head1">Volume</th>
</tr>
</table>
```

These are the table and column headings for the current stock values. In the next step, you'll create a template that writes the code for the individual table rows that display each stock's value.

7. Create a template for the today element that writes the following HTML code to the result document:

```
<tr>
    <td>
        symbol
    </td>
    <td class="numbers">
        current
    </td>
    <td class="numbers">
        open
    </td>
    <td class="numbers">
        high
```

```
      </td>
      <td class="numbers">
          low
      </td>
      <td class="numbers">
          volume
      </td>
  </tr>
```

where *symbol*, *current*, *open*, *high*, *low*, and *volume* are each stock's symbol, current value, opening value, high value, low value, and volume. (*Hint*: To display the stock symbol, use the relative path "../name/@symbol".)

8. Return to the root template and apply the today template before the closing </table> tag.

9. Create a template for the stock element that writes the following HTML code to the result document:

```
<h3>
    name
</h3>
<table align="left" hspace="15" border="10" class="summtable">
<tr>
    <td class="head2">Category</td>
    <td>category</td>
</tr>
<tr>
    <td class="head2">Year High</td>
    <td class="numbers">year_high</td>
</tr>
<tr>
    <td class="head2">Year Low</td>
    <td class="numbers">year_low</td>
</tr>
<tr>
    <td class="head2">P/E Ratio</td>
    <td class="numbers>pe_ratio</td>
</tr>
<tr>
    <td class="head2">Earnings</td>
    <td class="numbers">earnings</td>
</tr>
<tr>
    <td class="head2">Yield</td>
    <td class="numbers">yield</td>
</tr>
</table>
<p>
    description
</p>
```

where *category*, *year_high*, *year_low*, *pe_ratio*, *earnings*, *yield*, and *description* are the values of elements taken from the stock2.xml document.

10. Return to the root template and apply the stock template above the closing </body> tag.

11. Next you'll add a graphic to the Stock Values table to indicate whether each stock is increasing, decreasing, or staying the same in value. These graphics are stored in the up.gif, down.gif, and same.gif files in your tutorial.06x/review folder.

Return to the today template and use the <xsl:choose> element to modify the HTML for the table cell that displays each stock's symbol. If the stock's current value is higher than its opening value, the HTML code is:

```
<td>
    <img src="up.gif">
    symbol
</td>
```

If the stock is decreasing in value, the code is:

```
<td>
    <img src="down.gif">
    symbol
</td>
```

otherwise, the code is:

```
<td>
    <img src="same.gif">
    symbol
</td>
```

where *symbol* is the stock's symbol.

Next you'll create a hyperlink between the stock symbol and the paragraph that describes the stock, by enclosing the stock symbol and the stock name in <a> tags. For example, the hypertext link for the Alcoa stock is:

```
<a href="#AA">AA</a>
```

and the HTML code for the stock name would be:

```
<a name="AA">Aluminum Company of America</a>
```

Explore 12. To create the hypertext link, first go to the today template and use the <xsl:element> and <xsl:attribute> elements to display the symbol text as:

```
<a href="#symbol">symbol</a>
```

where *symbol* is the stock's symbol. *Hint*: The value for the href attribute should be entered as:

```
#<xsl:value-of select="../name/@symbol" />
```

Explore 13. Next, go to the stock template and use the <xsl:element> and <xsl:attribute> elements to display the name of the stock as:

```
<a name="symbol">
    <h3>name</h3>
</a>
```

where *symbol* is the stock's symbol and *name* is the stock's name.

Explore 14. Finally, Kevin wants the stocks sorted by symbol. Go to the root template and revise the <xsl:apply-templates> element for both the today and stock templates, sorting those templates by stock symbol. (*Hint*: For the today template, the value of the select attribute should be "../name/@symbol", and for the stock template, the value of the select attribute should be "name/@symbol".)

15. Save your changes to the **stock2.xsl** file.

16. Use XML Spy to create the result document as a separate file named **stock2.htm**. Open **stock2.htm** in your Web browser and verify that the layout matches that shown in Figure 6-40, and that the hypertext links in the Stock Values table jump the user to the stock's summary paragraph, located lower down on the Web page.

17. Hand in your files to your instructor.

CASE PROBLEMS

Case 1. SkyWeb Astronomy Dr. Andrew Weiss of Central Ohio University uses XML to store astronomical data. One of his XML files contains information on the Messier catalog, a list of deep sky objects of particular interest to astronomers and amateur observers. Figure 6-41 describes the elements and attributes in his document.

Figure 6-41

ELEMENT	DESCRIPTION
messier	The root element of the document
object	A single Messier object. The id attribute of the <object> tag indicates the Messier catalog number.
name	The name of the Messier object
description	A description of the Messier object
p	An element used to divide the object description into paragraphs
image	The filename of a graphic image of the Messier object
data	An element containing data on the Messier object
distance	The distance to the object in light years
size	The apparent size of the object (in arc minutes)
mag	The magnitude of the object
ra	The object's right ascension in the night sky
dec	The object's declination in the night sky

Dr. Weiss wants to display information from his XML document on the Web. He asks for your help in creating an XSLT style sheet to transform his document into a Web page. A preview of the result document is shown in Figure 6-42.

Figure 6-42

$kyWeb

The Messier Objects

M1: The Crab Nebula

The Crab Nebula, is one of the most famous supernova remnants in the night sky. The supernova was first noted on July 4, 1054 by Chinese astronomers. At its height, the supernova was about 4 times brighter than Venus and could be seen during the day for a period of more than three weeks.

The remnant of the this supernova was discovered in 1731 by the British astronomer, John Bevis. Messier himself found it in 1758 while looking for Halley's comet. He soon realized it was no comet and the Crab Nebula became the first entry in Messier's famous catalog of celestial objects.

Distance (light years)	Size (arc min)	Magnitude	Right Ascension	Declination
7200	6 x 4	8.4	05:34.5	+22:01

M13: The Hercules Globular Cluster

The Hercules Cluster is one of the most prominent and best known globular clusters of the Northern sky. It was discovered in 1714 by the noted English astronomer, Edmond Halley. Located in the Hercules constellation, M13 is visible to the naked eye on clear nights in dark sky locations.

The cluster contains perhaps as many as 500,000 stars, though some estimates push that number even up to a million. M13 is estimated to be about 14 billion years old, which places the date of its origin near to the date of the galaxy's birth.

Distance (light years)	Size (arc min)	Magnitude	Right Ascension	Declination
2200	10	5.7	16:41.7	+36:27

To complete this task:

1. Using your text editor, open **messtxt.xml** located in the tutorial.06x/cases folder of your Data Disk and save the file as **messier.xml**.

2. Add a processing instruction after the XML declaration to attach this XML document to an XSLT style sheet file named "messier.xsl." Save your changes to the document and close it.

3. Using your text editor, create a blank document named **messier.xsl** and save the file in the tutorial.06x/cases folder of your Data Disk. Establish this document as an XSLT style sheet by creating the required XML declaration, stylesheet root element, and XSLT namespace. Add an output method that instructs the XSLT processor to create an HTML version 4.0 file.

4. Create a root template that writes the following HTML code to the result document:

```
<html>
<head>
<title>The Messier Objects</title>
<style>
    h1, h2 {font-family: sans-serif}
</style>
</head>
<body>
<center><img src="skyweb.jpg" /></center>
<h1 id="title">The Messier Objects</h1>
</body>
</html>
```

5. Create a template for the object element that writes the following HTML code:

```
<div style="clear:left; width: 640; margin-top: 20">

<h2>
    id:name
</h2>

</div>
```

6. Insert the following HTML code immediately above the </div> tag in the object template for each occurrence of the description/p element. *Hint*: Use the <xsl:for-each> element:

```
<p>description paragraph</p>
```

7. Create a template for the data element that displays the following HTML code:

```
<table border="5" width="640">
<tr>
    <th>Distance (light years)</th>
    <th>Size (arc min)</th>
    <th>Magnitude</th>
    <th>Right Ascension</th>
    <th>Declination</th>
</tr>
<tr>
    <td align="right">distance</td>
    <td align="right">size</td>
    <td align="right">magnitude</td>
    <td align="right">ra</td>
    <td align="right">declination</td>
</tr>
</table>
```

where *distance*, *size*, *magnitude*, *ra*, and *declination* are data values for each Messier object.

8. Return to the object template and insert the data template directly before the </div> tag.

9. Return to the root template and insert the object template directly below the h1 heading. Sort the object template by the value of the id attribute.

Explore ▶ 10. Create an attribute-set named "image_att" that contains the following attributes and values:

```
align="left" hspace="5" width="100" height="82"
```

Note that you'll use these attributes to format the inline images of the Messier objects.

11. Return to the object template. Directly below the closing </h2> tag, create an <img> element that uses the image_att attribute-set. Create the following additional attribute for the <img> element:

    src="*image*"

    where *image* is the name of the image file for the Messier object image. For example, the <img> tag for the M1 Messier object should be:

    <img src="M01.jpg" align="left" hspace="5" width="100" height ="82">

12. Save your changes to messier.xsl.

13. Using XML Spy, generate the result document and name the result document **messier.htm**.

14. Using your Web browser, open **messier.htm** and verify that it resembles the Web page shown in Figure 6-42.

15. Hand in all of the Messier files to your instructor.

Explore *Case 2. Generating an XML Document* Linda Sanchez is a freelance programmer who uses XML with a checking account application. The structure of her document is shown in Figure 6-43.

Figure 6-43

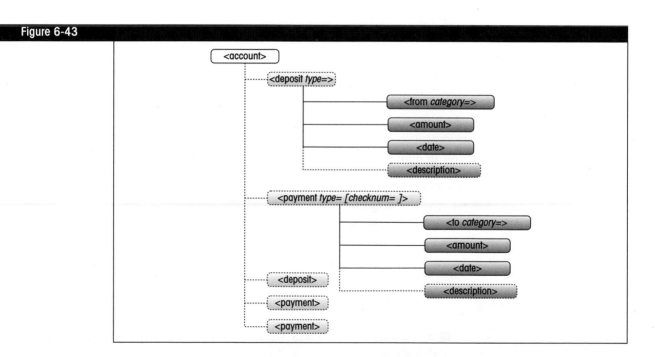

Linda wants to generate an XML document that displays only the checks written in the account. She envisions a simpler XML document with the structure shown in Figure 6-44.

Figure 6-44

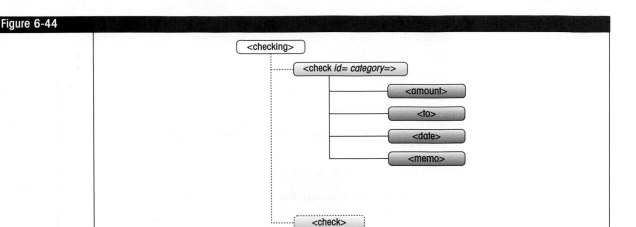

Linda knows that she can transform one XML document into another by using XSLT, and she wants your help in writing the style sheet.

To complete this task:

1. Using your text editor, open **acctxt.xml** located in the tutorial.06x/cases folder of your Data Disk and save the file as **account.xml**.

2. Add a processing instruction after the XML declaration that attaches this XML document to an XSLT style sheet file named "checks.xsl." Review the document structure to become familiar with its elements and attributes. Save your changes to the document and close it.

3. Using your text editor, create a blank document named **checks.xsl** and save the file in the tutorial.06x/cases folder of your Data Disk. Set up this document as an XSLT style sheet by creating the required XML declaration, stylesheet root element, and XSLT namespace.

Explore   4. Add an output method to the style sheet that instructs the XSLT processor that the result document is an XML version 1.0 document. In addition, have the processor add a !DOCTYPE tag to the result document that attaches the document to a DTD file named "checking.dtd."

5. Create a template for the payment element, and within this template, create an element named "check" for each payment element in the source document.

6. For the check element, create two attributes: one named "id" equal to the value of the checknum attribute, and the second named "category" equal to the category attribute of the element from the source document.

7. Also within the check element, create the following four elements:

   ■ The amount element with a value equal to the amount element from the source document

   ■ The to element with a value equal to the to element of the source document

   ■ The date element with a value equal to the date element of the source document

   ■ The memo element with a value equal to the description element of the source document

8. Create the root template, and within the root template, create an element named "checking."

9. Within the checking element, apply the payment template, but use a predicate to select only those payment nodes whose type attribute is equal to "check."

10. Sort the payment template in descending order based on the amount element. (*Hint*: Be sure to sort the amount values numerically.)

11. Save your changes to checks.xsl.

12. Using XML Spy, generate the result document. Store the result document as **checking.xml** in the tutorial.06x/cases folder of your Data Disk.

13. Using XML Spy, verify that the checking.xml document is valid and follows the specifications of the checking.dtd DTD file.

14. Hand in your files to your instructor.

Case 3. Creating an Employee Web Page for Freezing Point Refrigerators Catherine Davis is the personnel manager at Freezing Point Refrigerators, an online company that manufactures and sells kitchen appliances. Catherine stores employee data in XML documents. Figure 6-45 shows the structure of her XML document.

Figure 6-45

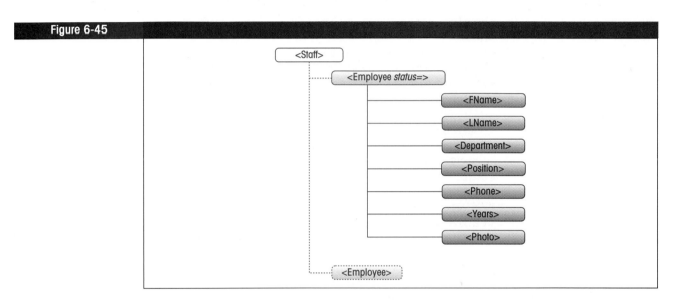

She wants to view this data on a Web page with an easy-to-use layout. Knowing that XSLT can be used to transform her XML document into an HTML file, she asks for your help in creating the style sheet. A preview of the Web page is shown in Figure 6-46.

Figure 6-46

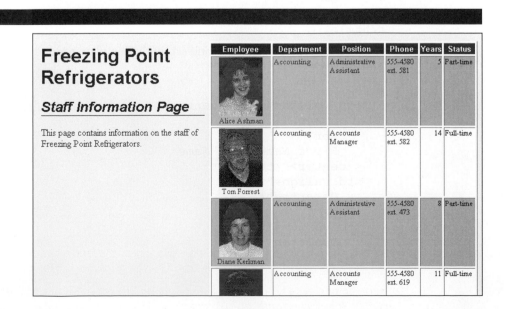

To complete this task:

1. Using your text editor, open **fptxt.xml** located in the tutorial.06x/cases folder of your Data Disk and save the file as **fp.xml**.

2. Add a processing instruction after the XML declaration to attach this XML document to an XSLT style sheet file named "fp.xsl." Save your changes to the document and close it.

3. Using your text editor, create a blank document named **fp.xsl** and save the file in the tutorial.06x/cases folder of your Data Disk. Define this document as an XSLT style sheet by creating the required XML declaration, stylesheet root element, and XSLT namespace. Add an output method that instructs the XSLT processor to create an HTML version 4.0 file.

4. Create the root template, adding the following HTML code to the template:

```
<html>
<head>
<title>Employees at Freezing Point</title>
<link href="fp.css" rel="stylesheet" type="text/css" />
</head>
<body>
<div id="Page_Data">
   <h1 id="Title">Freezing Point Refrigerators</h1>
   <h2 id="Subtitle">Staff Information Page</h2>
   <p>This page contains information on the staff of Freezing
Point Refrigerators.
   </p>
</div>
<table width="460" border="1" class="etable">
<tr>
   <th class="etable" width="100">Employee</th>
   <th class="etable" width="90">Department</th>
   <th class="etable" width="100">Position</th>
   <th class="etable" width="80">Phone</th>
   <th class="etable" width="30">Years</th>
   <th class="etable" width="50">Status</th>
</tr>
</table>
</body>
</html>
```

5. Create the Employee template and set up the template to send the following HTML code for each employee:

```
<tr>
   <td valign="top"><center>
      image
      <br>
      First_Name Last_Name
   </center></td>
   <td valign="top">
      Department
   </td>
   <td valign="top">
      Position
```

```
      </td>
      <td valign="top">
         Phone
      </td>
      <td valign="top" align="right">
         Years />
      </td>
      <td valign="top">
         Status
      </td>
   </tr>
```

where *First_Name*, *Last_Name*, *Department*, *Position*, *Phone*, *Years*, and *Status* are values taken from the fp.xml source document. For the *image* object, insert the inline image of the employee. The filename for the inline image is stored in the Photo element of the source document.

6. Apply the Employee template directly above the </table> tag in the root template.

Explore 7. Sort the Employee node by department, employee last name, and employee first name.

Explore 8. Return to the Employee template and revise the template so that if the employee's status is part-time, the table row tag is:

```
<tr bgcolor="silver">
```

but otherwise, the table row tag is:

```
<tr>
```

(*Hint*: Create the <tr> tag using the <xsl:element> and <xsl:attribute> elements. Determine whether there is a bgcolor attribute in the <tr> tag using the <xsl:if> element.)

9. Save your changes to fp.xsl and close the file.

10. Using XML Spy, generate the result document and store the file as **fp.htm** in the tutorial.06x/cases folder of your Data Disk.

11. Using your Web browser, open **fp.htm** and verify that the table is sorted in the proper order and that the part-time employees appear on a silver background.

12. Hand in your files to your instructor.

Explore **Case 4. Displaying a Box Score for the Baseball Abstract** Roy Packard is a statistician for the *Baseball Abstract*, an online publication reporting on daily activities of Major League Baseball. Roy has been migrating all his data to XML documents, and created an XML document with statistics from a ballgame. Figure 6-47 shows the layout of the box score from that game.

Figure 6-47

Minnesota at Boston

Final	1	2	3	4	5	6	7	8	9	Runs	Hits	Errors
Minnesota	1	0	0	0	0	0	0	0	2	3	6	0
Boston	0	2	0	1	0	0	1	0	x	4	10	0

Minnesota

Batters								
Player	AB	R	H	RBI	BB	SO	LOB	Avg.
L. Lawrence	4	0	0	0	0	1	0	0.255
S. Kemper	4	1	1	2	0	2	1	0.302
B. Aaron	4	1	0	0	0	0	0	0.286
C. Collins	4	0	1	1	0	2	1	0.303
D. Light	3	0	1	0	1	0	1	0.301
U. Guess	3	0	1	1	0	0	0	0.299
R. Dension	3	0	0	0	0	1	1	0.277
K. Kaufmann	2	0	1	0	0	0	0	0.252
L. Sanchez	2	0	0	0	0	0	1	0.279
J. Cho	3	1	1	0	0	1	0	0.281

Pitchers								
Player	IP	H	R	ER	BB	SO	HR	ERA
M. Li (L, 3-9)	7	8	4	3	3	4	0	3.85
R. Rawlings	2	2	0	0	0	2	0	4.20

Boston

Batters								
Player	AB	R	H	RBI	BB	SO	LOB	Avg.
J. Kasie	4	0	0	0	0	2	3	0.295
A. Wilson	4	1	2	2	0	0	1	0.268
M. Turner	4	1	2	0	0	0	1	0.316
R. Bonds	4	0	1	1	0	1	2	0.311
L. Wilkes	3	0	0	0	1	0	1	0.223
J. Hayes	3	0	1	1	0	0	0	0.251
B. Stevens	3	0	0	0	0	1	1	0.271
J. Sheridan	2	0	2	0	0	0	0	0.241
S. Stevens	1	0	0	0	0	1	0	0.302
M. Mitchell	3	1	1	0	1	0	1	0.225
A. White	2	0	1	0	1	0	0	0.281
B. Alvarez	2	1	0	0	0	1	0	0.277

Pitchers								
Player	IP	H	R	ER	BB	SO	HR	ERA
K. Mays (W, 16-2)	8	6	3	2	0	6	0	2.14
S. Wolf (S, 21)	1	0	0	0	0	3	0	3.51

Time: 2:22
Attendance: 32,018

The XML document for this box score is stored in the file scoretxt.xml. Your job is to create a style sheet to transform the XML document into a Web page displaying the source document in a box score-type layout.

To complete this task:

1. Using your text editor, open **scoretxt.xml** from the tutorial.06x/cases folder of your Data Disk and save it as **score.xml**.

2. Attach score.xml to an XSLT style sheet named "score.xsl" and specify HTML 4.0 as the output method for the result document.

3. Review the content and structure of score.xml and compare the contents of the file with Figure 6-47.

4. The design and layout of the result document are up to you. It should display the inning-by-inning results of the game in a tabular format, with the total runs, hits, and errors appearing at the end of the table.

5. Tables should also be created for the batting and pitching statistics of individual players.

6. The result document should also display the length of the game and the total attendance.

7. When you complete the XSLT style sheet, generate a result document using XML Spy.

8. Save the result document as **score.htm** in the tutorial.06x/cases folder of your Data Disk.

9. Hand in your files to your instructor.

QUICK | CHECK ANSWERS

Session 6.1

1. XSLT is the XSL language used to transform XML content into a presentation format. XPath is used to locate information from an XML document and perform operations and calculations upon that content. XSL-FO is used to implement page layout and design.

2. `<?xml-stylesheet type="text/xsl" href="styles.xsl" ?>`

3. /books/book/title

4. ../title

5. /books/book/title/@isbn

6. //author

7. No, it refers to the entire document. The root template refers to the root node, which is at the top of node tree and contains all nodes in the source document, including the root element of that document.

8. Literal result elements are elements that are not processed by the XSLT processor, and are sent as text to the result document.

9. `<xsl:output method="text" />`

   You would create a text document if you were creating a result document for a format other than HTML and XML—such as a PDF (portable document format) file or an RTF (rich text format) file.

Session 6.2

1. `<h1><xsl:value-of select="title" /></h1>`

2. `<xsl:for-each select="book">`
   `<h1><xsl:value-of select="title" /></h1>`
   `</xsl:for-each>`

3. The text of all elements in the document, using either the built-in template, which displays only the text, or the element's template, if one is defined

4. `<xsl:apply-templates select="category" />`

5. `<xsl:value-of select="@book" />`

Session 6.3

1. `<xsl:for-each select="/books/book">`
   `    <xsl:sort select="title" />`
   `</xsl:for-each>`

2. Alphabetically

3. ```
<xsl:if test="@category = 'Non-fiction'">
    <xsl:value-of select="title" />
</xsl:if>
```

4. ```
<xsl:choose>
    <xsl:when test="@category = 'Fiction'">
      <h3><xsl:value-of select="title" /></h3>
    </xsl:when>
    <xsl:when test="@category = 'Non-fiction'">
      <h2><xsl:value-of select="title" /></h2>
    </xsl:when>
</xsl:choose>
```

5. ```
test="sales < 20000"
```

6. ```
<xsl:value-of select="book[title="Non-fiction"] />
```

7. ```
books/book[1]
books/book[last()]
```

8. ```
<xsl:element name="inventory">
    15000
</xsl:element>
```

9. ```
<xsl:element name="inventory">
    <xsl:attribute name="amount">
       15000
    </xsl:attribute>
</xsl:element>
```

10. ```
<xsl:processing-instruction name="xml-stylesheet">
 href="styles.xsl" type="text/xsl"
</xsl:processing-instruction>
```

OBJECTIVES

In this appendix you will:

- Learn how to install the XML Spy software

- Receive an evaluation key-code

- Start XML Spy and explore how to work with the Project window

- View an XML document in Enhanced Grid view

- Explore the different parts of the XML Spy window

INSTALLING AND WORKING WITH XML SPY

SESSION A1.1

In this appendix, you'll learn how to install XML Spy on your computer and how to register the software. You'll learn how to start XML Spy and work with XML Spy's Project window. You'll also explore how to view the contents of an XML document in different formats.

Introducing XML Spy

XML Spy is a family of products designed to facilitate the development of XML applications. XML Spy consists of the XML Spy IDE and the XML Spy Document Framework. The **XML Spy IDE** is an application used to develop and manage XML documents, DTDs, schemas, and XSLT style sheets. The **XML Spy Document Framework** consists of two components:

- **XSLT Designer** uses an intuitive drag-and-drop interface to automate the process of writing complex XSLT style sheets. You can also use XSLT Designer to create advanced electronic forms for use with the XML Spy Document Editor.
- **XML Spy Form Editor** is a word processor type editor that supports electronic form-based data input, graphical elements, tables, and real-time data validation using XML Schema.

In this appendix we'll concentrate on working with XML Spy IDE to create and edit simple XML documents and to perform data validation using DTDs and schemas.

Installing XML Spy

An evaluation copy of XML Spy is on the CD that accompanies this book. You can use the evaluation copy, free of charge, for 120 days after installation. If you intend to use XML Spy after the evaluation period, you can purchase the application at Altova at *http://www.xmlspy.com*.

To install XML Spy:

1. Insert the XML Spy 4.3 CD that accompanies this book into the CD drive of your computer. If the setup program does not start, locate the **setup43.exe** file on the CD and double-click it to run the program.

2. Click **Install XML Spy Suite** to begin installing XML Spy.

3. Click the **Next** button to continue the installation routine.

4. Click the **Browse** button to select a location for XML Spy's setup files, or click the **Next** button to accept the default installation location (C:\Program Files\Altova\Setup Files\XML Spy Suite 4.3).

5. Click the **Next** button.

6. Click the option button to accept the software license agreement and click the **Next** button.

7. Click the **Change** button to select a location for the XML Spy program files, or click the **Next** button to accept the default location (C:\Program Files\Altova\XML Spy Suite\).

8. This dialog box allows you to customize XML Spy features for your work environment. Click the checkboxes for any of the following options you want to enable, and then click the **Next** button.

   ■ Make XML Spy the default editor for your XML-related files.

   ■ Add the "Edit with XML Spy" command to Internet Explorer's menu and toolbar.

   ■ Allow XML Spy to validate HTML files under the XHTML specifications.

9. Click the **Complete** option button, and then click the **Next** button.

10. Click the **Install** button to begin the installation.

    The installation procedure can take several minutes.

11. Click the **Finish** button after the installation is complete.

12. Click **Exit** twice to exit the XML Spy setup program.

    TROUBLE? Depending on your computer system, your instructor may give you more detailed instructions on how your version of XML Spy should be installed on your computer.

After the XML Spy Suite has been installed on your computer, it needs to be registered before you can use it. When you register XML Spy at the Altova Web site, you receive a key-code via e-mail. When you run XML Spy for the first time, you are prompted to enter the key-code.

To register XML Spy:

1. Click the **Start** button on your Taskbar, point to **Programs**, point to **XML Spy Suite**, and select **XML Spy IDE** from the menu.

   XML Spy displays the XML Spy Licensing Manager window shown in Figure A-1.

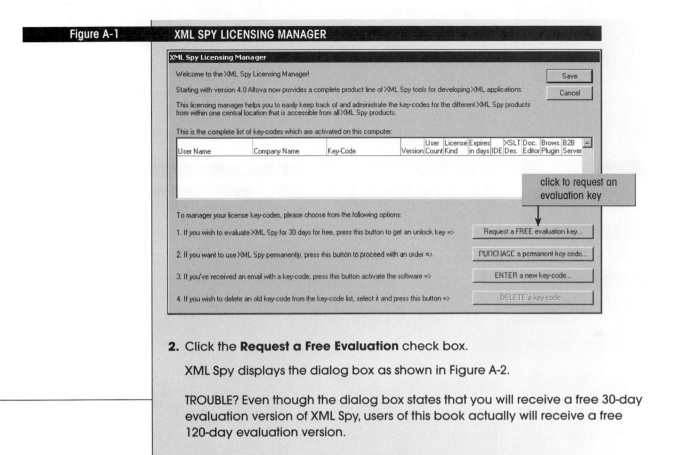

Figure A-1   **XML SPY LICENSING MANAGER**

2. Click the **Request a Free Evaluation** check box.

XML Spy displays the dialog box as shown in Figure A-2.

TROUBLE? Even though the dialog box states that you will receive a free 30-day evaluation version of XML Spy, users of this book actually will receive a free 120-day evaluation version.

3. Complete the form, being sure to include your e-mail address.

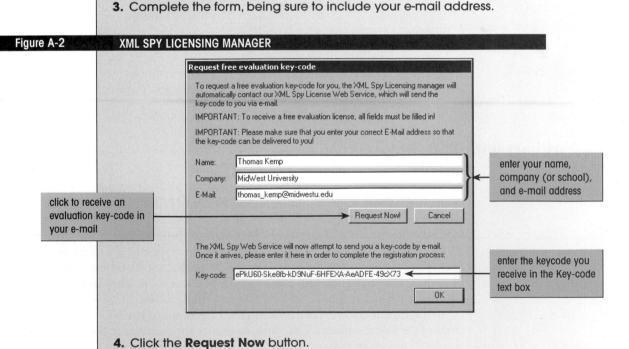

Figure A-2   **XML SPY LICENSING MANAGER**

4. Click the **Request Now** button.

The window expands revealing a text box for you to enter your key-code. Within a few minutes, you'll receive an email from the Altova Web site with your evaluation copy key-code.

5. Enter the key-code you received in your e-mail from Altova into the Key-code text box and click the **OK** button.

TROUBLE? If XML Spy refuses to accept the key-code, verify that you've entered the key-code correctly, including upper- and lowercase letters.

Click the **Save** button to save the key-code. XML Spy IDE starts on your computer and displays the document window as shown in Figure A-3.

Figure A-3	THE OPENING XML SPY WINDOW

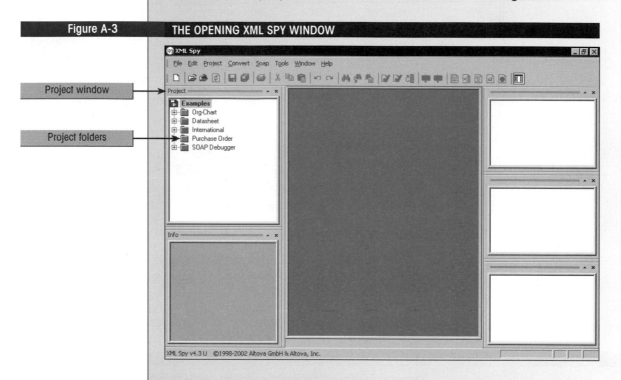

TROUBLE? Your document window may look different than the one in Figure A-3 depending on the options you chose when you installed XML Spy.

Working with XML Projects

XML Spy allows you to organize documents into a single project. A **project** is a collection of the XML documents, DTDs, schemas, XSL and HTML files, and other supporting documents that make up a single XML application. XML Spy allows you to organize these files into separate folders and display the hierarchy of those folders in the **Project window**.

The folders displayed in the Project window represent a logical organization of your files. The folders do not necessarily represent the location of these files on your computer's hard disk, although they can. For example, you can use folders to keep common file types together such as keeping all schema files in a single folder.

To display the contents of a folder in the Project window, click the [+] box that is located in front of the folder name. Try this now, to display the contents of the Purchase Order folder.

To display the contents of the Purchase Order folder:

1. Click the **(+)** box located in front of the Purchase Order folder in the Project window.

2. Click the **(+)** box located in front of the XML Files folder.

3. XML Spy displays the contents of the XML Files folder as shown in Figure A-4. In this case the folder contains a single file, ipo.xml.

Figure A-4	NAVIGATING THE PROJECT WINDOW

TROUBLE? If XML Spy did not automatically open the contents of the Example project, click Open Project from the Project menu, and then open Examples.spp located in the C:\Program Files\Altova\XML Spy Suite\Examples folder.

TROUBLE? If you did not choose to install the example files when you installed XML Spy, you can continue through the remainder of the appendix, but you will be unable to perform the exercises without access to the example files.

You can use the commands in the Project menu to work with the properties of your XML project. From this menu you can:

- close, open, and save old projects, and create new projects
- add files and URLs to projects
- create new project folders
- add external folders or Web folders to projects

Additionally, you can rearrange the contents of your XML projects by dragging file icons in the Project window to other project folders.

Viewing the Contents of an XML Document

To view the contents of an XML document, you can either open the document with the Open command on the File menu, or you can open the file from the Project window. Because we've already accessed ipo.xml in the XML Files folder, let's view its contents.

To view the contents of an XML document:

1. Double-click the **ipo.xml** document icon located in the Project window.

   The document is displayed in a separate window.

2. Click the **Maximize** button ▫ to expand the contents of the window to fill the available space (see Figure A-5).

Figure A-5	DISPLAYING AN XML FILE IN ENHANCED GRID VIEW

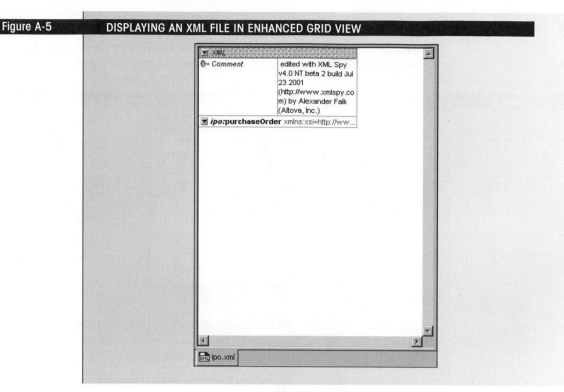

By default, XML Spy displays XML documents in **enhanced grid view**, which shows the hierarchical structure of the document through a set of nested containers. The containers can be expanded or collapsed to provide a clear picture of the document's structure. Elements that contain child elements are identified by a down arrow ▼. To close an open container, click the up arrow ▲.

To view the structure of ipo.xml:

1. Click the **down arrow** icon ▼ located in front of the ipo:purchaseOrder entry.

2. Click the **down arrow** icon ▼ located in front of the shipTo entry. The expanded structure of ipo.xml is displayed in Figure A-6.

Figure A-6	EXPANDING THE GRID VIEW

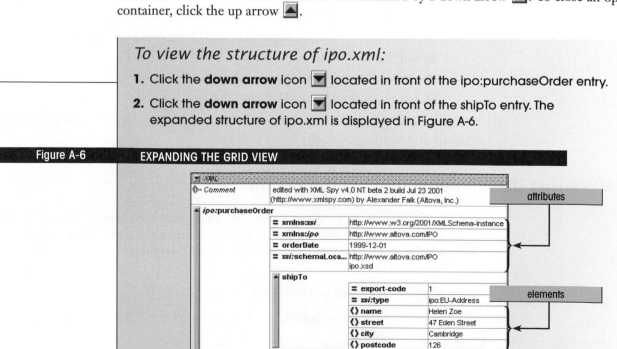

Attributes in the enhanced grid view are identified by the = symbol. Elements that contain text are indicated with a set of opening and closing brackets, < >. The attribute and element values are displayed following the attribute and element names. For example, the shipTo element, as shown in Figure A-6, contains two attributes: export-code and xsi:type. The xsi is a namespace prefix. The values of these attributes are 1 and ipo:EU-Address respectively. The shipTo element also contains four child elements: name, street, city, and postcode. A sample name and address is provided for each of these elements.

Working **with Entry Helper Windows**

If your XML document is associated with a schema or a DTD, you can use one of three entry helper windows to aid you in entering elements and attributes. The entry helper windows are stacked vertically and located to the right of the main window. The **Element Entry helper** window displays the elements that can be added at the current location in the XML document. You can choose to append an element, insert an element before the currently selected element, or add a child element to the currently selected element. Mandatory elements are identified with an exclamation point (!). Elements that can be added within the current parent element, but not at the position of the current selection, are shown in gray.

The **Attribute Entry helper** window displays the attributes that are available for the element you're currently editing. As with elements, mandatory attributes are identified with an exclamation point.

The **Entity Entry helper** window displays a list of predefined entities or parameter entities that can be used with the current XML document.

To view the contents of an entry helper window:

1. Click on the **shipTo** element located in the main window. The entire shipTo element area is highlighted.

2. XML Spy displays the attributes, elements, and entities, in their respective entry helper window, that are available within the XML document (see Figure A-7).

| Figure A-7 | ENTRY HELPER WINDOWS |

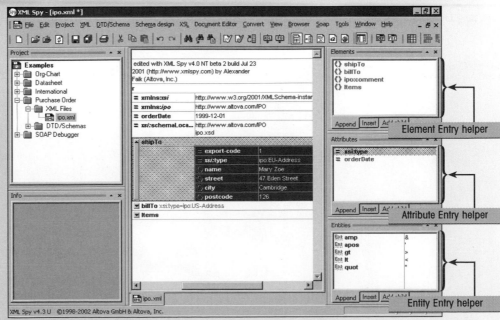

Note that the contents of both the Element Entry and the Attribute Entry helper windows are grayed out, indicating that these elements are allowed within the shipTo element, but not for the current selection.

Finally, another window you can use in developing your XML document is the Info window. The **Info** window displays information about the currently selected element or attribute in the XML document.

Now that you've explored the various parts of the XML Spy IDE, you can exit the application.

To close XML Spy IDE:

1. Click **File** and **Exit** from the XML Spy menu bar.

2. Click the **No** button when prompted to save your changes.

You can learn more about XML Spy using the online help available with the program. Also, Tutorial 3 and Tutorial 4 of this book contain examples of using XML Spy to open, edit, and validate the contents of an XML document.

XSLT Elements and Attributes

The following table describes XSLT elements and attributes. The IE and Netscape columns indicate the earliest version of Internet Explorer and Netscape that support each XSLT element.

ELEMENTS AND ATTRIBUTES	DESCRIPTION	IE	NETSCAPE
xsl:apply-imports	**Applies a template from an imported style sheet**	**6.0**	
Attributes			
none			
xsl:apply-templates	**Applies a template to the current element**	**5.0**	**6.0**
Attributes			
select	Optional. Specifies the node to be processed. If no select attribute is specified, the context node and its descendants are processed using the built-in templates or templates defined in the style sheet.		
mode	Optional. Allows for multiple processing methods for the same element.		
xsl:attribute	**Adds an attribute to an element**	**5.0**	**6.0**
Attributes			
name	Required. Specifies the attribute name.		
namespace	Optional. Specifies the URI of the namespace for the attribute.		
xsl:attribute-set	**Defines a set of attributes**	**6.0**	**6.0**
Attributes			
name	Required. Specifies the name of the attribute set.		
use-attribute-sets	Optional. A list of additional attribute-sets to use with the current attribute set.		
xsl:call-template	**Calls a named template**	**6.0**	**6.0**
Attributes			
name	Required. Specifies the name of the template to be called.		

ELEMENTS AND ATTRIBUTES	DESCRIPTION	IE	NETSCAPE
xsl:choose	**Used with the <xsl:when> and <xsl:otherwise> elements to create conditional tests for the result document**	**5.0**	**6.0**
Attributes			
none			
xsl:comment	**Creates a comment in the result document**	**5.0**	**6.0**
Attributes			
none			
xsl:copy	**Creates a copy of the context node without the child nodes and attributes**	**5.0**	**6.0**
Attributes			
use-attribute-sets	Optional. A list of attribute-sets to apply to the output element node.		
xsl:copy-of	**Creates a copy of the context node including the child nodes and attributes**	**6.0**	**6.0**
Attributes			
use-attribute-sets	Optional. A list of attribute-sets to apply to the output element node.		
xsl:decimal-format	**Defines the format to be used when converting numbers into strings**	**6.0**	
Attributes			
name	Optional. Specifies the format name.		
decimal-separator	Optional. Specifies the decimal point character. The default is ".".		
grouping-separator	Optional. Specifies the thousands separator. The default is ",".		
infinity	Optional. Specifies the text string used to represent infinity. The default is "infinity".		
minus-sign	Optional. Specifies the character to represent negative values. The default is "–".		
NaN	Optional. Specifies the text string used when the value is not a number. The default is "NaN".		
percent	Optional. Specifies the percent sign character. The default is "%".		

ELEMENTS AND ATTRIBUTES	DESCRIPTION	IE	NETSCAPE
per-mille	Optional. Specifies the per thousand sign character. The default is "⁰/₀₀".		
zero-digit	Optional. Specifies the zero character. The default is "0".		
digit	Optional. Specifies the character used to indicate a place where a digit is required. The default is "#".		
pattern-separator	Optional. Specifies the character used to separate formats for positive and negative values. The default is ";".		
xsl:element	**Creates an element node in the result document**	**5.0**	**6.0**
Attributes			
name	Required. Specifies the name of the element to be created.		
namespace	Optional. Specifies the URI for the namespace of the element.		
use-attribute-sets	Optional. A list of attribute-sets to apply to the output element node.		
xsl:fallback	**Specifies alternate code in the event that the XSLT processor does not support an extension element**	**6.0**	
Attributes			
none			
xsl:for-each	**Loops through each node in the specified node set**	**5.0**	**6.0**
Attributes			
select	Required. The node set to be processed.		
xsl:if	**Specifies that an XSLT or literal result element is processed only if a specified condition is met**	**5.0**	**6.0**
Attributes			
test	Required. Specifies the condition that must be met.		
xsl:import	**Imports the contents of one XSLT style sheet into another**	**6.0**	**6.0**
Attributes			
href	Required. The URI of the style sheet to be imported.		
xsl:include	**Includes the contents of one XSLT style sheet in another**	**6.0**	**6.0**
Attributes			
href	Required. The URI of the style sheet to be included.		
xsl:key	**Declares a named key to be used with the key() function**	**6.0**	**6.0**
Attributes			
name	Required. Specifies the name of the key.		

ELEMENTS AND ATTRIBUTES	DESCRIPTION	IE	NETSCAPE
match	Required. Defines the nodes that the key is applied to.		
use	Required. The key value for each of the nodes.		
xsl:message	**Writes a system message to the output string**	**6.0**	**6.0**
Attributes			
terminate	Optional. A value of "no" (the default) allows the processing to continue. A value of "yes" terminates the processing after the message is written to the output.		
xsl:namespace-alias	**Replaces a namespace in the style sheet with a different namespace in the result document**	**6.0**	
Attributes			
stylesheet-prefix	Required. Specifies the namespace to be changed.		
result-prefix	Required. Specifies the new namespace for the result document.		
xsl:number	**Displays the position of the context node**	**6.0**	**6.0**
Attributes			
count	Optional. An XPath expression that specifies what nodes are counted.		
level	Optional. Controls how the sequence is applied. Values are "single" (the default), "multiple", or "any". The value "any" is not supported by Netscape.		
from	Optional. An XPath expression that specifies where to start counting.		
value	Optional. Specifies a number to override a sequence-generated number.		
format	Optional. Specifies the output format for a number. Possible values are: "1" 1, 2, 3, ... "01" 01, 02, 03, ... (not supported by Netscape) "a" a, b, c, ... "A" A, B, C, ... "i" i, ii, iii, iv, ... "I" I, II, III, IV, ...		
lang	Optional. Specifies the language used in the numbering and is not supported by Netscape.		
letter-value	Optional. Specifies alphabetic (the default) or traditional numbering.		

ELEMENTS AND ATTRIBUTES	DESCRIPTION	IE	NETSCAPE
grouping-separator	Optional. Specifies the character used to separate groups of digits. The default is ",".		
grouping-size	Optional. Specifies the size of digit groups. The default is "3".		
xsl:otherwise	**The default action for the <xsl:choose> element**	**5.0**	**6.0**
Attributes			
none			
xsl:output	**Defines the format of the result document**	**6.0**	**6.0**
Attributes			
method	Optional. Defines the output format of the result document. The possible values are: "xml" (the default), "html", "text", or "name". Netscape supports the "xml" and "hmtl" values.		
version	Optional. Sets the version of the output format and is used only with XML and HTML output.		
encoding	Optional. Specifies the text encoding for the result document.		
omit-xml-declaration	Optional. Specifies that the XML declaration be omitted from the result document and be used only with XML result documents. A value of "no" (the default) includes the declaration; a value of "yes" omits the declaration.		
standalone	Optional. A value of "no" (the default) prohibits standalone declarations. A value of "yes" permits standalone declarations in the result document.This attribute is not supported by Netscape.		
doctype-public	Optional. Sets the value of the PUBLIC attribute of the DOCTYPE declaration in the result document.		
doctype-system	Optional. Sets the value of the SYSTEM attribute of the DOCTYPE declaration in the result document.		
cdata-section-elements	Optional. A list of elements that should be placed in CDATA sections in the result document.		
indent	Optional. A value of "yes" (the default) specifies that the elements in the result document are indented following the structure of the document. A value of "no" does not indent the elements in the result document. This attribute is not supported by Netscape.		
media-type	Optional. Defines the MIME type for the result document. The default is "text/xml". This attribute is not supported by Netscape.		

ELEMENTS AND ATTRIBUTES	DESCRIPTION	IE	NETSCAPE
xsl:param	**Declares a parameter**	**6.0**	**6.0**
Attributes			
name	Required. Specifies the name of the parameter.		
select	Optional. Specifies an XPath expression that indicates the default value of the parameter.		
xsl:preserve-space	**Indicates the elements in which white space should be preserved**	**6.0**	**6.0**
Attributes			
elements	Required. A list of elements for which white space should be preserved.		
xsl:processing-instruction	**Writes a processing instruction to the result document**	**5.0**	**6.0**
Attributes			
name	Required. Specifies the name of the processing instruction.		
xsl:sort	**Sorts the output of the context node**	**6.0**	**6.0**
Attributes			
select	Optional. An XPath expression that indicates the nodes by which to sort the context node.		
lang	Optional. Specifies the language used in the sorting.		
data-type	Optional. Specifies the data-type of the data to be sorted. Possible values are "text" (the default), "number", or "qname".		
order	Optional. Specifies the sort order. Possible values are "ascending" (the default) or "descending".		
case-order	Optional. Specifies whether to sort by uppercase or lowercase letters first. Possible values are "upper-first" and "lower-first" (the default).		
xsl:strip-space	**Indicates the elements in which white space should be removed**	**6.0**	**6.0**
Attributes			
elements	Required. A list of elements for which white space should be removed.		
xsl:stylesheet	**Defines the root element of the style sheet**	**5.0**	**6.0**
Attributes			
version	Required. Specifies the XSLT version of the style sheet.		

ELEMENTS AND ATTRIBUTES	DESCRIPTION	IE	NETSCAPE
extension-element-prefixes	Optional. A list of namespace elements used for extended elements.		
exclude-result-prefixes	Optional. A list of namespace prefixes not to be included in the result document.		
id	Optional. A unique id for the style sheet. This attribute is not supported by Netscape.		
xsl:template	**Stores code that can be applied to a specific node in the source document or run as a function**	**5.0**	**6.0**
Attributes			
name	Optional. Specifies a name for the template.		
match	Optional. An XPath expression for the template.		
mode	Optional. Specifies a mode for the template.		
priority	Optional. A number indicating the numeric priority of the template.		
xsl:text	**Writes literal text to the result document**	**5.0**	**6.0**
Attributes			
disable-output-escaping	Optional. A value of "no" (the default) indicates that such characters are replaced by their escape values such as: "<". A value of "yes" indicates that special characters (like "<") are to be output as is. This attribute is not supported by Netscape.		
xsl:transform	**Defines the root element of the style sheet**	**5.0**	**6.0**
Attributes			
version	Required. Specifies the XSLT version of the style sheet.		
extension-element-prefixes	Optional. A list of namespace elements used for extended elements.		
exclude-result-prefixes	Optional. A list of namespace prefixes not to be included in the result document.		
id	Optional. A unique id for the style sheet. This attribute is not supported by Netscape.		
xsl:value-of	**Displays the value of the selected node**	**5.0**	**6.0**
Attributes			
select	Required. An XPath expression that indicates the node or attribute to display.		

ELEMENTS AND ATTRIBUTES	DESCRIPTION	IE	NETSCAPE
disable-output-escaping	Optional. A value of "no" (the default) indicates that such characters are to be replaced by their escape values such as "<". A value of "yes" indicates that special characters such as "<" are to be output as is.		
xsl:variable	**Declares a variable**	**6.0**	**6.0**
Attributes			
name	Required. The name of the variable.		
select	Optional. Specifies the value of the variable.		
xsl:when	**Specifies an action used with the xsl:choose element**	**5.0**	**6.0**
Attributes			
test	Required. Specifies an expression to be tested.		
xsl:with-param	**Defines the value of a parameter to be passed to a template**	**6.0**	**6.0**
Attributes			
name	Required. Specifies the name of the parameter.		
select	Optional. An XPath expression that defines the value of the parameter.		

TASK	PAGE #	RECOMMENDED METHOD/NOTES
ANY content, declare in a DTD	XML 3.08	Use the declaration: `<!ELEMENT element ANY>`
Attribute list, declare in a DTD	XML 3.17	See Reference Window: Declaring an Attribute List
Attribute node, create a reference to	XML 6.11	Use the XPath expression: `@attribute` where *attribute* is the name of the attribute.
Attribute, add to an element	XML 1.18	`<element_name attribute="value">` where *attribute* is the name of the attribute, and *value* is the attribute's value. A single element can have several attributes.
Attribute, create a	XML 6.54	See Reference Window: Creating Elements and Attributes
Attribute, declare in a schema	XML 4.25	See Reference Window: Declaring an Attribute
Background image, add with CSS	XML 5.49	See Reference Window: Using a Background Image

Batch of nodes, processing a	XML 6.22	Use the XSLT code:
		`<xsl:for-each select="XPath Expression">`
		`    XSLT and Literal Result Elements`
		`</xsl:for-each>`
		where *XPath Expression* defines the group of nodes to which the XSLT and Literal Result Elements are applied.

Border color, set with CSS	XML 5.32	Use the styles:
		`border-top-color: color`
		`border-right-color: color`
		`border-bottom-color: color`
		`border-left-color: color`
		where *color* is the border color.

Border style, set with CSS	XML 5.32	Use the styles:
		`border-top-style: type`
		`border-right-style: type`
		`border-bottom-style: type`
		`border-left-style: type`
		where *type* is the border style.

Border width, set with CSS	XML 5.32	Use the styles:
		`border-top-width: value`
		`border-right-width: value`
		`border-bottom-width: value`
		`border-left-width: value`
		where *value* is the size of the border in absolute units or as a percentage of the width of the parent element.

Cascading style sheet, attach to	XML 5.07	Add the following declaration to the XML document: `<?xml-stylesheet type="text/css" href="URL" ?>` where *URL* is the name and location of the cascading style sheet.

TASK	PAGE #	RECOMMENDED METHOD/NOTES
Cascading style, create	XML 5.07	Add the following declaration to the cascading style sheet: `selector {attribute1:value1; attribute2:value2; ...}` where *selector* are the items in the XML document that receive the style, *attribute1*, *attribute2*, and so forth are the CSS attributes, and *value1*, *value2*, and so forth are the values of those attributes.
CDATA section, create a	XML 1.23	`<![CDATA[` `     Text Block` `]]>` where *Text Block* is the block of character text.
Character content, declare in a DTD	XML 3.09	Use the declaration: `<!ELEMENT element (#PCDATA)>`
Character reference, insert a	XML 1.21	See Reference Window: Inserting a Character Reference
Child elements, declare in a DTD	XML 3.09	Use the declaration: `<!ELEMENT element (child_elements)>` where *child_elements* is a list of the elements contained by *element*.
Clip rectangle, set with CSS	XML 5.18	Use the style: `clip: rect(top, right, bottom, left)` where *top*, *right*, *bottom*, and *left* define the coordinates of the rectangular region.
Color, set with CSS	XML 5.29	See Reference Window: Working with Color
Comment, create a	XML 6.56	See Reference Window: Creating Comments and Processing Instructions
Comment, insert a	XML 1.14	`<!-- comment text -->` where *comment text* is the text of the comment.
Complex type element, declare in a schema	XML 4.22	See Reference Window: Declaring Simple and Complex Types
Condition section, create in a DTD	XML 3.38	To ignore declarations in a DTD, use the structure: `<![IGNORE` `     declarations` `]]>` To include declarations in a DTD, use the structure: `<![INCLUDE` `     declarations` `]]>`
Data format, apply to a bound HTML element	XML 2.12	Include the attribute: `dataformatas="format"` in the HTML element tag, where *format* is either "text" or "html".
Data Island, create a	XML 2.08	See Reference Window: Creating a Data Island

TASK	PAGE #	RECOMMENDED METHOD/NOTES
Data type, derive a new	XML 4.48	See Reference Window: Deriving New Data Types
Default attribute value, declare in a DTD	XML 3.22	See Reference Window: Specifying an Attribute Default
Display type, set with CSS	XML 5.13	See Reference Window: Determining a Display Type
DTD, declare a	XML 3.06	See Reference Window: Creating a DOCTYPE Declaration
Element choice, declare in a DTD	XML 3.11	See Reference Window: Specifying a Sequence or Choice of Child Elements
Element node, create a reference to	XML 6.11	Use the XPath expression: `//descendant` where *descendant* is the name of the descendant node.
Element node, create absolute reference to	XML 6.10	Use the XPath expression: `/child1/child2/child3/ ...` where *child1*, *child2*, *child3*, and so forth are descendants from the root node.
Element sequence, declare in a DTD	XML 3.11	See Reference Window: Specifying a Sequence or Choice of Child Elements

Element, create a	XML 6.51	Use the XSLT code:
		`<xsl:element name="name" namespace="URI"`
		`    use-attribute-sets="namelist">`
		`  XSLT and Literal Result Elements`
		`</xsl:element>`
		where the name attribute assigns a name to the element, the namespace attribute provides a namespace, and the use-attribute-sets attribute provides a list of attribute sets.

Element, create a closed	XML 1.14	`<element_name>Content<element_name>` where *element_name* is the name of the XML element, and *Content* is the element's content.
Element, create a root	XML 1.16	The top level element in any XML document is the root element.
Element, create an empty	XML 1.17	`<element_name/>` where *element_name* is the name of the XML element.
Elements, declare in a DTD	XML 3.07	Use the declaration: `<!ELEMENT element content-model>` where *element* is the element's name and *content-model* specifies what type of content the element contains.
EMPTY content, declare in a DTD	XML 3.08	Use the declaration: `<!ELEMENT element EMPTY>`
Entity, declare a general parameter	XML 3.32	See Reference Window: Declaring and Using a General Parameter Entity

TASK	PAGE #	RECOMMENDED METHOD/NOTES
Entity, use a	XML 3.36	See Reference Window: Declaring and Using a Parameter Entity
Enumerated attribute, declare in a DTD	XML 3.18	Use the attribute type: `attribute (value1 | value2 | value3 | ...)` where *value1*, *value2*, *value3*, and so forth are the enumerated values of the attribute.
Flat Design, create	XML 4.40	Declare all elements of the instance document globally in the schema.
Font size, set with CSS	XML 5.38	Use the style: `font-size: value` where *value* is the size of the font.
Font style, set with CSS	XML 5.41	Use the style: `font-style: type` where *type* is normal, italic, or oblique.
Font weight, set with CSS	XML 5.42	Use the style: `font-weight: weight` where *weight* is the font weight.
Font, set with CSS	XML 5.36	Use the style: `font-family: fonts` where *fonts* is a list of possible fonts, separated by commas.
Height, set with CSS	XML 5.18	Use the style: `height: value` where *value* is expressed as a percentage of the height of the parent element, or in absolute units.
HTML element, bind XML field to an	XML 2.11	See Reference Window: Binding an HTML Tag to a Field
HTML tags, insert into an XML document	XML 5.56	See Reference Window: Mixing HTML and XML
Implied attribute value, declare in a DTD	XML 3.21	Use the keyword, #IMPLIED, in the attribute declaration.
Letter spacing, set with CSS	XML 5.40	Use the style: `letter-spacing: value` where *value* is the size of the letter spacing.

List data type, derive in a schema	XML 4.46	Use the command structure:
		`<simpleType name="name">`
		`        <list itemType="type" />`
		`</simpleType>`
		where *name* is the name assigned to the data type, and *type* is the data type of the base type.

List, create with CSS	XML 5.14	To display an element as a list, use the style: `display: list-item`

TASK	PAGE #	RECOMMENDED METHOD/NOTES
List, define with CSS	XML 5.15	To control the appearance of list-items use the style: `list-style: type position` where *type* defines the list bullet (disc, circle, square, decimal, lower-alpha, upper-alpha, lower-roman, upper-roman, or a graphic file) and *position* is either inside or outside.

Margins, set with CSS	XML 5.31	Use the styles:
		`margin-top: value`
		`margin-right: value`
		`margin-bottom: value`
		`margin-left: value`
		where *value* is the size of the margin in absolute units or as a percentage of the width of the parent element.

Mixed content, declare in a DTD	XML 3.13	Use the declaration: `<!ELEMENT element (#PCDATA | child1 | child2 | ..)*>` where *element* is the parent element, and *child1*, *child2*, and so forth are the names of the child elements.
Mixed content, specify in a schema	XML 4.24	Add the mixed="true" attribute to a complex type element declaration.
Modifying symbols, apply to a declaration	XML 3.12	See Reference Window: Applying Modifying Symbols to a Declaration

Named attribute group, create in a schema	XML 4.43	Use the command structure:
		`<attributeGroup name="name">`
		`        attribute declarations`
		`</attributeGroup>`
		where *name* is the name of the attribute group, and *attribute declarations* are the declarations for the individual attributes in the group.

Named complex type, create in a schema	XML 4.22	Add the name="name" attribute to the element type declaration.

Named model group, create in a schema	XML 4.42	Use the command structure:
		`<group name="name">`
		`        element declarations`
		`</group>`
		where *name* is the name of the group, and *element declarations* are the declarations for the individual elements in the group.

Namespace, apply to an attribute	XML 4.09	Insert the namespace prefix before the attribute name as follows: `prefix:attribute="value"`

Namespace, apply to an element	XML 4.07	Insert the namespace prefix before the element name as follows:
		`<prefix:element>`
		`        content`
		`</prefix:element>`

TASK	PAGE #	RECOMMENDED METHOD/NOTES
Namespace, attach a schema to	XML 4.31	See Reference Window: Attaching a Schema to a Namespace
Namespace, declare in an element	XML 4.08	Within an element, insert the attribute: `xmlns:prefix="URI"` where *URI* is the namespace URI, and *prefix* is the namespace prefix.
Namespace, declare in a document prolog	XML 4.05	Within the XML document, insert the command: `<?xml:namespace ns="URI" prefix="prefix"?>` where *URI* is the namespace URI, and *prefix* is the namespace prefix.
Namespace, use with DTDs	XML 4.11	Use the namespace prefixes in the element and attribute declarations as if they were part of the element and attribute names.
Node value, insert into the result document	XML 6.19	Use the XSLT element: `<xsl:value-of select="XPath Expression" />` where *XPath Expression* is an expression that identifies the node from the source document.
Node, create a conditional	XML 6.43	See Reference Window: Applying a Conditional Node
Node, sort a	XML 6.40	See Reference Window: Sorting a Node
Occurrence of an element, specify in a schema	XML 4.24	Add the minOccurs="*value*" maxOccurs="*value*" attributes to a simple type element declaration indicating the minimum and maximum times the element can occur.
Output method, set a	XML 6.15	Add the following declaration to the XSL style sheet: `<xsl:output attributes />` where *attributes* are the attributes that define the output format of the result document.
Overflow, set with CSS	XML 5.18	Use the style: `overflow: type` where *type* is either visible, hidden, scroll, or auto.

Padding, set with CSS	XML 5.35	Use the styles:
		`Padding-top: value`
		`Padding-right: value`
		`Padding-bottom: value`
		`Padding-left: value`
		where *value* is the size of the padding in absolute units or as a percentage of the width of the parent element.

Position, float with CSS	XML 5.22	To float an element with CSS use the style: `float: margin` where *margin* is either left, right, or both to position the element on the left, right, or both margins.

TASK	PAGE #	RECOMMENDED METHOD/NOTES
Position, set with CSS	XML 5.19	To position an element with CSS use the style: `position:type; top:value; right:value; bottom:value; left:value` where *type* indicates the type of position applied to the element (absolute, relative, fixed, or static) and the top, right, bottom, and left attributes define the coordinates of the element. You usually only have to define the top and left positions.
Predicate, create a	XML 6.48	The XSLT element for predicates is: `node[expression]` where *node* is a node from the source document and *expression* is an expression for a condition that the node must fulfill.
Processing instruction, create a	XML 6.56	See Reference Window: Creating Comments and Processing Instructions
Record, determine whether the current record is the first	XML 2.22	`id.recordset.BOF` where *id* is the name of the data island.
Record, determine whether the current record is the last	XML 2.22	`id.recordset.EOF` where *id* is the name of the data island.
Recordset, work with hierarchical	XML 2.32	See Reference Window: Working with a Hierarchical Recordset
Required attribute value, declare in a DTD	XML 3.21	Use the keyword, #REQUIRED, in the attribute declaration.
Restricted data type, derive in a schema	XML 4.47	Use the command structure: `<simpleType name="name">` `<restriction base="type">` `<facet1 value="value1" />` `<facet2 value="value2" />` `<facet3 value="value3" />` `</restriction>` `</simpleType>` where *name* is the name assigned to the data type, *facet1*, *facet2*, *facet3*, etc. are constraining facets, and *value1*, *value2*, *value3*, etc. are values for each constraining facet.
Russian Doll Design, create a	XML 4.39	Declare the root element of the instance document globally in the schema; nest all other element declarations within that declaration.
Schema, annotate a	XML 4.54	See Reference Window: Annotating a Schema
Schema, attach a document to a	XML 4.34	See Reference Window: Attaching a Document to a Schema
Schema, create a	XML 4.17	See Reference Window: Creating a Schema
Selectors, working with	XML 5.08	See Reference Window: Working with Selectors

TASK	PAGE #	RECOMMENDED METHOD/NOTES
Simple type element, declare in a schema	XML 4.19	Use the command: `<element name="name" type="type"/>` where *name* is the name of the simple element and *type* is the data type.
String Attribute, declare in a DTD	XML 3.18	Use the attribute type: `attribute CDATA`
Style sheet, link to	XML 1.29	See Reference Window: Attaching an XML Document to a Style Sheet

Table pages, navigate	XML 2.28	Use the JavaScript command:
		`id.firstPage()`
		to move to the first page of the table, where *id* is the name of the HTML table.
		Use:
		`id.lastPage()`
		`id.nextPage()`
		`id.previousPage()`
		to move to the last, next, and previous table page.

Table, bind XML data to a	XML 2.26	See Reference Window: Binding Data to a Table
Table, specify a page size for	XML 2.28	Include the attribute: `dataPageSize="value"` in the <table> element tag, where *value* is the number of rows in a single page.

Template, applying a	XML 6.24	Use the XSLT expression:
		`<xsl:apply-templates`
		`        select="XPath Expression" />`
		where *XPath Expression* indicates the node template to be applied.

Template, create a	XML 6.13	See Reference Window: Creating a Template
Text, align horizontally with CSS	XML 5.43	Use the style: `text-align: alignment` where *alignment* is left, center, right, or justify.
Text, align vertically with CSS	XML 5.44	Use the style: `vertical-align: alignment` where *alignment* is baseline, bottom, middle, sub, super, text-bottom, text-top, or top.
Text, change case with CSS	XML 5.45	Use the style: `text-transform: case` where *case* is uppercase, lowercase, or none.
Text, create a variant with CSS	XML 5.46	Use the style: `font-variant: type` where *type* is none or small-caps.

TASK	PAGE #	RECOMMENDED METHOD/NOTES
Text, decorate with CSS	XML 5.45	Use the style: `text-decoration: type` where *type* is none, underline, overline, or line-through.
Text, indent with CSS	XML 5.45	Use the style: `text-indent: value` where *value* is the size of the indentation in either absolute or relative units or as a percentage of the width of the element.
Token attribute, declare in a DTD	XML 3.19	Use the attribute type: `attribute token` where *token* is one of the tokenized types.

Union data type, derive in a schema	XML 4.46	Use the command structure:
		`<simpleType name="name">`
		`        <union memberTypes="type1 type2 type3 ..."/>`
		`</simpleType>`
		where *name* is the name assigned to the data type, and *type1*, *type2*, *type3*, and so forth are the different data types being united.

Unparsed entity, use a	XML 3.38	See Reference Window: Declaring an Unparsed Entity
Venetian Blind Design, create	XML 4.44	In the schema, use named complex types, model groups, and attribute groups to declare the various elements of the instance document.
Web browser, display an XML document in a	XML 1.25	Open the XML document in the Web browser. Internet Explorer will show the document in a hierarchical tree. Netscape will only show the element values.
Width, set with CSS	XML 5.17	Use the style: `width: value` where *value* is expressed as a percentage of the width of the parent element, or in absolute units.
Word spacing, set with CSS	XML 5.40	Use the style: `word-spacing: value` where *value* is the size of the word spacing.
XML, create a declaration	XML 1.13	See Reference Window: Creating an XML Declaration
XSLT style sheet, attach to	XML 6.06	Add the following declaration to the XML document: `<?xml-stylesheet type="text/xsl" href="URL" ?>` where *URL* is the name and location of the XSL style sheet.
XSLT style sheet, set up	XML 6.07	See Reference Window: Setting Up an XSLT Style Sheet

File Finder

Location in Tutorial	Name and Location of Data File	Student Saves File As ...	Student Creates New File
Tutorial 1			
Session 1.1			
Session 1.2			Tutorial.01X\Tutorial\Jazz.xml
Session 1.3	Tutorial.01X\Tutorial\Jazz.xml (saved from last session) JW.css	Jazz.xml	
Review Assignment	Tutorial.01X\Review\Rare.txt Tutorial.01X\Review\JW2.css	Rare.xml	
Case Problem 1	Tutorial.01X\Cases\FAQ.txt Tutorial.01X\Cases\FAQ.css	FAQ.xml	
Case Problem 2	Tutorial.01X\Cases\Hamlet.txt Tutorial.01X\Cases\Plays.css	Hamlet.xml	
Case Problem 3	Tutorial.01X\Cases\Staff1.xml	Staff2.xml	
Case Problem 4	Tutorial.01X\Cases\Accounts.txt Tutorial.01X\Cases\Delton.css		Accounts.xml
Tutorial 2			
Session 2.1	Tutorial.02X\Tutorial\FP1text.htm Tutorial.02X\Tutorial\FPInfo.xml	FP1.htm	
Session 2.2	Tutorial.02X\Tutorial\FP1.htm (saved from last session) Tutorial.02X\Tutorial\FPInfo.xml Tutorial.02X\Tutorial\Emp1.xml *Multiple jpg files*	FP1.htm	
Session 2.3	Tutorial.02X\Tutorial\FP2text.htm Tutorial.02X\Tutorial\FPInfo.xml Tutorial.02X\Tutorial\Emp1.xml Tutorial.02X\Tutorial\FP3text.htm Tutorial.02X\Tutorial\Emp2.xml *Multiple jpg files*	FP2.htm FP3.htm	
Review Assignment	Tutorial.02X\Review\Invtxt1.htm Tutorial.02X\Review\Invtxt2.htm Tutorial.02X\Review\Invtxt3.htm Tutorial.02X\Review\Refg1.xml Tutorial.02X\Review\Refg2.xml Tutorial.02X\Review\Refg3.xml *Multiple jpg files*	Inv1.htm Inv2.htm Inv3.htm	
Case Problem 1	Tutorial.02X\Cases\OEInvtxt.htm Tutorial.02X\Cases\OETitles.xml Tutorial.02X\Cases\OE.xml	OEInv.htm	
Case Problem 2	Tutorial.02X\Cases\SListtxt.htm Tutorial.02X\Cases\CHList.xml Tutorial.02X\Cases\bwills.jpg Tutorial.02X\Cases\czims.jpg Tutorial.02X\Cases\emcd.jpg Tutorial.02X\Cases\rshapiro.jpg Tutorial.02X\Cases\taaron.jpg Tutorial.02X\Cases\tdavis.jpg	SList.htm	
Case Problem 3	Tutorial.02X\Cases\AMtxt.htm Tutorial.02X\Cases\AutoOrd.xml	AM.htm	
Case Problem 4	Tutorial.02X\Cases\tour.xml Tutorial.02X\Cases\Castles.jpg Tutorial.02X\Cases\Hebrides.jpg Tutorial.02X\Cases\Highland.jpg Tutorial.02X\Cases\Lake.jpg		Scotland.htm

File Finder

Location in Tutorial	Name and Location of Data File	Student Saves File As ...	Student Creates New File
Tutorial 3			
Session 3.1	Tutorial.03X\Tutorial\Ordertxt.xml	Order.xml	
Session 3.2	Tutorial.03X\Tutorial\Order.xml (saved from last session)	Order.xml	
Session 3.3	Tutorial.03X\Tutorial\Order.xml (saved from last session) Tutorial.03X\Tutorial\Items.dtd	Order.xml	
Review Assignment	Tutorial.03X\Cases\Pixaltxt.xml Tutorial.03X\Cases\SWListtxt.xml Tutorial.03X\Cases\HWListtxt.xml	Pixal.xml SWList.xml HWList.xml	SW.dtd HW.dtd
Case Problem 1	Tutorial.03X\Cases\EDLtxt.xml	EDL.xml	DL.dtd
Case Problem 2	Tutorial.03X\Cases\newstxt.xml Tutorial.03X\Cases\images.dtd Tutorial.03X\Cases\full_txt.dtd	news.xml	stories.dtd WNS.xml
Case Problem 3	Tutorial.03X\Cases\accounttxt.xml	account.xml	checking.dtd
Case Problem 4	Tutorial.03X\Cases\Members.txt		List.xml
Tutorial 4			
Session 4.1	Tutorial.04X\Tutorial\UHosptxt.xml Tutorial.04X\Tutorial\UHDTDtxt.dtd	UHosp.xml UHDTD.dtd	
Session 4.2	Tutorial.04X\Tutorial\Pattxt.xml UHosp.xml (saved from last session)	Patient.xml UHosp.xml	PSchema1.xsd
Session 4.3	Tutorial.04X\Tutorial\Patient.xml (saved from last session) Tutorial.04X\Tutorial\UHosp.xml Tutorial.04X\Tutorial\Venetian.xsd Tutorial.04X\Tutorial\Flat.xsd	Patient.xml UHosp.xml PSchema2.xsd	
Review Assignment	Tutorial.04X\Review\CCCtxt.xml	CCC.xml	SSchema.xsd
Case Problem 1	Tutorial.04X\Cases\JWtxt.xml	JW.xml	CD.xsd
Case Problem 2	Tutorial.04X\Cases\Listtxt.xml	List.xml	LSchema.xsd
Case Problem 3	Tutorial.04X\Cases\Partstxt.xml Tutorial.04X\Cases\Grilltxt.xml	Parts.xml Grills.xml	PTSchema.xsd GRSchema.xsd GRStock.xml
Case Problem 4	Tutorial.04X\Cases\Books.txt Tutorial.04X\Cases\Movies.txt Tutorial.04X\Cases\Music.txt		Books.xml Movies.xml Music.xml BSchema.xsd MoSchema.xsd MuSchema.xsd MMart.xml
Tutorial 5			
Session 5.1	tutorial.05x\tutorial\biketxt.xml	bike.xml	bike.css
Session 5.2	tutorial.05x\tutorial\bike.xml (saved from last session) tutorial.05x\tutorial\bike.css (saved from last session)	bike.xml bike.css	
Session 5.3	tutorial.05x\tutorial\bike.xml (saved from last session) tutorial.05\tutorial\bike.css (saved from last session) tutorial.05x\tutorial\c100.jpg tutorial.05x\tutorial\c200.jpg tutorial.05x\tutorial\combo750.jpg tutorial.05x\tutorial\tnation.jpg tutorial.05x\tutorial\tour250.jpg tutorial.05x\tutorial\tri200.jpg	bike.xml bike.css	

File Finder

Location in Tutorial	Name and Location of Data File	Student Saves File As ...	Student Creates New File
Review Assignment	tutorial.05x\review\bike2txt.xml tutorial.05x\tutorial\c100.jpg tutorial.05x\tutorial\c200.jpg tutorial.05x\tutorial\combo750.jpg tutorial.05x\tutorial\tnation.jpg tutorial.05x\tutorial\tour250.jpg tutorial.05x\tutorial\tri200.jpg	bike2.xml	bike2.css
Case Problem 1	tutorial.05x\cases\nasdtxt.xml tutorial.05x\cases\down.gif tutorial.05x\cases\up.gif	nasdaq.xml	nasdaq.css
Case Problem 2	tutorial.05x\cases\schedtxt.xml	schedule.xml	schedule.css
Case Problem 3	tutorial.05x\cases\elemtxt.xml	elements.xml	pchart.css
Case Problem 4	tutorial.05x\cases\mealstxt.xml	meals.xml	meals.css
Tutorial 6			
Session 6.1	tutorial.06x\tutorial\stocktxt.xml tutorial.06x\tutorial\stock.css	stock.xml	stock.xsl stock.htm
Session 6.2	tutorial.06x\tutorial\stock.xml (saved from last session) tutorial.06x\tutorial\stock.xsl (saved from last session)	stock.xml stock.xsl	stock.htm
Session 6.3	tutorial.06x\tutorial\stock.xml (saved from last session) tutorial.06x\tutorial\stock.xsl (saved from last session) tutorial.06x\tutorial\down.gif tutorial.06x\tutorial\same.gif tutorial.06x\tutorial\up.gif	stock.xml stock.xsl	stock.htm
Review Assignment	tutorial.06x\review\stocktxt.xml tutorial.06x\review\stock2.css tutorial.06x\review\down.gif tutorial.06x\tutorial\same.gif tutorial.06x\tutorial\up.gif	stock2.xml	stock2.xsl stock2.htm
Case Problem 1	tutorial.06x\cases\messtxt.xml tutorial.06x\cases\m01.jpg tutorial.06x\cases\m13.jpg tutorial.06x\cases\m16.jpg tutorial.06x\cases\m20.jpg tutorial.06x\cases\m27.jpg tutorial.06x\cases\m31.jpg tutorial.06x\cases\m42.jpg tutorial.06x\cases\m51.jpg tutorial.06x\cases\m57.jpg tutorial.06x\cases\skyweb.jpg	messier.xml	messier.xsl messier.htm
Case Problem 2	tutorial.06x\cases\acctxt.xml tutorial.06x\cases\checking.dtd	account.xml	checks.xsl checking.xml

File Finder

Location in Tutorial	Name and Location of Data File	Student Saves File As ...	Student Creates New File
Case Problem 3	tutorial.06x\cases\fptxt.xml tutorial.06x\cases\Ashman.jpg tutorial.06x\cases\Bester.jpg tutorial.06x\cases\Brown.jpg tutorial.06x\cases\Charnas.jpg tutorial.06x\cases\DuMont.jpg tutorial.06x\cases\Forrest.jpg tutorial.06x\cases\Howard.jpg tutorial.06x\cases\Jacobs.jpg tutorial.06x\cases\Kerkman.jpg tutorial.06x\cases\Kuhlman.jpg tutorial.06x\cases\Laurence.jpg tutorial.06x\cases\Lawson.jpg tutorial.06x\cases\Nelson.jpg tutorial.06x\cases\Oneil.jpg tutorial.06x\cases\Paulson.jpg tutorial.06x\cases\Staford.jpg tutorial.06x\cases\Tompkins.jpg tutorial.06x\cases\Unwin.jpg tutorial.06x\cases\Watkins.jpg tutorial.06x\cases\Winston.jpg	fp.xml	fp.xsl fp.htm
Case Problem 4	tutorial.06x\cases\scoretxt.xml	score.xml	score.xsl score.htm